Midwest Studies in Philosophy
Volume XXXVIII

Many papers in MIDWEST STUDIES IN PHILOSOPHY are invited and all are previously unpublished. The editors will consider unsolicited manuscripts that are received by January of the year preceding the appearance of a volume. All manuscripts must be pertinent to the topic area of the volume for which they are submitted. Address manuscripts to MIDWEST STUDIES IN PHILOSOPHY, Department of Philosophy, University of California, Riverside, CA 92521.

The articles in MIDWEST STUDIES IN PHILOSOPHY are indexed in THE PHILOSOPHER'S INDEX.

Midwest Studies
in
Philosophy
Volume
XXXVIII
Forward-Looking Collective
Responsibility

Editors

Peter A. French
Arizona State University

Howard K. Wettstein
University of California, Riverside

WILEY PERIODICALS, INC. • BOSTON, MA & OXFORD, UK

Midwest Studies in Philosophy (ISSN 0363-6550 print; ISSN 1475-4975 online) is published annually as a supplement to the *Journal of Social Philosophy* (Spring, Summer, Fall and Winter) by Wiley Subscription Services, Inc., a Wiley Company, 111 River St., Hoboken, NJ 07030-5774. Periodical postage paid at Hoboken, NJ and additional offices. Postmaster: Send all address changes to MIDWEST STUDIES IN PHILOSOPHY, Journal Customer Services, John Wiley & Sons Inc., 350 Main St., Malden, MA 02148-5020.

INFORMATION FOR SUBSCRIBERS *Midwest Studies in Philosophy* is published annually as a supplement to the *Journal of Social Philosophy* (Spring, Summer, Fall and Winter).
Institutional subscription prices for 2014 are: Print & Online: US$636 (The Americas), US$985 (Rest of the World), €639 (Europe), £503(UK). Prices are exclusive of tax. Asia Pacific GST, Canadian GST and European VAT will be applied at the appropriate rates. For more information on current tax rates, please go to wileyonlinelibrary.com/tax-vat. The prices includes online access to the current and online back files to January 1st 1998, where available. For other pricing options, including access information and terms and conditions, please visit wileyonlinelibrary.com/access www.wileyonlinelibrary.com/access

DELIVERY TERMS AND LEGAL TITLE Prices include delivery of print journals to the recipient's address. Delivery terms are Delivered Duty Unpaid (DDU); the recipient is responsible for paying any import duty or taxes. Legal title passes to the customer on despatch by our distributors.

PUBLISHER *Midwest Studies in Philosophy* is published by Wiley Periodicals, Inc., Commerce Place, 350 Main Street, Malden, MA 02148; Telephone: 781 388 8200; Fax: 781 388 8210. Wiley Periodicals, Inc. is now part of John Wiley & Sons.

JOURNAL CUSTOMER SERVICES For ordering information, claims and any enquiry concerning your journal subscription please go to wileyonlinelibrary.com/support or contact your nearest office.
Americas: Email: cs-journals@wiley.com; Tel: + 1 781 388 8598 or +1 1800 835 6770 (Toll free in the USA & Canada)
Europe, Middle East and Africa: Email: cs-journals@wiley.com; Tel: +44 (0) 1865 778315
Asia Pacific: Email: cs-journals@wiley.com; Tel: +65 6511 8000
Japan: For Japanese speaking support, Email: cs-japan@wiley.com; Tel: +65 6511 8010 or Tel (Toll-free) 005 316 50 480
Visit our Online Customer Self Help available in 7 languages at http://onlinelibrary.custhelp.com

PRODUCTION EDITOR Abigail Gutierrez (email: MISP@wiley.com)

This journal is available online at Wiley Online Library. Visit wileyonlinelibrary.com to search the articles and register for table of contents e-mail alerts.

BACK ISSUES Single issues from current and recent volumes are available at the current single issue price from customerservices@blackwellpublishing.com. Earlier issues may be obtained from Periodicals Service Company, 11 Main Street, Germantown, NY 12526, USA. Tel: +1 518 537 4700, Fax: +1 518 537 5899, Email: psc@periodicals.com.

MICROFILM The journal is available on Microfilm. For microfilm service, address inquiries to University Microfilms International, 300 North Zeeb Road, Ann Arbor, MI 48106-1346, USA.

ABSTRACTING AND INDEXING The journal is indexed by the Arts & Humanities Citation Index; CatchWord; Ingenta; Online Computer Library Center FirstSearch Electronic Collections Online; Philosopher's Index; and POIESIS: Philosophy Online Serials.

DISCLAIMER The Publisher and Editors cannot be held responsible for errors or any consequences arising from the use of information contained in this journal; the views and opinions expressed do not necessarily reflect those of the Publisher and Editors, neither does the publication of advertisements constitute any endorsement by the Publisher and Editors of the products advertised.

ISSN 0363-6550 (Print)
ISSN 1475-4975 (Online)

For submission instructions, subscription and all other information visit: wileyonlinelibrary.com

Printed in USA by The Sheridan Press.

MIDWEST STUDIES IN PHILOSOPHY
Volume XXXVIII
Forward-Looking Collective Responsibility

Midwest Studies in Philosophy
Volume XXXVIII

Future-Looking Collective Responsibility:
A Preliminary Analysis

MARION SMILEY

How can we make sense of future-looking collective responsibility (FLCR)? What is its moral basis and how—under what conditions—can we ascribe it to particular groups? I address these questions below on a preliminary basis. I begin in Part I by exploring the nature of FLCR itself. I argue in Part II that FLCR is not, as we sometimes assume, grounded exclusively in backward-looking collective responsibility (BLCR). Instead, it is grounded in a cluster of moral considerations having to do with fairness, the need to prevent harm, and the identity of the collective entity in question. I conclude by pointing out that while BLCR may not ground FLCR, it does play an important role in prioritizing the moral tasks associated with it.

I.

Future-looking collective responsibility (FLCR), like its backward-looking counterpart (BLCR), focuses on a group's responsibility for a particular state of affairs in the world. But, unlike BLCR, it does not make responsibility out to be a matter of having caused an existing—morally problematic—state of affairs. Instead, it makes responsibility out to be a matter of being morally charged with—responsible for—bringing about a state of affairs which we as a community take to be desirable. Hence, when we ascribe FLCR to a group, we do not tell a story about its causal history. Instead, we point to what we think the group should now do.

Not surprisingly, we often focus on the particular tasks that we think a group should carry out and we call these tasks *responsibilities*. But we need to be careful here. For FLCR is not simply a matter of carrying out particular tasks. Instead, it is a matter of being morally charged with bringing about a state of affairs that is, by virtue of the ascription of FLCR itself, now part of the group's moral business. Hence, in discussions of FLCR, we do not simply say of a group that it *has responsibilities*. Instead, we also say of it that it *is responsible for* bringing about X and/or that it should *take responsibility* for making sure that X comes about in practice.

Since FLCR requires—and not just asks—a group to bring about a desirable state of affairs, it has much in common with *being morally obliged.* But the emphasis is different. So, too, is the level of flexibility afforded to the moral agent. In cases where we use the language of moral obligation, we make clear that a group *has* to do a particular thing. In cases where we use the language of responsibility, we allow a group to use its own judgment in figuring out how best to bring about a particular state of affairs and we charge it with exercising such judgment wisely.

Interestingly enough, the term "future" may not be required here, since being responsible for doing something takes a group into the future by necessity and since the major difference between the two kinds of collective responsibility is not in any case temporal. Instead, it is a matter of the kind of moral claim that we are making about a group's relationship to harm. In the case of BLCR, we are claiming that a group caused harm. In the case of FLCR, we are claiming that it should do what it can to remedy harm and to prevent harm from occurring in the future.[1]

The moral importance of each kind of collective responsibility follows accordingly. BLCR is morally important because of its association with moral blameworthiness. In cases where BLCR is modeled on the traditional, Kantian, notion of moral responsibility, moral blameworthiness is supposedly inherent in group causation itself.[2] In cases where BLCR is a condition, rather than the source, of moral blameworthiness, BLCR requires us to ask other questions of the group after judging it causally responsible for harm, for example, whether it can provide us with a valid excuse. But even in these cases the possibility of moral blameworthiness is key.

While FLCR is not completely removed from matters of blame—we sometimes blame those who do not fulfill their responsibilities—its moral importance

1. While some of those writing on collective responsibility emphasize the importance of timeline in distinguishing between past and future responsibility, others choose to distinguish between the two kinds of responsibility in the language of "outcome responsibility" (i.e., causal responsibility) versus "remedial responsibility." Iris Young provides an example of the first approach in *Responsibility for Justice* (Oxford: Oxford University Press, 2011). David Miller provides an example of the second in *National Responsibility and Global Justice* (Oxford: Oxford University Press, 2007). While FLCR is frequently associated with the need to remedy a bad state of affairs, it does not have to be remedial. Indeed, FLCR can be ascribed to a group for bringing about a state of affairs without reference to harm, for example, if our concern is to ensure moral, social, or political progress. Not surprisingly, we overlook these latter cases when we assume that FLCR is grounded in BLCR.

2. The capacity of group agency to sustain a notion of moral blameworthiness is absolutely crucial to the coherence of a Kantian approach to collective moral responsibility. I argue elsewhere that group agency cannot sustain a notion of moral blameworthiness and that a Kantian approach to collective moral responsibility is ill-advised. See Marion Smiley, "From Moral Agency to Collective Wrongs: Rethinking Collective Moral Responsibility," *Journal of Law and Policy* 19 (2010–11): 171–202.

does not lie with an association between it and moral blameworthiness. (Nor, for that matter, does it have moral blameworthiness as part of it.) Instead, it is morally important because of its association with two other things of value: the state of affairs that we hope will result from the group's taking responsibility for the state of affair's coming about and the virtuous character of a responsible group, that is, a group that is careful and attentive in pursuing those projects assigned to it.[3]

Since BLCR requires that a group be able to cause harm in the sense required by moral blameworthiness, it requires both that groups be able to act collectively and to form "we intentions" of the kind relevant to moral blameworthiness. In other words, it requires that a very steep set of metaphysical conditions be met—conditions that many of those now writing on collective responsibility argue cannot be met or cannot be met in many cases. (How, critics ask, can collectives form intentions and/or be morally blameworthy by virtue of causing harm?)[4]

While FLCR, like its backward-looking counterpart, requires us to make sense of how groups, as distinct from their individual members, can bring about a state of affairs in the world, it does not, like BLCR, require us to make sense of "we intentions." Nor does it, like BLCR in its traditional, Kantian form, require us to show how moral blameworthiness can be inherent in group causation itself. Instead, it requires only that we be able to make sense of a group *doing something* in the world and *taking responsibility* for bringing about a state of affairs.[5]

Since FLCR requires only that a group be able to do something and to take responsibility here, it does not present us with any serious metaphysical challenges. Nor do we have to worry about not finding at least some groups that are capable of doing and taking responsibility. For, *doing* something, unlike *acting*, entails only that an agent be able to produce a change in the world and *taking responsibility*, unlike *being morally blameworthy*, entails only that a group be able to take control over a situation to the extent that it can produce such a change.

While FLCR does not raise metaphysical red flags in the way that its backward-looking counterpart does, it does raise a set of difficult questions concerning both the kinds of groups capable of FLCR and the moral basis for ascribing FLCR in practice. What kinds of groups, we have to ask, are capable of doing something in the world and taking responsibility for bringing about a desirable state of affairs? How—on what basis—can say of a group that it is morally charged

---

3. While virtue ethics has historically been associated with individuals, it can be reformulated to speak to the moral traits of groups—as long as the traits in question are understood as group characteristics. For excellent examples of how this works in the political and corporate realms respectively, see Bernard Yack, chapter 5: "Political Justice," in *The Problems of a Political Animal* (Berkeley: University of California Press, 1993); Donald Beggs, "The Idea of Group Moral Virtue," *Journal of Social Philosophy* 34 (2003): 457–74, and G. Moore, "Corporate Character: Modern Virtue Ethics and the Virtuous Corporation," *Business Ethics Quarterly* 15, no. 4 (2005): 659–85.

4. For a very helpful review of these critical perspectives, see David Schwelkard and Hans Bernhard Schmid, "Collective Intentionality," *Stanford Encyclopedia of Philosophy*, ed. Edward Zalta (2013).

5. I make the case for requiring only that a collective entity be able to *do* something or *produce* a state of affairs, as distinct from freely will an action, elsewhere. See Marion Smiley, "Collective Responsibility," *Stanford Encyclopedia of Philosophy*, ed. Edward Zalta (2010).

with bringing about a state of affairs that we consider desirable? Where do the group's responsibilities come from? How—on what basis—can we justify them as moral?

What kinds of groups are capable of FLCR? Since being capable of FLCR requires exercising the kind of control cited above, random groups of individuals—for example, mobs—will not do in this context, even if random groups are, as some argue, capable of collective action and "we-intentions."[6] Nor will groups that are not organized or that do not have a governing structure, for example, groups that are constituted with reference only to the shared racial, gender, or cultural identities of their members. Indeed, the only groups that will do here are those that, in Peter French's terms, are organized and capable of carrying out projects in a purposeful fashion.[7]

I defer here to French's judgments about which groups—families, corporations, clubs, nation states, and so on—are capable of meeting the above standards, and focus in the next section instead on how we ascribe FLCR to groups in practice. I do so, moreover, with a particular example in mind that others have explored in detail, namely, the claim that the United States is responsible for both countering racism in its midst and providing its members with the means of satisfying their basic needs. How—on what moral basis—can we say that the United States is morally charged with doing these things? How—on what moral basis—can we say that it is not?

II.

Interestingly enough, questions of forward-looking collective responsibility are not generally posed in an open-ended fashion or geared to figuring out what states of affairs a particular group might be morally responsible for bringing about overall. Instead, they are posed about a particular state of affairs and are geared to assessing whether the group in question is responsible for bringing the latter about. In other words, they are questions like: "Is Corporation X responsible for ensuring that the world's poor have adequate amounts of food and medical care?" "Is the United States responsible for eradicating racism and poverty in its midst?"

In responding to these questions, moral philosophers sometimes make straightforwardly utilitarian claims about who is in the best position to remedy the harm.[8] But more often than not, they fall back on claims about who is causally responsible for harm and then proceed to use these claims to ascribe FLCR to the particular groups under scrutiny. In other words, they assume that because, say, a particular corporation is causally responsible for suffering around the world or

6. The controversy surrounding the collective responsibility for random groups is articulated in Virginia Held's classic article on the subject: Virginia Held, "Can a Collection of Random Individuals Be Responsible?," *Journal of Philosophy* 67 (1970): 471–86.

7. Peter French, *Collective and Corporate Responsibility* (New York: Columbia University Press, 1984).

8. The classic utilitarian argument for such responsibilities is Peter Singer's "Famine, Affluence, and Morality," *Philosophy and Public Affairs* 1, no. 3 (1972): 229–43.

because, say, the United States is causally responsible for both racism and poverty at home, they (the two groups) are FLCR for providing the required remedies to the harm in question.[9]

What are we to make of the choice to ground FLCR in causal responsibility?

Let me turn very briefly to the case of the United States and its purported responsibility to eradicate racism and poverty in its midst. Since FLCR here is attached to a group and since the group we are talking about is the United States, we cannot—no matter how we want to ground FLCR—focus simply on what individuals, classes (e.g., the wealthy), or races (e.g., whites) have done to create the myriad of problems now confronting the poor and those who have been badly affected by racism over the years. Instead, we have to point to something integral to the political community itself—which often means either official policies or larger institutional structures.

David Lyons provides an elaborate—and historically compelling—set of historical claims about how the United States' economic and race-based policies, as well as its lack of government regulation, have severely restricted the life chances of African Americans over the years. He then goes on to use these claims to ascribe moral responsibility to the United States for both eliminating racism itself and providing African Americans with those educational and employment opportunities deemed necessary to the creation of "favorable life prospects" for them.

> [T]he Federal government has a primary obligation to insure equal opportunities—to insure that social arrangements provide a fair share or favorable life prospects for each child. No morally defensible system of social organization would fail in that responsibility. Given the historical background that was articulated above, it also seems undeniable that the government is morally bound to eliminate unfair inequalities in opportunity that it has wrongfully promoted.[10]

Iris Young also invokes the causal responsibility of the United States for racism and poverty to ground what she takes to be the United States' FLCR. But, unlike Lyons, she focuses primarily on the social, economic, and political structures associated with the United States, rather than on particular historical policies, and emphasizes unregulated capitalism overall. According to Young, it is because these structures cause harm to the poor by depriving them of employment and fair wages that the United States, as well as various other groups that benefit from the structures in question, is morally responsible for challenging and replacing these structures now and into the future.

9. Robert Goodin, who distances himself from this position, states it very succinctly when he writes: "Task responsibility is often thought to flow, automatically, from blame responsibility. To determine whose responsibility it should be to correct some unfortunate state of affairs, we should on such logic simply determine who was responsible for having caused that state of affairs in the first place. Those who are responsible for causing an unfortunate situation are responsible for fixing it." Robert Goodin, *Social Welfare and Individual Responsibility: For and Against* (Cambridge: Cambridge University Press, 1998), 151.

10. David Lyons, "Corrective Justice, Equal Opportunity and the Legacy of Slavery and Jim Crow," *Boston University Law Review* 84 (2004): 1402.

Young makes clear that while future-looking collective responsibility builds on causal responsibility, it requires *taking responsibility* for doing the right thing now and into the future. "What," she asks, "is future looking responsibility?"

> With future looking responsibility . . . one has the responsibility always now, in relation to current events and in relation to future consequences. . . . The fact of having such responsibilities implies an imperative to *take* responsibility. If we see injustices or crimes being committed by the institutions of which we are a part, then we have a responsibility to speak out against them and oppose them.[11]

Lyons and Young provide compelling evidence for why the United States is causally responsible for harm. But they cannot, contrary to appearances, move directly from their claims of causal responsibility to ascriptions of FLCR to a group for remedying harm. (In other words, they cannot, contrary to appearances, ground FLCR exclusively in causal responsibility.) Nor can anyone else. Instead, we have to take into consideration a variety of normative and practical matters—ranging from how to prioritize our moral projects to what needs to be done to remedy the harm in question—and to acknowledge the place of these considerations in ascribing FLCR.

All of these measures are required because of three realities that we have to face when we set about to ascribe FLCR in practice. First of all, in many cases, the particular group under scrutiny (i.e., the group we are associating with FLCR) will not be the only candidate for causal status with respect to harm. Nor will its causal contribution necessarily be as great as that of others. Second, FLCR is ascribed for the purpose of ensuring the success of a particular moral project rather than for the purpose of gauging the moral agency of a particular group. Third, there are many important moral projects in the world to pursue and we cannot pursue them all.

Let me turn first to the matter of multiple candidates for causal status.

In the case of racism and poverty, it is difficult to deny that both U.S. policy and unregulated capitalism are causally responsible for harm. But in both cases, there are many other candidates for causal status. In the case of racism, we can point to political ideologies as well as to other groups (e.g., communities of racists). In the case of poverty, we can point to cultural formations and classes, as well as to economic forces. And of course we will not always agree on the causal status of the above. (Indeed, one of the most heated debates now surrounding welfare reform concerns whether the poor are causally responsible for their own poverty.)

How can we deal with multiple causes in this context? Which groups that contributed significantly to harm are FLCR for remedying it? Since ranking groups here in terms of their causal contribution to harm is near impossible, we might want to conclude simply that all of the groups (and individuals) that contributed significantly to the harm are morally responsible for remedying it. In other words, we might want to introduce a notion of *shared collective responsibility* and assume that

---

11. Iris Marion Young, *Responsibility for Justice* (Oxford: Oxford University Press, 2011), 92.

what is important is not *how* FLCR is shared, that is, in what amounts or in association with what particular moral tasks, but that all of the groups have it.

Recall, though, that the moral salience of FLCR does not, like that of BLCR, lie with what it tells us about the moral standing of an agent. Instead, it lies with what it does to help us bring about a desirable state of affairs. Hence, we cannot be satisfied with simply knowing that FLCR is shared in some general way among moral agents. Nor can we remain concerned solely with who caused harm. Instead, we have to be concerned with how FLCR can be configured—and distributed—across moral agents in such a way that the sought-after state of affairs comes about in a relatively efficient fashion.

All of this is to say that practical considerations about how to remedy harm are crucial to FCLR by virtue of its very nature. Moreover, such considerations are crucial to FLCR even in cases where our overriding concern is with the responsibility of one group in particular, rather than with all groups together, since the responsibility of one group has to be configured within a more all-encompassing discussion of how to distribute FLCR across groups and in accordance with the requirements of the moral project at hand. (What distribution—and configuration—of FLCR, we have to ask, will enable us to pursue this moral project effectively?)

While practical considerations of this kind are crucial to the ascription of FLCR by virtue of the very nature of FLCR itself, they are not the only noncausal norms that we find necessary to fall back on in ascribing FLCR in practice. Nor do we remain squarely in the consequentialist camp in any case. Indeed, as recent debates over the responsibility of the United States to provide welfare benefits to citizens attest, we take a whole host of more purely normative matters into consideration when ascribing FLCR, including both fairness (which I explore briefly below) and the relative value of those moral projects that can—and should—be associated with FLCR.

Not surprisingly, we fall back on assumptions of relative value here primarily in cases where we cannot pursue all of our moral projects—eradicating racism and poverty, bringing up healthy children, creating jobs, reversing global warming—at once or even at all. But these cases are not few in number. Indeed, they capture much of our moral life. Hence, we should not be surprised to discover that such assumptions of relative value, along with judgment about the feasibility of our moral projects, lie behind many of our ascriptions of FLCE in practice.

While we incorporate assumptions about relative value into FLCR most commonly in cases where we have to choose among projects, we also incorporate such assumptions into FLCR—frequently unselfconsciously—in cases where the same set of structures or institutions can be held causally responsible for both harm and something we value. In these cases, we may think that we are simply focusing on a particular institution because it is causally responsible for harm. But as long as we are holding a group responsible for challenging this institution on the basis of its causal responsibility for harm, we are prioritizing one state of affairs over another.

Young's own example of capitalism is instructive here. While capitalism may indeed be causally responsible for both racism and poverty, it may also be causally responsible for significant improvements in healthcare, better schools, the production of food on a mass scale, and (depending on one's political outlook) the separation of economic and political power. Hence, while we can ascribe responsibility to the United States for challenging capitalism, we cannot contend that our ascription is based solely on causal matters. Instead, we have to acknowledge that we are making a value judgment about the relative importance of the projects in play.

Moreover, if we want to ascribe FLCR responsibly—that is, in a way that avoids both arbitrariness and bias when valuing particular moral projects over others—we will have to argue explicitly about what we value as a community. In other words, we will have to ask: What kinds of moral projects are most valuable to us and how do they rank alongside other valuable projects in cases where we cannot pursue them all? Whose needs and interests are furthered by these projects? How, if at all, might we ensure that everyone's needs and interests are being taken into consideration? Where, if at all, do concerns about a project's feasibility come into play?

All of these are straightforwardly normative and practical questions. But even if we could skirt them in discussions of causal responsibility, we would still not be able to move directly from causal responsibility to FLCR in practice. (Nor, for that matter, could we provide an out for ourselves by insinuating that FLCR is *inherent* in causal responsibility.) Instead, we would have to justify our privileging of causal responsibility here by providing a *reason* for why a group (or any other kind of moral agent) should be held responsible for remedying harm to which it made a significant (causal) contribution. How might we do so?

If we could treat *being causally responsible for harm* as a matter of *doing something morally wrong*, we might be able to supply a retributivist-like reason for privileging causal responsibility in this context. In other words, we might be able to claim—on the basis of a retributivist theory of justice—that a group that is causally responsible for poverty and racism and that has as such done something morally wrong is responsible for righting this wrong by either providing reparations to those harmed or instituting the kinds of educational and employment programs that Lyons suggests are necessary to overcome the legacy of racism.[12]

While such a retributivist-like approach to grounding FLCR in BLCR might have a chance in cases where a group self-consciously caused harm,[13] it would not appear to work at all in cases where a group unselfconsciously caused harm through its support of institutions that, say, keep African Americans and financially poor people in subordinate positions. For, retributivism requires, at the very least, self-conscious moral agents, and if unselfconscious moral agents are left out of FLCR, the chances of the harm being remedied would go way down. (Indeed, by so circumscribing FLCR, we would inevitably render FLCR self-defeating.)

But even if this approach worked to bring BLCR together with FLCR in all cases, it could not provide us with a way of grounding FLCR exclusively in BLCR

12. Retributivist claims to punishment would presumably be out of the question here unless laws were broken—and in any case such claims would not be in keeping with the spirit of forward-looking, as distinct from backward-looking, collective responsibility.
13. Obviously, this would be the case only if retributivism is itself coherent as a moral theory.

or moving directly from BLCR to FLCR in ascribing the latter in particular contexts. For, we would still be faced with the need to coordinate our responsibilities in such a way that our moral projects were pursued effectively. In other words, we would still be faced with the need to ascribe FLCR with an eye to all of the practical and normative considerations cited above. How, if we cannot ground our ascriptions of FLCR exclusively in causal responsibility, can we ground them?

Since the practical and normative considerations cited above are so important to FLCR, we might do well to place them, rather than causal responsibility, at the center of our attention in our efforts to ascribe FLCR responsibly. Moreover, in doing so, we might want to focus on the capacity of particular groups to carry out the moral projects in question as a basis for our ascriptions of FLCR. Robert Goodin takes such an approach in his own arguments for why the United States should be held collectively responsible for providing the poor with welfare benefits.

> It is forward-looking, task-oriented collective responsibility that I am championing. . . . There are good reasons for pursuing certain sorts of goals through some sort of coordinated, collective apparatus like the state. . . . Responsibilities get collectivized simply because that is the only realistic way (or, anyway, much the most effective way) of discharging them.[14]

Goodin's approach here is, I think, the most promising approach that we can take to ascribing FLCR in a responsible fashion, since, among other things, it speaks directly to the purposes behind ascribing responsibilities in general, namely, the realization of a designated moral good, and it is very well suited to incorporating practical questions into itself, including not only those about who is in the best position to bring about the sought-after state of affairs but also those like "How will pursuing the project at hand, e.g., expanding federal welfare assistance, affect other projects? What costs will it incur? Whose interests will be served?"

Moreover, even though Goodin's approach does not now ask about the relative value of our moral projects, it could easily refer to such rankings and use them to configure—and distribute—FLCR across competing moral projects in ways that are both efficient and reflective of our moral priorities. In Goodin's own case, this would mean not only comparing the value of federal welfare assistance to the value of other federally funded projects, for example, the military or space exploration, but both also figuring out how the U.S. government might distribute FLCR across these projects according to the moral principles and practical criteria deemed appropriate.

While a focus such as Goodin's on the capacity of particular groups to carry out the moral projects that we value is very helpful, it cannot be construed as *the* basis for ascribing FLCR any more than causal responsibility can be construed as *the* basis for doing so. (In other words, we cannot simply substitute *capacity* for *causation* in this context by way of developing another single-value theory of FLCR.) For, there are other values that we have to take into consideration when

14. Robert Goodin, *Social Welfare and Individual Responsibility: For and Against* (Cambridge: Cambridge University Press, 1998), 50–55.

ascribing FLCR, including those that, critics suggest, are necessary to temper the supposedly radical implications of the capacity approach to FLCR itself.

Take, for example, the value of fairness. How, critics ask, can we square the capacity approach to FLCR with the need to be fair to those who may ultimately bear the burdens of bringing about the sought-after state of affairs, that is, be ascribed most of the responsibilities? David Schmitz, Goodin's sparring partner in the debate over the United States' collective responsibility for providing welfare assistance, argues that to hold taxpayers (the group he associates with the United States in this context) collectively responsible for providing assistance to the poor unfairly burdens those who have worked hard to achieve their superior capacity for change.[15]

Not surprisingly, the value of fairness gets introduced most frequently into discussions of collective responsibility via claims of unfairness. Alexander Brown, in his plea for personal responsibility, claims that while the U.K. government has a collective responsibility to do many things for the poor, it should not have to make up for behavioral lapses on the latter's part. Indeed, to expect the U.K. government to do so, according to Brown, would be unfair. Interestingly enough, Brown chooses to talk about fairness here in terms of causal responsibility.

> If a person is causally responsible for becoming an addict, then he cannot fairly expect our assistance in getting him off of drugs. . . . The government can only be expected to do so much.[16]

Michael Walzer takes things in a very different direction in his own arguments about the collective responsibility of the United States for taking care of the poor. Walzer also considers fairness to be key. But fairness for him is not a matter of who worked the hardest. Nor is it a matter of who caused harm. Instead, it is a matter of communal membership, that is, who belongs to our community and what we owe members of it. According to Walzer, we owe community members those things that will enable them to be dignified members of the community, including, among other things, both a national healthcare system and a welfare state.

Walzer makes clear that we owe them these things, not because of an elaborate theory of obligation, but because of the nature of the collective in question, that is, a political community.

> Membership is important because of what the members of a political community owe to one another. And the first thing that they owe is the communal provision of security and welfare. . . . Political community for the sake of provision. . . . There has never been a political community that did not provide, or claim to provide, for the needs of its members.[17]

15. David Schmitz, *Social Welfare and Individual Responsibility: For and Against* (Cambridge: Cambridge University Press, 1998), 46.

16. Alexander Brown, *Personal Responsibility: Why it Matters* (London: Continuum, 2009), 151.

17. Michael Walzer, *Spheres of Justice* (New York: Basic Books, 1983), 64–68.

All of these claims together suggest both that fairness is key to ascriptions of FLCR and that it is highly controversial in discussions of the collective responsibility of the United States for providing welfare in particular. Indeed, even the notion of fairness itself deemed relevant to FLCR turns out to be a site of normative contestation. In some cases, it is taken to be a matter of the rights of those who have the capacity to make things better. In other cases, it has to do with who is at fault. In still other cases, it has to do with the nature of the collective entity in question.

I gesture here both to the importance of fairness in ascribing FLCR and to the controversies surrounding what is fair in this context not to claim anything about fairness in this context but rather, by way of conclusion, to make three more general points about FLCR itself. First of all, while we would do well to focus our attention initially on configuring—and distributing—FLCR in ways that help us to bring about desirable states of affairs in the world, we cannot treat capacity to do good as the only (or even as the primary) basis of ascribing FLCR. Instead, we have to make room for a host of other practical and normative judgments, including who is causally responsible for harm (fault), how we value particular projects, whose interests count in the community, where our rights lie, and fairness.

Second, these judgments are not simply add-ons to the issue of FLCR. Nor are they the kind of judgments that we can always agree on or hope to pass for all time. Instead, they are judgments that are both integral to FLCR and normatively open-ended. Hence, we cannot treat them as peripheral to the question at hand. Instead, have to place them at the center of normative inquiry about both FLCR in general and its manifestations in particular contexts. Likewise, in doing so, we have to remember that ascriptions of FLCR depend, not just on an assessment of a particular group's responsibilities, but on how responsibilities can best be organized overall.

Finally, while the salience of the various practical and normative considerations cited above will presumably vary from case to case—and do so in accordance with the nature of each case, for example, whether scarcity is an issue or not—we cannot privilege any one of these considerations over the others theoretically by treating it as of overriding importance to FLCR in all cases. Nor can we treat any one of these considerations as *the* basis of FLCR. Instead, we have to bring them together into a pluralistic framework for ascribing FLCR responsibly.

Midwest Studies In Philosophy, XXXVIII (2014)

Forward-Looking Collective Responsibility:
A Metaphysical Reframing of the Issue

CAROL ROVANE

The word "responsibility" immediately puts in mind the retrospective case. Backward-looking responsibility is a matter of *bearing* responsibility for what we have already done, in the sense of deserving praise and blame for it.

A natural first thought about how we might construe the forward-looking case is that it is a matter of anticipating future backward-looking responsibility—a matter of anticipating future desert of praise and blame. But I think we should reject this natural-seeming thought, because it overlooks the way in which any attempt to anticipate future backward-looking responsibility will inevitably return our attention to the present. For any determination that we might make in the present, concerning how doing one or another of the options before us will lead to future desert of praise or blame, will automatically supply us with a determination of which of those options it would be better or worse to do *now*. I do not see why this should necessarily count as a *forward-looking* view at all. It will only be forward-looking if our decisions about what to do now are informed by a concern about what will actually happen in the future. So, as I see it, we should construe forward-looking responsibility not as a matter of *bearing* responsibility in the future for our present (or past) deeds, but rather as a matter of *taking* responsibility for what will happen in the future, by doing things in the present with an eye to what their future consequences will be. That, at any rate, is how I shall construe it for the purposes of this article.

Before trying to address the issue of our forward-looking *collective* responsibility, we would do well to consider, what are the conditions of responsible agency in general? That is the task of Section 1 below, in which I first offer an intuitive conception of responsibility which (I hope) is widely shared, and then raise a familiar puzzle about collective responsibility. It is my working view that this puzzle cannot be solved simply by arguing for the existence of irreducibly social facts. As far as I can see, the puzzle is generated by the fact that our intuitive conception of responsibility can intelligibly apply only to individual agents. Let the facts about collective agency be as irreducibly *social* as you like—they still won't qualify as individual agents to whom our intuitive conception of responsibility can intelligibly apply.

In Section 2, I distinguish the case of *group agency* from the case of collective agency as it is normally understood. Unlike a collective, a group agent does qualify as an individual agent in its own right, and as a result, there is no particular puzzle about how it can be a locus of responsibility. But the important point is not that our intuitive conception of responsibility can intelligibly be applied to group agents. What is important is that the argument for group agency unsettles the underlying picture of individual agency that informs it. The argument shows that the existence of an individual agent is never a metaphysical given, but always a product of effort and will—or to put it another way, every individual agent exists for the sake of the ends that its existence makes it possible to pursue.

Armed with these insights, I turn, finally, to Section 3 to address the issue of our forward-looking collective responsibility.

1. SOME INTUITIONS ABOUT RESPONSIBILITY, AND A *PRIMA FACIE* PUZZLE ABOUT COLLECTIVE RESPONSIBILITY

Here are two powerful intuitions about the conditions of responsibility. First, we are responsible only for what lies within our causal power to do it (or bring about). Second, responsible agency requires a point of view from which to deliberate. This does not mean that the domain of our responsibility is confined to cases where we actually take the time to deliberate before acting. It means rather that agency has a normative dimension that is unintelligible apart from the idea of a point of view from which deliberation *can* proceed, where the aim of deliberation is to answer the normative question, what would it be best for me to do?

These intuitions about the conditions of responsibility rest on a highly individualist picture of agency. They take for granted that each individual agent has *her own* domain of causal control and *her own* point of view from which to deliberate. They also take for granted that the aim of any individual agent—you might even call it the constitutive goal of agency—is to bring what falls within the domain of her own causal control into line with her own point of view, so that what she actually does accords with her normative sense of what she ought to do.

What, then, is the puzzle about collective responsibility? In general, the need and opportunity for collective agency arises when many agents believe that there is an end that does not lie within their causal power to bring about on their own, but they believe it can be brought about if they coordinate their agency in suitable ways. If these agents then proceed to coordinate their agency for the sake of that end—call it a "collective end"—it seems that none of them can either bear or take responsibility for it, because by hypothesis it does not lie within their individual causal power to bring *it* about, as opposed to their individual contributions to it. But of course, we often have a moral interest in finding a locus of responsibility for a collective outcome *as such*, and not merely this or that individual agent's contribution to it.

If we were to focus just on the causal condition of responsibility, it might seem that we could reasonably locate responsibility for a collective outcome with the larger collective that actually produces it. But the moral interest that we take in collective responsibility requires that the normative condition of responsibility also be in place—and this requires a point of view from which deliberation and action can proceed, and which can be engaged for the purposes of praise and blame. But of course there is no collective point of view from which a collective end is evaluated or embraced, because what makes collective agency *collective* is precisely that it is the agency of *many* agents, each with her own point of view. So what is puzzling is how there can be a proper locus of collective responsibility in a plurality of distinct points of view.

We might try to solve this puzzle by locating collective responsibility with *each* of the agents involved in a collective action, on the ground that each of them embraces the collective end from her own point of view. In that case, no matter how small a contribution an agent might make to a collective outcome, she will still be responsible for it—that is, for the collective outcome as such. This solution to the puzzle would obviously leave room for some serious mismatches between the moral significance of an agent's contribution to a collective outcome and the moral significance of the outcome itself—the former might be so small that it barely holds any moral significance at all when considered on its own, apart from latter. And then we might well wonder why responsibility for the collective outcome requires that an agent make any causal contribution to it at all. Why wouldn't it suffice to merely endorse the collective end? If this doesn't suffice—if an agent must make some causal contribution to the collective outcome in order to be a locus of responsibility for it—then it is unclear to me why her responsibility for it shouldn't be proportional to her contribution. But then, of course, we would be holding individual agents responsible just for their individual contributions to the collective outcome, and we wouldn't be thinking of them as loci of responsibility for the collective outcome as such.

In the last paragraph or so, as well as in the next few, it may seem that I am focusing almost exclusively on the backward-looking case—on how to find a locus of responsibility for collective outcomes already produced. But no harm will be done at this stage of the dialectic if I don't always take care to explicitly discuss the forward-looking case. For on the intuitive conception of responsibility that makes collective responsibility so puzzling, there is an extremely close connection—you might even say parity—between the backward and the forward view: What an individual agent bears backward-looking responsibility for, concerning her past actions, is something that she should have taken forward-looking responsibility for at the time of action. However, that being said, I should register that this connection, or parity, between the two views will look less perfect in the wake of the arguments to come in Sections 2 and 3—it is only in this section that I am taking it for granted.

I said in my introductory remarks that it is my working view that we cannot solve the puzzle about collective responsibility by bringing in arguments to show that there are irreducibly social facts—that is, arguments to show that the facts about collective agency cannot be reduced to facts about the individual psychologies of the members who comprise the collective.[1] My view is not driven by any conviction that such arguments are bound to fail—in fact, I am completely open minded about the possibility that there are irreducibly social facts. My difficulty is that I do not see how we can find, within an irreducibly social reality, the features of agency that our intuitive conception of responsibility requires.

Take, for example, the claim that agents who participate in collective agency form intentions that make ineliminable references to collective ends, as well as to the larger collective processes through which those ends are to be achieved. Frankly, I do not know if this requires the introduction of such notions as plural subjects or we-intentions, which are irreducible to our notions of individual subjects and individual intentions. But let us suppose for the sake of argument that it does. I simply do not see how that supposition can undermine the following reasoning: There can be no social facts without social relations; there can be no social relations without social relata; these relata must be individuals, who in some sense *remain* individuals even as they stand in social relations, or else it wouldn't be *social* relations in which they stand; these individuals will possess separate points of view from which to deliberate and act; whatever they are doing when they coordinate their efforts for the sake of collective ends, they do not thereby become *one* agent with *one* point of view from which to exert causal control for the sake of collective outcomes; precisely because they are *many* rather than one, there is a puzzle about where to find a locus of responsibility for the outcomes that they collectively produce.

The philosophical literature on agency does describe some social phenomena in ways that make it appear as though they might have the features of agency that are required by our intuitive conception of responsibility, and so might perhaps be plausible candidates to serve as loci of collective responsibility—I have in mind references to such things as "group identities" and "group points of view."[2] But such talk is not usually meant to be taken literally. The phrase "group identity" usually refers to the idea that membership in a group confers an identity on *each* of its members, thereby providing each with a sense of who she is, where this leaves each metaphysically intact as an individual agent in her own right. Similarly, the phrase "group point of view" usually refers to a set of attitudes that the members of a group hold in common—where again, this leaves each of them intact as an

---

1. There is a large and still growing literature in social ontology and the related topics of collective agency and responsibility. To name just a few book-length contributions: Peter French, *Corporate and Collective Responsibility* (New York: Columbia University Press, 1984); Margaret Gilbert, *On Social Facts* (Princeton: Princeton University Press, 1989); John Searle, *The Construction of Social Reality* (New York: Free Press, 1995); Raimo Tuomela, *The Philosophy of Sociality: The Shared Point of View* (Oxford: Oxford University Press, 2007).

2. An illustrative example can be found in Elizabeth Anderson, "Unstrapping the Straightjacket of 'Preference': A Comment on Amartya Sen's Contributions to Philosophy and Economics," *Economics and Philosophy* 17 (2001): 21–38.

individual agent who must act on those shared attitudes from her own individual point of view. When talk of "group identity" and "group point of view" is understood along these lines, it does not point to a locus of responsibility for collective outcomes as such.

I turn in the next section to a case in which talk about a group point of view *can* be taken literally.

2. THE DIFFERENCE BETWEEN GROUP AGENCY AND COLLECTIVE AGENCY

Here is what I mean by a *group agent*: a group of human beings functions as an individual agent in its own right, with its own point of view from which to deliberate and act.

I have argued at length elsewhere for the possibility of group agency in this sense.[3] I cannot reproduce that argument in full here, but only some relevant portions of it—and those, too, in the briefest terms.

The argument proceeds from some relatively uncontroversial assumptions about the nature of individual agency. Any individual agent who possesses the sort of reflective rationality by virtue of which it can be a locus of individual responsibility (whether it be forward-looking or backward-looking) must be committed to realizing certain rational requirements that define what it is for an individual agent to be fully, or ideally, rational. It doesn't matter for the purposes of my argument what the specific requirements of rationality are, but here is a sample list: consistency of belief, transitivity of preferences, and closure. What really matters for the purposes of my argument is this: Whatever the specific requirements of individual rationality may be, each of them invites a characteristic rational activity, where all of these rational activities are directed at contributing to an overarching rational requirement, which is to arrive at and act upon all-things-considered judgments, about what it would be best to do. Thus, on the sample list of rational requirements I just gave: The requirement of consistency invites an agent to resolve any inconsistencies she may find among her beliefs; the requirement of transitivity of preferences invites her to rank her preferences on a single scale; the requirement of closure invites her to accept the implications of her attitudes. Carrying out all of these specific rational activities puts an agent in a position from which to work out the joint rational significance of all that she thinks, for the question what it would be best for her to do—where to work this out is to arrive at an all-things-considered judgment.

(A brief aside about how this connects with my discussion in the last section: When I referred to *deliberation*, I was referring to the sorts of rational activities I just described above, whose common rational aim is indeed to arrive at all things-considered judgments. When I referred to the *constitutive goal of agency*, I characterized that goal as one of bringing what lies within one's own domain of causal control into line with one's own point of view, so that what one actually does accords with one's normative sense of what one *ought* to do. What I've now

---

3. For a book-length treatment, see my *Bounds of Agency: An Essay in Revisionary Metaphysics* (Princeton: Princeton University Press, 1998).

clarified is that when an agent is ideally or fully rational, she will arrive at her normative sense of what she ought to do by arriving at all-things-considered judgments.)

There is no reason why the various rational activities through which an agent arrives at all-things-considered judgments must be carried out within a single sphere of consciousness that is housed in a single human body. Consider that two human beings can carry out a conversation in which they reason together about how best to solve a certain philosophical problem, and that the logical structure of their conversation can coincide perfectly with the logical structure of a chain of thought that might have be carried out by one of them mutely. In the course of their conversation, the two human beings are, literally, reasoning *as one*. Furthermore, when they do this, they are reasoning from a single, albeit two-headed, point of view—which is to say, a group point of view.

The sort of philosophical conversation in which two human beings reason as one stands in stark contrast to another characteristically philosophical activity, namely, argument. In the context of argument, each party reasons from her own point of view and tries to persuade the other. Although each party may be open to being persuaded by the other, it is crucial to see that there is no rational necessity that either should reconsider her own views in the light of what the other thinks— each can rationally refuse to do this, so long as she sincerely believes that what the other thinks is in some way importantly *mistaken*. This shows that the parties to an argument are not committed to discovering the all-things-considered significance of a common pool of deliberative considerations; and insofar as they deliberate from *separate* pools of deliberative considerations they are deliberating from *distinct* points of view. In contrast, when two human beings reason together in the way I described above, they *are* deliberating from a common pool of considerations; and insofar as they are deliberating from a *common* pool of deliberative considerations, they are deliberating from a *single* point of view. It might seem like an exaggeration to say that two human beings would become a single group agent simply by engaging in a cooperative, as opposed to argumentative, philosophical conversation. Yet it is striking that if they did engage in such a conversation, then it would be possible for us to address them *as* a single agent for the purposes of finding out what they had thought and done with respect to the philosophical problem that they were trying to solve. And we would be on our way to recognizing the pair as a single agent that can be held responsible for *its* philosophical views.

Next, consider a philosophy department that wishes to decide on the degree requirements for the PhD in philosophy. The members of the department are accustomed to a fairly discordant life, in which they arrive at department meetings with antecedently settled opinions about which they then argue, never making much headway in persuading one another, and finding that they can resolve the issues before them only by voting. But when they take up the task of settling the degree requirements for the PhD in philosophy, they recognize that it calls for a *reasoned* position. Assuming that the department is not a dictatorship, this could not be the position of any one of its members, but would have to be a position of the *whole*, and there is only one way in which such a position can be arrived at. The faculty must cease to argue from their separate points of view.

What they must do instead is gather their various thoughts into a common pool of deliberative considerations. This will involve putting all of the possible degree requirements that are up for consideration on the table, along with all of the various reasons that speak for and against them, and then working out the joint implications of that entire set of deliberative considerations for the question, what is the best set of degree requirements for the PhD in philosophy. If the department were to proceed in this way, it would be reasoning *as one* in just the same sense as in the simpler example above, in which two human beings reason as one in order to solve a philosophical problem. In both cases, the reasoning would proceed from a single, group point of view. And in the case of the philosophy department, I think it should be clear that that group point of view is, importantly, a locus of responsibility. It is a point of view from which the department *takes* forward-looking responsibility for certain future states of affairs, concerning the quality and achievements of its graduates. And it is a point of view from which the department *bears* backward-looking responsibility for the decisions it has taken with respect to its PhD program, and as such, it is point of view that can be engaged for the purposes of praising and blaming it as we see fit.

The reason it makes sense to hold the department *itself* responsible for what it does, is that it really does meet the conditions of individual agency. Or, to put it another way, it does *not* function as a *collective*. Yet this is not to say that the existence of the departmental point of view would somehow obliterate the points of view of its individual faculty members. On the contrary. When the department's deliberations are concluded, the individual faculty go home, and then they are all free to reflect, from their own points of view, about what the department has done. In the normal course of things, they will each experience some level of *disagreement* with the department. This stands to reason, since the pool of considerations from which the department deliberates is much larger than the pool of considerations from which any individual faculty member would deliberate. In a real case, my own sense of disagreement with the Columbia Philosophy Department over the issue of requirements for the PhD was acute. I happen to believe that the only requirement that should be imposed for the PhD in philosophy is a defensible dissertation that makes an original scholarly contribution. This means that, from my own point of view, I rejected virtually *all* of the considerations from which the Columbia department actually deliberated, as it arrived at a fairly hefty slate of requirements. Although my colleagues' disagreements with the departmental point of view were probably less acute than mine, they were all nevertheless in a similar situation: None of them personally would deliberate from exactly the set of pooled deliberative considerations that formed the basis of the department's deliberations, and precisely because that was so, they were bound to find themselves in disagreement with at least some part of the department's reasoning and conclusions.

But if the existence of the departmental point of view does not obliterate the points of view of its individual faculty, we must take care not to draw the wrong conclusion from this fact. We must not suppose that the process that is the department's deliberations can be analyzed in terms of deliberations on the part of its individual faculty members. *That* would make it a case of *collective* agency involving many distinct agents, as opposed to a group *itself* being a case of *individual* agency in the way that I have just described.[4]

When philosophers officially acknowledge the possibility of group agency, they tend to wrongly assimilate it to a case of collective agency.[5] They tend to be driven to this assimilation by a commitment to the thesis of *metaphysical individualism*, according to which each human being qualifies as an individual agent in its own right, and its status as an individual agent in its own right, with its own point of view, can never be undermined or altered by involvements in group agency. (This thesis of metaphysical individualism is not to be confused with the thesis of methodological individualism. The latter is opposed by social ontologists when they argue for irreducibly social facts. But their arguments typically leave the former in place, and this shouldn't really be surprising since, as I explained above, there can be no social facts without social relations, and there can be no social relations without social relata, that is, individuals who stand in social relations. The point I want to underscore now is that these relata are typically conceived in accord with the thesis of metaphysical individualism, as individual human beings whose status as individual agents in their own rights is a metaphysical given that is neither undermined nor altered by their involvements in group agency.) Now, it may seem as though I have already implicitly conceded this thesis, by conceding that the existence of a departmental view would not obliterate the points of view of its individual faculty. But that is not so. For I never claimed that the individual faculty members are individual human beings! What else could they be? I claim they are agents of somewhat smaller than human size. Why? Because *some* of the intentional activities that go on in within the human beings that are the sites of their existence do not belong to their lives but belong instead to the life of the department. Going back to my own case. During the Columbia department's deliberations about its PhD requirements, an utterance issued from the human body that is the site of my existence, observing that distribution requirements are probably better than comprehensive examinations, because what is learned in courses has a better chance of being remembered. And then later, an utterance issued from that same human body, pronouncing to the student seated before it that she must fulfill the foreign language requirement in order to graduate. While we might colloquially say that both utterances were "mine" there is a clear sense in which they were not really intentional episodes in *my* life at all. The observation about distribution requirements was a moment in the *department's* deliberations, which were proceeding from its own group point of view—a point of view very different from mine as I just explained above; and the pronouncement enforcing the foreign language requirement was an expression of the *department's* will, not my own. This shows that the human being that is the site of my existence is not, in itself, an individual

4. This is not an obvious point. See my "Group Agency and Individualism," *Erkenntnis* 79 (2014), for an extended discussion of why we cannot model the deliberations of a group agent in collective terms, as a function of deliberations on the part of its human constituents.

5. Recent work that acknowledge the possibility of group agents in a sense close to the one I have in mind, include Philip Pettit and Christian List, *Group Agency: The Possibility, Design and Status of Corporate Agents* (Oxford: Oxford University Press, 2011), and Peter French, "The Corporation as a Moral Person," *American Philosophical Quarterly* 6 (1979): 207–15.

agent. It is the site of one agent that is smaller than human size—me; and it is also the site of intentional activity that proceeds from the point of view of a much larger group agent—the Columbia Philosophy Department.

What I have just brought out is that a human being can be a site of *rational fragmentation*. But according to metaphysical individualism, the natural condition of the human being is not rational fragmentation but *rational unity*. That is, it is the natural condition of a human being to be *one* agent, with a single point of view from which deliberation is to proceed in accord with the requirements of individual rationality. So if rational fragmentation were ever to occur within a human life, it would be a disruption of this natural condition. It would also be a rational failing—a falling short of the sort of overall rational unity that an individual human being, qua individual agent, should ideally achieve. Yet I do not see any rational failure in the situation I just described above. My brain and body are sites of intentional activities that figure in the life of the Columbia Philosophy Department, and as such, they do not figure in my own life as an individual agent who is distinct from the department. Even when I disagree with the department about what it does, I also believe that it is better that the department exist than not—because what it does is worth doing. I also believe that it is better that the department has reasoned positions on such things as requirements for the PhD even though they are not positions that I would personally put in place if I were dictator of the department. Finally, I believe that it is better that no one member of the department, including myself, should be dictator of the department—it is better that the department reason about the options before it *as a department*, from a departmental point of view that includes all that its members bring to the table as a basis for its deliberations. To believe all of these things is to have a reason to accept rational fragmentation within the human being that is the site of my existence; and it is to accept as well an existence and identity that makes me smaller than human size.

I realize that these are extremely nonstandard attitudes to take towards my own existence and identity. They are nonstandard precisely because they challenge the thesis of metaphysical individualism, by suggesting that my existence and identity are somehow *up to me*. This may seem a paradoxical suggestion. But here is a less paradoxical way of putting it: What is metaphysically given in human life is the existence of the human organism and its biological nature, which includes a biologically given capacity for reflective rational agency. But human beings are not born fully equipped with rational points of view from which to exercise that capacity. They are born as *wantons* who don't deliberate at all, but act impulsively on the present thought, whatever it may be. They *come* to deliberate when they see *reasons* to do so—when they see *opportunities* to pursue ends that require *coordinated* thought and action. Their first steps in this direction tend to be directed at certain sorts of long-term projects that require coordinated thought and effort over some period of time that is far shorter than a whole human life—projects such as building something, training for a sport, mastering a musical instrument, and so on. These projects provide reasons not to act wantonly, but to deliberate before acting by taking into account how the various things one might do would affect one's larger projects. If the scope of these initial deliberations that occur early in a human life is not yet very large, it is because the ends that prompt them do not require very large scope. But when the scope of deliberations is small, so is the point of view from which they proceed, for the point of view emerges with those deliberations. In other words, I'm saying that it is only *through* embracing and pursuing ends, and carrying out whatever deliberations those ends require, that individual agents with determinate points of view of their own come to exist. It follows that their existence is *not* a metaphysical given, but rather a product of effort and will.

It is very much part of this picture of agency that the overall philosophical claim I am making with it can be generalized to go in *both* directions of size. That is to say, *there can be multiple agents within a human being as well as group agents composed of many human beings.* So there are really *three* possibilities here, the two I have just mentioned in the last sentence, and then, of course, there can be (and are in the usual case we are so familiar with) agents of human size. Fictional cases of pathological multiplicity of agency—both benign and sinister—have been explored in books, films, and television, and we can glean from them what it might be like to actually encounter multiple points of view within a human being. But it is less noticed that involvements in group agency tend to induce multiplicity as well. Well, it *is* noticed in real life, only it is not correctly understood. We may visit our "friend" in the corporation and find that instead of encountering her familiar friendly point of view, we are faced with a mouthpiece for the corporate point of view. But we tend not to explicitly conceive these cases as cases of rational fragmentation; and so we tend not to draw the inference that our "friend" is not really an agent of human size, but somewhat smaller than that—a kind of "multiple" who coexists in the same body with another, only that "other" is a very large agent who doesn't reside wholly in her body but spans many other bodies as well. Yet we *should* view these cases in this way, because it helps us to direct our moral attention appropriately, away from the human constituents of the corporate agent, and toward the corporate agent itself, and *its* point of view, and *its* responsibility. For there often *is* a real locus of responsibility there.

We may find it morally unsatisfying to be told that in cases of group agency it is inappropriate to try to locate responsibility for group actions with the human constituents of the group agent. But this just reflects a residual commitment to metaphysical individualism, and perhaps to methodological individualism as well—we want to see human beings as the original, and also ultimate, individuals in whom all real responsibility resides. But the argument for group agency shows that there are no such original, ultimate individuals. What individuals there are have emerged for the sake of ends that their existence makes it possible to pursue. They need not fall one-to-one with human lives, and often do not. And each of them, no matter what their size, is properly regarded as a real locus of responsibility.

I claim, then, that it makes sense to regard a group agent as a locus of responsibility. But I do not claim that this should remove our sense of puzzlement about collective responsibility. On the contrary, it only helps to make the puzzle all the more vivid. If we can apply our intuitive conception of responsibility to group agents, it is because they have the features of individual agency that the conception takes for granted—because a group agent functions, literally, as an individual agent in its own right, with its own point of view. And if we find collective agency puzzling, it is because a collective does *not* function as an individual agent in its own right—because what makes collective agency collective is that it involves the agency of many.

3. FORWARD-LOOKING COLLECTIVE RESPONSIBILITY REFRAMED

Although merely *introducing* the distinction between group agency and collective agency doesn't solve the puzzle about collective responsibility, we've seen that it does unsettle many of our commonsense assumptions about the nature of individual agency. I now want to explain how this, in turn, can help to reframe the entire individualist picture of responsibility that gives rise to our puzzlement, so that we can better see where we might usefully direct our attention as we address the issue of our forward-looking collective responsibility.

But first a remark about what I take forward-looking collective responsibility to be. I have said that, in general, forward-looking responsibility is a matter of *taking* responsibility for what will happen in the future by acting in the present with an eye to future consequences. It follows that forward-looking *collective* responsibility is a matter of taking responsibility for what will happen in the future by undertaking collective action in the present with an eye to future consequences.

If the general idea of collective responsibility seems puzzling, the more specific idea of forward-looking collective responsibility may seem impossible. It is difficult enough to solve the problem of motivation that attends all cases of forward-looking responsibility—the problem of why we should *ever* act in the present for the sake of future consequences, especially when those consequences might not concern *us* at all, but rather future generations. Now, if this difficulty were to be solved by an individual—if she came to have real concern for the future—then we think she could surely act effectively, in the sense that she would be free to exercise whatever causal control she has at her disposal. So we think *an individual* really could *take* some responsibility for future states of affairs. But precisely because there is no locus of collective responsibility, we may doubt whether there is any parallel scope for *taking* collective responsibility for future states of affairs.

Given the intuitive picture of responsible agency, the difference between the individual and the collective case will naturally appear to turn on the presence versus absence of a definite domain of causal control. But if we view the nature of individual agency through the lens of the argument for group agency, we can see that this apparent difference is illusory.

The argument showed that agents exist for the sake of ends that their existence makes it possible to pursue. But it also showed that agents are emergent things that are *posterior* to the ends for the sake of which they exist. It is a characteristic feature of the process by which they emerge that ends are recognized as ends that might be pursued by *some* agent, even though that agent does not yet exist. And then, it is only through the actual pursuit of that end that the agent actually comes to exist. There is no significant assumption of causal control here. It is much more like a situation of cooperation—a recognition of an opportunity to pursue an end that will rest on voluntary "follow through" of one sort or another, that cannot be secured in advance. Thus, when an agent undertakes a long-term project, such as writing a philosophical book, she sees an opportunity to accomplish something that will take much coordinated effort over time—but at no time during the writing does she have control over whether her present efforts will be answered by future efforts that will complete what she has started. But she writes all the same, because she thinks she sees that somewhere in the future there is a common will that is equally interested in her long-term end. The same holds for the group projects that provide the reasons why group agents come to be. And the same holds for collective projects, too.

When, then, is the difference between these forms of agency? Only a difference in the nature of the ends at issue and the sort of coordination of effort they require. When ends are the reasons for an individual agent's existence, they demand the kind of overall rational unity that characterizes individual rationality. The example in the last section, of a philosophy department, is a case in point—the end of running a PhD program in philosophy mandates a *reasoned position* on many things, not on the part of this or that faculty member, but on the part of the department as a whole. Other ends require a similar rational unity but within different boundaries. Having a marriage and children, for example, mandate overall rational unity within a whole human life, or at least most of one. Still other ends might require some coordination of effort on the part of many human beings, but without achieving overall rational unity across them—sit-ins and rallies, for example. These ends would call for *collective* agency as opposed to *group* agency.

So one way to look at the issue, then, is that taking responsibility for future states of affairs is not best thought of as a matter of exercising causal control in the present with an eye to future consequences—though it is bound to involve that to some extent. It is better thought of as an openness to the various ends that might be embraced and pursued, insofar as we see opportunities to pursue them, and insofar as we think that pursuing them would indeed bring about good future consequences.

A parallel point can be made about the other major condition on responsible agency according to the intuitive individualist picture—not having one's own domain of causal control, but having one's own point of view from which to deliberate. Insofar as we really are open to all of the practical possibilities before us, we shall have to be open to the possibility that there might be good reason to cease existing as the size agents we are, so that we can help bring into existence agents of others sizes who could pursue ends we judge to be more important than the ends for the sake of which we currently exist. Of course these would be judgments made from our own points of view. But they wouldn't be anything like ordinary deliberative judgments that work out which, of the things that lie within the domain of one's *own* causal control, it would be best to pursue. They would be judgments made in a quite different spirit—a more opportunistic spirit. Indeed, I think what I'm describing is an *agency of opportunism*—finding ends worth pursuing, and finding ways of being that would afford pursuing them, where this would involve generating points of view from which to pursue them. Sometimes these ways of pursuing ends will involve individual agency of one scale or another, and sometimes they will involve collective agency.

I will end this article with one concrete proposal and one abstract moral observation.

The concrete proposal is to explore how the vision of agency that I've put forward in this article might relate to the issue of climate change, and how we might appropriately take forward-looking responsibility for the future state of the climate. That general end is too vague to be action-guiding. If we look about in the opportunistic spirit that I'm recommending, it becomes readily apparent that there are lots of different ends that call for different kinds and scales of coordinated effort. On the one hand, we can envisage a global collective project, in which each individual agent that exists (no matter what its size) aims to reduce its consumption of energy, as best it can, for the sake of the collective end of reducing aggregate energy consumption to such an extent as to make a global difference. On the other hand, we can also envisage the formation of group agents, modeled on the Manhattan Project, whose end would be to develop, as rapidly as possible, technologies that would benefit the climate. (I've argued elsewhere that the Manhattan Project was indeed the project of a group agent.[6])

The more abstract observation is to link the metaphysical vision of this article with a corresponding moral vision. I call it *moral opportunism.*

When I was first asked to think about forward-looking collective responsibility for this volume of *Midwest Studies,* the first thing that occurred to me was that we now feel ever-increasing pressure to extend the scope of our moral concerns, and to do so in an increasingly consequentialist spirit. It is obvious that these increased pressures are due to two related developments: increased knowledge about suffering on the part of distant others, and increased scope for coordinated action that can be aimed at alleviating that suffering. Both have been facilitated by technological advances in the media. But the latter has to do as well with our highly interdependent socioeconomic condition. As a result of these developments, we are now faced with new opportunities for taking meaningful large-scale consequentialist action. Yet it seems to me that there has always been available a simple chain of reasoning that could have led any of us to be sympathetic to a utilitarian moral point of view. It begins with the idea that the occasion for moral reflection is the recognition that there are other points of view from which things matter besides one's own. It then notes that the point of action is to bring things about. It proceeds to observe that if one is rational, one will aim bring about better consequences rather than worse, and also, that more good consequences are better. And it concludes that this is a morally significant point, insofar as the consequences we bring about will matter from other points of view as well as our own. I wouldn't want to suggest that this little argument for utilitarianism should eclipse all other moral arguments for competing moral visions. But I do want to reiterate that it has always been readily available to anyone who is capable of moral reflection. And this should lead us to ask: Why is it that an explicit formulation and defense of the principle of utility came so late in the history of Western moral philosophy? I think one good answer to this question is simply that, when Bentham put it forward, he was responding to new moral opportunities that were not present before then.

---

6. See "What is an Agent?," *Synthese* 140 (2004): 181–98.

Thus, my thought is that even if everyone could previously have agreed in the abstract that more good consequences are better, there was little scope for moral response to that moral insight. Whereas, in Bentham's lifetime, there were new socioeconomic conditions that were creating large-scale suffering (a newly created class of urban working poor), and new political conditions that might afford meaningful action toward alleviating that suffering (through progressive legislation). The lesson I take is that the more important thing he did was to respond to the moral opportunities around him, rather than produce a moral theory—or perhaps to make the lesson a little more palatable to the moral theorists among us, we should not have any illusions that it makes sense to engage in moral theorizing without being attuned to the actual moral problems and opportunities we face, which are not the same in all times and place—indeed, some of the most urgent problems and opportunities we now face have to do with precisely the topic of this special issue, and also how to muster, as well as cope with, the various forms of group and collective agency that they invite.

Midwest Studies In Philosophy, XXXVIII (2014)

Historical Memory as Forward- and Backward-Looking Collective Responsibility

LINDA RADZIK

1. STUMBLING BLOCKS

Visitors to Berlin, if they spend enough time walking through the various neighborhoods, will eventually have their eyes caught by a glimmer in the pavement. Every so often, one of the cobblestones is made of brass. Sometimes one sees a cluster of brass stones. Eventually, the visitor will stop for a closer look and see that that the stone is engraved. It will say something like this:

> Here lived
> ERNA SCHLESINGER
> née Apolant
> b. 1891
> Deported 1943
> Auschwitz
> Murdered 1.13.1943

To the left of Erna Schlesinger's stone, which lies in the newly trendy Neukölln neighborhood, is another:

> Here lived
> DR. DAGOBERT SCHLESINGER
> b. 1876
> Disenfranchised/Humiliated

Took Refuge in Death
7.20.1941[1]

These are *stolpersteine*, or "stumbling blocks." In the city of Berlin alone, 5,391 victims of Nazi crimes are memorialized with similar stones, not to mention the numerous other memorials and museums in the city.[2] One is always running into the Nazi past in Berlin. For a visitor from the United States, a country that is notably less forthcoming about the injustices of its own history, the bluntness of the *stolpersteine* is breathtaking. As you happily wander the streets of this vibrant city, window-shopping or eating ice cream, the stones wink up at you, "Erna Schlesinger lived *here*. She was *murdered*." That is a heavy reflection for a spring afternoon.

As one learns more about the *stolpersteine* and the culture of memory in Germany, it becomes clear that at least many contemporary Germans believe themselves to have a special responsibility to preserve the memory of the Nazi atrocities. What this has meant in practice is accepting the burden of living with continual and explicit reminders of the brutal histories of their ancestors and their cities. It has meant, for example, living with a plaque in front of your home (where you are building your life and perhaps raising your children) that declares that this is the very same place where people were driven to suicide or from which they were dragged off to a concentration camp. Given that contemporary Germans are almost all members of generations born too late to bear any sort of causal relation to the Nazi crimes, the moral intuition that they yet stand in some form of responsibility relation to those crimes requires justification.

If future generations of a wrongdoing group do indeed have a responsibility to preserve the memory of the past, what kind of responsibility is it? What manner of burden is it? And should we be troubled by the suggestion that it can be not only distributed to individuals but also inherited by future generations? As we will see in the *stolpersteine* case, a collective responsibility to preserve memory is often presented as less worrisome than other sorts of collective moral burdens, or, indeed, as not morally problematic at all. It is not interpreted as a form of collective punishment or atonement, but as something positive. Discussions often emphasize the "forward-looking" or "future-oriented" characteristics of memory work. In preserving the memory of the past atrocities, one is fighting anti-Semitism and other forms of discrimination, strengthening democracy, and working to ensure that such things never happen again. Being associated with a "forward-looking responsibility" such as this offers benefits to one's own community as well as to others, and is much less psychically threatening than being associated with moral

1. These are my translations of the German texts. What I have rendered here as "took refuge is death" is "Flucht in den Tod." This is how the stones indicate suicide. An image of the Schlesingers' stones is available at <http://kultur-neukoelln.de/gedenken-stolpersteine-in-neukoelln.php> (retrieved March 20, 2014).

2. <http://www.Stolpersteine-berlin.de/de/orte-biografien/suche/liste> (retrieved March 20, 2014). This may not translate into 5,391 separate stones, however, since the artist, Gunter Demnig, also makes larger "threshold" stones that list several persons. See also <http://www.Stolpersteine.eu/technik/> (retrieved March 12, 2014).

blame, guilt, or punishment. Therefore, one might argue, there is nothing amiss if forward-looking responsibilities are held collectively.

My aim for this essay is relatively modest. I will argue that the labels backward-looking and forward-looking, as they have been used in the literature to date, hide some conceptual ambiguities. Once these ambiguities are clarified, we will see that contemporary Germans' responsibility to preserve the memory of Nazi era crimes may well be forward-looking in one sense while being backward-looking in another and that, if this is so, moral worries about the attribution of collective responsibility resurface. In Section 2, I will tell the reader more about the *stolpersteine* memorial project. I will introduce the project in the terms of a loose forward-looking responsibility framework, which I think is tempting to use, but which I will go on to argue as problematic. Section 3 offers some suggestions as to how we can disambiguate the language of both forward- and backward-looking responsibility. Section 4 then uses these distinctions to offer some alternative interpretations of the kind of responsibility contemporary Germans have to preserve the memory of the past. Although I will provide a brief argument for my own preferred interpretation, my main point in that section will be to show that we can pose these alternatives and the moral issues to which they give rise more clearly once we attend to the distinctions drawn in Section 3.

2. THE HISTORY AND RECEPTION OF THE *STOLPERSTEINE*

The *stolpersteine* are the creation of the Cologne artist Gunter Demnig, who made the first stones in the mid-1990s. On his website, he describes it as "an art project that commemorates the victims of National Socialism, keeping alive the memory of all Jews, Roma and Sinti, homosexuals, dissidents, Jehovah's Witnesses and victims of euthanasia who were deported and exterminated."[3] The stones name and provide details for individual victims of Nazi crimes and are placed where the victim lived, worked, or studied before his or her death. As of December 2013, a total of 43,500 memorial stones had so far been placed;[4] the overwhelming majority of these are to be found in Germany,[5] but the project has now expanded into 16 other European countries as well.[6]

While Demnig is certainly the central figure in the creation of the *stolpersteine* project, the widespread success of the project is due to the participation of large numbers of people, who sponsor stones by donating labor or money. Each stone costs 120 Euros to produce and install. Research must also be done in order to establish the biographical details about each victim and the proper location for each installation (e.g., the last place of residence before deportation). Additionally, someone must secure permission from city or town authorities. Finally, the stones require cleaning and maintenance over time. Some sponsors are relatives of the people memorialized by the stones. However, most stones are

3. Gunter Demnig, <http://www.Stolpersteine.eu/en/> (retrieved March 20, 2014).
4. <http://www.Stolpersteine.eu/technik/> (retrieved March 12, 2014).
5. Linde Apel counts 40,000 stones in Germany. See Linde Apel, "Stumbling Blocks in Germany," *Rethinking History: The Journal of Theory and Practice* 17 (2013): 1–14.
6. <http://www.Stolpersteine.eu/technik/> (Accessed March 12, 2014).

sponsored by schools, churches, or clubs that have no relation to the person memorialized other than sharing a neighborhood.[7] Larger cities sometimes have *stolpersteine* organizations that offer tours or help visitors to their cities locate stones memorializing loved ones.[8]

On the whole, the *stolpersteine* project has been well received. There are some exceptions. In the early years of the project, cities debated whether to grant permits for the stones. Property values came into the discussion as well as issues of the burdens of memory. Some smaller towns continue those debates, but Munich is now the only large city that does not grant permits.[9] A prominent leader of the Jewish community in Munich objected to the imagery of German boots walking over Jewish names.[10] Some members of the Roma and Sinti communities have been similarly discomfited either with the idea of people walking on the memorials or with Roma and Sinti surnames being publicized as such, given continuing discrimination. As a result, some stones have been removed and others have been altered so as to read, for example, "Here lived a Sinto . . ."[11] Also, stones are sometimes stolen or vandalized, apparently by people with neo-Nazi leanings.[12]

Still, the growth of the *stolpersteine* project seems to be limited mostly by Demnig's own dedication to laying each stone himself. When school or neighborhood groups contact Demnig with research identifying a person to memorialize, a place to lay a stone, a city permit for the work, and the funds to pay for the project, they are told they must wait approximately one year for an appointment.[13] Demnig is on the road 255–300 days a year with the *stolpersteine* project. When he does arrive, the installation is often accompanied by a small ceremony arranged by the sponsoring group. They narrate whatever they were able to learn about the victim's biography, lay flowers, or say a prayer. Surviving relatives are sometimes located and invited.[14]

When Demnig himself is asked why it is important to remember the past, he explicitly denies the idea that it is a response to a collective form of guilt.[15] However, it is also clear that he is deeply troubled by the idea that the past will be forgotten. His idea for the *stolpersteine* project came when he was involved in another public art exhibit marking the deportation of Roma and Sinti people

7. Apel, 4.

8. See, for example, the websites for the groups in Berlin, <http://www.Stolpersteine-berlin.de/> (retrieved March 20, 2014); and Hamburg, <http://www.Stolpersteine-hamburg.de/> (retrieved March 20, 2014). Free smartphone apps for locating stones in Berlin and the suburbs of Munich were also available at the iTunes App Store at the time of this writing.

9. Kirsten Grieshaber, "Plaques for Nazi Victims Offer a Personal Impact," *New York Times*, 23 November, 2003, B23.

10. Alan Mairson, "Embedded Memories," *National Geographic* 205, no. 6 (2004).

11. Apel, 8.

12. Colin Nickerson, "Artist Lays Down Plaques for Victims of the Nazis," *International Herald Tribune*, 14 January, 2007.

13. These details are provided by Matthew Cook and Micheline van Riemsdijk, "Agents of Memorialization: Gunter Demnig's Stolpersteine and the Individual (Re-)Creation of a Holocaust Landscape in Berlin," *Journal of Historical Geography* 43 (2014): 138–47.

14. An author describes being invited to such an event in honor of his own relatives, in Marty Blatt, "Holocaust Memory and Germany," *The Public Historian* 34, no. 4 (2002): 53–66.

15. Nickerson.

through the streets of Cologne. "An old lady stopped by and scolded my work, insisting there had never been any Gypsies in Cologne," Demnig recalled.[16] The felt need to counteract this sort of denial and forgetting has now become Demnig's life's work.

The fact that the *stolpersteine* project is a memorial means that it involves at least some backward-looking elements, by which I mean here simply elements that are focused on the past. The *stolpersteine* look to past insofar as they are an effort to remember and display respect for the dead. However, when we think about the nature of the sense of responsibility being exhibited in this work of memory, the most compelling interpretation may well be the forward-looking one. It has many of the markers associated with the language of forward-looking responsibility.

First of all, the term "backward-looking responsibility" is often used to denote a status that one finds oneself with as a result of wrongdoing. If I have wronged you, then I am guilty. Because I have that status, I may be required to act by, say, repairing the damage I created. In contrast, the language of forward-looking responsibility is often used to indicate someone "taking responsibility" or "undertaking responsibility," that is, stepping forward to do important work.[17] In 2007, Hamburg mayor Ole von Beust, who himself sponsored four stones for Jewish relatives lost in the Holocaust, described the project as "the largest citizens' initiative in the world."[18] While I would not hazard to evaluate the superlative, the description of Demnig's project as a "citizens' initiative" is fitting. Forward-looking responsibilities are often associated with the concept of seeing that something ought to be done and doing it for that reason, not because one is being pressed by another into doing so. In turn, "taking responsibility" is associated with the virtue of "being responsible." Demnig has been the recipient of numerous awards and honors, which commend him and his project as virtuous.[19]

Another indication that the form of responsibility being exercised by the participants in the *stolpersteine* project is forward-looking is the emphasis that they place on the future. Many discussions cite the importance of understanding the past to avoid repeating it in the future. Demnig has described his work as a piece of performance art, wherein the stones are meant to prompt discussion and bring the memory of the past into everyday life.[20] He himself has said, "This is not a project for the past but for the future."[21] Historian and *stolperstein* volunteer Linde Apel emphasizes the educational importance of the project, which allows ordinary people to understand history in a way with which they emotionally connect at a

16. Quoted in Grieshaber.
17. See Henry S. Richardson, "Institutionally Divided Moral Responsibility," *Social Philosophy and Policy* 16, no. 2 (1999): 218–49; and David Enoch, "Being Responsible, Taking Responsibility, and Penumbral Agency," in *Luck, Value and Commitment: Themes from the Ethics of Bernard Williams*, ed. Ulrike Heuer and Gerald Lang (New York: Oxford, 2012), 103–13. Enoch notes that we sometimes use the phrase "taking responsibility" in a different, "epistemic" sense in which one might "take" responsibility for past wrongdoing simply in the sense that one acknowledges that one is guilty of past wrongdoing (Enoch, 103–4).
18. Quoted in Apel (2013), 2.
19. <http://www.stolpersteine.eu/en/biography/> (retrieved April 22, 2014).
20. Gilman (2007).
21. Gilman (2007).

time when fewer and fewer will have the opportunity to meaningfully interact with a survivor themselves.[22] Kirsten Harjes draws upon the biblical origin of the metaphor of the stumbling stone to interpret the forward-looking task of the *stolpersteine*,

> To the prophet Isaiah (8:14), the symbolic stone over which a wrongdoer or an entire people living in violation of God's law must stumble is a reminder to live life in fear of God and a gauge that tells whether one has lived the proper life or not. In the New Testament, the stumbling stone makes those fall who disobeyed the word of God, but it is a blessing to the faithful, a cornerstone of their godly lives.[23]

In other words, the purpose of the stumbling stone is not punitive but educative. It is meant to prompt reflection and future good behavior. So, while the *stolpersteine* activists are sincere in their desire to memorialize individual victims of the Nazis, and to prevent these people from being lost in an anonymous set of statistics, we can also see why James E. Young argues that, "These are memorials by and for the Germans," rather than, say, for the Jewish community or the surviving families.[24]

A further reason for interpreting the task of the *stolpersteine* to be something other than an expression of a backward-looking status such as guilt, or an attempt to expiate such guilt through self-punishment, can be found in the fact that the stones can be, and sometimes are, sponsored by descendants of victims and others who have no particular connection to the wrongdoers. They have been placed in countries, such as Norway and Hungary, where the local populations are not descended from groups who were generally complicit in the Nazi crimes. Yet these stones seem to play a very similar role to the German-sponsored stones in Berlin.[25] They cause pedestrians to stop, to picture the events in their minds as they unfolded on that spot (the arrival of the deportation notice, the Gestapo arriving, the last departure, the neighbors watching or averting their eyes . . .), to contemplate the lives lost, to ponder how atrocities likes these could have happened in the past, to talk about whether they could happen again, and to ask themselves what they would do if they did.

3. DIMENSIONS OF RESPONSIBILITY: ORIENTATION VERSUS JUSTIFICATION

So far I have provided some reasons for thinking that, despite its character as an act of memorialization, the sense of collective responsibility that seems to be exhibited by the *stolpersteine* activists is a forward-looking sense of responsibility. Such a conclusion would be, I believe, an interesting one because, if this is all that a collective responsibility to remember past atrocities amounts to—basically,

22. Apel (2013).
23. Harjes, 144.
24. Quoted in Lois Gilman, "Memory Blocks—Artist Gunter Demnig Builds a Holocaust Memorial One Stone at a Time," <http://www.smithsonian.com>, October 11, 2007 (retrieved April 3, 2014).
25. Thanks to Robert R. Shandley for this observation.

a burden that members of one's group can choose to take on and that provides opportunity for virtuous activity, such as participation in valuable projects of moral education—then, though the work might indeed be burdensome, there is nothing morally worrying about this form of collective responsibility. Yet this interpretation of the sense of responsibility at work in the case of the *stolpersteine* leaves out something crucial, namely the fact that it is a project that is being carried out largely by the contemporary members of the nation that, in the past, perpetrated the crimes in question. The stones placed in the sidewalks of Berlin would have a significantly different meaning were they funded, produced, and maintained entirely or even primarily through international efforts and merely tolerated by the local population. Instead, the *stolpersteine*, in addition to the myriad other memorials and evidence of a culture of memory in Germany, suggest that at least many contemporary Germans perceive themselves as having a special duty to remember the past because of their identity as Germans. In this thought, a backward- rather than a forward-looking conception of responsibility seems to be at work.

At this point, one might simply conclude that the responsibility to remember past atrocities is both forward- and backward-looking. However, given the ways these terms have been used in the literature, such a statement might well have problematic implications, raising associations of collective guilt and punishment. In this section, I will argue that the concepts of both backward- and forward-looking responsibility are ambiguous in ways that need to be explored. In order to examine these distinctions in a more manageable way, it will help to switch for a while from cases of collective responsibility for atrocities to more mundane cases of individual responsibility.

Let's begin by thinking about the various ideas associated with backward-looking responsibility in cases where one individual has wronged another. Suppose Jim wrongfully harmed me, by betraying my trust or recklessly damaging my property. If he had no justification or excuse, then he is responsible for that past act in the sense that he is liable to responses such as blame, resentment, guilt, retribution, and, where some form of compensable material damage was done, demands for restitution. The type of responsibility at issue here is "backward-looking" in two senses. First, what I will call the *orientation* of the responsibility—the main focus of moral attention and concern of the people enforcing or satisfying the responsibility, the character of the responses they make—can be described as backward-looking.[26] I resent Jim for the wrongful act, which occurred at a particular point in time, now past. His guilt, too, focuses on that past act. Indeed, on standard analyses, the attitudes of resentment and guilt require the judgment that a wrongful action has taken place.[27] In paying restitution to me, he will again look backward to determine what he owes me now. If Jim is punished in accordance with the logic of

---

26. Backward-oriented responsibility in cases of virtuous actions (e.g., Jim protecting me from harm) would involve things like pride, praise, admiration, and reward.

27. They *require* that judgment in the sense that, if the judgment is absent, then the attitude or emotion being experienced is either not really resentment or guilt, but another emotion (such as jealousy or shame), or not rational (as in the case when we resent the door we walked into or feel "survivor guilt").

retribution (the purely backward-*oriented* version of punishment), the authorities look to the character of his past act and past state of mind to determine the proportionate level of suffering to impose upon him now.

The second dimension of responsibility, which I would like to delineate here, is justification. In Jim's case, the type of responsibility at issue can aptly be described as backward-looking insofar as this characterizes the kind of *reason* or *justification* that the victim and the community have for responding to Jim the way we do (resenting him, blaming him, calling for his punishment, demanding restitution), or the kind of *reason* or *justification* that Jim has for responding as he does (feeling guilty, apologizing, accepting legitimate punishment, paying fair restitution). In the cases with which backward-looking language is usually associated, it is the fact that Jim wrongfully harmed me in the past that now justifies these responses. Here we look to a past act of wrongdoing as the source of negative desert. But we might also use this sort of language in cases where someone comes to have a responsibility through a past action of another kind, such as signing a contract or making a promise. The key idea is that backward-*justified* responsibilities are supported by desert-based or justice-based claims rather than by the good consequences that might be brought about by the enforcement or satisfaction of such responsibilities. Indeed, the legitimacy of Jim's backward-justified responsibilities toward me, the victim of his misdeed, is fully independent of future consequences. Even if Jim knows that I will only spend the money he owes me in a way that I will live to regret (say, by purchasing an unreliable used car), he still has a backward-justified responsibility to pay me that money.

Let us now consider what the dimensions of orientation and justification look like in the category of forward-looking responsibilities. A responsibility that is forward-looking in orientation involves accepting a role in the future. Henry S. Richardson's examples from his classic paper include a man taking responsibility for supervising a group of children in a swimming pool and a teenage boy accepting a job as a babysitter.[28] The main focus of attention and concern for these two people is the children's welfare. Childcare is sensibly characterized as a forward-oriented concern because it requires a readiness to meet whatever challenges the future holds. While the lifeguard's and the babysitter's responsibilities can often be traced back to particular past acts, namely the moments when they promised to take on the supervisory duties, those acts do not fully determine the character of actions they should take. Richardson argues that it is folly to attempt to reduce something like the responsibility of being a babysitter to a set of rules to which one binds oneself at the moment that one makes the promise.[29] In taking on responsibilities like these, we are taking on roles that will require us to decide when circumstances demand that rules be revised or broken. For example, "Don't leave the house" should be ignored in the case of a fire or armed intruder. It is the orientation to dealing with what the future might bring that characterizes what are called forward-looking responsibilities in Richardson's discussion.

28. Richardson (1999).
29. Richardson (1999), 220–21.

Other commentators simply define "forward-looking responsibilities" in terms of what I have called the dimension of justification rather than orientation.[30] For them, forward-looking responsibilities are those that are justified by an appeal to consequences or by pragmatic considerations rather than desert- or justice-based considerations. On this construal, someone has a forward-looking responsibility to watch the children if the reason for doing so is the good that would result from playing that role. I will refer to these hereafter as "forward-justified" responsibilities.

Defining forward-justified responsibilities in this way makes for a clean contrast to backward-justified responsibilities, but it also worth noting that it places in a single category cases one might be inclined to separate. For example, this category might include both duties that are assigned to a person on consequentialist grounds and situations that are best described as supererogatory, that is, where a person takes on a responsibility that no one could legitimately claim was her duty prior to her voluntarily "taking" it as own.[31] In the supererogatory case, the point of describing the responsibility as forward-looking would be to emphasize that there is no desert- or justice-based claim against this person in virtue of which someone could demand that she take up the responsibility. However, once she does voluntarily adopt the responsibility (say, by promising to watch the children as they swim in the pool), she comes to have a backward-justified responsibility to fulfill her promise.

The distinction between what I am calling the orientation and the justification of responsibility talk is subtle, especially on the backward-looking side of things, and the reader might wonder whether it can really be maintained. But that there is a distinction to be drawn becomes clearer in those cases where we get different combinations of the backward- and forward-looking categories. For example, when a teenager is required to take on the responsibility of babysitting her younger siblings as a punishment for breaking her curfew, then the orientation of her responsibility is primarily forward, but the justification for her having that responsibility is backward. She deserves to be saddled with the burdens and sacrifices of babysitting on a Saturday night as her "just desert" for her transgression, yet the focus of her concern and attention in carrying out the responsibility of a babysitter is properly future-oriented. Similarly, Bishop Butler's defense of the reactive attitude of resentment emphasizes its role in defending the self, promoting justice in the community, and training up the moral conscience.[32] Resentment, by definition, is a negative emotional reaction to a perceived past wrong, and so is

30. See, for example, Jeffrey Blustein, *The Moral Demands of Memory* (New York: Cambridge University Press, 2008), 220; and David Miller, "Distributing Responsibilities," *Journal of Political Philosophy* 9, no. 4 (2001): 466.

31. Some discussions of "forward-looking responsibility" seem to place special emphasis on the idea that these responsibilities are adopted somewhat voluntarily. For example, Richardson (1999) and Enoch (2012) both emphasize the idea of forward-looking responsibilities being responsibilities that a person takes on. Yet they seem willing, in the end, to accept that there can be duties to take on such responsibilities.

32. Joseph Butler, *Fifteen Sermons Preached at the Rolls Chapel* (Boston: Hilliard, Gray, Little and Wilkins, 1827), Sermon VIII.

backward-oriented. Yet the justification for God giving us the capacity for this attitude in the first place, according to Butler, is largely based on the consequences of our holding such attitudes; resentment is forward-justified. These examples suggest (though we will have to look at the matter more closely in the next section) that the distinctions between backward- and forward-looking orientation and justification are orthogonal to and independent of one another.

4. ALTERNATIVE INTERPRETATIONS OF THE RESPONSIBILITY TO REMEMBER

With these distinctions at hand, let us return to the case of the *stolpersteine*. Let us take seriously the moral intuition that contemporary Germans have a special responsibility to preserve the memory of the Nazi crimes and their victims, a responsibility that is met, in part, with efforts such as the *stolpersteine* memorials. If this is the case, what kind of responsibility could this be?

Let us start with the *orientation* of the responsibility. Are the responses the *stolpersteine* volunteers are making primarily oriented toward the past or toward the future? What is the main focus of their moral attention and concern? When the question is put in this way, we can now see that, of course, the moral attention and concern go in both temporal directions. There is a backward-oriented element in that the stones are memorials meant to honor the dead. As such, the information they include about the person must be accurate and convey something of the gravity of the wrongs done to him or her. But this backward-oriented element is connected to the fact that the task at hand is memorialization, rather than the fact that it is a response to wrongdoing. Notice, the need to be accurate and respectful in one's depiction of the dead remains even when the work of preserving memory is taken up by a person who has no individual or group-based relationship at all to the history of the Nazi crimes. It is there even if the person being memorialized is not a victim of an atrocity but only of a tragedy. So, the presence of this sort of backward-oriented element in the responsibility of memory does not send up any particular red flags to a theorist who is worried about the assignment of collective responsibility to future generations of wrongdoing groups.

Continuing with the question of the orientation of the responsibility of those carrying out the *stolpersteine* project, our attention is next drawn to the forward-oriented elements. The reasons for thinking that the orientation is toward the future is the explicit emphasis placed on the role of the *stolpersteine* project in moral and political education—both in the education of the people who participate in researching the lives of particular victims and placing the stones, and the education that takes place when people stumble over the stones in their daily lives and are led to reflect or converse with others about the meaning of the past and its relevance for their own lives. The debates that almost inevitably surround the form of memorial projects—whether the symbols they have chosen are appropriate and tasteful—also serve as some evidence of their forward-orientation. Memorials are not simply ways of paying off debts for which there are relatively stable standards (which would fit a backward-oriented model). They must answer to their contemporary audience's aesthetic, moral, and political sensibilities and, because memorials are built to last, try to anticipate how they will be received in the future. As Richardson's discussion emphasized, this is the sort of responsibility where one cannot simply rely on established moral rules but can only fulfill one's responsibility through a more open-ended engagement with the possibilities the future might hold.

So it appears that the *stolpersteine* project is properly interpreted as at least primarily forward-looking in orientation. This leaves open the question of whether it is forward- or backward-looking in justification. In other words, we might still ask, given that this forward-oriented responsibility to remember the Nazi past is a kind of burden to be born, what justifies its being born *by these people?* Notice, the chief advantage of distinguishing between the dimensions of orientation and justification is that it makes it clear that this question needs to be asked. Otherwise, simply insisting that the responsibility to preserve memory is forward-looking (in one sense) might simply deflect one from asking whether it is also backward-looking (in another sense).

A purely forward-looking justification of the collective responsibility to preserve memory would appeal solely to consequences. Perhaps contemporary Germans are simply the *best-placed* geographically, linguistically, etc., to continue the work of memory. On such an account, their being the contemporary members of the same national group that committed the atrocities would, in itself, have no significance. If some other group, for some reason, became better equipped to do the work of memory, the burden would pass to them instead. The main appeal of a purely forward-justified account such as this would be, of course, that it managed to assign some kind of collective responsibility without endorsing collective blame, guilt, or punishment.

On the other side of the spectrum, one might embrace just such a framework and use it to interpret the *stolpersteine* case. In other words, one might argue that Germany's collective guilt for the crimes of the Nazi era, which also justified the payment of costly reparations in the postwar years, continues to this day. The passage of time has merely resulted in a gentler form of collective penalty—a duty to preserve the memory of the past. On this reading, then, the case of historical memory parallels the case of the teenage girl who must babysit her siblings as a penalty for breaking her curfew. The responsibility is forward-oriented (preserving memory, babysitting), but the justification for the responsibility is backward-justified (as retribution for negative desert). In both cases, the punishments are somewhat burdensome, but not inherently painful or humbling; they even offer benefits to the ones being punished and opportunities for virtue. But they are still punishments because the justification for the distribution of the burden is punitive.

If this account is right then, according to my terminology, it turns out that the responsibilities in question (preserving memory, babysitting) are paradigmatically backward-oriented in addition to being forward-oriented. They are responses to past wrongdoing that fit within the standard paradigm, which is oriented toward guilt, blame, and punishment. One might suspect that all cases of backward-justification will turn out like this. *Whenever* we are dealing with a case where a responsibility is justified by negative desert, we will also have a case where these paradigmatic backward-oriented responses are merited. In other words, although I have suggested above that the dimensions of orientation and justification are orthogonal to and independent of one another, many will disagree. They will argue instead that negative desert and the legitimacy of the guilt, blame, and punishment must go together. In fact, I suspect many people believe the connection is simply analytic. To have negative desert just is to be *to blame* for something, *to be guilty* for it, and *to deserve punishment* for it.

I believe that it is precisely this assumption that makes so many theorists resistant to the notion of collective responsibility. I also believe that it is an unnecessary assumption and that we should be open to conceiving of different varieties of responsibility in terms of the different kinds of responses that they make appropriate. Guilt, blame, and punishment are not appropriate responses to people who bear no individual causal connection to wrongful actions; though we may be able to hold those people responsible in other sorts of way, such as requiring their group to pay reparations.[33]

For me, then, the question raised by the *stolpersteine* project is this: Can we make sense of the intuition that contemporary Germans' special responsibility to preserve the memory of the past is rooted in their historical connection to the wrongdoers without attributing any guilt or blame to them? In other words, can we provide a backward-justification for this responsibility to preserve memory without inadvertently pushing its meaning back into the old guilt-blame-and-punishment paradigm?

Answering this question requires asking ourselves how we should continue to conceive of the wrongs in question. How do we think of the legacy of the atrocities of the past? People used to think of sin like a stain on the soul that could only be purified by suffering. (Some still do.) The prospect of claiming that a whole people have a collective blot and are in need of a collective dose of suffering is horrifying. To the degree that these ancient notions of sin and atonement are still at work in any of our conceptions of collective responsibility or retribution, critics are right to object. Others conceive of the wrongs of the past on the model of a debt. Yet this model is objectionable, too, in that it suggests that wrongs such as murder, torture, and genocide could be (if only we are given enough time and information) measured, compared, paid off with something of equivalent value, and left behind forever. A more satisfactory conception of the continuing legacy of the past will conceive of it, not as a stain on the soul or as a debt, but as a set of ongoing problems in a series of relationships—the relationships between the former wrongdoing group and the formerly victimized groups, between the former wrongdoing group and the larger community of nations, and among the members of the former wrongdoing group.[34] While some of these problems can sensibly be captured on the model of debt and repayment, others cannot. They are instead a matter of rebuilding trust.[35]

33. Linda Radzik, "Collective Responsibility and Duties to Respond," *Social Theory and Practice* 27, no. 3 (2001): 455–71.

34. See Linda Radzik, *Making Amends: Atonement in Morality, Law, and Politics* (New York: Oxford University Press, 2009), especially chap 7.

35. One need only attend to Germany's diplomatic relations with Poland to see that this remains a work in progress.

If we read the *stolpersteine* project with this framework in mind, then I think we have another interpretation according to which the responsibility in question is forward-oriented yet backward-justified. The reason why contemporary Germans have a special responsibility to preserve the memory of the past is because it is crucial to reestablishing their place as a trustworthy member within the community of nations. In other words, they are assigned this role, not simply because they are well placed to play it efficiently, but because they are burdened by history— because their ancestors were the wrongdoers. However, to say this does not imply that contemporary Germans are themselves to blame for the actions of their ancestors. It is merely to say that it is not unreasonable for other groups to maintain a moderate degree of caution and suspicion with respect to their group given that past.[36] (How much caution and suspicion is, of course, itself a morally significant question and should reasonably change over time.) To say that contemporary Germans' responsibility to preserve the memory of the past is backward-justified is simply to say that it is not unfair for them to bear this part of the burden of responding to the legacy of that past. Alternatively, to avoid the suggestion that this is a history with which one could ever be "finished," we might say that a willingness to deal honestly with this past is a condition of trust.

5. CONCLUSION

My primary goal in this article has been to disambiguate the language of forward- and backward-looking responsibility, so as to raise questions about collective responsibility and the ethics of memory in a clearer way. But I will also be happy if I have drawn philosophers' attention to the *stolpersteine*, which are a particularly eloquent expression of the culture of memory in Germany, where the past is frequently acknowledged without excuse or deflection. Again, it is worth pausing to ponder the contrast between this example and the memory of slavery, or the memory of the genocide of Native Americans, in the United States.

In this essay, I have suggested that we can interpret the work of preserving the memory of historical atrocities as primarily an expression of moral concern for the future, at the same time that is also an expression of respect for the dead. For this reason, it makes sense to describe the *orientation* of the sense of responsibility displayed as forward-looking. However, I have argued that though the work of memory looks primarily forward in this sense, whether the *justification* of the responsibility is forward- or backward-looking is an independent question. The former sort of justification would appeal solely to future good consequences, while the latter would look to the past to ground the responsibility in a desert- or justice-based claim.

In the last section, I suggested that there at least three ways in which a collective responsibility to preserve the memory of the past could be forward-oriented yet backward-justified. Its justification could be rooted in negative desert and a principle of retribution. It could be grounded in a collective debt and an appeal to a principle of restitution. Finally, the collective responsibility to preserve

36. For more on the notion of reasonable distrust, see Radzik (2001).

memory could be justified by appeal to the claim that it is not unfair for the descendants of a wrongdoing group to bear the burden of responding to the distrust that reasonably came to be attached to their group because of the actions of their ancestors. I believe that the third alternative is the most attractive. But both of the latter two interpretations have the advantage of being able to make sense of the intuition that a historical connection to the wrongdoing group can yield a special responsibility to preserve the memory of the past without also suggesting that the latter generation bears any guilt or blame for the wrongs in question.[37]

37. Thanks for comments on an earlier draft of his essay are due to Colleen Murphy, Robert R. Shandley, and Rebecca Wittman.

Midwest Studies In Philosophy, XXXVIII (2014)

Collective Responsibility and Collective Obligation

TRACY ISAACS

When we think of collective responsibility, most often we are thinking of retrospective assessments of the actions of collective agents according to which they are blameworthy or praiseworthy. If they acted wrongly, then they are blameworthy for those actions. If they acted as they ought or even better, then they are praiseworthy for those actions. Is there an analogous forward-looking concept of collective responsibility, according to which collective agents are responsible for actions in the future? In this paper, I argue that responsibility in the retrospective sense is quite different from responsibility in the forward-looking sense. When we are looking ahead to actions in the future, we do better to think in terms of the equally significant normative concept of collective obligation.

Consider the following case:

Coordinated Bystander: Four bystanders are relaxing on a riverbank when six children on a raft run into trouble when their raft ends up in rapids. They are hurtling helplessly toward a dangerous waterfall downriver and are unlikely to survive if they go over it. Nothing any of the four bystanders can do as an individual will make a difference. But there is an obvious course of coordinated action they could take to divert the raft into calmer waters. This measure would pose little risk to the bystanders and would save all of the children.

This case has an obvious solution—that is, to save the children by diverting the raft—and an obvious collective agent who could bring the solution about—that is, the collective agent constituted by the four bystanders at the side of the river. When there is a clear collective solution to a perilous circumstance such as that in which the children find themselves and a clear collective agent who could carry it out, the case is one of forward-looking collective responsibility, or, to put it more succinctly, of collective obligation.

Not every case of collective obligation is like the Coordinated Bystander case. The coordinated bystanders do not, as the case is described, have any prior involvement in the children's perilous situation. Nor do they stand to gain if the children are not saved. They are neither causes nor beneficiaries.

In some circumstances, by contrast, at least some of the people who are able to make a difference or alleviate harm were causally implicated in the harm to be addressed. And sometimes, at least some of those who may make a difference benefit from the harm to be addressed. Arguably in these cases, their prior connection and/or continued benefit serve as grounds for a heavier burden of obligation.

I argue that agents who are causally implicated and who benefit do indeed bear a heavier burden of obligation for alleviating harmful circumstances. Where collective obligation is concerned, these connections to the harm or wrong not only make some collective agents more obligated than others, but also these factors play a role in determining the identity of the collective agent who has the collective obligation.

In order to illustrate and support both the claim that causal implication, on the one hand, and continued benefit, on the other hand, can ground heavier burdens of obligation, I draw attention to two different cases. The first is Canada's treatment of its First Nations (Aboriginal) people and the collective obligations to which the history of poor treatment and wrongful practice give rise. The second is men's collective responsibility for the prevalence of sexual violence against women. Larry May and Robert Strikwerda have argued that men as a group are responsible for the prevalence of rape.[1] Their provocative claim and the arguments they offer in its support provide a rich ground for discussion of the idea that some groups might be more responsible than others for alleviating harms that require collective solutions.

I begin with a discussion of some background and terminology concerning my view of collective moral responsibility.

I. BACKGROUND AND TERMINOLOGY

Let us understand *moral responsibility* as, quite simply, the praiseworthiness or blameworthiness of moral agents. It is backward-looking in so far as it involves a moral assessment of an agent in light of the agent's past actions—if those actions were wrong, then the agent is, other things being equal, blameworthy for them; if right or good, then the agent is, other things being equal, not blameworthy and may even be praiseworthy.[2]

1. Larry May and Robert Strikwerda, "Men in Groups: Collective Responsibility for Rape," *Hypatia* 9, no. 2 (Spring 1994): 134–51.

2. Right action is the default standard to which all moral agents should adhere. For this reason, it is not the case that agents will necessarily be praiseworthy for doing as they ought. However, when an agent is praiseworthy it is for morally right/good behavior.

Individual human agents or collective agents such as corporations or institutions may be morally responsible. *Collective moral responsibility* is the moral responsibility of collective agents. It is an altogether different level of moral responsibility from that of the individuals who might make up collectives or be members of collectives.

There are several different types of collective agents, and not all collectives have the requisite capacities for agency. Non-agent collectives, such as the audience at a sports event or the people on a beach, do not constitute collective agents because they do not have the relevant structure to produce intentional actions. This is not to say that they could not gain it under appropriate circumstances, such as the bystanders in the Coordinated Bystander case. But unless they mobilize into goal-oriented collectives, they lack agency.

Only collectives with agency may be considered morally responsible. I focus on collective agents and distinguish between two kinds of collective moral agents: *organizations* and *goal-oriented collectives*. Organizations are more structured than goal-oriented collectives and have clear role definition, decision procedures, and mechanisms for acting in the world that might be outlined in terms of corporate structures and policies, the specification of corporate interests and the like.[3] Corporations are paradigmatic organizations, but institutions such as universities or governments are also organizations, as are nonprofit groups, militaries, and even lots of clubs. Organizations are capable of intentional actions and are for this reason agents, even if in a minimal sense. Therefore, they are legitimate subjects of praise and blame.

Goal-oriented collectives are more loosely structured than organizations and arise out of shared understandings and a sense of common purpose. They also have collective intentions, that is, intentions that are distinct from the intentions of individual members and that propel the collective's actions toward the achievement of its goals. Goal-oriented collectives are more varied in their cohesiveness than organizations and some might not manifest the same level of collectivity as organizations or as other goal-oriented collectives. There is more variance, and their collectivity comes in degrees.

Aside from organizations and goal-oriented collectives, both of which exhibit agency, there are also *social groups*, in which people are grouped together because of some feature that they share or are assumed to share (such as the social group women). Some are even more loosely defined collections of people who are neither organized nor share a common goal or purpose and who might share just one feature on the basis of which we can group them together, such as citizens of the same country, members of the same community, or workers in the same field, such as piano instructors or cashiers. With respect to collective moral responsibility, the focus ought to be entirely on collective agents. However, with respect to the more forward-looking collective obligation, groups that may have the potential to become effective collective agents also warrant our attention. Remember the Coordinated Bystander case with which I began. At the outset, these people did not

---

3. Peter French spells out the idea of organizations as I see it in his influential paper, "The Corporation as a Moral Person," *American Philosophical Quarterly* 16, no. 3 (1979): 207–15.

constitute any sort of collective agent. However, the obvious solution to the children's plight cannot happen unless the bystanders form themselves into a collective agent with the intention of diverting the raft into safe waters. And many of the large scale global challenges facing us today—social injustice, poverty, hunger, disease, climate change and other threats to the planet's ability to sustain life—require collective action solutions and yet the collective agent who might achieve them, much like the bystanders by the river, have not yet formed as such.

In collective contexts, moral responsibility operates at two levels: the collective level and the individual level. Elsewhere,[4] I argue that these are two distinct levels of responsibility, and that claims about the responsibility of a collective agent do not automatically yield claims about the responsibility of individuals who are members of that collective. Thus, just because a corporation is blameworthy, it is not necessarily the case that every member of the corporation is blameworthy. This fact about collective moral responsibility helps in response to the frequently cited concern that collective moral responsibility holds some responsible for the misdeeds of others, and thus has a punitive effect on innocent individuals.[5] In my view, there is no necessary connection between collective blameworthiness and individual blameworthiness. Therefore, we do not automatically implicate innocent individuals when we make attributions of blameworthy responsibility at the collective level. This claim holds true both for organizations and for goal-oriented collectives, since both have intentional structures that allow for collective intentions and actions that are distinct from the intentions and actions of individuals.[6]

A brief reflection on word "responsibility" reveals that it has multiple meanings. For our purposes, we need to distinguish between responsibility, in the sense of blameworthiness and praiseworthiness, and responsibilities, in the sense of duties and obligations. Because both senses of responsibility have normative dimensions to them, they are easy to conflate. I maintain that they are fundamentally different from each other. Blameworthiness and praiseworthiness are assessments of agents. They are qualities or evaluations we might attribute to agents based on actions they have taken. Thus, they have a retrospective quality to them that does not translate neatly into a future-oriented concept.

We can of course think in terms of collective actions that would yield attributions of blameworthiness or praiseworthiness if they were to be taken. For example, we might say that British Petroleum (BP) would be blameworthy if it had a second major oil spill anytime in the near future, or would be praiseworthy if it became an industry leader in developing best practices for safe drilling. But that does not yet articulate a course of action for BP. I claim that to be prospectively responsible is simply to have a responsibility to perform some action in the future. This notion is best understood in the terms having a responsibility or having responsibilities, that is, of having collective obligations or duties. Contrast it with the idea of being responsible, that is, being praiseworthy or blameworthy for one's

---

4. Tracy Isaacs, *Moral Responsibility in Collective Contexts* (New York: Oxford University Press, 2011), 8–12, 52–70.

5. Jan Narveson, "Collective Responsibility," *Journal of Ethics* 6, no. 2 (2002): 179–98.

6. I argue for this claim extensively in my *Moral Responsibility in Collective Contexts* (2011), chap. 2.

behavior. Collective obligations are obligations that collective agents have to perform actions in the future. This way of thinking about "forward-looking collective responsibility" distinguishes it in kind from the backward-looking concept of collective responsibility that is the usual subject matter of philosophical discussion. Though both have normative dimensions, they have different normative functions. Where collective responsibility (retrospective) is evaluative, collective obligation (future-oriented) has a primarily prescriptive function.

So far, I have outlined some basic terms and argued that if we want to think about collective moral responsibility in a forward-looking sense, it is best understood not as a corollary of backward-looking collective moral responsibility, but rather as collective obligation. Rather than thinking of it in terms of blameworthiness and praiseworthiness, we do better to think of it as normatively prescriptive for collective agents. It specifies what they are required or responsible to do. In other words, it specifies their duties and obligations. For the remainder of the paper, "collective responsibility" will refer to the retrospective, evaluative concept and "collective obligation" will refer to the future-oriented, prescriptive concept.

Collective moral obligation is an important normative concept, particularly in the face of large-scale global challenges such as world hunger and disease, the global distribution of food and medical care, environmental degradation and climate change that results from the way humans occupy the planet, the extinction of species of plants and animals that results from humanity's way of life, the eradication of oppression and unjust social practices, and so forth. These ticking time bombs require collective solutions, and the notion of collective obligation can play a key role in mobilizing groups of people to act effectively in response to mounting evidence that our industrialized way of life is destroying the planet, that the global economic structure is ghettoizing populations in the global south, and that social injustice, oppression, and the legacy of colonialism are keeping large proportions of the world's population, even in the most affluent countries, in states of systemic and structural disadvantage, denying them access to the seats of power and opportunities to enjoy an adequate quality of life.

The most straightforward way of understanding collective obligation is as the obligations of collective moral agents. Organizations have obligations, such as Nike's obligation to pay its employees a reasonable wage for their labor, and BP's obligation to clean up its mess in the Gulf after the disastrous oil leak in 2010. Collective obligations are not limited to organizations. Goal-oriented collectives may also have obligations. For example, a group of people who have come together to raise funds for cancer research, perhaps by organizing a race in which participants can collect sponsors to raise money for the cause, has the obligation to do what they say they will do with the money, to alert the requisite authorities that there will be a race that day, and to make sure the city approved it.

But in some cases, such as the pressing scenarios outlined above—world poverty and hunger, global warming, and so on—though it is clear that a collective response is necessary, it is not clear who the collective agent is, be it organization or goal-oriented collective. That lack of clarity muddies the waters considerably because it is difficult to grasp how an agent that has not yet come into being might have obligations to act.

I develop this point at length elsewhere[7] and will outline the main points here. Some situations demand a clear collective solution, and when they do, collective obligations can attach to putative or potential collective agents, and these obligations can, in turn, help to narrow the field of individual obligation, thus providing some direction for individuals to act in relation to the groups to which they belong. The Coordinated Bystander case cited earlier helps to secure this point. As we observed at the beginning, the collective agent who could save the children had not yet been formed. Larry May introduces the language of *putative*, as opposed to actual, groups or collective agents.[8] Despite the putative nature of the collective agent, it is clear what that collective agent should look like.

In the Coordinated Bystander case, its potential members are the four bystanders on the riverbank. All four need to act together to divert the raft, and it is clear both who should participate and what they need to do. In the case as described, even though the collective has not yet formed, the putative group has a putative obligation. Moreover, the putative collective obligation helps to shape the individuals' obligations in this situation. Each is individually obligated to do her or his part in achieving the collective goal, namely, to save the children. In the absence of a collective effort, there is no way that they could achieve the goal.

We may invoke here a condition of clarity, an idea introduced by Virginia Held in her discussion of responsibility and random collections.[9] Held claims that when the course of action required of a random collection of people is clear, then there is a collective obligation for them to form into a group and act accordingly to reach the goal. Similarly we may claim that the clarity condition, when met, generates a putative collective obligation, that is, an obligation that will apply to the group but, in the absence of the group forming, helps to shape and mediate the obligations of the individuals who are involved. To the extent, then, that the course of action that the situation demands is clear (to the reasonable person), there is adequate support for the claim that the individuals, as individuals, ought to act so as to promote a collective goal. I argue the following:

> Clarity at the collective level does not always translate into equal clarity at the individual level. However, once it is clear what is required of the collective, the collective obligation has a derivative impact on the obligations of individuals. Members are, in virtue of their position in a collective with an obligation to act, required to sort out appropriate roles and tasks such that the collective action can take place. The presence of even a putative collective obligation, therefore, begins to impose some order on the actions and obligations of individuals acting in the service of a collective end. To the extent that a means for achieving the end is in reach, the putative collective obligation grounds actual obligations for individuals. When there is no clear

7. Isaacs, *Moral Responsibility in Collective Contexts* (2011), chap. 5.

8. See Larry May, "Collective Inaction and Responsibility," in Peter French, *Individual and Collective Responsibility* (Rochester, VT: Schenkman Books, 1998), 218.

9. Virgina Held, "Can a Random Collection of People Be Morally Responsible?" in *Collective Responsibility: Five Decades of Debate in Theoretical and Applied Ethics*, ed. Larry May and Stacey Hoffman (Savage, MD: Rowman & Littlefield, 1991), 89–100.

putative collective obligation in sight, then there is no mechanism for morally requiring that individuals coordinate their actions in a manner that would address the issue at hand. Not every unacceptable situation has—though it may at some point come to have—a clear moral solution, collective or otherwise.[10]

Having outlined the main lines of my view of collective obligation both with respect to actual and putative collective agents, I turn now to discussion of how collective responsibility (backward-looking) might be connected to collective obligation (forward-looking).[11]

II. COLLECTIVE RESPONSIBILITY AND COLLECTIVE OBLIGATION

In what follows, I consider how collective responsibility, particularly collective wrongdoing, might be connected to collective obligation. The view of collective obligation offered above provides criteria—a clear collective solution and a clear collective agent or putative agent to enact that solution—that do not require that we take the past into account. For example, in the Coordinated Bystander case as described, the bystanders take the plight of the children as they find it. Some might see the strictly forward-looking nature of this account of collective obligation as a merit. When only a collective solution will suffice, then it may be that taking the situation as we find it, with a forward-looking stance focused on a solution, will be more constructive than a backward-looking assessment of responsibility.

In some scenarios, however, questions could arise that press us to consider the relationship between collective responsibility and collective obligation. For example, in matters of collective obligation it might make a difference whether anyone stands to benefit from the situation that requires a response, or whether an agent or agents, be they individual or collective, have an intentional or even unintentional causal connection to the circumstance that a collective obligation would address. One of the perils of looking ahead and only ahead is that we might erase morally relevant historical facts. These facts could well contribute a deeper and more nuanced understanding of how to individuate the collective agents who have collective obligations to address complex moral problems. It may be the case that not all who are well-positioned to act are equally obligated to do so, and this difference could be a feature of collective agents as much as (or even more than) of individual agents.

In order to highlight some of the reasons for thinking the connection between collective responsibility and collective obligation has normative significance, we will consider two cases. The first is the case of Canada's Aboriginal People[12]—a clear example of systemic social injustice. The second is the case of

10. Isaacs, *Moral Responsibility in Collective Contexts*, 149–50.
11. For a fuller discussion of the view outlined, please see my *Moral Responsibility in Collective Contexts*, chap. 5.
12. The term "Aboriginal People" refers to the indigenous inhabitants of Canada and includes the Inuit, First Nations people, and Métis. See "A Note on Terminology" on the Inuit Tapiriit Kanatami Web site: https://www.itk.ca/note-terminology-inuit-metis-first-nations-and-aboriginal.

responsibility for the prevalence of violence against women, which Larry May and Robert Strikwerda have claimed falls heavily onto men as a group.

II.i Case One: Canada's Aboriginal People

Canada's Aboriginal People are the descendents of the indigenous population who inhabited the territory that is now Canada when Europeans began to establish permanent settlements (in the seventeenth and eighteenth centuries). Today, a great many of Canada's Aboriginal people live in impoverished and under-resourced conditions on reserves across the country. Those who live in urban centers do not on average fare much better.[13] Aboriginal people have higher rates of poverty and lower levels of education than the average Canadian citizen, and the youth suicide rate on reserves is three times the national average (by age group) and in general life expectancy is shorter. In relation to their percentage of the population of Canada, they make up a disproportionate percentage of those incarcerated in federal and provincial prisons[14] and of the homeless population in urban centers. Many struggle with alcoholism, addiction, and other mental health issues, with few resources and supports at their disposal.

Present conditions alone dictate that a collective response is necessary to address the circumstances of this vulnerable group. And yet history is also morally significant in determining collective obligation. The present plight of Canada's indigenous population can be traced directly back to colonization and colonialism, the attempt to assimilate them through residential schools, as well as a history of racism and systemic discrimination against them, poor education and health care, isolation, and discriminatory policies concerning status designed to minimize the impact of land claims.[15] How significant is the historical context in determining collective obligation in this matter? If much of the damage is from white settlement, and if subsequent to that immigrants and the descendents of settlers have been and continue to be the beneficiaries of colonization, then they might bear a heavier burden of collective obligation because of their backward-looking connection—possibly a connection of blameworthy collective responsibility—to present circumstances.

13. According to the 2006 Canadian Census, 54 percent of Canada's Aboriginal population lived in urban areas. See Statistics Canada Census Report, 2006 Analysis Series, 97-558-XIE2006001 http://www12.statcan.ca/census-recensement/2006/as-sa/97-558/p1-eng.cfm.

14. See *Canada Juristat, Canadian Centre for Justice Statistics*, Statistics Canada—Catalogue no. 85-002-XIE Vol. 26, No. 3 (June 2006).

15. For example, up until 1985 the Indian Act required that women with Aboriginal status would permanently lose that status if they married a nonstatus man and also required anyone with status to make a choice between status and enfranchisement. Bill C-31, introduced in 1985, enabled those who had lost their status through marriage or enfranchisement to apply for reinstatement of their lost status. See "Indian Act and Women's Status: Discrimination via Bill C-31, Bill C-3," Working Effectively with Aboriginal Peoples TM (Web site): http://workingeffectivelywithaboriginalpeoples.com/womens-status-discrimination-via-bill-c-31-bill-c-3. See also "Guide to Bill C-31," Native Women Association of Canada (1986), 6–8. http://workingeffectivelywithaboriginalpeoples.com/womens-status-discrimination-via-bill-c-31-bill-c-3.

Recall that collective blame and collective obligation operate at the level of collective agents. The most obvious collective candidate for blame and obligation in this case is Canada or the government of Canada that represents it and acts on its behalf. Though the state was not established until 1867, the historical roots of its creation and its continuity as an identifiable collective entity afterward make it a plausible candidate for a collective agent of the organizational type.

The First Nations example helps to illustrate that collective responsibility stands in an important relationship to collective obligation and ought not be ignored when it is relevant. This relationship is important for two reasons. First, recognizing collective responsibility helps us to individuate collective agents in cases requiring collective solutions in the form of collective obligations. In the case of the Aboriginal peoples, for example, we might legitimately look to the government of Canada not just because the government is responsible for the social good of all Canadians, but also because the government represents the nation that systematically undermined Aboriginal people and whose non-Aboriginal citizens have benefitted from that undermining. Canada is an enduring and identifiable collective entity, causally connected to the history of wrongdoing against First Nations. For these reasons, Canada and its (nonstatus) citizens share in blame for past wrongs.

Second, identifying collective responsibility for past wrongs and establishing collective obligation on that basis prevents us from erasing important histories. The erasure of these histories would misrepresent present conditions in a way that might lead to blaming those who are most vulnerable and disadvantaged by those conditions. Furthermore, ignoring the historical reasons for current conditions might frame responses to these dire conditions as supererogatory gestures of good will or charity rather than morally required fulfillments of collective obligations.

Some might point out that current Canadians and the current Canadian government had nothing to do with what happened so far in the past, and so ought not be considered responsible because in the strict sense we cannot establish a causal connection. No one who was involved in past violations of colonization lives still today. Indeed, Canada as a nation was not established until 1867, quite some time later than the first settlers began to change the terms of life for Indigenous people.

There are a number of responses to this objection. First, it is of course true that no one involved in the original colonization is still alive today. Yet it is also true that Canada grew out of the original settlement and was established as a direct result of it. Moreover, Canada has operated as a continuous and identifiable collective agent since it was established in 1867. There is no metaphysical reason to deny Canada's status as a collective agent, or to ignore the historical trajectory that led to it becoming a country. To deny that today's Canada is accountable for the wrongs (and the results of those wrongs) of Canada in the past is similar to denying that my current self should is not to be held accountable for anything I have done in the past. This conclusion flies in the face of commonsense; we assume continuity over time in the case of individual agents, and we ought to do the same in the case of collective agents.

Second, even if we conclude that Canada is only responsible for wrongs and harms from 1867 onward and set aside the harms of early colonization, it is arguable that the most egregious of social damage to the First Nations resulted from the residential schools and the *Indian Act*, both established after Canada became a nation. The schools began very shortly after Canada became a state and had the explicit goal of assimilating First Nations into white society and destroying their languages and culture.[16] Similarly, Canada's parliament enacted the *Indian Act* in 1876, giving the Canadian government exclusive authority to determine who should have Indian status and to legislate the sale of Indian lands.[17] The *Act* was amended a number of times and significantly revised in 1985. Thus, government policies and legislation since Canada became a country have done a great deal of social, cultural, and psychological damage to First Nations communities.

In addition, the Canada we know today and many of the Canadians who live here are the beneficiaries of past injustices. It is not the case that those who are disadvantaged by current social structure have no obligations with respect to changing it, but it makes sense to see them as differently placed from those whom the structures benefit. That also helps to justify a collective obligation to the results of past injustice that have led to the current social hierarchy, to the disadvantage of some and the advantage of others. Being a beneficiary of harm or wrongdoing is different from being causally implicated in it.[18] It may not even be a solid basis for collective responsibility. But it is still a relevant consideration. If the benefit flows from past wrongs, it is held at the expense of those wronged. When coupled with the claim of collective responsibility that has its basis in Canada's historical part, as a collective agent, in creating the conditions in which the First Nations live today, the continued benefit has its roots in injustice and helps to support the claim that Canada has a collective obligation to take action to improve the situation of people in Aboriginal communities.

Given these considerations, the claim that no one involved in the original colonization or in the founding of Canada in 1867 is alive today does not constitute a strong objection to the possibility that Canada's collective obligations in this matter flow from prior collective responsibility. This example illustrates well that agents who are collectively responsible for a wrong or harm have a stronger collective obligation to address it than they might have in the absence of collective responsibility.

We now turn to a second illustration of this point, the case of men's responsibility, as a group, for the prevalence of sexual violence against women.

16. For a concise history of the residential schools, their abolition, lasting impact, and eventual apology by the Canadian government in 2008, see Erin Hanson, "The Residential School System," Indigenous Foundations.arts.ubc.ca (Web site), http://indigenousfoundations.arts.ubc.ca/home/government-policy/the-residential-school-system.html. See also Canada: Royal Commission on Aboriginal Peoples, "Residential Schools," in *Report of the Royal Commission on Aboriginal Peoples, Volume 1: Looking Forward, Looking Back* (Ottawa: Supply and Services Canada, 1996), chap. 10; and the Truth and Reconciliation Commission of Canada, whose Web site is: http://www.trc.ca/websites/trcinstitution/index.php?p=3.

17. See above, footnote 15.

18. Wayne Sumner drew this point about the significant difference between those who are complicit or causally implicated and those who are beneficiaries.

II.ii Collective Responsibility and Sexual Violence against Women

In 2011, a police officer giving a talk about women's safety at York University in Toronto[19] said that a woman could protect herself from sexual assault by not dressing "like a slut."[20] He prefaced his remarks, saying he was aware that he shouldn't be saying it, but he said it anyway. The outrage the remark generated gave rise to a series of "Slut Walks" in which women walked together dressed in all manner of outfits to make the point that many women have been called sluts or subjected to sexual assault even when dressed in jeans and a t-shirt or a business suit.

Independently of this incident and its fallout, a list entitled "Preventing Sexual Assault: Tips Guaranteed to Work" has been making the rounds on the internet for a few years.[21] Lists about women's safety usually include a panoply of suggestions about what women can do to keep themselves safe, suggesting that it is women's responsibility to prevent sexual assault. But the "Tips Guaranteed to Prevent Sexual Assault" contains quite different suggestions. It focuses on actions that men can take:

1. Don't put drugs in people's drinks in order to control their behavior.
2. When you see someone walking by themselves, leave them alone!
3. If you pull over to help someone with car problems, remember not to assault them!
4. NEVER open an unlocked door or window uninvited.
5. If you are in an elevator and someone else gets in, DON'T ASSAULT THEM!
6. Remember, people go to laundry to do their laundry, do not attempt to molest someone who is alone in a laundry room.
7. USE THE BUDDY SYSTEM! If you are not able to stop yourself from assaulting people, ask a friend to stay with you while you are in public.
8. Always be honest with people! Don't pretend to be a caring friend in order to gain the trust of someone you want to assault. Consider telling them you plan to assault them. If you don't communicate your intentions, the other person may take that as a sign that you do not plan to rape them.
9. Don't forget: you can't have sex with someone unless they are awake!
10. Carry a whistle! If you are worried you might assault someone "on accident" you can hand it to the person you are with, so they can blow it if you do.

---

19. York is situated in the north end of the City of Toronto. Its sprawling campus has a reputation for being dangerous, particularly for women walking alone after dark.

20. "Toronto police officer offers inappropriate safety tip," *Globe and Mail*, Thursday, February 17, 2011. See article online at http://www.theglobeandmail.com/life/the-hot-button/toronto-police-officer-offers-inappropriate-safety-tip/article611859/.

21. See the list posted on the Feminist Philosophers blog (Web site): http://feminist philosophers.wordpress.com/2009/09/22/preventing-sexual-assault-tips-guaranteed-to-work/.

The list rings both funny and true. If followed, its suggestions would, as guaranteed, prevent sexual assault. If men did not attack women, there would be no problem. The list turns the usual story on its head by situating accountability with the men who violate women instead of with the women whom they violate. That is an important shift in focus.

Larry May and Robert Strikwerda, with less humor and more philosophical analysis, have made a similar point and taken it further, introducing a second important change in the way we view sexual assault by viewing it as a matter of collective responsibility.[22] They argue that men as a group are collectively responsible for rape. They maintain that men can collectively do something about it by changing men's cultural attitudes toward women and men's sense of sexual entitlement over women.

In the terms outlined earlier, we might say that men constitute a putative group with respect to this issue. With a coordinated effort, they could constitute themselves into a goal-oriented collective agent, much like the bystanders on the banks of the river. In this way, men could effectively eradicate sexual violence against women. May and Strikwerda's analysis offers one significant difference between men concerning this issue and the bystanders concerning the children in peril: though men do not constitute a collective agent with an intention to perpetuate a society in which sexual violence is rampant,[23] their collective obligation might flow not only from their capacity to make a difference but also from men's causal contribution as a social group to the situation as it exists today.

The authors argue that "insofar as male bonding and socialization in groups contributes to the prevalence of rape in Western societies, men in those societies should feel responsible for the prevalence of rape and should feel motivated to counteract such violence and rape."[24] More specifically, they claim that:

(1) Insofar as most perpetrators of rape are men, then these men are responsible, in most cases, for the rapes they committed. (2) Insofar as some men, by the way they interact with other (especially younger) men, contribute to a climate in our society where rape is made more prevalent, then they are collaborators in the rape culture and for this reason share in responsibility for rapes committed in that culture. (3) Also, insofar as some men are not unlike the rapist, since they would be rapists if they had the opportunity to be placed into a situation where their inhibitions against rape were removed, then these men share responsibility with actual rapists for the harms of rape. (4) In addition, insofar as many other men could have prevented fellow men from raping, but did not act to prevent these actual rapes, then these men also

---

22. Larry May and Robert Strikwerda, "Men in Groups: Collective Responsibility for Rape," *Hypatia* 9, no. 2 (Spring 1994): 134–51.

23. See Maire Sinha (editor), "Measuring Violence against Women: Statistical Trends," Canadian Centre for Justice Statistics, February 25, 2013, Statistics Canada, and "The Facts about Violence against Women," Canadian Women's Foundation (Web site), http://www.canadianwomen.org/facts-about-violence.

24. May and Strikwerda, 135.

share responsibility along with the rapists. (5) Finally, insofar as some men benefit from the existence of rape in our society, these men also share responsibility along with the rapists.[25]

May and Strikwerda call upon men to change their behavior, to call their friends out on their behavior, and as a group to alter their culture so that sexual assault against women is reduced because men themselves are taking action to prevent it.[26] The significant point for the purposes of this section is the claim that men's collective obligations in this matter flow from their past causal contributions to the present culture. The authors claim men's collective responsibility for rape, responsibility in the retrospective sense. Even if they do not constitute a collective agent at present, men's cumulative behavior has contributed to a culture in which sexual violence is prevalent. This causal role could suggests sufficient complicity to ground a stronger collective obligation than that of others who might be equally well-positioned to make a difference (though it is arguable whether women are as well-positioned to do so, as the tipsheet tries to show). This prior connection in the form of a causal role stands as ground for collective obligation.

According to my view, men do not constitute a collective agent and so cannot be responsible as a group in quite that way. They can however be implicated by a cumulative causal role and we can identify them as a putative agent. Some may think of it as a shortcoming of my view that only organizations and goal-oriented collectives count as collective agents.[27] Social groups such as men, social forces, or even cultures are often cited as responsible. While it's true that these sorts of things make causal contributions to harmful states of affairs, they fall short with respect to satisfying a minimal condition for responsible agency, namely the capacity for intentional action. Because of this shortfall, it makes little sense to attribute moral blame to them. We can, however, cite their causal role and at least in some cases, such as men as a group, establish a collective obligation to incite change.

Some might argue that attributing a stronger collective obligation to men because of their role in creating the culture of violence unfairly implicates men who have never subjected any women to violence or even entertained the idea of doing so, making them as responsible as every other man as part of the goal-oriented collective of men who have the collective obligation to make significant changes in this area of social practice. May and Strikwerda point out that even if particular men are not themselves violent toward women, all men benefit from the prevalence of rape "in that many women are made to feel dependent on men for protection against potential rapists" and women feel required to take precautions and restrict their movements, particularly after dark, in ways that men do not. Because women need to restrict themselves in these ways, their opportunities to thrive are curtailed relative to men's. The authors note that at a department

25. May and Strikwerda, 146.
26. And such action is not completely unheard of. Both the White Ribbon Campaign (http://www.whiteribbon.ca/) and the My Strength Is Not for Hurting Campaign (http://www.mystrength.org/) are the initiatives of men who seek to eradicate sexual violence.
27. Dan Hicks raised this point as an objection to my analysis.

meeting, the men were remarking how beautiful the campus looked at night. The women had not noticed because they did not feel comfortable being on campus at night, and if they were, they were far too preoccupied with staying alert and making it safely from their offices or the library to their vehicle to focus on how the campus looked. Thus, their colleagues who were women were disadvantaged professionally by the culture of sexual violence in so far as their time at the workplace was shorter than the time their male colleagues could comfortably spend there. May and Strikwerda claim that "just as the benefit to men distributes throughout the male population in a given society, so the responsibility should distribute as well." We saw much the same sort of argument in the previous example when we considered the objection that none of the Canadians alive today was involved in the original colonization that resulted in the steady decline in the quality of life of First Nations people.

This issue of benefit is different from the issue of causal contribution because benefit comes after the fact. However, given that the benefit is a consequence of a harmful state of affairs that men as a group are well-positioned to address, their continued benefit provides a further reason to think that men bear a heavier collective obligation because of it.

Some might quarrel with the claim that there is a clear course of action available to address sexual assault and that men constitute a clear putative collective agent who could address it. May and Strikwerda's reading of the broad contribution men make to supporting the culture is not a mainstream commonplace. They widen the base of responsibility beyond actual perpetrators, offering a collective analysis of crimes that are ordinarily thought to be individual in nature. Despite the obviousness of the "tips" offered in the "tips for preventing sexual assault" list, and despite the claims that May and Strikwerda have made concerning men's responsibility for rape, the idea of holding men as a group responsible and of believing that men as a group are collectively obligated to change the culture comes across as radical.

Most men will claim (truthfully) that they are not rapists, would never commit sexual assault, and have never even entertained the idea of so doing. They will therefore resist being thrown into the same collective as those who are in fact perpetrators. And yet May and Strikwerda's analysis fails unless all or almost all men are responsible and unless all or almost all men are part of the collective agent—the goal-oriented collective of men opposed to rape—that has the obligation to make a difference. They claim that rape is a crime against humanity, and as such ought not be viewed only as a crime against individual women but against humanity itself. Moreover, "rape is a crime perpetrated by men as a group, not merely by the individual rapist" because male bonding and socialization contributes to the prevalence of rape in Western societies.[28]

The objection that their claim condemns men as a collective for crimes that are ordinarily considered to be the acts of individuals is a more specific instance of a version of an objection that often arises against collective responsibility more generally. Many philosophers have argued that collective moral responsibility is

---

28. May and Strikwerda, 135.

suspect because it holds some people responsible for the misdeeds of others.[29] What they have in mind is that when a collective agent is held responsible, the net is cast too wide, thereby implicating more individuals than the individuals who actually participated in the action. Similarly in this case, the claim might be that not only does this collective analysis of rape hold more men responsible than it ought to, but it also makes more men obligated to change their behavior than it ought—that is, with respect to the forward-looking context, the net of collective obligation may be cast too wide.

Elsewhere, I have addressed the first objection in a number of ways, primarily by pointing out that collective responsibility operates at a different level of responsibility from individual responsibility. An attribution of collective responsibility—that is, responsibility of a collective—does not draw any necessary connection of blame between the collective as a whole and the individuals who might be members of the collective. The moral responsibility of individuals as individuals in the collective is a separate question.

There is definitely a sense in which those who are members of the collective are more likely to be implicated than those who are not, but the reason for this is not that collective responsibility distributes among individuals. The mere fact of collective responsibility does not mean that we may make a justified attribution of blame in the case of every man as an individual. A central point in May and Strikwerda's analysis is that the collective context generates the culture that condones sexual assault. They give some clear criteria for who is implicated, in turn making the individuation of the collective clearer. My view of their analysis complicates the issue in some respects because I have denied the collective agency of the social group, men. But my view does not support an automatic condemnation of individuals just because they are members of blameworthy collectives. Collective blame befalls the collective itself.

The relationship between being implicated in the collective and being individually responsible is complicated. Because of the collective nature of collective actions, I argue that individuals cannot be responsible, as individuals, for collective wrongdoing.[30] Collective wrongdoing is, by definition, wrongdoing of collective agents, not of individual agents. This two-level analysis allows for some slippage, therefore, between what individuals are responsible for as individuals, and what collectives are responsible for as collectives. In this case, for example, it is clear that no one person can be responsible for the prevalence of rape in society. It just doesn't work that way. I have also noted that men *as a collective agent* are not collectively responsible (in the retrospective sense) because the group, as it stands, is a non-agent collective. It is neither an organization nor a goal-oriented collective. But agency comes into play more clearly is in terms of the collective solution. Recall the discussion of putative collective agents. Collective agents of a putative

29. See, for example, H. D. Lewis, "Collective Responsibility," in *Collective Responsibility: Five Decades of Debate in Theoretical and Applied Ethics*, ed. May and Hoffman (Savage, MD: Rowman & Littlefield, 1991), 17–33, and Jan Narveson, "Collective Responsibility," *Journal of Ethics* 6, no. 2 (2002): 179–98.

30. See Isaacs, *Moral Responsibility in Collective Contexts* (New York: Oxford University Press, 2011), 54–55.

kind can have obligations collectively, and these collective obligations can play a mediating role in determining what individuals are required to do as individuals. They are required to contribute to the fulfillment of the collective obligation, qua members of the collective that is so required.

If outright blame seems too strong in some of these cases, then perhaps wrongdoing with an excuse might fare better. Cheshire Calhoun draws a useful distinction here between moral knowledge in normal moral contexts and moral knowledge in abnormal moral contexts.[31] The idea is this. When people participate in wrongful social practices, such as practices that are oppressive to particular social groups, their participation in these practices is wrong. However, if they are acting out of moral ignorance in a social context that is *normal* with respect to the wrongness of that behavior, then they are acting wrongly with no excuse. In a normal moral context, reasonable people are aware of the wrongness of the relevant behavior.[32] In an abnormal moral context, however, things are different because the majority of the population is not aware that the behavior is morally wrong.[33] Therefore, it is more difficult for any one person to be aware that she or he is acting in a way that is morally dubious.

Now apply this distinction to the case at hand. Arguably, men's participation in perpetuating "rape culture" occurs in an abnormal moral context. A lot of the behaviors, such as conversations with friends in which random women on the street are cast as sex objects, or other aspects of male socialization, are not thought of as contributions to a rape culture. If it is correct to say that the moral context is abnormal with respect to this range of behaviors, then men's moral ignorance concerning the wrongness of their behavior in support of that culture is excusable. This does not make it any less wrong. Rather, it mitigates the blame.

Consider, however, how the analysis itself can make that ignorance less excusable. As we bring these issues to light, for example as we consider the tips and think through some of the points that May and Strikwerda have made, as campaigns against male violence against women, such the "My Strength is not for Hurting Campaign,"[34] take hold, as the culture shifts even slightly, it becomes less plausible to maintain ignorance about the acceptability of many of the behaviors they point to as contributing to a culture of violence against women. Reflecting on the tipsheet, it is almost impossible not to see the truth in it. If all men followed it, then sexual assault would be eliminated completely.

But the tipsheet is directed specifically at perpetrators. May and Strikwerda claim that the complicity reaches much further and to a broad range of more subtle behaviors that support cultural attitudes that are harmful to women. A coordinated effort mobilizing the potential for collective agency is required for the necessary culture shift. Individuals cannot perform collective actions as individuals. These actions are, by definition, the actions of collective agents. That is what makes them *collective* actions. Because individuals cannot perform collective actions, they

---

31. Calhoun, "Responsibility and Reproach," *Ethics* (1989).
32. Calhoun, 394–96.
33. Calhoun, 396.
34. http://www.mystrength.org/.

cannot be morally responsible for them. The same reasoning explains why individuals cannot undertake to fulfill collective obligations as individuals. Collective obligations operate at the level of the collective. Joining together with others is necessary. However, individuals contribute to collective actions and responsible for their individual parts in collective actions, including actions to fulfill collective obligations.[35]

Return now to the reason for raising this case. My contention is that we need in some cases to attend to the relationship between prior involvement and current obligation in order to establish which collective agents bear the stronger burden of collective obligation in addressing some issues that require collective action solutions. May and Strikwerda's discussion helps to support this point because they maintain that men as a collective are responsible for the prevalence of sexual assault against women in Western societies and that they are also collectively obligated for changing the culture. This analysis challenges the status quo, which often makes prevention of sexual violence against women an issue for women, requiring changes in their behavior. Thus, like the First Nations case, this case illustrates how attending to the historical roots of current harms can help to identify and, where putative groups are concerned, to individuate, the collective agents with the stronger obligations. Though my own analysis challenges their claim that men as a group constitute a collective agent, my view is nonetheless consistent with the claim that their causal relationship of complicity yields a stronger collective obligation and identifies them as a putative collective agent of the goal-oriented type.

III. CONCLUSION

The preceding discussion aims to show that collective responsibility and collective obligation stand in an important relationship to each other. The connection is especially important as we attempt to address large-scale harms such as global warming, global poverty and malnutrition, oppression and other structural injustices, and other similar challenges that require collective solutions. Prior contribution helps identify those collective agents, be they actual or putative, who bear a heavier or more significant collective obligation in undertaking solutions even when there are others who are equally placed to act. Matters become more complicated when the collective agent in question as yet to be mobilized as an agent.

In those cases, past contribution and continued benefit both serve as relevant criteria for determining where the heaviest burden of collective obligation lies. It can be equally helpful for identifying existing collective agents or, when there is sufficient clarity, for individuating potential or putative collective agents.

There are those who would take issue with the possibility that something putative could have any real impact on something actual. But there is no lack of clarity about what would, if pursued, remedy some of the large-scale harms our world faces. When we see one another as potential members of effective collective

---

35. See my *Moral Responsibility in Collective Contexts*, chap. 4, for a more detailed discussion of this claim.

agents, opportunities arise and more plausible solutions become possible.[36] Since so many of the challenges that need our attention as moral agents today are unsolvable at the level of individuals only, it is necessary to think about putative collective agents and their obligations as a way of imagining effective solutions. That is, we must think of the context as a collective. Then we can see ourselves as functioning within a collective agent. Thus, though it is true that the collective level of action and the individual level of action are distinct from each other, and it is true that when collectives are blameworthy this does not necessarily say anything about the blameworthiness of the individuals who are their members, the context of a putative agent and its obligations is a bit different. It is different in the sense that under the right conditions, being a possible member of a group that could effectively take action to address an obvious issue that needs addressing can influence a person's individual obligations. We should see this as a good thing because, in fact, though many of us want to act in ways that might make a difference, it is morally discouraging to recognize that you cannot make a difference all on your own.[37] This awareness can lead quickly to moral inertia or even paralysis. However, as in the Coordinated Bystanders case, when there is a clear course of action and a clear group of people who, if they banded together as a goal-oriented collective, could pursue that course of action, then they ought to take it. This in turn generates individual obligations that derive directly from the collective nature of the context. While I cannot perform a collective action as an individual, I can participate in one.

The second half of the article more fully explores the connection between collective responsibility and collective obligation. The examples of Canada's treatment of its Aboriginal peoples and of men's responsibility in the prevalence of sexual assault illustrate that when a group has been complicit in or responsible for a situation in need of remedy, the larger burden of collective obligation falls on the group who is responsible in the backward-looking sense. This increased obligation holds even if others are equally placed to address the issue. The collectively responsible group has a larger burden precisely because of its prior contribution to (or the complicity of its members in) the problem requiring attention, and quite possibly because of the continuing privilege and benefit that the group's members collectively enjoy as a result of the current state of affairs.

---

36. I develop the idea of the importance for effective collective action of seeing one another as selves in relation in Tracy Isaacs, "Feminism and Agency," in *Feminist Moral Theory, Canadian Journal of Philosophy Supplementary Volume*, ed. Samantha Brennan (Calgary: University of Calgary Press, 2003), 129–54.

37. Isaacs, *Moral Responsibility in Collective Contexts*, 2011.

Joint Moral Duties

ANNE SCHWENKENBECHER

1. THE PROBLEM OF COLLECTIVE INACTION

In his book *Sharing Responsibility*, Larry May paraphrases Edmund Burke, saying that "All that is necessary for evil to triumph in the world is for good people to do nothing" (May 1992, 105). And further down he notes: "Inaction leads to serious harm in the world, just as certainly as intentional, active wrongdoing" (105–06). He argues that many problems that cannot be solved by individuals can be addressed by collective action.

May is right. There are countless situations and circumstances in which individuals *could* act together to prevent something morally bad from happening or to remedy a morally bad situation, but often they do not. But when *ought* individuals to act together in order to bring about a morally important outcome? This is the question that this article seeks to answer. In order to do so, I will put forward the notion of a particular type of duty that individuals in random groups may have: a joint duty to perform an action together.

2. JOINT ACTION EXPLAINED

Many scholars hold that groups can be agents (e.g., Erskine 2003; French 1984; List and Pettit 2011). They argue that states, business corporations, and all kinds of other organizations with a formal structure can be considered entities capable of performing actions. My argument, however, does not make this assumption.

In this article, I am not interested in so-called "group agents" and their moral status. Instead, I want to think about individuals in so-called random or unstructured groups. I will investigate the moral status that these groups have, and the moral duties that their members can hold. Calling random collections of individuals "groups" may already seem to presuppose too much. In order to avoid any confusion, let me clarify: Random or unstructured groups are not group agents, because they have no established decision-making procedures or an identity independent of that of their members, for instance.[1] I will use the term "group" loosely to apply to all groups including unstructured ones.

A number of authors have argued that individuals in some unstructured groups may be in a position to act jointly, or collectively (Collins 2013; Cripps 2011, 2013; Held 1970; Lawford-Smith 2012; Pettit and Schweikard 2006; Schwenkenbecher 2013; Wringe 2005, 2010, 2014). In order for joint action to be possible, most scholars agree that some minimal conditions need to be met. These include a joint goal that individuals share, and a condition of mutual belief and knowledge regarding other people's contributions to that goal: People who act jointly with others do so because they believe that these others will contribute their share toward the joint goal (see, e.g., Lawford-Smith 2012; Pettit and Schweikard 2006, 23). On this account, people who accidentally or ignorantly contribute to the same outcome do not act jointly.

In this article, I will adopt the account of joint action put forward by Pettit and Schweikard (2006). For the individual agents, a joint action is "something they combine to perform" (Pettit and Schweikard 2006, 19). According to Pettit and Schweikard (2006, 19), people do not just produce a joint effect, but act jointly; apart from an individual action, there is an action that is performed together. Pettit and Schweikard argue that a joint action is always performed with a certain intention (20). Furthermore, if people perform a joint action intentionally, then they must each be focused on a common target (21):

A number of people in a plurality perform a joint action in enacting a certain performance together only if:

(i) they each intend that they enact the performance;
(ii) they each intend to do their bit in this performance;
(iii) they each believe that others intend to do their bit;
(iv) they each intend to do their bit because of believing this; and
(v) they each believe in common that the other clauses hold.

We think that the five clauses given here are not just individually necessary but jointly sufficient in order for the enactment of a joint performance- for the behavior involved in a joint performance to count as a properly joint action. (Pettit and Schweikard 2006, 23–24)

---

1. Regarding criteria for group agency, see Toni Erskine, ed., "Assigning Responsibility to Institutional Moral Agents: The Case of States and 'Quasi States'." In *Can Institutions Have Responsibilities? Collective Moral Agency and International Relations* (Basingstoke UK: Palgrave Macmillan, 2003), 19–40.

Pettit and Schweikard emphasize that in a joint action agents "go beyond the case where a number of different agents perform different actions and bring about a joint effect." However, agents acting jointly do not necessarily constitute a novel agent with own intentions (30). Examples for this type of joint action abound. The following actions meet Pettit's and Schweikard's definition:

(i)   Two people who dance together.
(ii) Four people who lift a table together.
(iii) A choir and an orchestra who perform Johann Sebastian Bach's *Magnificat* together.

None of these actions involves a novel group agent emerging in the course of the collaboration. Rather, individual agents perform an action together that—in these particular cases—can only be performed by more than one person. The individuals in the above examples perform joint actions.

On the account sketched above, people can spontaneously act jointly, or they can act jointly according to prior planning and agreement. Sometimes, random individuals who are not part of an established practice or institution or who do not belong to a group agent in a narrow sense are in a position to act together. They might not even know each other. But they may have the potential to perform a joint action.

3. JOINT MORAL DUTIES DEFENDED

Provided that individuals *can* sometimes act together in the way described above: Is it plausible to think that they sometimes *ought to* act together in the way described above? According to Larry May (1992, 105–06), collective inaction can be just as wrong as intentional wrongdoing. Let us assume for the sake of argument that (positive) duties of assistance are as stringent as (negative) duties not to harm. In this article, I want to argue that individuals can sometimes hold duties to jointly assist others in need. In short: There are joint duties to assist. To start with, let us look at a number of examples.

Car accident. Let us use one of an abundant number of examples where random passersby jointly assist the victim of a traffic accident. Here is the description of a scene that was filmed by coincidence and reported by Associated Press on September 13, 2011[2]: a motorcyclist is trapped underneath a burning car after a collision. Passersby approach the car realizing that in order to retrieve him, the car must be lifted. After a couple of unsuccessful attempts with insufficient people, eight people eventually manage to jointly lift the car off the injured man, saving his life. Would we say that the passersby were under an obligation to team up and lift the car to save him? I am confident that most of us would be very inclined to think that the individuals walking past the car were under some kind of obligation to

---

2. <http://www.youtube.com/watch?v=aIGTyANMFb4>.

help the injured motorcyclist if no other help (police, ambulance, or the like) was available.

Held's bystanders to a violent attack. A famous example used by Virginia Held has us imagine a situation in which a person is being beaten to death by another while bystanders who could collectively prevent the crime refrain from doing so. She argues that if "[i]t is extremely probable that action by two or more of the group to subdue him [the attacker, author's initials.] would have succeeded, with no serious injury to themselves . . . I think that in such a case we would hold the random collection morally responsible for its failure to act as a group" (Held 1970, 94f). Again, I am confident that most people would agree that the bystanders have some kind of duty to remedy the situation or work toward its remedial, provided no other form of help is available (police or security officers, etc.). What kind of duties are these and who holds them?

In order to answer this question, let us look at two principles that are usually considered necessary (though not sufficient) for ascribing moral duties: the agency principle and the capacity principle (or the principle that "ought" implies "can"):

Agency principle: Only agents can hold moral duties.

Capacity principle: An agent can only hold a moral duty if the agent is capable of discharging that duty.

According to the agency principle, only agents can hold duties. In the examples above—the bystanders and the passersby—there are individual agents who can be described as members of a random group merely on the basis of their being at the same place at the same time. However, there are no—structured—group agents or members thereof present. The random strangers do not constitute a group agent *before* they act together, nor do they (necessarily) become one *as* they act together. Still, the individual agents can perform individual actions toward a joint goal. And they can perform actions jointly: They can stop the attackers and free the trapped motorcyclist, therewith saving their lives. If the agency principle is to be upheld, these individual agents can hold duties to assist, but there is no group agent that could hold such duties.

Let us now turn to the capacity principle. According to this principle, there is no "ought" without a "can." In the previously described examples, none of the individuals who intervene to help can achieve the desired outcome of saving another person's life on their own. Individually, each person's duty is limited by each individual agent's capacity. No individual agent has the capacity to either subdue the attacker or lift the car off the trapped motorcyclist. Individually, all that any of them would be capable of doing is to call the ambulance or the police. However, in both scenarios the urgency of the situation requires immediate action if the person under attack and the trapped driver are to be saved. It seems then that if nothing any of the individuals could do would actually help those in danger, that individual has no moral duty to assist. The individual agents with their (limited) abilities do not satisfy the capacity principle, as long as the principle is taken to apply to individual capacities only. However, most people would think that the individual persons in the examples above have some kind of duty to attempt to save those in danger, together with others. And in fact, the individuals *jointly can* achieve the desired outcome(s). The individual agents jointly can save the motor-cyclist and the person under attack. If the action that is required in order to save those in danger is a joint or collective action and if the individual agents have duties to perform that joint action, does this mean that they *jointly ought*? And what would that mean? There are two[3] possibilities for framing such a joint "ought":

(i) The first reading is *individualistic* in terms of the moral duties involved:
According to the individualistic reading, the individual members of the group (passersby or bystanders) hold no duty to overwhelm the attacker or to lift the car. Such a duty simply does not exist because there is no agent that could hold that duty given that there is no agent that could discharge the duty. The indi-viduals, however, have moral duties to perform individual actions toward a joint goal. In the examples used above, this would be actions such as helping to estab-lish communication between members of the random group, suggesting possible individual actions to other members, and, if necessary, performing a contributory action toward the joint goal such as contributing to lifting the car or contributing to overwhelming the attacker. The agency principle is satisfied, given that there are no "free-floating" duties, that is, no duties that are not held by a particular agent.

   The individualistic reading satisfies the capacity principle by suggesting that in the examples above, each individual holds a moral duty to perform an action toward solving the problem. The capacity principle is met, because no individual member of the group has duties beyond his/her capacity. As a result, however, no one holds a duty to solve the problem—retrieve the driver from underneath the burning car or subdue the attacker—*as such*. No agent ought to do so because no agent can do so.

(ii) The second reading proposes a nonindividualistic interpretation of the duties involved in the two assistance scenarios:
According to the second reading, the individuals involved can and ought to perform individual actions, but they also can and ought to perform a joint action. The passersby, for instance, each put their hands against the car's body and push. Together they eventually lift the car. They perform individual actions as part of, or contribution to, a joint action. The individuals act jointly with others if, apart from acting toward a shared goal, they act with the belief that others contribute to that same goal and with the intention to jointly perform an action, and so forth (Pettit

---

3. Arguably, there is—at least—one more possibility: the joint "ought" could be understood as a duty of the individual members of the random group to "collectivise," that is, to form a group agent. This possibility has been discussed in detail by Stephanie Collins (2013). I agree with Collins in that in some cases a group agent might be needed in order to perform the required action. However, I think there are cases where joint action that falls short of being group action will suffice. These are the ones I focus on in this article.

and Schweikard 2006). For example, in each of the above scenarios, the individual members of the random group can jointly perform the action necessary for saving another person's life.

The second reading suggests that the individual members of the random group of bystanders and passersby jointly hold duties to assist in these cases. They jointly ought to perform these actions and each of them individually ought to contribute to the joint goal. That is, *jointly*, the individuals hold a duty to lift the car, for example, and *individually* each holds the duty to do their part. The capacity principle can be satisfied if we are prepared to extend it to include joint actions and jointly acting agents:

> *Singular-agent capacity principle:* For singular—individual or group—agents "ought" implies "can" means that if the singular agent ought to do x, this implies that she can do x, and if she cannot do x then she need not do x.

> *Plurality-of-agents capacity principle:* For a plurality of—individual or group—agents "ought" implies "can" means that if agents jointly ought to do x, this implies that they jointly can do x, and if they cannot jointly do x then they need not jointly do x.

The capacity principle is satisfied because the agents *jointly can* discharge the duty. The agency principle is satisfied because it is the individual group members who hold moral duties to assist. On this account, the individuals in situations which clearly require cooperation have

(a) a duty to establish whether there exists a joint duty;
(b) if there exists a joint duty, a duty to contribute their part; and
(c) if there exists no joint duty, depending on what looks more successful, they each have
   o a duty to either establish the conditions for a joint duty to exist, namely to establish the conditions for joint ability, or
   o a duty to do whatever else they can do to help.

After introducing these two fundamentally different approaches to the moral duties involved in the above-described scenarios, let me now turn to my argument in defence of the second, nonindividualistic, reading. There are a several reasons why the nonindividualistic reading of joint "oughts" may be preferred to the individualistic reading.

The first reason has to do with intuitive ascriptions of wrongdoing in the above scenarios. One could argue that the nonindividualistic reading of duties follows our intuitions more closely than the individualistic reading. Imagine that the people walking past the attacker bashing his victim quickly walk away knowing that their failure to intervene will probably mean that the victim dies. In that case, according to the first, individualist interpretation, we could only accuse the defectors of not doing their part (whatever that involves). But we could not accuse them of bearing responsibility for the death of the victim or for failing to comply with a duty to save him. But intuition tells us otherwise. We think that the defectors are responsible for the victim's death and culpable because they walked away when they could and should have helped (I will look at the problem of noncompliance in more detail in part 6 of this article).

The nonindividualistic reading avoids the individualistic view's implication that the duty to perform the action which is most likely to save the life of the person in danger remains unallocated. If there are potential bearers of that duty then there is someone who is culpable of wrongdoing, and potentially deserving of reactive attitudes such as blame or praise should the duty (not) be discharged. Under the individualistic reading, no one can be held culpable of not saving the person's life because no one held that duty in the first place. Under the nonindividualistic reading, in contrast, the individuals are culpable of *jointly* failing to assist the victim of the attack.

At this point one might object to *joint* duties by saying that there is no need for such a notion. In the above cases, one could argue, all that we need to be able to say is that individuals have moral duties to contribute to some kind of joint or collaborative action. Each individual, we could say, ought to perform the action(s) necessary for effectively assisting those in danger. If assisting those in need requires the passersby and the bystanders to team up with others, then this is simply what it takes to discharge their individual duty to assist. Bill Wringe calls this the "primitive obligation to co-operate account."

One argument in favor of the "primitive obligation to cooperate account" is that it appears simpler than the account proposed here, because it operates with only one kind of moral duty instead of two kinds (Wringe 2014, 12). However, Wringe argues, whether or not the resulting theory is really simpler than one that accepts collective duties cannot be shown without seeing them both worked out in detail. Furthermore, "we should notice that it is not clear that collective obligations are a distinct kind of obligation rather than a familiar kind of obligation falling on a new kind of thing" (12). This takes us to the second argument in favor of the nonindividualist reading of the duties involved in the above scenario: the notion of collective duties gives us "a more unified picture of the moral scene, since it postulates one underlying obligation which explains a range of individual obliga-tions, rather than a large number of unconnected primitive obligations" (12).

The third reason to prefer the nonindividualist reading is that the joint duty seems more basic, or logically prior, to the individual (contributory) duties. The "primitive account" ignores that we somehow have to account for the existence of the duty to assist in the first place. If we do not have the capacity to assist someone, we are under no obligation to do so. In the above-described cases, capacity to assist results from the fact that the individuals have a joint ability but no individual ability to assist. Only together with others can the individual passersby and bystanders help those in need. Their individual action would not have any effect if it were not part of a joint action, that is, if others did not perform corresponding actions toward a joint goal. Hence, the individual bystanders cannot be required to throw themselves onto the attacker by virtue of their individual duty to assist. They can only be required to do so as in the context of a joint action. Furthermore, they cannot hold individual duties to collaborate with others, because whether or not others collaborate is outside their control and power. One cannot have moral duties to do things that are outside one's control. Hence, the duty to collaborate in order to assist cannot be an individual duty.

It makes sense, then, to consider the individual obligations to contribute as arising or resulting from the collective or joint obligation. According to Wringe, that the latter are more basic than the former is shown by the fact that the collective obligation remains the same even if the individuals who hold respective contributory duties change (Wringe 2014, 11).[4] Apart from being more basic, the existence of the joint obligation *explains* the existence of the individual obligation, as Wringe (2014, 9) has argued. In sum, the view defended here is that—under certain circumstances—individuals can jointly hold a moral duty to assist, resulting in individual duties to contribute to that joint action.

In the following, I will spell out the notion of joint moral duties in more detail. However, we have to be careful about several issues here. Most of all, we have to be aware that "can" does not imply "ought." There is a great temptation to think that, once we accept the existence of joint duties, all kinds of individuals in all kinds of random groups, people who have no shared or joint goals and so on, could still have moral duties to act upon moral pressing issues by virtue of the fact that they *could* act jointly. But surely, the mere fact that individuals *could* act jointly toward morally worthy end, does not imply that they *should* in the sense that they ought to do so. And while the capacity principle seems to hold for nonindividualistic interpretation of joint duties, we have to make sure we determine the limits of such joint duties.

4. THE LIMITS OF JOINT MORAL DUTIES

What, then, are the limits of such joint moral duties provided they exist? When do individuals in random groups who could act together have duties to act together? Again, let us start with simple claims and proceed to more difficult ones:

(I) It seems reasonable to think that joint moral duties are—at least—subject to the same general limitations that all moral duties are subject to
   (a) demandingness, and
   (b) competing duties.

(Ia) Limitations concerning *demandingness*.
Joint moral duties should not be overly demanding. According to Robert Goodin, "[t]he greater the moral gains in view, the greater the sacrifice that can properly be morally demanded" (Goodin 2009, 6). Furthermore, if satisfying a moral duty would require a person to sacrifice (or forgo) something of "disproportionate moral worth," that person is excused from that duty. Goodin argues that "If there are great gains in view, a morality is not wrong to demand proportionately great sacrifices from people to secure them" (2009, 8).

---

4. This undermines, according to Wringe, two types of reductionist claims about collective duties: analytic and ontic reductionism. "Both forms of reductionism are undermined by the fact that in many cases the sorts of individual obligations to which both sorts of reductionist appeal arise out of, and are explained by the existence of collective obligations" (Wringe 2014, 14). Wringe goes on the argue that collective obligations supervene on individual obligations (16 ff.).

Similar limitations to the permissibility of moral demands should apply to groups of individuals who could perform a joint action. Because several individuals are involved, the sacrifices on part of the individual members of the random group will have to be weighed against the gains of their action. Should they be weighed individually or collectively (or in aggregation)? For instance, if the gain of the joint action was to save the victim of the attacker but all helpers would suffer injuries, should these injuries be added up? I suggest that each individual agent's sacrifice be weighed separately against the moral gain. A moral duty would be overly demanding if it required at least one agent involved in discharging it to sacrifice something of disproportionate moral worth. However, it would not be overly demanding in cases when there are more people than necessary to perform the joint action and the disproportionately burdened individual does not need to be part of the joint performance.

(Ib) Limitations concerning *competing duties.*
Joint moral duties are *pro tanto* duties. They should be subject to the same limitations imposed by competing duties as "ordinary" individual *pro tanto* duties are. To give a straightforward and noncontentious example: If a person must choose between saving a child from drowning in a pond or returning home on time because her partner is waiting with dinner, surely the duty to save a life overrides the duty to keep the promise to be home on time in this case.

Something similar should apply to the duties of agents performing—or capable of performing—a joint action on both the individual and the group levels. If there exists an overriding competing (individual) duty, then a member of a random collective has no duty to contribute to a joint action. What could an overriding competing duty be in the case of the accident scenario? It would have to be a duty that is weighty enough to override a duty to save the trapped driver's life. To use a simple example: if a passerby had to choose between contributing to the action of saving the one driver or contributing to (or performing) the action of saving ten drivers trapped underneath another car, then that person should, arguably, contribute to (or perform) the action that will secure the greater benefit. Provided that she cannot do both, that person never acquires an all-out duty to contribute to the joint action of saving the one. She has an all-out duty to assist the ten.

The same would apply on the group level. If two persons jointly can save one trapped driver or ten trapped drivers, then they never acquire an all-out moral duty to save the one driver, provided that they cannot do both and provided one accepts that it is morally imperative to save then ten over the one.

(II) Apart from "standard" limitations, joint moral duties are subject to some limitations that individual moral duties are not subject to. These limitations have to do with
  (a) the right type of action, and
  (b) the group's "joint ability": the capacity of the members of the random group to perform a joint action.

(IIa) Limitations concerning *the right type of action*.
Sometimes, joint action might not be the "right type of action" to respond to a problem. Given that joint action is more difficult to establish, it has a higher potential to fail than individual action. In situations of particular urgency, the latter may be a more appropriate response to the problem than the former. Hence, under certain circumstances, it might be best to perform an individual action given time (or other) constraints when joint action is also possible but less likely or less efficient.

Similarly, group action, that is, an action performed by a group agent, may sometimes be more appropriate and promising than joint actions (which falls short of being group action). If a group agent exists, that agent may be in a better position to remedy the problem. Consider a scenario where joint action is not sufficient for saving the person in need, but where group action is needed. Group action is a type of joint action that is performed by a group as a (novel) agent. A group agent, that is, has a decision-making structure and corresponding procedures. Arguably, the more complex the task, the more it requires a group agent rather than "mere" joint action. Stephanie Collins (2013) has argued that individuals in random groups can sometimes have duties to collectivize, that is, to form a group agent with the aim of remedying a morally pressing problem. I will not discuss her suggestion here, but instead I will—for now—accept that individuals may have duties other than that of contributing to and performing a joint action if other types of action are clearly more promising and more likely to succeed in solving the problem.

(IIb) Limitations concerning *the group's "joint ability"*.
Establishing joint action is—typically—more difficult than establishing (and performing an) individual action. I have control over my own actions, but I do not have control over other people's actions. In this sense, the barrier to acting jointly seems to generally be higher than the barrier to acting individually. It looks like we need to take that barrier into account for deciding whether or not there *exists* a joint duty for any given random group of agents. It is the mutual dependence (or responsiveness) of group members when it comes to establishing joint action that we need to account for.

The ease with which joint action can be established or a joint action can be performed by a number of individuals in a random group may differ greatly depending on their circumstances. Hence, the mere *existence* of a joint duty would seem to depend not only on each individual member's capacity to perform their contributory action, but also on the capacity of the group, of the collection of individuals, to establish joint action, that is, to communicate, coordinate, and cooperate. Whether or not the members of a random group hold a joint duty is contingent on interdependent factors.

This means that whether or not individuals in a random group can hold joint duties depends on their individual abilities and features, as well as the relationship between these. The capacity to act jointly could, for instance, be severely constrained by communication barriers. Random individuals who cannot communicate (or who are not even aware of each other's existence) are incapable of performing a joint action.[5] They also cannot hold a joint duty. Or else, if the people walking past the accident site are—in combination—physically unable to lift the car of the trapped driver, then they have no capacity to act jointly and hence—given the capacity principle—they have no duty to act jointly (but they may arguably still have individual duties to do something to improve her situation if they can).

Let us now look at the positive conditions that allow for joint action. What are the situations like where individual agents have a duty to act together? What do the two cases—passersby and bystanders—have in common?

We saw that in each of the examples given, the individual members of the group were in the same place at the same time: They were in a position to communicate, observe each other, and have a grasp of the situation (the emergency), its seriousness and urgency. They were furthermore individually capable of performing the necessary contributory actions. The scenarios described so far had characteristics that only apply to a narrow selection of cases:

  (i)   *Situational simplicity:* concrete aim/goal; concrete beneficiary; concrete group; concrete place/location; limited in time/immediacy; one-off.
 (ii)   *Joint ability:* acting together is not only possible but relatively easy; individuals are capable of discharging contributory action.
(iii)   *Epistemic simplicity:* it is clear what needs to be done; it is clear what each individual needs to do; it is clear when the goal has been accomplished; it looks like there is a good chance of achieving the outcome.
 (iv)   *Limited demandingness:* no disproportionate sacrifice required.

Which of these characteristics are essential to ascribing a joint duty? Joint ability (ii) and epistemic simplicity (iii) appear to be necessary conditions. The latter, because individual agents can only have moral duties to assist when it is rather obvious what must be done. Limited demandingness (iii) is also a necessary conditions for joint duties.

However, while situational simplicity (i) is necessary, it need not include all the above criteria. It is essential that there be a concrete aim or goal. Having a concrete aim or goal usually means that it is clear who benefits from assistance. In *bystanders* and *passersby*, the need for assistance is immediate. They are emergencies: This aspect contributes largely to making the case for duties to assist compelling. To what extent we can have joint moral duties to assist in cases that are not emergencies is yet to be determined, but it seems that such duties would be much less stringent and would less often become all-out duties. *Bystanders* and *passersby* are one-off situations. If an unstructured group such as *bystanders* encounters violence repeatedly, they repeatedly accrue duties to assist, so long as these are not overly demanding. However, if the problem is a lack in public safety generally, institutional action is required, above all. Situational simplicity furthermore

---

5. Common limitations include:
○ members cannot communicate;
○ they cannot communicate and act together *in time*; and
○ they could do the above, but it is not very likely, they only have a small chance.

requires there to be a concrete group of duty bearers. This aspect is crucial, both for epistemic simplicity (individuals must know that they are part of a group) and for determining whether there exists a duty in the first place (if there is no concrete group, joint ability and the level of demandingness cannot be established).

If these are the minimal conditions which need to be in place in order for a random group to have joint ability (the ability to perform a joint action) then the random groups who have such joint ability are rather few. Members of an unstructured group need not necessarily be at the same place or location. However, with very extended random collectives consisting of people who are physically apart or who do not know each other, people who live on different continents or only in different cities, joint ability is not a given. Moreover, until recently, it would have been almost impossible to establish. Still, even with the means of modern of communication and the Internet today, the level of joint ability of random groups—such as the citizens of industrialized countries—is rather low.

It makes sense to think of a group's capacity to perform a joint action—its joint ability—as temporal. A group can have joint ability at one moment in time and lose that ability in the next moment, for instance, if there are no longer enough group members to perform the task. A group's joint ability can vary in degree. For the cases described above, it was assumed that the group's joint ability was high. Hence, its members acquired joint obligations to save the lives of the persons in danger. At the other end of the spectrum, groups with no joint ability cannot hold joint moral duties.[6] Then there would be groups that have some level of joint ability, but not the maximum level. A random group's joint ability can be diminished by a number of factors, including obstacles to communication or limitations to the group members' individual abilities to perform the contributory action. If the obstacles are too great, then the group has no joint ability and its members do not hold joint duties.

5. LIMITS OF INDIVIDUAL DUTIES

What do the previously discussed issues imply for individuals who find themselves in situations where they could contribute to a joint action to remedy a morally problematic situation? In situations in need of remedy, individuals could often perform a variety of actions, individual contributory actions to a joint action being one of several options. What should an individual do in light of the uncertainty of whether or not joint action will be established and/or successful?

In order to answer this question, let us return to the example of the bystander of the attack. Any individual bystander of the attack could either

---

6. Again, I am using the term "group" very loosely here. In the way I use it, any two random individuals anywhere on the planet can be a group. A psychologist from China and a dairy farmer from Southern France are a random group in this loose sense of group. As a random group, they have a certain level of joint ability which depends on the particular circumstances. If they are unaware of each other's existence, for instance, their joint ability is zero.

(i) work toward establishing joint action, including starting to communicate with others about intervening to assist the victim of the attack,

OR

(ii) perform an individual action (with no view to a joint outcome). For instance, she could walk to the next phone booth and call the police. (In doing so, she would be potentially lowering the chances of a joint intervention of the remaining bystanders on behalf of the victim, and dangerously increasing the chances of the attack being fatal.)

Let us assume, for the sake of argument, that a successful joint action's outcome is preferable over a successful individual action's outcome here. Suppose that the successful joint action's outcome involves immediately overwhelming the attacker and saving the victim's life and physical integrity while a successful individual action's outcome would involve the arrival of police at a later point in time with a high chance of the victim having died as a result of the attack by then. Hence, if option (i) is better, and if this is obvious to a reasonable observer, what ought the individual bystander to do when arriving at the crime scene?

In this situation, whether or not she should choose the *pro tanto* better option (i) or option (ii) depends on her reasonable assessment of her own and the other group members' ability to cooperate, communicate, and contribute to a joint action. If she has reasonable doubts that the group, including her, has joint ability, then she is under no obligation to contribute to a joint outcome or to enact her part of the joint performance.

If she has no good reason to believe that joint action cannot be established, she ought to work toward or contribute to the joint action until she has reason to believe that the joint goal has been achieved or that a number of other agents willing to contribute are insufficient for the joint goal to be achieved (see Lawford-Smith 2012). If, in the process of establishing joint action, she realizes (or has good reason to believe) that an insufficient number of members will contribute, then she must (usually) fall back on individual obligations and actions. If z_{joint} (= saving the victim jointly instantaneously) cannot be achieved by the group, then z_{indiv} may still be achievable by an individual agent and her individual action.

To sum up: Individual members of a random group confronted with a situation in need of remedy will need to make a choice between (1) performing individual contributory action(s) to a joint action with the other agents present with a view to contributing toward a joint goal, or (2) performing an individual action toward an individual goal.

How does an individual member of a random group know that they have a contributory duty? I argue that in order for an individual to have a contributory duty, the following conditions must be met:

(i) The group must have joint duty (to assist) as specified in Section 4.
(ii) The individual has good reason to believe that the group has a joint duty.

(iii) The individual has no good reason to believe that
    (a) an insufficient number of others would contribute, or
    (b) a sufficient number of others are contributing already.

This implies that an individual can fail in his/her contributory duty even if the joint outcome is achieved. This would be the case, for example, if she walked away from the accident scene, before she can be certain that enough others will contribute to pushing the car of the trapped motorcyclist. Each individual's duty involves a conditional such that they are required to contribute to the joint action unless and until they have good reason to believe that sufficient others are already contributing.

6. NONCOMPLIANCE WITH JOINT MORAL DUTIES EXPLAINED

We can now turn to the question of what it means to fail to comply with joint duties. As we established, joint duties are held by individual agents together (or jointly) and they always give rise to another type of duty: individual (contributory) duties. Noncompliance with a joint duty must then entail noncompliance with an individual duty. At first glance, there seem to be two ways of failing to comply with a joint moral duty:

(i) The individuals in the random group do perform a joint action but that action is unsuccessful. That is, it does not achieve the joint goal of retrieving the trapped motorcyclist or of subduing the attacker.
(ii) The individuals in the random group fail to perform a joint action.
    (a) One or more individual members of the random group bail on the rest and undermine the group's joint ability.
    (b) People embark on a joint action but one or more individuals fail to perform their contributory action.
    (c) No one does anything. They all just stand there and watch the person being killed by the attacker or the motorcyclist being killed by the flames.

As to the first option: If the individuals perform a joint action without achieving their goal, this could be due to a number of factors. First, the individuals might not have been jointly capable of performing the duty. In this case, insufficient joint ability existed, which means that the group did not have a duty in the first place. Second, the individual members of the group did their very best to contribute to the joint goal, and they performed a joint action, but other circumstances prevented them from achieving that goal or they were simply unlucky. In such cases, we could say that they failed to discharge their duty but are blameless for that failure.[7] However, this seems to put too much into the concept of moral duty. Surely, their duty is to perform an action with a view to achieving a particular goal, but there cannot be a duty to perform that action successfully, that is, to actually

---

7. I thank Michael Rubin for mentioning this possibility.

achieve that goal regardless of the circumstances. Therefore, it seems appropriate to say that the individuals discharged their joint duty despite their action being ultimately unsuccessful. Hence, only the second option remains: Failing to comply with a joint duty means to fail to perform the required joint action.[8]

As to the second option, there are several possibilities, too. First, one or more individual members of the random group can bail on the rest and undermine the group's joint ability. For instance, if all individual agents' contributions are necessary for performing the joint action, then any single agent bailing undermines the group's joint ability.[9] In that situation, the remaining members of the random group cease to have a moral duty to act jointly as soon as the group loses its joint ability. Their failure to comply with their joint duty (which they held while they still had joint ability) is due exclusively to the bailing agent's action.[10] That single agent would be morally blameworthy for the failure of the random group to perform the joint action.

The second possibility has people embark on a joint action, but one or more individuals fail to perform their contributory action. While the group has joint ability, one or more of its members just do not act toward the joint goal. Again, if their individual contributions were necessary for performing the joint action and they have no excuse for failing to contribute, then they are morally blameworthy not only for the failure to perform that individual action, but also for the group's failure to perform the joint action.

Regarding the first and second possibilities: If, due to one or more agents' defection, a random group does not achieve the joint outcome, the remaining individual members of that group are not accountable for that failure and not blameworthy if

(i) they did contribute or took credible steps toward establishing joint action, and
(ii) as a result they had good reason to believe that an insufficient number of others would not contribute.[11]

The third possibility is that the individuals in the random group fail to perform the joint action because no one does anything. They might just stand there and watch

8. Another possibility is that the individuals are jointly doing the wrong thing. In this case, individuals would act together toward the joint goal but their action would be unsuccessful because it was the wrong kind of response to the problem. Again, we have to allow for our agents to err. Even if they make a mistake, they may still have complied with their joint duty. However, if the mistake was easily avoidable or resulted from negligence or slackness, then they may have failed in their duty and be morally blameworthy.

9. Holly Lawford-Smith (2012) calls these cases of "joint necessity."

10. See also Robert Goodin's (2012) solution to cases where individual group members mutually excuse each other from a joint duty. He describes the case in which individual group members give each other reason to believe that an insufficient number of individuals will contribute to the joint action which means that they no longer hold a joint duty. Goodin suggests a solution to this problem, which I think is successful and which I will not discuss here.

11. This condition ensures that group members who do not care to find out whether others are willing to contribute, or who give other group members no reason to believe that they are willing to contribute, are not off the hook.

the person being beaten to death or the motorcyclist being killed by the flames. In this case, we would definitely want to say that individually they have failed in their duty to make their individual contributions. However, we would probably want to say more than that: The individuals have also failed to comply with their joint duty: They failed in a duty to assist the victim of the attack and the trapped motorcyclist. If we think that together they failed to assist, this does not necessarily mean that they failed "as a group."[12] We established that the members of the random group do not form a group agent. Hence, the individuals' failure to act is not the failure of a group as a distinct agent. It remains the failure of the individual members.

Who would be the legitimate object of blame in that case? One thing is clear: If there is no group agent, but only individual agents (who can potentially act jointly), then blame cannot fall on this nonexistent group agent, but only on the individual agents. With regard to joint necessity cases, each of them could be individually blameworthy for the random group's failure, because one agent's refusal to act is individually sufficient for the joint action failure. The same should apply to cases where more individuals are present than required to perform the joint action. This is because each individual defection can be seen as sufficient for undermining the joint ability of a potential subgroup of willing agents.[13]

7. CONCLUDING REMARKS

What follows from the account of joint moral duties sketched here? If we accept that individuals in random groups can hold moral duties jointly, does this mean that each of us has more or different moral duties than those of which we are currently aware? Does it mean that we ought to team up with others in order to address problems that require joint action solutions? After all, if an individual agent's capacities are joined up with other individual agents' capacities, more and more complex moral problems can—in principle—be effectively addressed.

It appears that an incredibly large number of individuals in random groups could in principle act together if they only took the necessary steps toward establishing joint action. However, it was demonstrated that joint ability does not suffice for ascribing joint duties: Not every group of random individuals that is capable of acting jointly has a duty to act jointly. This article showed that in cases characterized by situational simplicity, epistemic simplicity, and limited demandingness, individuals in random groups with joint ability can have duties to spontaneously act together, that is, to perform a joint action with the aim of remedying the morally dire situation. This might mean that the circumstances under which individuals in

12. This is what Virginia Held (1970) seems to be suggesting.
13. That is, if there are six bystanders and only four of them need to take action, then each has a duty to contribute, unless there are four individuals contributing already. Each individual agent must consider herself to be part of the subgroup of four unless she has reason to believe that four other individuals comprise the subgroup of four and that she is in the subgroup of the remaining two. In case all six stand around and do nothing, no individual has reason to believe that she is not part of the subgroup of four. If she fails to take action then, she has failed to act as one out of four who were required to act. Her individual defection was sufficient for undermining the subgroup's ability.

random collectives acquire joint duties are very limited, too. As a matter of fact, joint action of random groups—which is often spontaneous, requires no complex decision-making or task-distribution and falls short of being group action—is most likely to be established and successful on a small scale and in settings where membership of the group is limited and unambiguous.[14,15]

REFERENCES

Collins, Stephanie. 2013. "Collectives' Duties and Collectivisation Duties." *Australasian Journal of Philosophy* 91(2): 231–48.

Cripps, Elizabeth. 2011. "Climate Change, Collective Harm and Legitimate Coercion." *Critical Review of International Social and Political Philosophy* 14(2): 171–93.

———. 2013. *Climate Change and the Moral Agent: Individual Duties in an interdependent World.* Oxford: Oxford University Press.

Erskine, Toni, ed. 2003. "Assigning Responsibility to Institutional Moral Agents: The Case of States and 'Quasi States'." In *Can Institutions Have Responsibilities? Collective Moral Agency and International Relations*, 19–40. Basingstoke, UK: Palgrave Macmillan.

French, Peter A. 1984. *Collective and Corporate Responsibility*. New York: Columbia University Press.

Goodin, Robert E. 2009. "Demandingness as a Virtue." *Journal of Ethics* 13(1): 1–13.

———. 2012. "Excused by the Unwillingness of Others?" *Analysis* 72(1): 18–24.

Held, Virginia. 1970. "Can a Random Collection of Individuals Be Morally Responsible?" *Journal of Philosophy* 67(14): 471–81.

Lawford-Smith, Holly. 2012. "The Feasibility of Collectives' Actions." *Australasian Journal of Philosophy* 90(3): 453–67.

List, Christian, and Pettit, Philip. 2011. *Group Agency: The Possibility, Design, and Status of Corporate Agents.* Oxford: Oxford University Press.

May, Larry. 1992. *Sharing Responsibility*. Chicago: University of Chicago Press.

Pettit, Philip, and Schweikard, David. 2006. "Joint Actions and Group Agents." *Philosophy of the Social Sciences* 36(1): 18–39.

Schwenkenbecher, Anne. 2013. "Joint Duties and Global Moral Obligations." *Ratio* 26(3): 310–28.

Wringe, Bill. 2005. "Needs, Rights, and Collective Obligations." *Royal Institute of Philosophy Supplement* 80(57): 187–207.

———. 2010. "Global Obligations and the Agency Objection." *Ratio* 23(2): 217–31.

———. 2014. "Collective Obligations: Their Existence, Their Explanatory Power, and Their Supervenience on the Obligations of Individuals." Advance online publication. *European Journal of Philosophy* 21(4).

14. We can also see that the argument put forward in this article does not suffice to justify a positive joint duty of beneficence held by the "global community" or other large and dispersed random collectives. The citizens of industrialized nations cannot hold joint duties of assistance to combat complex and large-scale moral problems, because the criteria for accruing such duties are not met. However, this is not to say that they cannot hold negative duties to combat climate change or global poverty, or that there are no other ways of justifying positive duties to assist for large and extended groups.

15. I would like to thank Stephanie Collins, Daniel Halliday, Christian Lee, Alejandra Mancilla, and Michael Rubin for their invaluable comments on earlier drafts of this article. I am also very grateful to audiences at the 2013 Australasian Association of Philosophy Annual Conference, The Centre for the Study of Mind in Nature in Oslo, Olaf Mueller's research seminar at Humboldt University of Berlin, Stefan Gosepath's research seminar at Free University of Berlin, the Philosophy and Economics Program at the University of Bayreuth, and the Philosophical Seminar at the University of Muenster.

Midwest Studies In Philosophy, XXXVIII (2014)

Small Impacts and Imperceptible Effects: Causing Harm with Others

KAI SPIEKERMANN

1. INTRODUCTION

In an increasingly crowded and interactive world, there are more and more ways to harm people in an indirect way. These "new harms" (Lichtenberg 2010, 558) are typically caused by many hands (Thompson 1980). Many people use too many plastic bags, drive their cars too much, eat too much meat or bluefin tuna, drink bottled water, and so on. Each individual act has a negligible effect, and may, as a singular act, not be harmful—but the same act performed by millions is. This gap between the (almost or perhaps entirely) harmless singular act and the harmful performance of the same act by many spells trouble for the moral evaluation of these acts and for assigning responsibility.

In a recent article, Shelly Kagan (2011) tries to dissolve some of these difficulties. In essence, Kagan claims that many small contributions must always encounter a threshold, such that a relevant harm is triggered. If that is so, Kagan argues, any single action contributes to expected harm because there is a nonzero probability that it crosses the relevant threshold. Julia Nefsky (2011) pokes holes in Kagan's argument, showing that Kagan proceeds too quickly in dismissing the challenge of sorites-like situations where each additional action does not incur additional perceived harm. This exchange shows that the issue of imperceptible effects and harms is still not conclusively settled thirty years after Derek Parfit's (1984) seminal discussion in *Reasons and Persons*.

I propose to take the imperceptibility challenge seriously. Our perception can be *minimal change insensitive* so that very small changes are impossible to perceive. And if the normatively relevant consequences of an action, holding all other actions fixed, cannot be perceived, then we are challenged to explain what makes the action wrong. My tentative answer is that an action cannot only be wrong because of its immediate effects, it can also be wrong because it can possibly cause an effect together with other actions. To avoid such wrong actions, an agent has to engage in forward-looking considerations as to how her actions, together with other actions that are possibly performed, can be harmful.

The article proceeds by specifying the decision situations of interest. Section 3 states four *prima facie* attractive propositions about problems of imperceptible effects, and shows that these four propositions are mutually inconsistent. Sections 4–7 discuss four attempts to avoid the inconsistency by relaxing different propositions. I sketch my preferred solution in Section 8 and conclude in Section 9.

2. ZOOMING IN ON THE PROBLEM

When many people make a small contribution to a large problem, we can distinguish between two schematic ways how these contributions lead to harm. Either the contributions are harmless until the overall contribution reaches a tipping point at which great harm is caused. Or the contributions gradually increase the level of harm, without any critical thresholds. In this article, the focus is exclusively on the latter case.

Many hands problems are particularly challenging when the individual consequences of actions cannot easily be associated with harm because the changes brought about by each individual are so miniscule that they do not register as harm (I will flesh out this thought in much greater detail below). Some collectively caused harms may appear to have that structure, but, under closer inspection, we can rule out some of them. For instance, jointly causing climate change is often seen as a paradigmatic example (see Sinnott-Armstrong 2005). When looking at the implications of individual acts of emissions, however, it turns out that they are often quite significant. The typical personal lifetime emissions in a developed country are expected to "wipe out more than six months of a healthy human life" in the calculations of John Broome (2012, chap. 5). Smaller emissions also have clear effects. Flying from London to New York causes about one tonne of CO_2 emissions. The damage from these emissions can be quantified as a double digit US$ amount,[1] so they are likely to register. This shows that many larger emissions do cause expected harm, and this harm can be quite significant indeed.[2]

Sinnott-Armstrong and others have in mind smaller emission amounts: the emission of a Sunday pleasure drive with your sport utility vehicle (SUV), for example. If the emission is quite small (perhaps a very short Sunday pleasure drive), it may not register on the scale of harm. These are the cases I am interested in here. Nevertheless, carbon emissions are not the best example to use. Even

---

1. In estimated carbon prices deemed necessary for effective mitigation action.
2. There may be objections against using *expected* rather than *actual* harm to morally evaluate these actions. It is true that, since the effect of the emissions may not linearly lead to more harm, one cannot claim that each individual emission will certainly lead to actual harm. However, increasing the probability of serious harm occuring in the future is surely morally wrong as well.

though single instances of small emissions may only cause imperceptible effects, a different way to individuate actions would make them components of larger actions that do trigger perceptible effects (Andreou 2006). So perhaps consequentialists have difficulties criticizing a single short pleasure drive, but they have the tools to criticize an individual's total annual emission pattern. In the case of emissions, that is the correct approach in the first place—what matters are aggregate emissions, after all.

The problem of many hands becomes much harder and more interesting if the individual actions (with imperceptible effects) are not performed repeatedly by the same individual. Consider a simplified version of Parfit's "harmless torturers" (Parfit 1984, 80). A group of n torturers can each push a button to increase the voltage of the electric shock the victim[3] receives by the amount 1,000 volt / n (one "notch"). The pain caused by 1,000 volts is excruciating. It is plausible to assume that there is a number of torturers n so large that the victim cannot distinguish between x torturers and $x + 1$ torturers for any x between 0 and $n - 1$. Suppose the torturers push their button only once. If the harm done is defined as the additional suffering caused, then, it can be argued, none of the single torturers causes any harm. And, unlike the case of carbon emissions, there is no larger individual action pattern that would cause any perceptible effects and could be criticized on the basis of the harm caused, since the torturers will not repeat their action.

3. THE CONTRADICTION

It is useful to make this setting more precise. Let there be a set N of individuals labeled $1, 2, \ldots, n$. Each individual can perform one of two actions, "contribute" or "not contribute." We denote a contribution by individual i with $a_i = 1$, and no contribution by $a_i = 0$. There are no other actions available to the individuals, which means that for all $i \in N$: $a_i \in \{0, 1\}$. We call the vector of all actions $\boldsymbol{a} = (a_1, a_2, \ldots, a_n)$ an action profile, while the sum of all contributions is $c = \Sigma \boldsymbol{a}$. For simplicity, assume that the individual actions are exchangeable, so that it does not matter who contributes, it only matters how many individuals contribute. The contributions make an impact m_c, and m is strictly increasing in c, such that each additional contribution increases the impact somewhat.

The impact can be measured precisely: the voltage, the poison emitted, the temperature increased by greenhouse gas emissions, and so on. Therefore, one might think that the harm produced can simply be measured directly in terms of the impact. But this view is mistaken. The impact as such is morally neutral—what is normatively relevant is how the impact determines a morally relevant property such as harm. What is needed is a bridge principle connecting empirical facts with normative propositions. Hedonists, for instance, take pleasure and pain as morally relevant and say that an impact leads to harm if it increases pain, relative to a baseline. Of course, many other such principles are conceivable and have been discussed, but, for simplicity, I stick with the hedonistic line here. The important

3. In Parfit's original example, the torturers have 1,000 victims, but this is not necessary for my discussion.

upshot is that the impact is *causally related* to the harm but it is not identical with the harm. Rather, the harm is a function of the impact, $h(m)$. I assume that the harm is weakly increasing in the impact (i.e., more impact will either lead to equal or more harm).

While we can often quantify impacts precisely, this may not be true of the harm caused by impacts. Think about Parfit's harmless torturers again. Even though there will be a difference in voltage (i.e., in impact) when comparing x and $x + 1$ torturers, there may be no difference in the perceived pain. And since Parfit proposes, at least initially, to measure harm in perceived pain, the torturers are a problem.

More generally, the problem of imperceptible effects arises as a contradiction between four (at least *prima facie*) plausible propositions:

Direct Act Consequences. Whether an action is wrong only depends on the consequences in a particular sense: the consequences of this particular action while holding all other relevant actions fixed.

Experienced Harm. For an action to be wrong (expected) experienced harm must be among the consequences.

No Stepwise Harm. There exist decision situations such that the individuals decide on their respective actions $a_1, a_2, \ldots, a_n$ and:

(i) if all individuals "contribute" ($c = n$) then the actions cause experienced harm, and if all individuals do "not contribute" ($c = 0$) the actions do not cause experienced harm.

Also, for any level of contribution $x \in (0, n - 1)$:

(ii) adding one more contribution, so that $\Sigma a = x + 1$, always makes a small positive contribution to the impact; but

(iii) adding one more contribution, so that $\Sigma a = x + 1$, never causes a change in experienced harm compared to x.

Contribution Is Wrong. Any action that contributes to the impact is wrong.

Direct Act Consequences, Experienced Harm, No Stepwise Harm, and *Contribution Is Wrong* are inconsistent, because (from *No Stepwise Harm*) there exist actions that do not cause experienced harm while holding all other actions fixed, even though they contribute to the impact. From *Direct Act Consequences* we know that we should only consider the immediate consequences of an action to determine whether it is wrong, holding all other actions fixed. Therefore (from *Experienced Harm*), these actions do not have the wrong-making property of causing (expected) harm and are not wrong. This contradicts *Contribution Is Wrong*.

How plausible are these propositions? Take *Direct Act Consequences* first. Act consequentialists are committed to the claim that the moral properties of an action depend on its consequences only. In fact, all reasonable ethical theories would take the consequences of actions, perhaps among other considerations, into account. The more controversial aspect of *Direct Act Consequences* is the claim that only the consequences of *this particular action, holding all other relevant actions fixed*, should be considered. The plausibility of this more stringent condition stems from considerations of control. To assess what is under the control of the acting person, we need to know what exact difference this person's action can make to the world. We work this out by comparing the consequences of performance and nonperformance, while holding everything else fixed.[4] *Direct Act Consequences* ensures that the rightness or wrongness of one's action depends only on the consequences one has control over.

Experienced Harm is a commitment to a specific conception of harm. According to *Experienced Harm*, one property that is required to make an action wrong is the expectation of experienced harm, or, more precisely, the *phenomenal* component of harm. The most obvious candidates here are pain and discomfort. Unsurprisingly, classical hedonist act-utilitarians will have no issue with *Experienced Harm*. However, even if most philosophers are probably unwilling to subscribe to *Experienced Harm* across the board, *Experienced Harm* may at least be plausibly applicable in those situations where no other bad effects can be identified except for the harm experienced by the victim.

Let us turn to *No Stepwise Harm*. If we assume *No Stepwise Harm*, each single additional contribution leads to an increase in the impact m but will not lead to an increase in experienced harm. How can this be? The explanation is that the experience of harm is *minimal change insensitive* (short: *insensitive*), such that adding or subtracting just one contribution never leads to a change in the perception of the current level of harm (here I am inspired by the formal treatment of the related concept of vagueness in van Rooij 2010).

To express this a little more technically, assume that we order the harms according to the relations $>_H$ ("is experienced as more harmful than") and an indifference relation $\sim_H$ ("is experienced as equally harmful as"). According to *No Stepwise Harm*, clause (iii), there exist decision situations such that any pair of harms that differ by just one additional or omitted contribution is indistinguishable. This results in a series of indistinguishable harm observation pairs:

$$h(m_{c=0}) \sim_H h(m_{c=1}) \wedge h(m_{c=1}) \sim_H h(m_{c=2}) \wedge \ldots \wedge h(m_{c=n-1}) \sim_H h(m_{c=n}). \qquad (1)$$

It is now clear that the relation $\sim_H$ cannot be an equivalence relation. If it was, it would follow immediately that $h(m_{c=0}) \sim_H h(m_{c=n})$, which would contradict clause (i) of *No Stepwise Harm*. Of course, some have taken this as a *reductio*, claiming that a premise like *No Stepwise Harm* must be rejected (e.g., Graff 2001). I will argue, however, that the insensitivity involved here makes it plausible to accept *No Stepwise Harm*.

For *No Stepwise Harm* to be consistent, we need to explain how the claim in clause (iii) can be true without directly contradicting (i). The key to this is the assumption that the relation $\sim_H$ can be *non-transitive*.[5] Therefore, all the conjuncts of (1) can be true, but, due to nontransitivity, this does not imply that $h(m_{c=0}) \sim_H$

---

4. How precisely the counterfactual is to be cashed out is a surprisingly difficult question, but here a rough sketch suffices. See Norcross (2005).

5. More technically, van Rooij (2010) and others before him account for this with semi-orders. Note that (1), together with the assumption of nontransitivity, does *not* give rise to the sorites paradox because (1) and nontransitivity do not imply the inductive premise needed for a sorites problem. I will revisit this point below.

$h(m_{c=n})$ and avoids the contradiction with (i). In other words: It is possible that adding or taking away the contribution of one individual never increases or lowers the experienced harm, but putting all (or more than one) actions together does.[6]

The vagueness[7] literature contains several proposals as to how relations like "is indistinguishable from," "feels just as," and so on, can be nontransitive. Here I state just one such proposal. According to one type of "contextualist" account, the relation of indistinguishability depends on context, and the context changes in a subtle way while moving through the series. For instance, if the relation "is experienced as equally harmful as" is a slightly different relation for some levels of contribution, then some of the relations in (1) are slightly different, and if some of the relations are different, transitivity cannot be applied across them all (e.g., Raffman 1996). After all, transitivity is a property of one and the same relation, it has no bearing on a series of subtly different relations. If we can accept such an interpretation of clause (iii), then *No Stepwise Harm* can plausibly be true. Further evidence that this is a plausible assumption comes from the literature on phenomenal sorites problems. Many philosophers[8] engaged in this debate endorse the view that it is possible to experience insensitivity in terms of color perception. If two color patches are *very* similar (even though we know from the way we produced them that they do not have exactly the same hue), then subjects cannot distinguish between them in pairwise comparison. A very similar phenomenal experience is plausible with regard to pain perception.

Last, we look at *Contribution Is Wrong*. This expresses a fairly common intuition about doing harm. If you play a contributing part in a causal process that harms people by increasing the impact, then this contributing action is wrong. This, according to *Contribution Is Wrong*, is independent from whether your action alone makes a perceptible difference, it suffices that you positively contribute to the impact.

To avoid the contradiction between *Direct Act Consequences*, *Experienced Harm*, *No Stepwise Harm*, and *Contribution Is Wrong*, we need to weaken or give up at least one of these four propositions. Using this framework, we can analyze the recent debate on imperceptible effects and "many hands problems." Different participants have proposed to relax different propositions, but very few have carefully considered the underlying background assumptions and possible trade-offs. The next four sections account for different attempts to relax one of the four propositions to avoid the contradiction. I sketch my preferred solution in Section 8.

4. RELAXING DIRECT ACT CONSEQUENCES

In *Reasons and Persons*, Parfit defines a view very similar to *Direct Act Consequences*, which he calls the Second Mistake:

6. Michael Otsuka (1991, 138), for example, explicitly endorses the view that such situations exist.

7. While the literature on vagueness inspires my approach, I prefer the term "insensitivity" to mark the fact that vagueness pertains to semantics, while insensitivity pertains to perception. I am grateful to Christian List for urging me to make this distinction.

8. Graff (2001) reviews the main players, but comes to endorse transitivity.

(The Second Mistake) If some act is right or wrong *because of its effects*, the only relevant effects are the effects of this particular act (Parfit 1984, 70).

Parfit argues that this view is mistaken because it leads to implausible implications in overdetermination cases. To demonstrate, Parfit discusses the famous "Two Assassins." If two snipers shoot at me at exactly the same time and the two bullets pierce my heart such that each of them would have been sufficient to kill me immediately, then each of the two assassins alone is not causally necessary for killing me.[9]

Parfit's preferred solution for problems of this sort is to suggest that even if individual acts do not produce harm, it is possible that individuals *together* can create harms:

(C7). Even if an act harms no one, this act may be wrong because it is one of a *set* of acts that *together* harm other people (Parfit 1984, 70).[10]

This principle states that acts can be wrong because they are part of a set of acts that causes harm, in contradiction to *Direct Act Consequences*. Even though one single act may be "harm-less" in the sense of *No Stepwise Harm*, the set of acts is not. For instance, even if Sinnott-Armstrong's pleasure driver is not causing any harm individually, his driving is part of a set of actions that do cause harm, namely all the acts leading to greenhouse gas emissions. Therefore, relaxing *Direct Act Consequences* by suggesting a principle along the lines of C7 has some appeal.

One difficulty with notions like "harming together" is to deliver a plausible explanation why the *individual* acts are impermissible if they cause harm *together* (Tannsjö 1989, 223). In addition, note that according to C7 an individual act is not *necessarily* wrong just because it is part of a harming set of acts. Parfit aims to qualify C7, since in his view, what is required of individuals depends on what the other individuals do. People are not required to withhold actions if there is no harm in the aggregate, or if the harm will happen anyhow. This is why, in *Reasons and Persons*, Parfit conditions the obligation on enough but not too many others acting in a similar way, and introduces a common knowledge assumption (see C10 on 77). In addition, as both Gruzalski (1986) and Otsuka (1991) point out, Parfit's "together" solution crucially depends on two inconsistent claims: that one can determine a most beneficial (and equivalently: least harming) set of actions, while at the same time assuming that adding or withdrawing one contribution makes no difference. These problems remain a challenge for Parfit's view.

9. Not everyone agrees with Parfit that the Second Mistake really is a mistake. Frank Jackson (1997) maintains that act-consequentialists should hold their nerve: In cases of overdetermination, they should maintain that the single acts are not wrong because they are not causally necessary to bring about the harm. If one wants to defend Jackson's line, it is important to be precise about the setup. In Jackson's discussion of the two assassins, it is *certain* that both of the two assassins will shoot, and they shoot independently from each other. In such a case, the action of one assassin alone truly does not cause any harm.

10. I quote (C7) rather than (C10), as Parfit has retracted on (C10) in his reaction to an argument presented by Gruzalski. See Parfit (1986) and Gruzalski (1986).

Overall, Parfit's proposal for relaxing *Direct Act Consequences*, while clearly intuitively attractive, has faced objections that have not been fully addressed. Below I will suggest a different way to relax *Direct Act Consequences* that, I hope to show, holds more promise.

5. RELAXING THE EXPERIENCED HARM ASSUMPTION

Rejections of *Experienced Harm* are frequent in the literature. Glover suggests that actions without experienced harm as a consequence are still wrong because they must be understood as producing *fractions* of perceptible harm:

> [The Principle of Divisibility] says that, in cases where harm is a matter of degree, subthreshold actions are wrong to the extent that they cause harm, and where a hundred acts like mine are necessary to cause a detectable difference I have caused 1/100 of that detectable harm. (Glover and Scott-Taggart 1975, 174)

Unfortunately, Glover's argument for the Principle of Divisibility is rather weak: He simply points to the unpalatable implications of rejecting that principle.

More promising are arguments that give us an explanation why actions that do not cause experienced harm can be wrong nevertheless. Several authors have observed that even if the addition of one more actions may not change the perceived harm, at some point the *report* of the overall level of pain must change. In Parfit's torturer case, every two situations that differ by only one step in the increase of voltage feel exactly the same when compared against each other, but at the same time it must be true that the subjects' experience of pain changes when the voltage gets notched up gradually. If absolutely *no* property changed while the voltage increases, it could not be true that there is no pain at voltage 0, but tremendous pain at voltage 1,000. The question is which property one should consider to avoid the problem. Kagan considers the subject's pain report:

> At some point the answer to the question "are you in pain?" must differ from the answer given immediately before—otherwise the victim would still be answering "no" at state 1,000 (just as they answered "no" at state 0), something we know to be false. (Kagan 2011, 132)

Kagan thus proposes to take the *pain report* as the relevant property. It is undoubtedly true that when the number of contributions c increases, at some number of contributions x the impact has increased enough for the experienced harm to be greater than the (lack of) harm at the beginning, that is to say $h(m_0) <_H h(m_x)$. From this Kagan infers that "at least one state must feel different from the one that came before" (Kagan 2011, 132). This last claim, however, is mistaken, and it contradicts what Kagan says earlier about such cases: "Each individual act makes no perceptible difference to anyone's pain" (115).

Kagan begins with a careful definition of the morally relevant measure, the perception of pain, only to gradually conflate it with other measures. The fact that *reported* pain must eventually change between two steps in the increase of voltage simply does not imply that the experienced pain is different between these two steps. The subject's report can consistently look like this:

. . .

Step x: Does the pain feel just like at step $x - 1$? "Yes"
    Are you in pain? "No"
Step $x + 1$: Does the pain feel just like at step x? "Yes"
    Are you in pain? "Yes"

At step $x + 1$ the subject may be thinking: "This feels just like the last step. But it really does feel painful now, so I say yes to the second question." Despite Kagan's best efforts to convince us otherwise, the subject does not make a mistake in reporting their perception (Nefsky 2011). What would be mistaken is the belief that *nothing* has changed—but that does not entail that the subject must therefore be able to distinguish the pain perception of step x and $x + 1$ in direct comparison.

Similar claims can be defended in analogous settings. Arguably, one can gradually change the temperature such that a subject can never tell the difference between any two notches, one can gradually fade from one color to another such that each two adjacent shades are indistinguishable, and so on. This does not prevent the subjects from realizing along the way that certain variables have changed. They begin to notice pain, they notice that the water that was cold at the beginning is now lukewarm, or that the green is now orange. What they cannot do is distinguish between adjacent steps. Consequently, they also cannot pinpoint the precise step where the change has taken place—even though they do notice the change.

What Kagan effectively proposes is a revision of *Experienced Harm*. Instead of considering experienced harm, he suggests considering *harm reports*. And since contributions are typically made under conditions of imperfect information, any contribution has a small probability to change the harm reported, such that the *expected reported harm* is positive for all contributions.[11]

Another way to revise *Experienced Harm* is to appeal to properties that are accessible by theoretical reasoning (Hansson 1999; Shrader-Frechette, 1987). Provided that the subjects are well informed about the setup, they know that even though they cannot feel a difference in pain when the contribution level changes slightly, they still know that the impact on them has changed. In the case of the harmless torturers, one could think about the subjects sitting in front of a voltmeter with very high measurement resolution, displaying the current voltage. One contribution is added. The subjects do not feel any difference, but they do see the increased voltage on the voltmeter. From this they infer that it has become more likely that their pain perception will change once further contributions are added.

Extending our limited cognitive abilities by theoretical reasoning or by measurement instruments is common in science and in everyday life. Suppose I cut a piece of butter into two equal halfs. They feel equally heavy to me. However,

---

11. A related, probabilistic version along the same lines was given earlier by Voorhoeve and Binmore (2006) and by Arntzenius and McCarthy (1997).

theoretical reasoning tells me that with a probability infinitely close to 1, one piece must be a tiny bit heavier than the other, and a sufficiently precise scale will tell me which one this is. It would be crazy to maintain that we should end the inquiry by insisting that the two lumps of butter are equally heavy because they feel equally heavy. And perhaps we should also use suitable reasoning and measurement tools to get a better empirical access to the causal process that leads to the harm the subjects are experiencing in our problem. That means that we should stop taking phenomenally experienced harm as the relevant wrong-making property; instead we should consider variables such as "contribution to the impact leading to harm."

I am broadly sympathetic to the proposal to replace *Experienced Harm* with a more theoretically and empirically informed measurement of harm. It avoids the inconsistency by correcting the limitations of our insensitivity in perception in a theoretically compelling way. However, as attractive as this solution is, it also comes with a challenge: A moral theory that departs from *Experienced Harm* must explain what makes an action wrong if no one experiences any consequences caused by this action. The challenge is complicated by the fact that not all contributions to an impact that causes harm are obviously wrong. For instance, suppose the torturers push their buttons sequentially. Let it be a known fact that 999 of the harmless torturers have already pushed their button. Is it wrong for the final torturer to also push her button? The action of the last torturer will not lead to any difference in pain, but it does add to the impact (in voltage). For what it's worth, my intuition is that the action of the last torturer is irrelevant and therefore not wrong. However, that sort of intuition does not sit well with with more theoretically informed measurements of harm, as just sketched. My preferred solution, described in Section 8, is better suited to deal with such cases.

6. RELAXING THE NO STEPWISE HARM ASSUMPTION

The only subclause of *No Stepwise Harm* that can plausibly be relaxed is (iii): that any single additional action does not cause any experienced harm, given all other actions.

A first revision would move from perceived harm to *perceivable* harm.[12] Proponents of this revision can concede that the subjects do not *actually* experience any difference in pain when one contribution is added or removed. They do maintain, however, that the subjects are mistaken in claiming that the pain is the same, and that the subjects would be able to notice the difference under ideal conditions of perception. Therefore, there is a perceivable, though unperceived, difference in harm whenever the level of contribution changes. I am unsure how to understand this argument. It may be that the difference becomes perceivable by using theoretical knowledge or tools of measurement as discussed in the previous section. If that is the case, the proposal looks like a revision of *Experienced Harm*,

---

12. An argument along this line was suggested but not necessarily endorsed by Gunnar Björnsson (personal communication).

as discussed above. Or it may be that the subjects perceive the difference without awareness, but are able to become aware of the differences (Mills 2002, 392). That latter claim is an empirical speculation, and there is no reason to believe that it would hold for extremely small differences in impact.

A second revision of *No Stepwise Harm* consists in contextualizing the comparisons between settings. Proponents of this solution are prepared to admit that changes of just one contribution do not cause additional experienced harm. However, for them that is beside the point. The harm increase from x contributions to $x + 1$ contributions will be noticed, it is claimed, once we compare these settings not only pairwise against each other, but with other levels of contributions. For example, Voorhoeve and Binmore suggest that

> Two adjacent notches might be indistinguishable in this way because [the subject's] pain experience at a particular notch might (because of some neurophysiological process that we need not understand) depend on the current she was exposed to before. Thus, it might be the case that if the previous current is very different, [the subject] experiences the current at notch n in one way, but if it is similar, (i. e. the difference between them is smaller than the just-noticeable difference) she experiences it in another way. (Voorhoeve and Binmore 2006, 105)

No matter how exactly the described phenomenon would be caused, Voorhoeve and Binmore want to suggest that the reported indistinguishability in pairwise comparisons is a mistake, and that this mistake could be avoided if, first, settings with quite different voltages are compared, and second, many such settings are tried, so that one can establish the frequencies of different pain reports. In effect, Voorhoeve and Binmore propose to revise both *No Stepwise Harm* and *Experienced Harm* to appeal to reflectively corrected harm judgements.

The question remains, however, why individuals ought to be compelled to make this rationality adjustment. To be clear, Voorhoeve and Binmore's proposal is not meant to address many hands problems but settings that threaten *individual* rationality, especially Quinn's famous "self torturer" (Quinn 1990). Getting what is worst for yourself through your own choices clearly is a failure of individual rationality. It makes sense to try to avoid this failure by rational reflection. This reflection will reveal that you ought not to prefer each one-step increase of voltage and you ought to correct your preference structure accordingly. In the interpersonal case of many hands, however, this line of reasoning does not apply so easily because the harm is neither self-inflicted nor caused by one and the same agent. Perhaps one could claim that despite forming judgements of pain perception with a nontransitive "is experienced as equally harmful as" relation, the victim ought to form *transitive preferences over the outcomes that can arise*. And if that is so, one could say that the torturers ought to orientate their actions according to these transitive preferences. However, this line of argument moves toward a quite different form of consequentialism, a "preference consequentialism" that requires a complete revision of *Experienced Harm* as well.

7. RELAXING THE WRONGNESS OF CONTRIBUTION ASSUMPTION

Contribution Is Wrong links contributions to wrongness, even if the individual action does not lead to experienced harm.[13] Relaxing this principle does not, on first sight, appear to be a promising way out.

One caveat applies: There may be settings in which the contribution to a causal process leading to harm is such that the rest of the causal process is entirely fixed. For example, assume that Bob sits on a dike in a major flood area. Huge amounts of waters are flowing, foreseeably leading to a humanitarian catastrophe further downstream. The amount of water flowing is due entirely to natural processes, and we can assume that it is a fixed amount. Also assume that tipping point effects can be ruled out. In this situation, Bob pours one pint of water into the floods. Bob's contribution is so small that it is not leading to any perceptible harm. Is it wrong for Bob to pour his pint?

According to *Contribution Is Wrong*, Bob minimally contributes to the impact, that is, the volume of water that causes harm downstream, and his action is therefore wrong. However, in such cases my intuition, at least, pulls in the other direction. For reasons that I will explore in greater detail in the next section, it makes a difference whether the causal process one deals with is fixed or the result of agential choices.

8. THE SKETCH OF A SOLUTION PROPOSAL

At the heart of the hardest many hands problems lies the insensitivity of harm perception. Taking this problem seriously means acknowledging that minimal increases in impact may not be perceptible. And if the effects of single actions are not perceptible, it *seems* to follow that the aggregate effects of many such actions are not perceptible either. I say "seems" because I think that this last step is mistaken. Put very roughly, it is mistaken because the imperceptibility of single actions does not imply that the aggregate effects of many actions are equally imperceptible. The error occurs because many have thought that the relation $\sim_H$ ("is experienced as equally harmful as") must be transitive. But this need not be the case. In this section I lay out the steps of the argument just sketched more carefully and discuss its normative implications.

Readers familiar with the sorites paradox literature will have noted that *No Stepwise Harm* does *not* set up a sorites paradox. To get the paradox, a stronger inductive premise is needed:

> *Base Premise.* When 0 torturers push the button, the victim is not in pain.
> *Inductive Premise.* If the victim is not in pain if x torturers push the button, then the victim is not in pain if $x + 1$ torturers push the button.
> *Conclusion.* The victim is not in pain if all torturers push the button.

---

13. However, actions that do not cause any change in impact are not necessarily wrong according to *Contribution Is Wrong*.

The paradox arises because we arrive at the absurd conclusion that the harmless torturers are indeed—harmless. A plausible diagnosis of the argument is that the Inductive Premise is false. However, clause (iii) in *No Stepwise Harm* is subtly weaker. The formalization from above makes this quite clear. *No Stepwise Harm* only postulates that the difference in each pairwise comparison between the pain at step x and at step $x + 1$ is imperceptible. This results in a series of pairwise relations:

$$h(m_{c=0}) \sim_H h(m_{c=1}) \wedge h(m_{c=1}) \sim_H h(m_{c=2}) \wedge \ldots \wedge h(m_{c=n-1}) \sim_H h(m_{c=n}). \tag{1}$$

The inductive premise, by contrast, implies this:

$$h(m_{c=0}) \sim_H h(m_{c=1}) \sim_H h(m_{c=2}) \sim \ldots \sim_H h(m_{c=n-1}) \sim_H h(m_{c=n}). \tag{2}$$

(1) entails (2) only if the relation $\sim_H$ is transitive. But it is the transitivity of $\sim_H$ that I deny.

Transitivity is often assumed without explicit argument because we tend to think about similarity relations in terms of equivalence relations or as the symmetrical part of a weak order. Moreover, transitivity is a fundamental rationality constraint for preferences. In the context of preferences it should not be abandoned lightly. In the context of perception, however, it is far from clear whether transitivity in similarity judgements obtains empirically. Also, unlike in the preference case, it is not a fundamental rationality constraint. Thus, assuming nontransitivity for similarity of harm perceptions is much less objectionable.

Two implications follow immediately. First, we can now account for the plausible claim that individuals cannot perceive a difference in harm if the difference in impact is very small. Second, this does not lead to a sorites paradox because the nontransitive pairwise rankings in (1) are weaker than the inductive premise required to set up the paradox. In particular, from the fact that $h(m_{c=x}) \sim_H h(m_{c=x+1})$ for any $x \in (0, n-1)$ it does *not* follow that $h(mc_{c=x}) \sim_H h(m_{c=x+2})$ for any $x \in (0, n-2)$. The fact that small steps are indistinguishable does not imply that larger steps are indistinguishable.

The last point has an important upshot: If larger steps are distinguishable in their harm, then aggregate actions can lead to perceptible harm even if they consist of many small actions that are individually not harmful. This opens up a potentially attractive solution to avoid the contradiction between *Direct Act Consequences*, *Experienced Harm*, *No Stepwise Harm*, and *Contribution Is Wrong*. More specifically, what is required is a revision of *Direct Act Consequences* such that individuals take into account how their action can be effective when it occurs with other actions, rather than keeping all other actions fixed. Here I will simply sketch the rough shape of the revision required, a detailed solution proposal and a thorough defense will have to wait for another time.

It is clear that each individual on her own, given the contributions of all other individuals, cannot change the harm perceived by the victim. At the same time, it is the case that several individuals *together* can change the victim's pain (this, of course, is also the motivation behind Parfit's solution). Therefore, it is useful to consider *minimal perceptible subsets* of the set of all actions. Minimal perceptible subsets are those sets that contain just enough actions such that together these actions avoid minimal change insensitivity—they can jointly make a perceptible difference. More specifically, if all actions in a minimal perceptible subset change from "not contribute" to "contribute" (or *vice versa*), the victim notices a difference.[14]

Consider individual i's action a_i. This action is an element in some of the minimal perceptible subsets. Each set can make a difference to harm if all actions in the set change from "not contribute" to "contribute" (and *vice versa*). Action a_i therefore contributes to expected harm together with others in a minimal perceptible subset if (i) a_i is "contribute" and (ii) there is a positive ex ante probability that all others actions in the set (except a_i) are "contribute" and a positive probability that they are all "not contribute." Condition (i) checks whether the individual contributes; condition (ii) whether there is a positive probability that the minimal perceptible subset can make a difference.

Crucially, whether a_i is in the position to increase expected harm depends on the joint probabilities of the other actions. If a_i cannot make a difference to the consequence this subset of actions has because, for example, other actions are fixed, then a_i does not increase expected harm by contributing with regard to that set. And if a_i cannot contribute to a difference in any of the minimal perceptible subsets it is an element of, then it does not increase expected harm at all.

A solution along the lines sketched here will have to revise *Direct Act Consequences* by incorporating a nonstandard conception of consequences. This nonstandard conception will have to say that contributing in suitable minimal perceptible subsets has the consequence of increasing expected experienced harm. This, in turn, will allow us to say that actions that are individually imperceptible are still wrong because they are expected to bring about harm together with other actions.

For example, the action of pushing a button in the harmless torturers setting leads to increased expected experienced harm for the victim. Even though the action does not *by itself* increase experienced harm, the action is expected to do so in the following sense: The action (to contribute to the voltage) will be part of minimal perceptible subsets of contributions such that the actions of these subsets together can be felt by the victim. And since there is a positive probability that all the actions in the subsets are "not contribute" or "contribute," there is a positive probability that these subsets can make a difference. For instance, suppose that the victim always experiences additional pain if two more torturers push the buttons, but never if just one additional torturer pushes the button. This means that the button pushing of one torturer is part of subsets with two elements that can be felt. And since there is a positive probability for a subset to make a difference in harm, contributing within such a subset leads to expected harm when adopting the nonstandard notion of consequences suggested in this section.

The solution sketched offers a suitably differentiated account of cases where the choices of other agents are either truly agential free choices, and cases where the

---

14. My solution is inspired by Braham and van Hees's (2009, 2012) treatment of moral and causal responsibility, though my sketch solution differs from theirs and my framework is much less general.

other contributions are fixed (and therefore not subject to choice). Suppose a single torturer shows up for work (cf. Parfit 1984, 81) and, as introduced above, 999 buttons are already pushed so that the victim suffers severe pain. If pushing or not pushing the button is the only available action, is it permissible to push one more button? Parfit is inclined to say "no," as he thinks that the "second mistake" is indeed that: a mistake. But according to my proposal, the single push of the button has a zero expectation to contribute to harm, and is therefore permissible. The reason is that while such an action is a member of minimal perceptible subsets, the probability that any of these subsets will jointly make a perceptible difference is zero, as all the other actions are fixed. Similar implications follow for other determined processes. If one pours a pint of water into a devastating flood and the amount of floodwater is already fully determined, this action is permissible. But it is not permissible if the amount of floodwater is not fully determined and one's pint could with some nonzero probability make a difference in combination with other stochastic processes (and this is the more realistic setting in the real world). These examples show that the solution I sketch here will also have to revise *Contribution Is Wrong*: Contributions are only wrong if they cause an increase in expected experienced harm, if they cannot make a difference to expected harm they are permissible.

Unlike Kagan, I do not rely on any actual thresholds being crossed by any specific contributing individual. In particular, I do not have to claim that, at some point, the action of one individual must trigger harm. And, again unlike Kagan (130), I do not have to deny the existence of genuine imperceptible effects cases. In fact, my proposal shows that Kagan's claim "that there could not possibly be cases of imperceptible difference" (130) is false. There can be cases of imperceptible difference if the relevant relation is nontransitive because of insensitivity. My solution can therefore preserve the empirically and conceptually plausible assumption that there exist changes in impact so small that they never register as additional harm. Toward the end of the paper, Kagan admits that the differences from notch to notch may not be "directly" (137) perceivable. If he weakens his view in that way, however, he concedes that one single action can be imperceptible, undermining his central conceptual claim. In any case, in his final discussion Kagan vacillates between denying *No Stepwise Harm* and denying *Experienced Harm*.

9. CONCLUSION

The hardest many hands problems are those where each individual action does not register in terms of perceived harm, but collectively the actions are very harmful. The solution I propose requires individuals who find themselves in such a situation to consider what the consequences of their action might be in combination with other actions. I do not simply claim that contributing individuals do wrong because they are part of a harming group. The contributing individuals do wrong because they ignore the risk that their action, even though it cannot be perceived while holding all other actions fixed, may well be perceived with others if we do not hold everything else fixed. The individual action can become perceivable in a set with other actions and therefore contributes to expected harm. I claim that performing actions that might become phenomenally effective together with others is wrong because the individual's action increases the chance that such a harm comes about. To avoid doing wrong, individuals must be forward-looking and think about how their contributions to the impact might lead to experienced harm.[15]

REFERENCES

Andreou, Chrisoula. 2006. "Environmental Damage and the Puzzle of the Self-Torturer." *Philosophy and Public Affairs* 34(1): 95–108.

Arntzenius, Frank, and McCarthy, David. 1997. "Self Torture and Group Beneficence." *Erkenntnis* 47(1): 129–44.

Braham, Matthew, and van Hees, Martin. 2009. "Degrees of Causation." *Erkenntnis* 71(3): 323–44.

———. 2012. "An Anatomy of Moral Responsibility." *Mind* 121(483): 606–34.

Broome, John. 2012. *Climate Matters: Ethics in a Warming World*. New York: W.W. Norton.

Glover, Jonathan, and Scott-Taggart, M. J. 1975. "It Makes No Difference Whether or Not I Do It." *Proceedings of the Aristotelian Society, Supplementary Volumes* 49: 171–209.

Graff, Delia. 2001. "Phenomenal Continua and the Sorites." *Mind* 110(440): 905–36.

Gruzalski, Bart. 1986. "Parfit's Impact on Utilitarianism." *Ethics* 96(4): 760–83.

Hansson, Sven Ove. 1999. "The Moral Significance of Indetectable Effects." *Risk: Health, Safety and Environment* 10: 101–08.

Jackson, Frank. 1997. "Which Effects?" In *Reading Parfit*, ed. Jonathan Dancy, 42–53. Oxford: Blackwell.

Kagan, Shelly. 2011. "Do I Make a Difference?" *Philosophy and Public Affairs* 39(2): 105–41.

Lichtenberg, Judith. 2010. "Negative Duties, Positive Duties, and the 'New Harms'." *Ethics* 120: 557–78.

Mills, Eugene. 2002. "Fallibility and the Phenomenal Sorites." *Noûs* 36(3): 384–407.

Nefsky, Julia. 2011. "Consequentialism and the Problem of Collective Harm: A Reply to Kagan." *Philosophy and Public Affairs* 39(4): 364–95.

Norcross, Alastair. 2005. "Harming In Context." *Philosophical Studies* 123(1–2): 149–73.

Otsuka, Michael. 1991. "The Paradox of Group Beneficence." *Philosophy and Public Affairs* 20(2): 132–49.

Parfit, Derek. 1984. *Reasons and Persons*. Oxford: Clarendon Press.

———. 1986. "Comments." *Ethics* 96(4): 832–72.

Quinn, Warren S. 1990. "The Puzzle of the Self-Torturer." *Philosophical Studies* 59(1): 79–90.

Raffman, Diana. 1996. "Vagueness and Context-Relativity." *Philosophical Studies* 81: 175–92.

Shrader-Frechette, Kristin. 1987. "Parfit and Mistakes in Moral Mathematics." *Ethics* 98(1): 50–60.

Sinnott-Armstrong, Walter. 2005. "It's Not My Fault: Global Warming and Individual Obligations." In *Perspectives on Climate Change: Science, Economics, Politics, Ethics*, ed. Walter Sinnott-Armstrong and Richard B. Howarth, 285–307. Amsterdam: Elsevier.

Tannsjö, Torbjörn. 1989. "The Morality of Collective Actions." *The Philosophical Quarterly* 39(155): 221–8.

Thompson, Dennis F. 1980. "Moral Responsibility of Public Officials: The Problem of Many Hands." *The American Political Science Review* 74(4): 905–16.

van Rooij, R. 2010. "Vagueness, Tolerance, and Non-Transitive Entailment." Manuscript. Retrieved July 13, 2014, from <http://web.logic.at/lomorevi/vaguebook/rooij.pdf>.

Voorhoeve, Alex, and Binmore, Ken. 2006. "Transitivity, the Sorites Paradox, and Similarity-Based Decision-Making." *Erkenntnis* 64(1): 101–14.

15. Ideas for this article were presented at the MANCEPT workshop on forward-looking collective obligations, at the NELPP seminar at the University of Newcastle, the Department of Government at the University of Essex, and the Collective Obligation Workshop in Manchester. I would like to thank all audiences for their comments and suggestions. I am particularly grateful to Christian List and Felix Pinkert for generous written comments. All errors are my own.

Midwest Studies In Philosophy, XXXVIII (2014)

A Plural Subject Approach to the Responsibilities of Groups and Institutions

LUDGER JANSEN

1. INTRODUCTION

Margaret Gilbert has defended the claim that her plural subject theory can give a reasonable account of retrospective (or backward-looking) collective responsibility. On one occasion, publishing in this periodical, she wrote that she deliberately left out the discussion of prospective (or forward-looking) collective responsibility, or the "responsibilities" of a collective.[1] In the present article, I want to show that plural subject theory, in fact, also allows accounting for prospective responsibilities of groups and institutions. In order to do so, I will first sketch the social ontological background of my discussion which is, in fact, an amended version of Gilbert's theory of plural subjects (Section 2). Based on the assumption that a prospective responsibility accrues from some kind of commissioning, I will then discuss a variety of possible sources of prospective collective responsibilities: self-commissioning, third-party commissioning, and what I will call commissioning by unique capability (Section 3). Having done so, I will discuss some consequences of this account and defend it against objections (Section 4).

---

1. Gilbert (2006), 95.

2. SOME BITS OF SOCIAL ONTOLOGY

2.1 From Pluralities of Subjects to Plural Subjects

In the following, I will expand on a three-tier social ontology: person aggregates, plural subjects, and institutions. These are, in fact, not three totally separate levels, but, as I will show, interconnected and interdependent layers of the social world.

First, there are person aggregates. Any number of persons can be considered an aggregate, as arbitrary as these persons are selected out of the totality of persons. Natural language provides several means for us to single out such aggregates, starting from personal pronouns in the plural ("we," "they") via enumeration ("Peter, Paul, and Mary") to description ("the people who lived on the hill"; "double income, no kids"). Gilbert's plural subject theory does now provide a link from person aggregates to more integrated social entities, that is, to plural subjects: A plural subject comes into being, when members of a person aggregate are jointly committed to some action. What has been a mere aggregate has then turned into a plural subject.[2]

Gilbert's pet example for this is a walking party.[3] Consider the following dialogue: Adam asks Eve whether she would like to go for a walk with him. Eve answers in the affirmative and encourages Adam to start immediately. In this dialogue, Adam and Eve agree to go for a walk together. In Gilbert's terms, they enter a joint commitment for having a walk together and by this they form a plural subject for this walk. So far, this plural subject is quite ephemeral, being a plural subject for a unique action, that is, this single walk. Adam and Eve's joint commitment imposes the obligation to participate in this joint walk on each of them. Would Adam rescind unilaterally, Eve would be justified in chiding him for not obeying his obligations. They can, of course, agree bilaterally to dissolve their plural subject; in this case, their obligations vanish and the plural subject ceases to exist before it fulfills its unique task.

Plural subjects for actions are, more precisely, plural subjects for a special attitude: They are plural subjects for action intentions. This account can be generalized: A plural subject is a plural subject for a certain attitude if and only if members are jointly committed to having this attitude. Moreover, members of plural subjects cannot only be jointly committed to a particular action, but also to action schemes, series of actions, or action patterns. Among such action patterns may also be decision structures, like the majority rule, voting systems, or delegations. With an act of delegation, a plural subject transfers decisions to a single person (who may or may not be one of its members) or to a committee (whose members may or may not be members of the plural subject in question).

By introducing decision procedures and delegations, joint commitments can come about in an indirect way. Think of Ruth and Paul planning their joint vacation. They agree that this year Ruth has her turn to decide on their destination. This is what Gilbert calls a basic commitment: It is formed by direct involvement of all

2. Cf. Gilbert (1989, 1996, 2000).
3. Cf. the talking title of Gilbert (1990).

members of the plural subject without the involvement of any authority. Now Ruth decides that the destination is going to be Paris. Given the assumptions of the example, Ruth and Paul then have a joint commitment to travel to Paris. However, this is not a basic commitment formed by participation of all members of the plural subject, but a nonbasic commitment, that is, one "engendered by authorities."[4]

2.2 From Plural Subjects to Institutional Subjects

So far, I have more or less simply rehearsed Gilbert's plural subject theory that provides the essential link, or so one could say, from mere collections of persons to collective persons. This is because plural subjects can be subjects of both actions and attitudes, which are also important features of natural persons. But there is more to say concerning the social world, and nonbasic commitments provide the crucial mechanism for explaining them. Consider the situation where a plural subject delegates its decisions to a committee. Now, such a committee is also a social entity, but it does not come into existence by its members fusing together via a joint commitment, but rather by mandate of the original plural subject, that is, from the outside. Not all social groups, that is, are established by the same mechanisms: While standard Gilbertian plural subjects are established by their members, not all groups are established this way. Some are established by founders that are not their members. They are established, so to speak, in a top-down manner using a pre-established institutional structure.

In order to envision an adequate picture of the social world, we must go one step further: We can also establish institutional structures that do not have any members at all, but only representatives and agents. Think of an Internet start-up company. It might have its beginnings somewhere in a garage with founders that are jointly committed to realizing a common project. On this stage, the company fits the standard Gilbertian picture of plural subjects: equals united by a joint commitment. Later, the founders may hire their first employees. These employees are agents of the original plural subject that consists of the company founders. The founders may even hire a manager and transfer all directorial power to her. Now the company has an institutional structure consisting of a decision-making management and decision-realizing workers, neither of whom belong to the original plural subject of the company's founders. Finally, the founders may sell the company, thus dissolving the connecting line between the company and its founding plural subject. Throughout this little story, the company acquires more and more institutional structure and it becomes more and more independent from its founding plural subject. Finally, the institutional structure is rich enough not only to persist independently of its founders, but also independently of (and without) any member.[5]

Just like joint commitments, acts of delegation can be direct or indirect. A direct act of delegation has the form of a contract (or, less formally, a joint

---

4. Gilbert (2006), 103.
5. Cf. also the fate of *American Electric*, a fictive company invented by Hacker (1964); cf. also Coleman (1982), 39–42.

commitment) between delegator and delegate. Direct delegations need bipartisan speech acts: The delegate has to accept the delegation for it to be successful. If, however, the delegate is already related to the delegator in a generic way, for example, as an employee, the delegator might be able to delegate in a one-sided way, for the employee has already agreed to be delegated to a wide range of unspecified tasks. In this case, the delegation can take on the form of a declarative speech act. The content of such declaration can have the form of John Searle's famous scheme "X counts as Y in context C."[6]

The growth of institutional structures starts with basic joint commitments, in particular with basic joint commitments for action patterns. But it does not end there. By forming joint commitments for decision procedures and delegation, by establishing networks of roles whose holders can interact with each other following predesigned patterns, the social world very much takes an institutional face. Henceforth, I will call any social subject that is committed to at least one rule, be it a rule for action patterns or for decision procedures, an institutional subject, or an institution for short.[7] This definition is rather broad. Many of these institutional subjects are Gilbertian plural subjects, but not all of them—and it is this fact that makes this new label necessary.[8]

In what follows, we have, thus, to consider three categories of social entities as potential bearers of collective responsibilities: person aggregates, plural subjects, and institutions. Equipped with this background theory in social ontology, I will now discuss potential sources of prospective responsibilities.

3. SOURCES OF PROSPECTIVE COLLECTIVE RESPONSIBILITIES

3.1 Self-Commissioning

Even a superficial look at the theory of plural subjects reveals that something like prospective responsibility is built-in in the very idea of a plural subject. Imagine that Peter and Paul establish a plural subject PP by signaling their readiness for a certain joint action X. As a result, there is a joint commitment of Peter and Paul to jointly perform X. In a way, performance of X is what the plural subject PP is there for: PP exists *in order to* perform X. If this is a case of forward-looking responsibility, we may say that it is a responsibility that is generated by self-commissioning: The commitment to do X is a self-imposed commitment. Without doubt, this is a future-directed collective phenomenon. But it might be questioned whether this is a case of (moral) responsibility. The joint commitment to do X gives Peter and Paul the right to call in the contribution of other members and to disapprove of any defunctive behavior of the other. But this disapproval would be, so to speak, internal: It is a disapproval of members with respect to other members. Peter and Paul would be obliged to participate in X, but this obligation is rooted in a contract.

6. Cf. Searle (1995, 2010).
7. To be sure, there are institutions (like money or political borders) that are not institutional subjects; cf. Jansen (2005). In this article, I can ignore this complication, as I only deal with institutional subjects here.
8. Cf. also the classification attempts in Jansen (2004).

Of course, *pacta sunt servanda* is a widely recognized moral norm. Hence, Peter and Paul are morally obliged to fulfill their contract, whatever it says. But there is no moral norm directly mandating their participation in X.

A good reason for not considering this as a moral responsibility is that, up to now, there is no disapproval from the outside, no authority Peter and Paul could be responsible to. That is, failure to fulfill the commitment to do X doesnot lead to moral reproval. Nobody will care; nobody will ask for a justification of their actions or omissions. If we wanted to generalize on this intuition, we could say that prospective responsibility implies retrospective responsibility in case of nonfulfillment. And there is neither need nor occasion for justification if Peter and Paul decide not to go for a walk together.

However, we can fill this gap by modifying our example. Up to now I left completely unspecified what kind of action X belongs to. There are obvious cases, like going for an enjoyable walk, where not much depends on X being performed or not. Not much is at stake in this case. Peter and Paul could jointly rescind their plan and there would be no reason for moral reproval. But we can change the example. Imagine that Peter and Paul are strolling along the reservoir. By chance they notice that there is a leak in the dam and it is in danger of breaking. They agree to hurry back to town in order to report that the dam is in danger of breaking. Now the setting has changed: It is important to all townspeople that Peter and Paul reach their destination in time, for their home and lives are in danger. Peter and Paul are only chance witnesses of the leak and people in town may not even know that Peter and Paul are strolling along the reservoir, but they have an interest in the warning arriving on time. If Peter and Paul rescind from hurrying—it does not matter here whether they do so in agreement or unilaterally—they can be reproached on behalf of the townspeople. That is, we now have an authority to which Peter and Paul are responsible. This role of authority can be taken either by the townspeople who are stakeholders in their joint action or by outside observers speaking on behalf of them.

We can tweak the example yet again. Imagine now that Peter and Paul are not alone at the reservoir. Others are with them and, after detecting the leak, there is a lively discussion about what to do. While the others are still debating, Peter takes Paul aside and after a very short exchange they decide to hurry together to town to warn the inhabitants. Note that this is the moment at which the joint commitment and with it the plural subject PP comes into existence. Peter and Paul announce their decision to the others and start their way down. Now we have another party to whom they can be responsible, namely the remaining group at the dam, for they will now rely on PP for warning the town. Had Peter and Paul not taken this task on themselves, others may have volunteered to do so. Note that this does not depend on the folks at the dam being a unified plural subject for rescuing the dam and the town. In the setup of the example, it is not the larger group that decides to warn the town and delegates this task to PP. It is the other way around: PP is established in order to warn the town and this decision is announced to the larger group which might still be undecided on what to do. Once the intention of PP is announced, however, the people remaining at the dam have good reason to assume that the task of warning the town is being cared for. If Peter and Paul rescind hurrying to town, the other folks have good reason to reproach them, for they relied on PP to fulfill this task. Hence, PP is prospectively responsible for warning the town. This shows that self-commissioning can, indeed, establish a prospective responsibility, though it would be an exaggeration to postulate prospective moral responsibility for any action a plural subject is committed to.

It could be objected that Peter is able to fulfill the task of warning the town on his own, and so is Paul. Hence, or so the objection goes, they are distributively responsible for warning the town.[9] This objection can easily be met by the additional assumption that they can only reach the town in time if they help each other, for example, when crossing an obstacle. I think, however, that the objection is mistaken: The self-ascription mechanism does not presuppose any unique ability. Whether Peter and Paul are individually able to fulfill the task in question is, thus, accidental to the question whether they are, as a plural subject, collectively responsible for that task.

3.2 Third-Party Commissioning

In the preceding paragraph I have argued that even ephemeral plural subjects, that is, plural subjects for exactly one action token, can acquire prospective responsibilities. I will now turn my attention to collective subjects with a richer structure and discuss institutional subjects in particular. Typical institutional subjects are companies, associations, nongovernmental organizations, and states.

A peculiarity of institutional subjects is their nested structure. Often, the nesting of institutions works in a bottom-up manner: Just as people can establish an association, associations can establish an umbrella organization—an association of associations. States can establish a defense alliance or other international organizations, like the European Union or the United Nations. But nesting also works from the top down: A committee, for example, can establish subcommittees. A state can establish a new government agency. A company can set up a new branch. In our time, institutions are normally established under the auspices of an overarching institution (i.e., a state that sets up rules for, say, starting a company or founding an association). In such a setting, founders of an association do not only have to signal their readiness for a joint commitment to establish this association—which would be the only requirement for a standard plural subject—they also have to abide by the rules of establishing, registering, and running an association that has been set up within the legal framework in which they are operating.

Institutional reality is complicated: We do not only have states as overarching structures regulating the establishment of institutions within their domain, we also have multinational companies or international associations stretching out across national borders, that is, working within the spheres of influence of more than one state.

With self-commissioning, responsibilities are imposed on plural subjects by their members. Now I want to discuss if and how responsibilities can be imposed on institutional subjects by other institutional subjects. One obvious case is bottom-up

---

9. I owe this objection to Kurt Bayertz.

commissioning, which is, in fact, a special case of self-commissioning. The only difference to the cases discussed before is that we now do not consider people forming a plural subject of people, but rather institutions establishing a plural subject of institutions. On the institutional level, just as on the individual level, institutions can signal their readiness to form a plural subject and commit themselves to, say, perform a certain action.

Another type is top-down commissioning. Top-down commissioning is a specific sort of delegation; it requires the existence of a nested institutional structure. In such a situation, the overarching institutional subject—say, a state—can establish institutional substructures and delegate certain tasks to them. Or the overarching institution may take an already existing group or institution and assign it a novel function.

3.3 Prospective Responsibility through Unique Capability

Often plural subjects are established for tasks that, by nature or dimension, cannot be performed by other subjects. Indeed, the development of new types of juridical persons like limited companies or joint-stock companies can be seen as the attempt to meet the needs of new economic challenges. How can forces be joined such that, for example, a railway can be built crossing a whole continent? Putting together a consortium for such a task would often mean bringing together a number of already existing institutional subjects rather than individual subjects, and rather than bringing together working power, these institutional subjects would join their financial forces—their venture capital. But this does not change the general theme: Subjects join to establish plural subjects in order to be capable to fulfill a certain task.

It is, thus, rarely disputed that by joining forces results can be obtained that would lie beyond the reach of individual subjects. No doubt there are important goals that can only be achieved, if at all, by massive cooperation. Rescuing thousands of victims after an earthquake, preventing global warming and fighting starvation are of this kind. While each individual subject might feel inclined to support these goals, no individual subject, on their own, is able to reach these goals.

In the debate on prospective responsibility, responsibility for a certain task is often ascribed to those who are capable of fulfilling this task. If 100 people witness someone drowning not too far from the beach, only those among them who are able to swim are able to rescue the drowning person. This example (which I will later refer to as the "drowning example") shows that there can be a certain prospective responsibility without a previous (official or unofficial) ascription of this responsibility: It is because of their sufficient abilities that the swimmers are responsible for rescuing drowning persons. But it can be argued that in the drowning example, as we have discussed it so far, this responsibility is in each case an individual responsibility: Each of the swimmers is individually responsible for rescuing the drowning person.

A typical move to reach the level of collective responsibility is to consider situations in which no individual subject can fulfill the task in question on its own.[10]

---

10. Cf., for example, Held (1970).

Consider the following situation (the "car crash example"): Suppose there are ten people that happen to witness a car accident. The crash victim needs help to be evacuated from the car. Rescuing him is too much for a single person, but three cooperating helpers could manage to free him from his wrecked car. In this situation we can argue as follows:

(i)   The individual subjects are not able to free the victim on their own; hence, as obligation implies ability, the individual subjects are not obliged to free the victim on their own.

(ii) The group contains enough potential helpers; hence, the group could free the victim. But it is an arbitrary group and arbitrary aggregates cannot act; hence, there can be no obligation of the group.

(iii) But each individual is able to communicate with other members of the group and turn this mere plurality of subjects into a plural subject for rescuing the crash victim.

Hence, even if we are cautious with respect to the responsibility of arbitrary groups, we can point to the individuals' obligation to act toward turning the arbitrary group into a nonarbitrary group, that is, a group that joins forces for a certain collective action.

When it comes to important collective tasks, turning an arbitrary group into a plural subject is not always necessary because plenty of plural subjects or institutional subjects committed to certain tasks already exist. If there is already a plural subject that is committed to the task in question, then it is not necessary to establish another one to fulfill the task in question. Suppose there is an important task T that can only be performed if enough persons cooperate. In the best case there is already a plural or institutional subject dedicated to perform T. Only if this is not the case, such a subject has to be created. An appropriate subject could, of course, be established bottom-up by means of basic joint commitments that create a new plural subject "from scratch." But it could also be created top-down by means of nonbasic joint commitments that are established by already existing overarching institutional subjects like states, companies, or nongovernmental organizations.

It is possible that several plural subjects are capable of performing an instance of the action type in question, or several plural subjects could be established from scratch in order to fulfill the task. Now which of these is responsible for performing the task? The case, of course, resembles the drowning example with several swimmers on the beach. And we can give the same answer that we are likely to give for that example: each of them. But we can also think of certain ranks of responsibility, or a hierarchy of responsibles, to generate rules of thumb to ease the coordination between subjects and determine who is going to perform the task. If, in the drowning example, among the capable swimmers there are lifeguards, the prospective responsibility can primarily be ascribed to them and only secondarily to other competent swimmers. Lifeguards are, of course, specifically trained and educated to rescue people. But they are more: They are also employed and mandated to do so. In addition to the general responsibility arising from their ability, there is a special responsibility arising from their role. If we now rank responsibilities using criteria referring to abilities and roles, we can set up what can be called rules of subsidiarity. One rule of subsidiarity is this: Among an aggregate of subjects that is prospectively responsible to perform a certain action, those subjects are primarily responsible that are capable of performing that action on their own. Now we can supplement this rule, already implicitly used above, with a second: Among such an aggregate of subjects, those subjects are primarily responsible to which the task has previously been assigned. These rules of subsidiarity can as well be applied to institutional subjects as to individual subjects.

4. PLURAL SUBJECT THEORY AND THE INDIVIDUALS

I have argued that Margaret Gilbert's theory of plural subjects can be extended to account for the ontology not only of groups but also of institutions. Plural subjects (groups) and institutional subjects can have forward-looking moral responsibilities. These responsibilities can be role-based if they are based on self-commissioning or third-party commissioning, or they can be ability-based if they are based on the unique capability of a group or institution to perform a certain task.

When it comes to backward-looking responsibility, it is often argued that it cannot apply to groups or institutions, as these are not suited for intentional actions at all and do not fulfill the necessary requirements for punishment: There is neither a wrong mind (*mens rea*) nor a wrong deed (*actus reus*) simply because there is neither a collective mind nor a collective body.[11] For similar reasons, it is said that punishing an institution is not feasible because an institution "has no soul to be damned and no body to be kicked," as an eighteenth century politician put it.[12] These misgivings have been answered by others,[13] but for the present context we can do away with many of them because we do not deal with backward-looking punishment. Instead, we need to check whether groups and institutions are apt for prospective responsibilities. For this they have to be capable of actions and they have to exist long enough to witness the situation in which they have to live up to their responsibilities. On the latter count, groups and institutions can obviously outperform individuals. Groups can gain new members when old ones die and, thus, stretch their existence long beyond the lifespan of human individuals and, analogously, institutions can find new role-holders for the roles in its institutional structure. In fact, institutions can be seen as mechanisms to transfer individual duties from one generation of role-holders to the next. Hence, according to this requirement, groups and institutions are much better suited for long-term prospective responsibilities. Indeed, for any task that transcends the normal lifespan of an individual, a group or institution is required as the bearer of the responsibility in question. Hence, it is no surprise that in the course of history certain tasks are only fulfilled if there is a group that takes on the appropriate responsibility. A typical example is the preservation of texts when these still had to be copied from

---

11. Cf., for example, Velazques (1983).
12. This quote is the motto of Coffee (1981).
13. Cf., for example, French (1979) and Korenjak, Ungericht, and Raith (2010).

manuscripts in order to hand them down to future generations. If there was a group of enthusiasts or an institution for which these texts were important, they were preserved, while other texts were lost. Another drastic example is the responsibility of handing down information about radioactive waste. Given a half-life of many thousands of years, this is not a task that could be performed by any individual subject, but is in want of an institution.

But are groups and institutions really agents? Peter French has argued that corporations, as opposed to mere aggregates of persons, are indeed moral persons capable of action because they have an internal decision structure that allows for tracking the corporation's decision-making process.[14] As we have seen above, plural subject theory permits us to generalize on this and to distinguish various different ways in which such a decision structure may be established, namely by joint commitments to accept certain decision procedures or delegations. At the most basic level, without at least some institutional structure, there is only one way to establish a decision, and this is unanimity: All members have to signal their readiness to join the commitment.

Still, individualists may find some consternation in my relaxed ascriptions of prospective responsibilities to both groups and institutions. Individualists should note that Gilbertian plural subject theory, on which I base my argument in this article, does, in fact, start with individuals. To be sure, the individuals with which I started were already socialized: They had a common language and they knew how to signal their readiness to share in a joint action.[15] It is also true that plural subject theory does not end with individual subjects. Nevertheless, for every single step in the evolution of plural subjects and institutional structures we can, in principle, point to those individual actions that constitute this step in institutional history, that is, to those individuals that signal their readiness to participate in a plural subject and to those individuals that are the delegates and representatives of the institutions in question. Nevertheless, talk about groups and institutions is necessary if we want to have a theory of prospective responsibility that is adequate for our complex social world that abounds in legal, economic, and civil institutional structures located at the communal, national, and even international level.[16]

A large advantage of having a social ontology with individuals, groups, and institutions is that we can do justice to the complex network of responsibilities in which at least three layers are meshed together. First, there are the responsibilities of "bare" individuals disregarding their allegiances to groups or their roles within institutional structures. Second, there are the responsibilities of individuals due to their direct involvement in basic joint commitments. Third, and most important in developed social structures, there are the responsibilities of individuals due to their

---

14. Cf. French (1979).

15. Gilbert (1989, esp. 132–45) argues that a common language is not necessary to bring about a joint commitment and that the very norms of language can itself be established by joint commitments. But each of the participants must know what a joint commitment is (and what it means to signal readiness to enter one) in order to use some appropriate means for this end. This knowledge can be acquired by learning a sufficiently rich language, and I take it that it is, in fact, normally acquired in the course of acquisition of such a language.

16. Cf. the data provided in Coleman (1982), 10–13.

involvement in nonbasic joint commitments. The responsibilities of this third kind rest on the institutional structure in which the individuals play certain roles. Explanatory priority is here on the side of the institutional subjects: If, for example, an individual changes its role within an institutional hierarchy, this will change the role-related responsibilities of the individual, but the responsibilities of the institutional subject will barely change. If, however, the institutional subject takes on a new responsibility, the role-related responsibilities of at least some individuals will change. Hence, it is the institutional structure that determines the individual's roles and, hence, it is not sufficient only to talk about individuals and their roles. In a way it is true that all institutional responsibilities fall back on individual subjects: There is no action of an institutional subject without any individual actions which are instrumental for it. But institutional responsibilities cannot be discarded without loss because the individual subjects whose actions are instrumental for the actions of the institutional subject have their responsibilities only because of their role within the institution. Hence, we do need to talk about institutional subjects if we want to yield an adequate picture of responsibilities in our complex social world. In this article I demonstrated how this talk can find a solid foundation in plural subject theory.

REFERENCES

Coffee, John C. 1981. " 'No Soul to Damn: No Body to Kick': An Unscandalized Inquiry into the Problem of Corporate Punishment." *Michigan Law Review* 79(3): 386–459.

Coleman, James S. 1982. *The Asymmetric Society*. Syracuse, NY: Syracuse University Press.

French, Peter A. 1979. "The Corporation as a Moral Person." *American Philosophical Quarterly* 16(3): 207–15.

Gilbert, Margaret. 1989. *On Social Facts*. Princeton, NJ: Princeton University Press.

———. 1990. "Walking Together: A Paradigmatic Social Phenomenon." *Midwest Studies in Philosophy* 15: 1–14. Reprinted in Gilbert (1996), 177–94.

———. 1996. *Living Together: Rationality, Sociality, and Obligation*. Lanham, MD: Rowman and Littlefield.

———. 2000. *Sociality and Responsibility: New Essays in Plural Subject Theory*. Lanham, MD: Rowman and Littlefield.

———. 2006. "Who is to Blame? Collective Moral Responsibility and Its Implications for Group Members." *Midwest Studies in Philosophy* 30: 94–114.

Hacker, Andrew. 1964. "Introduction: Corporate America." In *The Corporation Take-Over*, ed. Andrew Hacker, 1–14. New York: Harper & Row.

Held, Virginia. 1970. "Can a Randon Collection of Individuals Be Morally Responsible?" *Journal of Philosophy* 68: 471–81. Reprinted in May/Hoffman (1991), 89–100.

Jansen, Ludger. 2004. "We, They, You: Persons in the Plural." In *Selected Papers Contributed to the Sections of GAP.5, Fifth International Congress of the Society for Analytical Philosophy*, ed. Roland Bluhm and Christian Nimtz, 479–91. Paderborn, Germany: Mentis.

———. 2005. "Institutionen und die kategoriale Ontologie." In *Institutionen und ihre Ontologie*, ed. Gerhard Schönrich, 45–57. Frankfurt: Ontos.

Korenjak, Thomas, Ungericht, Bernhard, and Raith, Dirk. 2010. "Unternehmen als verantwortungsfähige Akteure. Ein Beitrag zur Zurechenbarkeit von Verantwortung im Zeitalter der Globalisierung." In *Kollektive Verantwortung und internationale Beziehungen*, ed. Doris Gerber and Véronique Zanetti, 137–59. Berlin: Suhrkamp.

May, Larry, and Hoffman, Stacey, eds. 1991. *Collective Responsibility: Five Decades of Debate in Theoretical and Applied Ethics*. Lanham, MD: Rowman and Littlefield.

Searle, John R. 1995. *The Construction of Social Reality*. New York: Free Press.

———. 2010. *Making the Social World: The Structure of Human Civilization*. Oxford: Oxford University Press.

Velazques, Manuel G. 1983. "Why Corporations Are Not Morally Responsible for Anything They Do." *Business and Professional Ethics Journal* 2(3): 1–18. Reprinted in May/Hoffman (1991), 111–32.

Midwest Studies In Philosophy, XXXVIII (2014)

Essentially Shared Obligations

GUNNAR BJÖRNSSON

1. INTRODUCTION

Consider:

> THE LAKE: Alice, Bertha, and Claudia live around Forest Lake, at some
> distance from each other. The ecosystem is sensitive, in particular to the
> solvent they have been using when painting their boats, and the lake is faring
> badly. Until recently, they had no way of knowing that the solvent would have
> this effect, but they just learned that it is in fact killing the fish in the lake, and
> that the fish would survive if the amount of solvent entering the lake were
> sufficiently decreased. Alice now thinks that she might be able to make a
> difference if she takes on the minor hassle of disposing of the solvent in a safe
> way. Bertha and Claudia each think similar thoughts. As a matter of fact, the
> fish would not be saved if only one of them stopped polluting, but it would be
> if at least two of them did.

Faced with a case like this, many would think that Alice, Bertha, and Claudia have
an obligation to save the fish. They can do it, and if the fish die, it would be because
they (or at least two of them) cared insufficiently. However, as far as the case is
described, it is not clear that any *one* of them has an obligation to save the fish.
Suppose that none of them will in fact stop polluting. Given that two of them
continue polluting, it cannot be that the third has an obligation to save the fish, for
she cannot save the fish. Or suppose instead that all will in fact stop polluting.

Given that two of them will stop polluting, it is unclear how the third could have an obligation to save the fish, as the fish will survive whether she stops polluting or not. (Set to the side notions of *an obligation to* φ that do not imply *an ability to* φ. Also distinguish an obligation *to save the fish* from an obligation *to stop polluting*. Each agent might have an obligation to stop polluting even if the others make it impossible for her to save the fish.)

Judging from cases like this, there seem to be *essentially shared* obligations. *Together*, Alice, Bertha, and Claudia seem to have an obligation to save the fish; *individually* they might not have, depending on what the others do.[1] Obviously, THE LAKE is a simplistic case—a toy example—but attributions of shared obligations, or shared prospective moral responsibility, are legion in folk morality. It is said, for example, that it is the responsibility of citizens to vote bad politicians out of office, that people witnessing violent assault ought to intervene if they are many enough to do so safely, or that the rich nations have an obligation to stop catastrophic climate change. One might object to some of the above attributions of shared obligation, or to ones that I assume later in the article. Perhaps nations cannot have obligations (perhaps they don't count as moral agents), and perhaps voters only have obligations to express their own preferences or conceptions of a good society, rather than obligations to achieve some outcome. Whatever one thinks about particular cases, however, it is clear that attributions of shared obligations are part of common sense, and these attributions raise a number of foundational or conceptual puzzles that might cast doubt on the very notion of shared obligation: puzzles about the nature of the groups that can share obligations and about the relation between shared and individual capacities and obligations.

The purpose of this article is twofold: to spell out some of these puzzles and to propose an analysis of obligations that suggests solutions. In Section 2, I raise four crucial questions for our understanding of shared obligations. The first question concerns to what extent or in what way individuals who share an obligation to secure some outcome with other individuals must be able to contribute, individually, to the securing of that outcome. The second concerns the possibility of a mismatch between shared obligations and individual obligations or reasons to contribute. The third concerns the principles determining whether some individual is a member of group sharing an obligation. The final question concerns the relation between shared obligations and agency, given that many groups, like the trio around the lake, do not themselves seem to constitute agents. In Section 3, I note that similar questions arise for the case of shared *retrospective* responsibility (or shared blameworthiness), and sketch a strategy that I have used elsewhere to answer those questions (Björnsson 2011). In brief, the strategy is to employ an account of moral responsibility designed to make sense of attributions of *individual* responsibility and to show how it could make sense of issues of shared responsibility too. In Section 4, I briefly motivate a similarly structured account of

---

1. One might think that a case like this violates the deontic distribution principle that if a conjunction ought to be the case, then each conjunct ought to be the case. However, to reach that conclusion we have to conflate the proposition that *A and B* φ and the proposition that *A* φs *and B* φs.

moral obligation, before applying it to the case of shared obligations in Section 5, explaining how it would answer the questions raised in Section 2.

A few clarificatory remarks will be helpful before we proceed. First, it should be noted that the discussion will rely on what I take to be commonly shared, theoretically untutored intuitions. In the end, one might conclude that such intuitions are conceptually or metaphysically confused, but that conclusion should only be drawn following a serious effort of charitable interpretation. Readers are asked to reserve objections until the proposed account of these intuitions has been presented.

Second, it should be said that the notion of obligation that concerns me here is one with intimate ties to notions of blameworthiness: If P has an obligation to φ in the relevant sense, then if P does not φ, P is blameworthy for not φ-ing. So if citizens fail to vote bad politicians out of office, bystanders fail to prevent an assault, or rich nations fail to stop catastrophic climate change, the claims that they had an obligation to do so imply that the continued corruption, assault, or climate change is *their fault* in such a way that they are to blame for this.[2]

Finally, note that my primary concern here is conceptual rather than substantive. The task is not to spell out what individuals ought to do in situations where it is unclear whether others will contribute towards a desired ideal, or clear that they would not (see e.g., Cohen 2000; Regan 1980; Zimmerman 1996, chap. 9). Rather, it is to understand how attributions of shared obligations can be intelligible, in spite of raising what might seem like intractable questions.

2. SOME QUESTIONS CONCERNING SHARED OBLIGATIONS

In this section, I canvas a number of interrelated questions raised if we assume the soundness of everyday attributions of shared obligations, briefly discussing some tempting but ultimately flawed answers, and make a few initial suggestions.

2.1 The Question of Individual Influence

For the species of obligation that concerns us here, an obligation to do something presupposes a capacity to do it. In particular, obligations to ensure a desirable outcome or prevent one that is undesirable typically rely on the possibility of influencing the outcome, or of making a difference. The same seems true for shared obligations: people share an obligation to ensure something only insofar as they can ensure it through some appropriate combination of (non-)actions. At the same time, however, the actions and dispositions of the individuals sharing an obligation are often such that some or all of the individuals lack the power to ensure, either on their own or by initiating coordinated action with others, the outcome that the

---

2. Blameworthiness is frequently connected to the blameworthy party's "quality of will" and knowledge of consequences; so is the relevant notion of obligation and corresponding notion of moral wrongness. Notions with such connections are well entrenched in ordinary parlance. Studies by Fiery Cushman (2008), for example, show that ordinary attributions of wrongness or permissibility are sensitive to just such aspects rather than to outcomes.

group has an obligation to ensure. In many cases, the outcome is a major event and individual agents can at most slightly influence its timing or scope, and not always for the better. This lack of influence is clearest in cases of what Jonathan Glover (1975, 173) called "absolute thresholds," where a certain number of contributions are needed to make a major difference to outcomes but where extra contributions under or over the threshold make no significant difference. Voting procedures provide some of the more striking examples—because of the voting dispositions of other citizens, any given citizen might be unable to affect the outcome of a referendum by her own voting or by influencing the voting of others. THE LAKE provides another.

While a shared obligation to ensure φ apparently does not require that any individual has the capacity to ensure φ, it seems to require some weaker or more indirect form of individual influence. At the very least, the way we characterize the group that has a shared obligation to ensure something seems to be sensitive to this. Part of the reason that one might think that stopping catastrophic climate change is primarily the obligation of *rich* countries, rather than countries in the Northern Hemisphere, say, is that one thinks that rich countries are in a better position to ensure this given their resources. Similarly, part of the reason that one might think that it is the obligation of *citizens of a state* to vote bad politicians in that state out of office is that they, and only they, can do so. The question of individual influence concerns *what sort* of influence is in fact required.

One might be tempted to think of influence in terms of potential to *facilitate* the process that would lead to or constitute the outcome in question (cf. Petersson 2004). But this does not seem to be required. Consider:

> DELAYED RECOVERY: Just like THE LAKE, but the recovery of the fish would be a little slower if all three agents stopped polluting than if only two did. (The more sudden drop in pollution would require more radical adaptive adjustments in the ecosystem.)

Suppose that all three agents will in fact stop polluting. Then given what the others will do, no one agent would facilitate the process by stopping. But it still seems that Alice, Bertha, and Claudia have an obligation to save the fish.

While facilitation is not required, it is also clear that potential individual influence needs to be stronger than mere causal involvement in the process. Consider Debra, a fourth person around the lake who had not been pouring solvent into the lake and is thus unable to cut down on the pollution. Suppose that she could add a nontoxic chemical to the lake that would change the exact chemical pathway by which the solvent killed the fish *without facilitating (or hindering) the process*. She would not thereby seem to have the right kind of influence over the outcome to be part of the group whose obligation it is to save the fish (cf. Björnsson 2011, 183–84).

Another tempting way to think about individual influence is the following. Whether a group of agents share an obligation to φ depends on whether they *can* φ, which would seem to depend on whether they *would* φ if enough of them wanted to. Perhaps, then, an agent is a member of a group with a certain obligation only if there is some possible combination of wills in that group given which the agent's will would determine whether the group fulfills the obligation or not.[3] This would make straightforward sense of THE LAKE, including the variation with Debra. It is true for each of Alice, Bertha, and Claudia that her decision will make a difference if only one of the two others decides to stop polluting, but whatever these three decide, Debra's contribution cannot make a difference. Similarly for the voting case. At the time of a procedurally fair election or referendum, there is typically some distribution of wills of eligible voters such that adding one more vote for or against a certain alternative determines whether that alternative wins. By contrast, there is no distribution of wills such that the will of someone not eligible to vote determines the outcome.

While promising, it is not clear that this suggestion handles cases where the outcome is just too coarse-grained or vaguely defined for one individual to make a difference. For example, inhabitants of a city with limited water supply might seem to have an obligation not to cause a severe water shortage. And this might seem so even though any individual inhabitants would be unable to make a difference as to whether there is such a shortage or not, independently of what the others do. There just is no sharp enough divide between what is and what is not a *severe* shortage (for discussion, see. e.g., Kagan 2011). (One might reject the metaphysical possibility of vagueness of this sort—perhaps there has to be a perfectly sharp divide— but the point here is that *conceiving* of the inhabitants as sharing an obligation to prevent severe water shortage does not require conceiving of the notion of severe water shortage as sharply delimited.)

2.2 The Question of Individual Reasons to Contribute

The case of THE LAKE illustrated how a shared obligation to φ does not require effective individual capacity to ensure φ-ing. Since individual obligations to φ require such capacities, the shared obligation cannot be understood as a mere aggregation of such individual responsibilities. And there is nothing unique about THE LAKE in this regard. Suppose that the rich countries do indeed have an obligation to stop catastrophic climate change, but that they are unwilling to do what is required. This does not seem to undermine their shared obligation—in general, unwillingness to fulfill an obligation does not void that obligation—but it might straightforwardly undermine the claim that one individual rich country, such

---

3. An idea of this sort is articulated by Alvin Goldman's (1972) analysis of social power, along roughly the following lines:

> An individual agent, A, has *some power* with respect to some alternative outcomes, O and ~O, if and only if: (i) there is some group, G, that can determine at will whether O or ~O happens (i.e., O would happen if each member wanted O and ~O would happen if each member wanted ~O), and (ii) A is a nondispensable member of G with respect to O and ~O (i.e., a member such that a group consisting of the members of G apart from A could not determine at will whether O or ~O happens independently of whether A wants O or ~O). (For some reason, Goldman's formulation on p. 240 only takes this to be a sufficient condition.)

Peter French (1984, chap. 5) relies on Goldman's suggestion in his discussion of the power of people in groups and corporations. A related account of (*retrospective*) moral responsibility has been proposed by Braham and van Hees (2012). For criticism, see Björnsson (2011), 184–85.

as Sweden, has an obligation to stop catastrophic climate change. Because of the unwillingness of the other rich countries, Sweden would be incapable of doing this, however willing it would be. Similarly, if Swedish citizens have an obligation to deny parliamentary representation to the violently anti-immigrant right, this does not mean that any one individual citizen has an obligation to do this, as it might be beyond his or her power given the wills of other voters. And so on.

Lack of individual influence makes for a mismatch not only between shared obligations and the obligations of individuals, but also between the reasons underlying the shared obligation and individuals' reasons to *contribute* toward its fulfillment. In many cases, the existence of a shared obligation seems to imply a *prima facie* reason for individuals to contribute. In THE LAKE, for example, it seems that Alice, Bertha, and Claudia each have some *prima facie* reason to stop polluting. But consider the following two variations:

> KNOWN RELUCTANCE: Just like THE LAKE, but each of the parties know that the others refuse to stop polluting, and knows that at least two need to stop in order to save the fish.

> KNOWN RELUCTANCE AND HASTENED DEMISE: Just like KNOWN RELUCTANCE, but each of the parties also knows that if she were to stop polluting, this would hasten the death of the fish somewhat (an insufficient drop in pollution would fail to prevent the deadly processes but would instead cause adaptive stress).

At least in KNOWN RELUCTANCE AND HASTENED DEMISE, it seems possible that a given individual not only lacks an obligation to ensure the outcome (because the individual cannot ensure it), but also lacks an obligation or even a normative reason to contribute or to do what would have contributed toward fulfilling the obligation had others cared appropriately. Indeed, it might seem that the individual has an obligation not to act in such a way. Moreover, this could be the predicament of all, each individual knowing that everyone else will in fact refuse to do their part, and that her contribution would only make things (a little) worse. So no individual might have an obligation or reason to stop pouring solvent into the lake, and might even have an obligation or reason not to stop, given what they know about the others. The upshot would be that while it is the shared obligation of the individuals around the lake to save the fish, none of them, taken individually, has any reason to contribute, let alone an obligation to do so. In the end, I will argue that this is a coherent set of judgments, but at a first glance it carries at least a whiff of paradox.

2.3 The Grouping Question

A question related to the questions of individual influence and contribution concerns the extent to which the parties need to be related to each other to share an obligation. To *share* an obligation, it seems, it is not enough that the parties each have obligations to ensure the same outcome. For example, suppose that, independently of each other, Joe has promised Eve that someone will meet her at the station, and Jill has promised Adam that someone will meet Eve at the station. Joe and Jill might each have an obligation to ensure that someone meets Eve at the station, but they do not thereby *share* an obligation to ensure this. Joe can fail to fulfill his obligation while Jill fulfills hers.

One initially tempting way to account for shared obligations is with reference to shared or collective agency or action; perhaps a set of agents share an obligation to φ insofar as these agents ought to jointly perform φ. This suggestion would lack substance if a jointly performed action were understood as nothing but an aggregate or mereological sum of individual actions, or the effect of such an aggregate. But substance can be added if the notion of a joint action is itself given substantive content, and a variety of interesting analyses has been offered lately. Some appeal to an interpersonal or joint commitment by members of a group (Gilbert 1989); others to various forms of intention to perform a joint action (Bratman 1999), or to intentions to act that are openly conditional on the intentions of others (Sadler 2006); still others appeal to a less theory-of-mind-laden understanding of coordinated teleological action (Petersson 2007). On none of these accounts do Joe and Jill share an obligation just because each has an obligation to ensure that someone meets Eve at the station.[4]

An appeal to joint agency seems tempting for at least three reasons. First, it seems to allow for a relaxed requirement of influence, as not everyone participating in a joint action (understood in any of the above ways) might have a real chance to substantially affect the outcome of that action. Second, an appeal to joint agency might seem to stay at least partly true to the commonplace assumption that moral obligations pertain to moral *agents*. Perhaps the parties have not yet engaged in joint action, but if they are capable of doing this, they at least constitute a *potential agent* (in some suitably weak sense). Third, an appeal to joint agency points to a way in which the paradox of contribution could be explained away. Since the shared obligation is an obligation of a (potential) agent with capacities logically distinct from those of the individual agents, it should be no surprise that there might be a mismatch between its obligations and reasons, and those of its constituting members.[5]

While the suggestion is tempting, I think that it is too restrictive: shared obligations are not essentially obligations to perform joint actions. While accounts of joint action differ in details, they all require that the individual agents participating in the joint action understand themselves as so doing, or understand how their individual contributions are joined. By contrast, it seems that a shared

4. Another form of collective responsibility discussed in the literature, beginning with French (1984), understands certain collectives—in particular certain corporations—as agents in their own right, with beliefs and plans independent of the beliefs and plans of members of the collectives (cf. Hess 2014; List and Pettit 2011; Rovane 1998; Tollefsen 2002). Though I think that there are such corporate agents, the examples considered here are not plausibly understood along such lines.
5. Compare David Copp's (2007) argument that collectives can have an agential moral property that no member of that collective has. For criticism, see Miller (2007).

obligation can be fulfilled without any sense of coordinated or shared agency among the parties. Consider:

> COINCIDING CLEAN HANDS: Just like THE LAKE, but in response to the news about the fish, each of Alice, Bertha, and Claudia thinks that the fish will die whatever she does but (independently) decides that she does not want to further contribute to the death of the fish—she wants to keep her hands clean from now on. Independently, they all stop polluting and the fish survive.

Though the fish were saved, and saved by the trio's actions, no agent intended to act together with the others; if anything, they intended *not* to act together with others. Nevertheless, it seems that the people around the lake saved the fish, thus avoiding the blame for the death of the fish that would have accrued to (at least two of) them if they had not saved the fish. If this is correct, shared obligations are not necessarily obligations to perform joint actions.

In fact, one might even wonder whether the agents in fact sharing an obligation need to think that others *can* play a role in fulfilling the obligation. Consider:

> SOLIPSISTIC POLLUTERS: Like THE LAKE, but each of Alice, Bertha, and Claudia is unaware that the others had also been polluting. Each thinks that she is the only one who can do anything to save the fish, and that she would be successful if she tried.

It still seems that they would be to blame for the death of the fish if they failed to save them, and that they would avoid blame for the death of the fish if they each (independently) decided to stop polluting, thus saving them.

Some might want to resist the claim that the group fulfilled their obligation to save the fish. In the absence of some kind of coordinated or joint effort, one might perhaps prefer to say that Alice, Bertha, and Claudia removed the grounds for their obligation, rather than say that they fulfilled it. But we should not in general take the fulfillment of obligations to φ to require coordinated efforts to φ. In fact, very few fulfillments of our strongest obligations result from such coordinated efforts. In satisfying obligations not to kill or steal, we are rarely considering the possibility of killing or stealing. Instead, the work is done by habitual focus on opportunities that do not involve killing or stealing, perhaps in conjunction with concerns to satisfy weaker demands, such as demands not to invade someone's physical space, or not to use someone's property against their wishes or without their permission. Of course, while we rarely engage in coordinated efforts to fulfill these strong obligations, it is no accident that such habits and concerns lead to their fulfillment. But it is similarly nonaccidental that the actions in COINCIDING CLEAN HANDS result in the survival of the fish: If agents independently refrain from practices that threaten to have bad effects when sufficiently common, this will often avoid such bad effects even in the absence of coordination.[6]

---

6. Obviously, to deny that shared obligation has to be obligation to perform a joint action is not to deny that a group of people might have a shared obligation to act jointly, in a coordinated fashion—to form a political party, say, or search systematically for a lost child.

2.4 The Question of Agency

I have denied that agents sharing an obligation to φ must have an individual obligation to φ, or even an individual obligation to contribute toward φ-ing, and I raised the possibility that, taken individually, *each* party might lack the relevant obligation. This raises a skeptical worry: How can there be an obligation to φ if no agent is obligated to φ? And, relatedly: How can there be an obligation to φ if there is no agent that *can* φ? Notice, too, that it does not obviously help to say, contrary to what I argued above, that shared obligations are obligations to perform joint actions, and that they are thus restricted to groups capable of performing such actions. The problem is that a group whose members could (given suitable motivation) come together so as to perform a joint action does not thereby seem to be an agent in any qualified sense *before* they have organized their actions.[7] While it might be natural to say that "the people around the lake can save the fish and are thus obligated to do so," the obligation and capacity are thus not attributed to the individuals in the group, nor, it seems, to any existing agent constituted by the group. Perhaps, then, intuitions of shared prospective obligations in such cases are illusory, based on confused assignments of agency or a confused grasp of what individuals are capable of.

2.5 Looking Ahead

Rather than proceeding piecemeal trying to answer each of the questions canvassed here, I will mimic a strategy that I have employed elsewhere to make sense of shared retrospective moral responsibility (Björnsson 2011). The strategy was to rely on an independently motivated account of attributions of *individual* retrospective moral responsibility and blameworthiness, and to argue that this account makes good sense of attributions of *shared* responsibility. Since that account answered questions analogous to those discussed here in Section 2, and since there are close links between retrospective responsibility and moral obligation of the sort that concerns us here, there is *prima facie* reason to think that an analogous strategy might help us to understand shared obligations. It is of course possible that we employ different notions of obligation when we consider individual and group obligations, but the conservative hypothesis is that the concept is the same in both cases, and the successful subsumption of individual and shared retrospective responsibility bolsters that assumption.

    I begin to pursue this strategy in Section 3, where I briefly explain how the questions were answered in the case of retrospective responsibility. In Section 4 I

---

7. One way to try avoiding this difficulty is to claim that any group of unorganized people is itself an agent. Taking this route, Torbjörn Tännsjö (2007, 302–03) suggests that such a group qualifies as an agent because its behavior is explained by the beliefs and desires of (the members of) the group, and furthermore that it is capable of acting wrongly because it has a weak form of compatibilist free will, that is, because the behavior of the group depends on its preferences (i.e., the preferences of its members). However, since the collective lacks the hallmark of agency— coordinated goal-directed action—this suggestion is hard to take seriously, except perhaps as a proposal for conceptual reform.

motivate a general analysis of the notion of moral obligation that I take to be at play in many ordinary judgments of individual obligation. In Section 5 I argue that this concept of obligation provides the keys to answering questions of individual influence, contribution, grouping, and agency. If the argument is correct, attributions of shared obligations, just like attributions of shared retrospective responsibility, can be as intelligible and clear-headed as attributions of individual obligations.

3. A SOLUTION TO RELATED PROBLEMS OF SHARED RETROSPECTIVE MORAL RESPONSIBILITY

If Alice, Bertha, and Claudia continue polluting out of sheer laziness and the fish die, it seems that they are (retrospectively) responsible, and to blame, for the death of the fish. They knew that the fish were dying, and if they had cared sufficiently they would have stopped the pollution and saved the fish. But such attributions of responsibility and blameworthiness raise the same questions as attributions of shared obligations. Given the actions of the others, there was nothing any *one* of them could have done to prevent the death of the fish, and so it seems that they cannot individually be blamed for that outcome.[8] Elsewhere, I have argued that this mismatch between individual and shared responsibility is not well understood on standard accounts of collective responsibility (Björnsson 2011). However, I also argued that this sort of responsibility *is* straightforwardly understood on the basis of an analysis developed for individual retrospective responsibility. Here is a simplified version of that analysis:

> THE EXPLANATION HYPOTHESIS: We take P to be retrospectively morally responsible for a morally significant event E insofar as we take it that the right sort of motivational structure of P is part of a normal significant explanation of E.[9]

A *motivational structure* is a structure that guides behavior in relation to circumstances. The *right sorts* of motivational structure are ones that tend to respond appropriately to our practices of holding each other responsible (sets of values and preferences say, as opposed to mechanisms driving compulsive behavior). A motivational structure of type M is part of a *normal* explanation of E only if E is a type of event such that type M structures have a sufficiently general tendency to explain this type of event in this way. Intuitively, and in typical cases, we hold an agent responsible for some bad outcome when it is explained by the agent's ill will (or lack of appropriate concern) in the way bad outcomes tend to be explained by such ill will. Similarly, we typically hold an agent responsible for some good outcome when it is explained by the agent's exceptionally good will in the way good outcomes tend to be explained by such good will.

---

8. Perhaps even more clearly than in the case of prospective shared responsibility, the parties need not even know of each other's existence.

9. For elaboration and defense, see Björnsson (2014); Björnsson and Persson (2012, 2013).

The EXPLANATION HYPOTHESIS, I have argued, accounts for a wide variety of both well-known and surprising features of our thinking about moral responsibility (Björnsson 2014; Björnsson and Persson 2009, 2012, 2013), including notorious skeptical worries about moral responsibility elicited by thoughts about determinism or luck. What is important here, however, is that the EXPLANATION HYPOTHESIS provides a straightforward account of essentially shared retrospective responsibility. First, it makes sense of our unwillingness to attribute ordinary individual, un-shared, responsibility and blame in our retrospective version of THE LAKE. Intuitively, we do not think that the fish died because *Alice* didn't care appropriately about their fate; after all, her lack of concern made no difference to the outcome. Second, it makes sense of our willingness to attribute shared responsibility to *Alice, Bertha, and Claudia* for the death of the fish. We naturally think that *their* lack of appropriate concern is part of a normal significant explanation of the death of the fish. The fish died because they didn't care enough, and this is just a special case of the common phenomenon that something valuable is harmed because people care too little about it to take insufficient precautions to protect or avoid harming it.

The EXPLANATION HYPOTHESIS also suggests answers to questions corresponding to those raised for shared obligations in Section 2. In explaining how we can attribute responsibility for an outcome to groups without attributing responsibility to some particular agent for that outcome, it answers *the question of agency* for retrospective responsibility. It also explains why we can find a group of people responsible and to blame for an outcome even in cases where each of them had good normative reasons not to help prevent that outcome, thus providing an answer to the question about the lack of connection between *individual reasons to contribute and shared responsibility*. If Alice, Bertha, and Claudia each knew that the others were too lazy to dispose of solvent in an appropriate way, and knew that if they alone stopped polluting, the fish would die even more quickly (as in KNOWN RELUCTANCE AND HASTENED DEMISE), each might well have good reason not to stop polluting (even if they do not in fact care about such reasons). But according to the EXPLANATION HYPOTHESIS, we can still see how they might share responsibility for the outcome. It might still be that the fish died *because they cared insufficiently*: If they had all cared appropriately, they would have known that the others would be likely to contribute, and so would themselves have cut down pollution enough to ensure the survival of the fish. The EXPLANATION HYPOTHESIS also directly suggests an answer to *the grouping question* and *the question of individual influence* for retrospective responsibility: a group of people share retrospective responsibility and blame for some event insofar as that event has a straightforward normal explanation in terms of the lack of proper concern of that particular group.[10]

10. An explanation appealing to the fact that *they didn't care enough* might be understood in two ways. On the one hand, it can be understood as collectively invoking the lack of sufficient care of each of the parties: the death of the fish is explained by the fact that each of A, B, C, and so on did not care appropriately. Under this (distributive) understanding, the explanatory requirement of the EXPLANATION HYPOTHESIS is applied to each of the parties; the upshot is that the attribution of shared responsibility to a group implies that each member of that group lacked the appropriate concern. On the other hand, it can be understood as invoking lack of appropriate concern more holistically: The death of the fish might be explained by the fact that there was too little concern

The Explanation Hypothesis promises to make good sense of attributions of retrospective responsibility and blame, solving puzzles about individual influence, agency, and grouping. The suggestion in the rest of the article will be that a parallel account can be given of our attributions of shared obligations. To make this suggestion plausible, I will first need to say something about the notion of obligation that is at play in many ordinary attributions of individual obligation, and which I think gives rise to the puzzling sets of intuitions canvassed in Section 2.

4. MORAL OBLIGATION

The concept of a moral obligation involved in the judgments that concern us here is the concept of a *practically relevant moral demand*. As a first stab at spelling out what practical relevance here amounts to, we might say that practically relevant demands are ones that *can be fulfilled by the subjects of the demands in appropriate response to the demands*. This distinguishes the kind of moral obligations that we are concerned with—the sort intimately connected to blameworthiness—from some other kinds of obligation. For example, it is a common experience that, through no fault of our own, we find ourselves in situations where we are unable to keep a promise we have made and so unable to fulfill an obligation to the promisee. Failure to fulfill this sort of possibility-insensitive obligation does not make us blameworthy.

The requirement that subjects of the demands in question be *able* to fulfill the demands must be taken in the right way. The requirement of practicality is not satisfied by *a mere chance* that the demand would be met if the subject were appropriately responsive. When there is a mere chance of success, what is demanded is at most that one *tries*. Rather, the requirement is (at least) that appropriate responsiveness to the demand would *ensure* that the demand is met. Moreover, it would have to be ensured in the right way. For example, consider:

> MISINFORMATION: Dr. Albert has medical information that she mistakenly but through no fault of her own thinks would alleviate the terrible pain of a former patient if she got it to him before leaving for the day. Suppose also that if she were appropriately responsive to the situation, she would head over to the ward to give the patient the information in person, as the ward cannot take incoming calls. But suppose further that the patient is about to call her to ask for the information. If she were inappropriately responsive and did *not* head over to the ward, the patient would call her and she would provide the incorrect information over the phone. If she decided to

for the environment in that group *as a whole*. Under this (nondistributive) understanding, individual members of that group might well have the appropriate concern, but their concern fails to make up for the lack of concern of other members. On the former understanding, each member is necessarily morally implicated in the outcome; on the latter, some members might not be. In neither case is it puzzling that a group can be retrospectively morally responsible for an outcome over which no individual had significant control. In Björnsson (2011), I looked primarily at the first sort of explanations, as the examples discussed there involved small enough groups for us to represent each individual. To simplify matters, I adhere to the same restriction here.

head over to the ward, however, another doctor would take the call, a doctor who would give him the correct information.

In MISINFORMATION, it is true that if Dr. Albert were to respond appropriately to the situation, the patient would be saved from terrible pain. But it is not true that Dr. Albert morally must save the patient from terrible pain in the relevant sense. If she does not respond as seems to be morally required and the patient suffers the terrible pain, she still cannot be blamed for the pain the patient experiences. She had every reason to think that the information she offered was correct, and it is only by luck that the patient would have received the correct information if she had been appropriately responsive. One might think that what goes wrong in this case is that the end is achieved in a way other than that intended by the agent. As noted in Section 2, however, appropriately responding agents often fulfill obligations without forming intentions of the relevant sort—intentions not to kill or harm, say. But the requirement that the relevant outcome is achieved in the intended manner can be generalized: What seems to be required for a practically relevant demand to φ is that a proper response to the demand would ensure φ-ing *in a normal way*. In the special case when the proper response involves an intention or plan to φ, φ-ing is ensured in a normal way when it is ensured according to plan.[11]

Thus far I have said that the practical relevance of a demand requires that appropriate responsiveness to the demand would ensure that the demand is met. The relevant notion of correct, proper, or appropriate responsiveness to a demand also needs clarification, with regard to what it means to *respond* to a demand, and to what it means to be *appropriately* responsive.

First, *responding* to a demand does not necessarily involve believing or knowing that one is subject to the demand. Rushing to catch a train, I have an obligation not to shove people who stand in my way as I make it around a corner, and I have this obligation even if time is too short to form the belief that I have the moral obligation. It is enough that various subpersonal perception-action routines of mine can respond to features associated (though not necessarily identical) with the core reason that grounds the obligation—that the others are sentient beings, say—by initiating nonaggressive solutions to the problem. What practical relevance requires, it seems, is only that if I were appropriately responsive to those features, this would ensure, in a normal fashion, that the demand is met. Moreover, as noted in Section 2, we fulfill most of our most serious obligations without any thoughts on our part that we have these obligations.

Second, to be *appropriately* responsive to features associated with the reasons that ground the obligation is to have a motivating sensitivity to these

---

11. A proper response should *ensure* that the demand is met, but need not *explain* why it is met. Most of the time we meet all sorts of obligations, especially negative duties, because we have no reason not to. In those cases, coming to think about having the obligations would have no effect on our behavior. Moreover, it is not required that the subject of a demand *knows* that the demand would be met if the subject responded appropriately. I can sensibly think that I have an obligation to save a person *if I can*. I then understand my obligation as conditional upon the possibility of saving the person, but not upon my knowledge of it.

reasons *of a sort that can be reasonably morally required.* What sensitivities can be reasonably morally required is of course a vexed issue, intricately related to issues in metaethics and normative ethics, as well as questions about what sort of free will is required for moral obligations. The account of moral obligations provided here is meant to be abstract enough to be compatible with most views in these areas.[12] Luckily, some things are relatively uncontroversial. Most agree that in order to be subject to moral demands, an agent must have a general capacity to grasp and act on the nature of these demands. For this reason, we think that small children and people with sufficient mental deficiencies are less appropriate subjects for moral demands, or at least subject to less stringent or sophisticated demands of this sort.

Summarizing the considerations discussed in this section and hypothesizing that they tell the full story (given suitable precisification of the admittedly vague terms involved), we get:

> MORAL OBLIGATION: P has a moral obligation to φ in C (is morally required to φ in C) if, and only if, were P in C to have the sort of motivational sensitivity that can be reasonably morally required of P, this would ensure, in normal ways, that P φ in C.[13]

12. Arguably, the account does not fit well with versions of act-consequentialism that identify our moral obligations with what would actually have the best consequences (rather than what has the highest expected value, say). At least if what can be reasonably morally required is a matter of what we can reasonably demand of each other on moral grounds, it often cannot reasonably be required that we should be sensitive to facts about what actions have the best actual consequences. But incompatibility with such forms of consequentialism is no objection to the current proposal, as these forms are antecedently implausible when understood as accounts of the sort of blame-related moral obligations discussed here.

13. Given this account of moral obligation, the following analysis of (blame-related) moral wrongness is tempting:

> MORAL WRONGNESS: It would be morally wrong of P to φ in C if, and only if, were P in C to have the sort of motivational sensitivity that can be reasonably morally required of P, this would ensure, in normal ways, that P does not φ in C.

One might worry that MORAL OBLIGATION (and MORAL WRONGNESS) is circular, defining obligations in terms of what can be reasonably morally required. However, the obligations in questions have activities as their objects, whereas the requirements in questions concern dispositions. The definition does not tell us what requirements are, but it does reduce obligations (or requirements) concerning actions to requirements concerning motivational sensitivities.

One might also worry that this account fails for various cases involving agents lacking sensitivities that could reasonably be demanded of them. Consider a version of an example from Gary Watson (1975), utilized by Michael Smith (1995) to illustrate a similar problem: I'm furious after losing a game of squash in a humiliating fashion. I consider shaking hands with my opponent, because this is what one normally does to show respect, but because I'm ill-tempered and self-centered, if I were to approach the opponent I would perhaps shake his hand, but not without insulting him or getting into an argument. Sensing this, it might seem that I have an obligation to take a minute or two to cool down before interacting with my opponent. But MORAL OBLIGATION might seem to imply that I had a moral obligation to shake hands with my opponent after the game. After all, this might be what I would have done if I had been less self-centered, and perhaps it can be reasonably demanded that I be less self-centered. Exactly what to say in response to apparent counterexamples like this—examples where the falsity of the antecedent of the conditional in our analysis of obligation itself seems morally relevant—is a difficult and complex matter that goes beyond what can be fully discussed here (for a discussion of the analogous "conditional

5. SHARED MORAL OBLIGATIONS

Given the requirement of practical relevance, one might think that subjects of moral obligations must be special kind of *agents*: entities capable of systematically meeting moral demands through a motivating sensitivity to the reasons grounding the demands, a sensitivity that can be reasonably morally required of them. This, of course, is exactly what seemed problematic when we looked at putative cases of shared obligation. For example, though it seemed that the trio around the lake had an obligation to save the fish, they were not required to act *as one agent*, and the agents, taken individually, lacked the capacity to ensure that the demand would be met. However, as I will now suggest, MORAL OBLIGATION allows that P is a plurality of agents, rather than an agent in its own right.

Recall first that P's φ-ing does not have to be a coordinated action directed at fulfilling the obligation; as noted in Section 2, it is rare that our strongest obligations are met via such coordinated efforts. Furthermore, when P is a group— Alice, Bertha, and Claudia, say—the sensitivities required need not be sensitivities of the group, understood as something beyond the three individuals, as opposed to sensitivities of the individuals in the group. What is required is merely that the subject of the obligation—*they*—can respond in the required way to the reasons grounding the obligation. Finally, it seems eminently plausible that the sensitivities required of the members of the group can be part of a normal explanation of why the group does something. Many or most of the sensitivities that can be required of individual agents are dispositions to facilitate or contribute to important outcomes that sometimes require the input of other agents, through an aggregation of actions (if enough people treat the environment well, important ecosystems survive; if enough people vote for one alternative, it wins) or through joint actions where people coordinate their efforts to produce the outcome.

If what I have said is correct, it provides the key to answering the questions outlined in Section 2.

First, it answers the question of agency. The full moral agency required for shared obligation is merely that of individual agents. However, the *capacity* to fulfill the obligation is one that pertains to the group as a whole, as the antecedent of

---

fallacy" problem for certain virtue ethical accounts of rightness, see Johnson 2003). But let me mention two natural (complementary) ways of modifying or clarifying MORAL OBLIGATION to handle cases like this. The first is to say that obligations to φ are, strictly speaking, restricted to "maximal" φs, that is, φs that are not themselves part of some more complex activity that would be ensured by the relevant motivational sensitivities. In this particular case, it would mean that I do not have an obligation to shake hands with my opponent, period, as the relevant motivational sensitivities would guarantee that I do so *in a polite manner*. (If you think that this would make the requirements too detailed, remember that motivational sensitivities that can be reasonably required might fall way short of full virtue, or full rationality.) The second thing to say is that what can be reasonably morally required is restricted to sensitivities that are in some relevant sense up to the agent. Perhaps I cannot shake my opponent's hands in a polite manner given my self-centered bad temper. But if my disposition to insult my opponent is not under my control in the relevant way, then if I were sensitive to this and other features of the situation in a way that could be reasonably required of me, I would refrain from shaking my opponents hand, knowing as I do that it would take an ugly turn.

the conditional in Moral Obligation is one that encompasses the sensitivities of all its members.

Second, Moral Obligation provides an account of the requirement of influence as pertaining to shared obligations, or rather an account of the absence of any strict requirement. What is required for a shared obligation is that if the members of the group were sensitive to features of the situation in ways that can reasonably be morally required, this would ensure, in normal ways, that the obligation is fulfilled.[14]

Third, the account makes it intelligible that a group has an obligation even though no individual agent has any obligation to contribute. Consider Known Reluctance, the variation of The Lake in which (1) all parties of the putative shared obligation lack the appropriate motivational dispositions and refuse to contribute toward the shared obligation; (2) all are known by all to do so; and (3) there is no way for one individual to make any significant difference without the contributions of one of the others. Under such epistemic circumstances, it seems highly plausible that, for each party, that party has no individual obligation to contribute: even with the appropriate concern, it would not contribute. But the mere fact that each member of a group is unwilling to contribute to a goal and knows that the others are equally unwilling should not be enough to remove their shared obligation to bring about the goal. Moral Obligation accounts for this: it might well be that *if* the members were appropriately responsive, they would each realize, or consider likely, or at least possible, that the other members of the group would be willing to contribute, and would then themselves do their part. The situations in which beliefs that others are unwilling to contribute most plausibly would undermine shared obligations, then, are situations where, *even if the parties all had the appropriate motivational structures*, they would believe that others were unwilling. But such situations might be quite uncommon, given the plausibility of something like the following principle:

> Signal Willingness: When people in a group would more likely achieve some important end if they were aware of the extent to which members have the motivational sensitivities that could reasonably be morally demanded of them, a member of the group has a *pro tanto* obligation to make others aware of her readiness to contribute toward that end (perhaps by explicit offer, or by some modest first contribution).

Given Signal Willingness, the existence of appropriate responsiveness among members of a group would typically ensure that when it is known that an important end can likely be achieved through and only through efforts by suitably motivated members, members know about the motivation of other members.

Fourth, Moral Obligation begins to answer the question of group membership. For the required sensitivities to explain the fulfillment of the obligation *in a normal way*, there must be a certain degree of *unity* to why and how members of the group would contribute if they were suitably motivated. Focusing on the case

---

14. Here it is important to bear in mind that a *normal* explanation of how an outcome is ensured is likely to be fairly programmatic, allowing for variations in various details.

of THE LAKE, the normal way in which appropriate sensitivities to possible damage from cumulative impact (cumulative pollution, wear and tear, pressure, etc.) prevent such damage is through sufficient actions that decrease the impact. Consequently, we would naturally think that the appropriate sensitivities of Alice, Bertha, and Claudia would ensure the survival of the fish in a normal way. By contrast, we would not naturally think that the appropriate sensitivities of Alice, Bertha, Claudia, *and Debra* would ensure the survival in a normal way (Debra, recall, was the character who could change but neither help nor hinder the process by which the fish were being killed). Whatever action or nonaction would be triggered by Debra's appropriate sensitivities would not be of the sort that decreases the impact (i.e., the pollution). Similarly in the case of Joe, Jill, Adam, and Eve. Here Joe and Jill might each have an obligation to see to it that someone meets Eve at the station, as there are normal ways in which appropriate sensitivities to existing promises ensure that the promise is kept. But there would be no *one* explanation of how someone would meet Eve pointing to Joe's *and* Jill's sensitivities, only two similar and parallel explanations.

6. CONCLUDING REMARKS

Although MORAL OBLIGATION makes sense of shared obligations and indicates answers to the questions raised in Section 2, the discussion in this article leaves a number of issues untouched, not least among which are issues concerning what can reasonably be demanded of people given various prospects of contributions from others, and issues concerning the importance or usefulness of focusing on shared rather than merely individual obligation. By explaining how essentially shared obligations are possible and no more mysterious than individual obligations, I nevertheless hope to have provided some tools for thinking more clearly about those issues.[15]

REFERENCES

Björnsson, Gunnar. 2011. "Joint Responsibility without Individual Control: Applying the Explanation Hypothesis." In *Compatibilist Responsibility: Beyond Free Will and Determinism*, ed. Jeroen van den Hoven, Ibo van de Poel, and Nicole Vincent, 181–99. Dordrecht: Springer.

———. 2014. "Incompatibilism and 'Bypassed' Agency'." In *Surrounding Free Will*, ed. Alfred Mele, 95–122. New York: Oxford University Press.

Björnsson, Gunnar, and Persson, Karl. 2009. "Judgments of Moral Responsibility—A Unified Account." In *Society for Philosophy and Psychology, 35th Annual Meeting, Bloomington, IN*. Retrieved July 18, 2014, from <http://philsci-archive.pitt.edu/4633/>.

———. 2012. "The Explanatory Component of Moral Responsibility." *Noûs* 46: 326–54.

———. 2013. "A Unified Empirical Account of Responsibility Judgments." *Philosophy and Phenomenological Research* 87: 611–39.

15. This article has benefitted from comments from audiences at MANCEPT 2011, London School of Economics, Umeå University, and University of Gothenburg. Special thanks to Kendy Hess for comments on a late version of the article. Work on this article has been funded by Stiftelsen Riksbankens Jubileumsfond.

Braham, Matthew, and van Hees, Martin. 2012. "An Anatomy of Moral Responsibility." *Mind* 121: 601–4.

Bratman, Michael E. 1999. *Faces of Intention: Selected Essays on Intention and Agency*. Cambridge: Cambridge University Press.

Cohen, Gerald A. 2000. "If You're an Egalitarian, How Come You're So Rich?" *Journal of Ethics* 4: 1–26.

Copp, David. 2007. "The Collective Moral Autonomy Thesis." *Journal of Social Philosophy* 38: 369–88.

Cushman, Fiery. 2008. "Crime and Punishment: Distinguishing the Roles of Causal and Intentional Analyses in Moral Judgment." *Cognition* 108: 353–80.

French, Peter A. 1984. *Collective and Corporate Responsibility*. New York: Columbia University Press.

Gilbert, Margaret. 1989. *On Social Facts*. London: Routledge.

Glover, Jonathan. 1975. "It Makes No Difference Whether or Not I Do It." *Proceedings of the Aristotelian Society, Supplementary Volumes* 49: 171–90.

Goldman, Alvin I. 1972. "Toward a Theory of Social Power." *Philosophical Studies* 23: 221–68.

Hess, Kendy M. 2014. "The Free Will of Corporations (and Other Collectives)." *Philosophical Studies* 168: 241–60.

Johnson, Robert N. 2003. "Virtue and Right." *Ethics* 113: 810–34.

Kagan, Shelly. 2011. "Do I Make a Difference?" *Philosophy and Public Affairs* 39: 105–41.

List, Christian, and Pettit, Philip. 2011. *Group Agency: The Possibility, Design, and Status of Corporate Agents*. Oxford: Oxford University Press.

Miller, Seumas. 2007. "Against the Collective Moral Autonomy Thesis." *Journal of Social Philosophy* 38: 389–409.

Petersson, Björn. 2004. "The Second Mistake in Moral Mathematics Is Not About the Worth of Mere Participation." *Utilitas* 16: 288–315.

———. 2007. "Collectivity and Circularity." *Journal of Philosophy* 104: 138–56.

Regan, Donald H. 1980. *Utilitarianism and Co-Operation*. Oxford: Clarendon Press.

Rovane, Carol A. 1998. *The Bounds of Agency: An Essay in Revisionary Metaphysics*. Princeton, NJ: Princeton University Press.

Sadler, Brook J. 2006. "Shared Intentions and Shared Responsibility." *Midwest Studies in Philosophy* 30: 115–44.

Smith, Michael. 1995. "Internal Reasons." *Philosophy and Phenomenological Research* 55: 109–31.

Tollefsen, Deborah. 2002. "Organizations as True Believers." *Journal of Social Philosophy* 33: 395–410.

Tännsjö, Torbjörn. 2007. "The Myth of Innocence: On Collective Responsibility and Collective Punishment." *Philosophical Papers* 36: 295–314.

Watson, Gary. 1975. "Free Agency." *The Journal of Philosophy* 72: 205–20.

Zimmerman, Michael J. 1996. *The Concept of Moral Obligation*. New York: Cambridge University Press.

Midwest Studies In Philosophy, XXXVIII (2014)

Beyond the Sins of the Fathers:
Responsibility for Inequality

DERRICK DARBY and NYLA R. BRANSCOMBE

Every generation, by virtue of being born into a historical continuum, is burdened by the sins of the fathers as it is blessed by the deeds of the ancestors. (Hannah Arendt)

When we speak of reducing social inequality, we often lose sight of or fail to capture the impact of organizational and collective processes that embody the social structure of inequality and have varied influences on different racial and ethnic groups. (William Julius Wilson)

INTRODUCTION

In the United States it is not uncommon to find black Americans perceiving white people as morally responsible for slavery and contemporary black/white inequality. Although doing this and inducing whites to feel collective guilt for the sins of their fathers can produce useful outcomes such as lowered racism and increased willingness to make various forms of reparations to blacks, this backward-looking strategy for assigning moral responsibility is not without problems. Some philosophers may object that only individuals, not collectives, can bear moral responsibility. And whenever individuals are held "collectively" responsible, this only makes sense if their personal deeds qualify them for membership in the group. While other philosophers are skeptical about collective guilt as such, they allow that a community of persons can indeed take political responsibility for the sins of their fathers, even though their own deeds do not causally connect them directly to the past wrong doing (Arendt 2003). Other proponents of political responsibility argue that a nonmysterious account requires an indirect, albeit quite complicated and diffuse, connection between persons and past wrongdoing and present unjust outcomes (Young 2011). We shall take it for granted that this notion of political responsibility is useful for thinking about our duty to do something about inequality. However, we shall argue for grounding it in a forward-looking manner given the limits of a backward-looking approach brought to light by social psychological data.

Black Americans might remain hopeful that whites en masse come to feel collective guilt and eventually take up political responsibility for historical injustice and its lingering effects. However, there are also nonphilosophical reasons for doubting that they will do so. Because dominant group members' identities are at stake and it is generally painful to see one's group as having acted immorally in the past and to feel guilt for having done so, people have a variety of defenses to avoid taking political responsibility for injustice or inequality. In previous work we consider the implications for philosophical theorizing about egalitarian justice of "shifting standards of injustice," namely the amount and nature of evidence that persons—depending on their class, race, or gender—rely upon to reach their conclusions about the fairness of inequality (Darby and Branscombe 2012). In keeping with our general view that normative political philosophy should consider how people actually think and behave as members of social groups, this sequel considers some of these responsibility-deflecting defenses and examines their ramifications for how we ought to ground political responsibility for unjust racial inequality.

In this article we argue that a forward-looking basis for grounding our shared political responsibility to address unjust racial inequality is attractive given what we know from empirical research in social psychology about the limits of playing the blame game (Sullivan et al. 2012), about how majority ingroup members frame inequality as a problem of minority disadvantage rather than majority privilege to avoid blame and collective guilt (Powell, Branscombe, and Schmitt 2005), and about how placing blame on the majority can be an obstacle to majority members forging the political solidarity with the minority that is necessary for collectively changing unjust social institutions (Subašić, Reynolds, and Turner 2008). We develop our argument by drawing upon the role that basic societal institutions—on which we all depend and have a stake in sustaining—play in shaping the distributive outcomes that stem from a unified system of social cooperation.

THE PSYCHOLOGY OF WHITE COLLECTIVE GUILT

When people categorize themselves as members of a social group that is associated with inequitable treatment or harm doing toward others, they can experience *collective guilt* even though they had no personal role in causing the harm. To the extent that they see their group (which is a part of the social self) as responsible for actions that they deem to be illegitimate, collective guilt for the group's past immoral actions can be felt (Branscombe 2004). Guilt for wrong doing—whether it be personal or collective—is a highly aversive emotion and is therefore one that people have powerful defenses they can deploy to help them avoid it. However, when the experience cannot be avoided, and the individual is forced to conclude that their group is responsible for injustice that has not been repaired, numerous positive social benefits can emerge.

First of all, people can be motivated to restore justice and repair the harm done. A variety of empirical studies have linked the experience of collective guilt (e.g., "I feel guilty about white Americans' harmful actions toward black Americans;" "I feel guilty about the negative things my ancestors did to black Americans") with willingness to make compensation in the form of monetary allocations, support for official apology for the ingroup's actions, and support for affirmative action to improve the outcomes of the previously harmed group (Branscombe, Slugoski, and Kappen 2004; Doosje et al. 1998; Iyer, Leach, and Crosby 2003; McGarty and Bliuc 2004). By perceiving one's group as illegitimately privileged at the expense of another group, which can induce collective guilt, racist attitudes can be reduced (Powell et al. 2005). This is consistent with Martin Luther King Jr.'s claim that "remorse can raise the moral threshold of a society." Collective guilt, which encompasses such remorse, can indeed promote the desire to correct unjust wrongs of the past.

When it can be induced, collective guilt clearly has benefits. But inducing it requires that we call attention to a group's negative history, and this is not without risks. In contrast to collectivist cultures where people define themselves in terms of their group memberships, in a highly individualistic culture such as the United States, where people often define themselves separate from the groups they belong to, it is especially easy for white individuals to deny collective responsibility and guilt for slavery (Triandis 1995). There are other defenses apart from denial they can employ to lessen their group's responsibility and hence the extent to which collective guilt for slavery is experienced. People can minimize the harm done. They can perceive the harm as impossible to correct. They can derogate the victims, which as Albert Bandura (1990) has pointed out allows perpetrator groups to be "less burdened by distress" when faced with their wrongdoing. And they can also legitimize the harm done as consistent with the times, with what other groups have done so not uniquely bad, or as having served some greater moral good (Branscombe and Miron 2004). Such defensive strategies can also affect attributions of collective responsibility by whites for why they are better off than blacks today on many measures of social inequality (Johnson et al. 2003; Miron, Warner, and Branscombe 2011; Sigelman and Welch 1991).

When people's valued social identities are at stake, they may be strongly tempted to defend that identity, and do so by legitimizing their group's "questionable" actions as a means of restoring the moral value of their group. To the extent that the differential outcomes of the groups can be seen as legitimate, collective guilt is undermined (Miron et al. 2006). Likewise, perceiving the costs of correcting the past as very difficult or impossible can reduce collective guilt and the motivation to do so (Schmitt et al. 2008). Thus, it is clear that perceiving the ingroup as responsible for past wrong doing will not inevitably evoke collective guilt, precisely because people can creatively legitimize those past actions and separate the current ingroup from members in the past who did the harm.

Moreover, it is not certain that people will perceive existing racial inequality as directly stemming from that past, and to the extent that they do not there will be little motivation to correct existing inequality. For instance, it has been noted that reparations for past wrongs are more likely to be supported when past harms experienced can be linked to present circumstances (Brooks 1999). But who we are (i.e., our political ideology, group membership) affects willingness to see links between unfair past victimization and the group's present situation. For white Americans, political conservatism predicts unwillingness to view historical injustice effects as persisting into the present and therefore low support for reparations. However, this is not the case for members of the group suffering the historical injustice. Political ideology in this case did not predict support for reparations; rather African Americans support reparations for both their own group as well as Native Americans, regardless of their own political orientation (Banfield, Ross, and Blatz 2014).

A further problem is that triggering these defenses is counter-productive to generating the multiracial collective societal effort necessary to reduce unjust racial inequality. William Julius Wilson (1999) argues against allowing racial ideology to undermine building the multiracial political coalitions necessary for structural change and reducing social inequality. In the same vein, we call for moving from a politics of individual blame to a politics of forward-looking shared political responsibility for racial inequality. The benefits of backward-looking shared responsibility and collective guilt notwithstanding, in view of other empirical evidence from social psychology, we think that playing the blame game poses a serious obstacle to building the diverse political coalitions necessary to combat racial inequality *when taking people as they are rather than as we wish or imagine them to be*. The foregoing evidence invites us to retool the philosophical case for why we must share responsibility for racial inequality.

THE LIMITS OF BACKWARD-LOOKING RESPONSIBILITY

The inducement of collective guilt encourages us to ground responsibility by looking backward. Because collective guilt is an emotional experience that people are typically motivated to avoid, and because we assume that normative arguments should be rooted in realistic assumptions about persons, we defend a less threatening means of motivating people to take political responsibility for doing something about unjust racial inequality. We do this by advocating a forward-looking approach to grounding political responsibility; however, we refrain from assuming that this approach is trouble-free, though we will not address its problems here. In this section we distinguish these approaches and discuss shortcomings of the backward-looking one.

Atrocities such as slavery, genocide, rape, sex trafficking, and apartheid provide an occasion for thinking about moral responsibility. These and other evils compel us to raise questions such as: Who is to blame? Who should be liable for harm? Is the passage of time, or the psychological state of the perpetrators, relevant to how and whether we attribute responsibility? Can collective agents as well as individuals be held responsible for atrocities? Should we distinguish between those who are directly responsible for bringing them about due to their actions and those who are indirectly responsible due to their omissions and is there a morally significant difference between the two? While these are among the important philosophical questions raised by atrocities, there is a further issue that gets to the nub of the matter we examine in this article.

For those who embrace the idea of collective moral responsibility, attributions of this sort can be backward-looking or forward-looking (Gilbert 2006). The former involve making a causal connection between agents' actions or inactions and the outcome for which they are being held morally responsible. "Sex traffickers are morally responsible for the physical and psychological harms done to victims of the sex trade" is an example of the former. If the trafficking was run by an oppressive government, which forced some of its citizens to participate, say, upon threat of death to a loved one, this would be a case where the traffickers were causally connected to the harm, though we might refrain from holding them morally responsible for it. Although a causal connection is necessary for assignment of backward-looking moral responsibility, it is not always sufficient since we must also rule out mitigating factors such as coercion. "Society is responsible for bearing the costs of treating victims of the sex trade" is an example of the latter. In cases of forward-looking responsibility, such as this one, a causal connection is not necessary to establish moral responsibility for doing something about the sex trade, anything from stopping it, alleviating current and future suffering of victims, or bearing the costs of enforcement or deterrence measures. A causal connection, in this case, is inessential for recognizing a collective moral duty to address the problem. This type of moral responsibility is more like holding one another collectively responsible for ameliorating the effects of Hurricane Katrina despite the fact that we are not causally responsible for the storm, the broken levees, or the inability of its victims to escape the devastation.

Moral atrocities like slavery, genocide, and sex trafficking, which we shall describe as instances of *manifest evil*, encourage us to adopt a backward-looking approach to shared moral responsibility. They invite us to look back to the past to determine guilt, to place blame, and to assign responsibility, sanctions, or remedies. Successful assignments of responsibility are predicated on identifying victims and perpetrators and establishing a plausible causal connection between harm done to the victims and the acts or omissions of perpetrators. But this can be difficult to establish, particularly when dealing with manifest evil that occurred further back in time such as black chattel slavery. For example, some critics will make the obvious point that there are no longer living slaves or slaveholders. So even if we grant that slaves are owed reparations, those who rightfully stand to benefit and those who are obliged to pay are long gone.

We certainly do not deny the importance of holding persons—either individually or collectively—responsible for manifest evil, nor do we reject the value of seeking some form of reparations for historical injustice. Yet it is important to realize that manifest evil does not provide the only occasion for taking up questions of responsibility. As recent arguments in favor of racial reparations for Jim Crow and its effects appreciate, social inequalities in the distribution of goods, resources, capabilities, and opportunities also provide such an occasion (Kaplan and Valls 2007; McCarthy 2004; Williams and Collins 2004). For instance, disproportionate sentencing of blacks and whites for similar drug offences, in receiving the death penalty, in who gets stopped and frisked, in the quality and safety of neighborhoods where they live, in their home values, in their educational achievement and attainment, in their levels of income and wealth, in their health outcomes such as infant mortality, obesity, and heart disease, and in the resilience of their communities to recover from natural disasters, also prompt us to think about responsibility. But these matters do not necessarily require us to look back to the past *with the aim of locating blame and assigning guilt*, though this has often been the case in practice. Indeed, this can even be counter-productive, particularly when the argument for shared political responsibility turns on what are bound to be controversial accounts of the causes of racial inequality, which are frequently complex, multiple, and difficult to disentangle (Darby 2009, 2010).

Critics of efforts to assign shared political responsibility for inequality may also question whether racial disparities are necessarily a problem from the standpoint of justice, while acknowledging that there may be other normative objections to them, for example, consequentialist ones (Wilkinson and Pickett 2010). It may be objected that such inequalities do not immediately raise cause for concern, especially if one thinks that they stem from the voluntary choices of persons rather than from what Ronald Dworkin calls bad brute luck or from circumstances beyond a person's control (Darby and Branscombe 2012). And, unfortunately, at least when it comes to racial inequality, this thought is fairly common in so-called "post-racial" America (Bobo 2012). An abiding feature of post-racial thought is that black disadvantage and racial inequality—by whatever socioeconomic indicator of well-being one is considering—is largely due to the choices or lack of effort of blacks rather than past or ongoing formal or informal racial discrimination (Darby and Saatcioglu 2014).

Recent survey data on racial attitudes concerning racial inequality and black disadvantage shows that this perspective is not anomalous (Bobo et al. 2012). If one holds some such view, as do many critics of government-sponsored efforts to ameliorate racial disparities, then the search for responsibility will be deemed warranted only if it stays focused on those persons (blacks) who have allegedly failed to make the right choices or to put in the right amount of effort to avoid disadvantage. And this will have consequences for whether or not white majority members are prepared to take political responsibility for doing something about racial inequality, whether it be supporting affirmative action, social welfare, school desegregation, or endorsing other strategies for enabling blacks to take full advantage of formal equality of opportunity (Powell et al. 2005).

Of course we can dismiss such explanations as mere ideology (in a pejorative sense), as race baiting, or as claims not supported by creditable empirical evidence. Although we find it incredulous to think that group-based racial inequalities can simply be chalked up to poor choices and lack of effort given empirical evidence to the contrary (Sidanius and Pratto 1999; Wilson 2009), at the same time, because of what we do know about group psychology, we think it is advisable to avoid tethering forward-looking political responsibility for doing something about inequality to backward-looking blameworthy responsibility for causing inequality.

Therefore, when considering social problems such as inequality and poverty, if we raise the same sorts of questions that we raise when considering manifest evil (e.g., who is to blame? who should pay?), and if we adopt the same backward-looking model for analyzing responsibility that we use in those cases, we will run into serious problems. Given what we know from empirical research on the psychology of groups, we will face substantial obstacles to persuading persons to take political responsibility for these inequalities and other social problems when they deny having responsibility for having "caused" them in the first place. Moreover, some data suggests that by following this model we also undermine efforts to get white majority group members to act in solidarity with blacks and other social reformers and to take political action to mitigate unjust racial inequalities (Subašić et al. 2008).

As we noted earlier in the case of responsibility for slavery, in view of various objections including concerns about the passage of time and establishing links between past wrongs and present circumstances, the best way of responding has been to consider the relationship between present (inequality) and less ancient evils (Jim Crow). But this strategy will have limited effect on those who place great significance on *Brown v. Board of Education*, the Civil Rights Movement, and Lyndon B. Johnson's Great Society programs, and view them as having driven the nail in the coffin of the dark legacy of racial injustice in America, wiping the slate clean, and finally realizing the ideal of equality of opportunity (Horowitz 2002). In response, we can certainly argue that we still have formal and informal racial discrimination in America and that we are still living with the effects of past wrongs (Feagin 2000; Sidanius and Pratto 1999). Yet we must acknowledge that these responses will have limited effect if the goal of recalling the past and linking it to the present is *primarily* to assign blame. At most, we can recall the past to under-stand where we are, how we got here, and to think from the standpoint of public policy about what to do moving forward. Nelson Mandela's politics of reconcilia-tion in post-apartheid South Africa is arguably the most familiar example of this strategy (Branscombe and Cronin 2010). And, along with Desmond Tutu's (1999) approach, it requires a forward-looking emphasis, without ignoring or forgetting the past.

Admittedly, this will be a much less radical argument than some progressives might hope for, but it may be the most we can do given the limits of playing the blame game. Ironically, as current research shows, some whites have themselves played this game to their benefit, which further complicates the blaming strategy. For example, black Americans are underrepresented in U.S. universities compared with whites (Epenshade and Radford 2009), which historically can be traced to past discrimination. Yet, when white Americans are focused on their group's responsi-bility for the disparity in college admissions, they respond in a "competitive victimhood" fashion (Sullivan et al. 2012). That is, whites uniquely claimed that it was their racial group that was discriminated against in the college admissions process. In contrast, when another group was considered responsible for the racial disparity, no such claims of "white victimization by racial discrimination" were made. This same process of defending one's group by claiming to be the "true victims" when it is accused of having committed harm against another group has been observed in other powerful groups such as men when accusations of harm to women are made. Thus, the threat that can be raised by implied ingroup respon-sibility for harmful actions toward another group encourages majority groups to defend their group's moral identity (over and above any concerns with material benefits that might be gained).

Grounding our obligation to change unjust social institutions, or to do something about unjust racial inequality, in forward-looking political responsibility is advisable in view of these empirical findings. However, as those who fought against racial apartheid in South Africa appreciated, ignoring or forgetting about the past and its connection to the present is not an attractive option—even if our best hope for fostering shared political responsibility may ultimately require that we refrain from assigning each other blame for the past sins of our fathers. Such knowledge of the past, and its present effects, is clearly vital for determining the content of public policy to mitigate unjust inequality and for addressing absolute disadvantage. Moreover, minority ingroup members will balk at forgetting the past and view this as an instance of disrespect, which will undoubtedly undermine their willingness to cooperate in a multi-racial, ethnic, and class coalition to mitigate unjust inequality and address absolute disadvantage (Huo and Molina 2006).

Consider, for instance, that American ethnic/racial minority group members who perceive that white Americans do not respect their history and experiences of discrimination have less positive attitudes toward America and display less trust in the existing justice system. Such "forgetting of the past" is perceived as disrespectful. Although playing the blame game has serious drawbacks, we cannot confront our shared political responsibility without addressing the host of injustices (e.g., inequality, poverty, joblessness, and the "New Jim Crow") that flow from the basic structure of society, which is comprised of the interrelated practices and processes that we all have a hand in sustaining in our capacity as citizens actively pursuing our individual good and rational plan of life in cooperation with others within shared social institutions. This idea, which will be familiar to readers of Rawls, is crucial to our argument for forward-looking responsibility for racial inequality.

INEQUALITY AND THE BASIC STRUCTURE

A backward-looking model for grounding political responsibility for racial inequality is limited under nonideal circumstances when we consider evidence concerning the various problems, risks, and defenses involved when we make such attributions. Attending to empirical data regarding the relationship between attributions of responsibility and our social identities, and to how identity-driven attributions can derail backward-looking attributions of political responsibility for racial inequality insofar as these entail playing the blame game, suggest the need for an alternative strategy for grounding shared political responsibility that is compatible with these findings. But before arguing that citizens have a forward-looking shared political responsibility for racial inequality, which satisfies this constraint, we must first elucidate the nature of what Rawls calls the basic structure of society and its relationship to social inequality more generally and racial inequality in particular.

Social practices, which are comprised of a set of formal or informal rules that assign roles to participants, generally specify how participants may or may not act in pursuit of certain goals. And these practices often provide incentives or sanctions to encourage participants to act in the proscribed ways. Competitive games such as soccer or basketball are instances of social practices with these features; but so too are organized political societies. Political philosophers and theorists have staked out various explanations of why we choose to form and maintain this particular social practice. For example, social contract theorists have long argued that we collectively participate in organized societies (whether democratic or nondemocratic) to achieve mutually beneficial goals such as pleasure, welfare, security, or, as Hobbes might say, to attain the things we desire for a commodious living. Others, especially thinkers within the liberal philosophical tradition, have argued that we form political societies to pursue our individual good or rational plans of life in cooperation with others. However the purpose of organized political societies is understood, if we focus on our participation as citizens within society, we need rules to specify the terms of our social cooperation within this distinctive social practice.

Following Rawls (1971, 7), we can use the term "social institutions" to describe the rules that constitute the basic structure of society, which "distribute fundamental rights and duties and determine the division of advantages from social cooperation." These institutions have the formal features generally described above: they assign roles, they specify the permitted range of action within the roles, and they provide persons with motivation for acting accordingly since they are generally backed up by various kinds of formal and informal sanctions. These major societal institutions, which collectively form a unified system of social cooperation, profoundly shape the life prospects of everyone participating in the practice. As Rawls (1971, 7) puts it, the institutions that make up the basic structure determine a person's "life prospects, what they can expect to be and how well they can hope to do."

Rawls identifies the political constitution, the economic system, which regulates markets and property, and the monogamous family as examples of major social institutions which, when considered together, comprise the basic structure of society. Political theorist Iris Young criticizes Rawls, somewhat unfairly, for seeking to identify some small subset of institutions within society that are more essential than others for determining our life prospects. She proposes instead that the injustice-generating features of society are not comprised of static institutions taken individually or collectively but rather are constituted by what she calls "social-structural processes," in which "the actions of masses of people within a large number of institutions converge in their efforts to produce [certain] patterns and positioning" in the distribution of goods, resources, and opportunities (Young 2011, 70).

Young's qualification has the virtue of emphasizing the interrelationship between individual agency and social institutions, and disabusing us of the idea that there is some evil rational planner pulling the strings of the basic structure to intentionally advantage some and disadvantage others. Yet we see no harm in acknowledging, as Rawls does, that some institutions play especially important roles in this process. Rawls concedes that "the concept of the basic structure is somewhat vague" and allows that it may be filled out in different ways. Indeed, we might add more precision to the concept, and in ways that highlight the processes Young has in mind, by attending to observations made by Wilson (1999, 98):

Among these processes are the institutional influences on mobility and opportunity, including activities of employers' associations and labor unions; the operation and organization of schools, the mechanisms of residential racial segregation and social isolation in poor neighborhoods; categorical forms of discrimination in hiring, promotion, and other work-related matters; ideologies of group differences shared by members of society and institutionalized in organizational practices and norms that affect social outcomes; and differential racial and ethnic group access to information concerning the labor market, financial markets, education and training, schools, and so on.

However we render the concept more precise, one thing is clear: the basic structure and processes have a profound and comprehensive impact on our life prospects from cradle to grave. As Young (2011, 34) observes, they have broad consequences for people's basic well-being, for the range of options available to them, and for their vulnerability to certain forms of oppression, domination, and deprivation. Moreover, as Wilson (1999, 98) notes, these "organizational and collective processes that embody the social structure of inequality have varied influences on different racial and ethnic groups."

This last point is particularly significant for our argument. Although the basic structure determines life prospects, it does so in well ordered societies by interacting with contingencies such as a person's social class background, their natural talents and abilities, their opportunities for education to develop these endowments, and their good or bad luck over their life course. In societies that are not well ordered, such as ones where all citizens do not enjoy equal rights and basic liberties or a fair chance to secure opportunities and offices open to others, additional contingencies such as race, ethnicity, gender, and sexual orientation may also contribute to the shaping of life prospects within the basic structure. They can do so either formally via exclusion based on group membership (e.g., racial segregation) or informally (e.g., subtle discrimination) or by affecting the abilities of the minority itself (e.g., stereotype threat). Therefore, given the ways in which these contingencies interact with the basic structure and the sorts of processes Wilson describes, some measure of social inequality in goods, resources, and opportunities appears to be an inevitable consequence of these background social practices that govern the terms of our cooperation. In well ordered societies we would expect these inequalities to be solely class-based, but in other societies such as the United States they will also be based on race and ethnicity.

For the argument we present in the next section, it would suffice simply to show that social inequality is a *consequence* of the basic structure. But Rawls (2005, 270) goes one step further in claiming that social inequality is also highly advantageous for maintaining effective social cooperation in well designed and effectively organized societies for various reasons including the need for incentives. If Rawls is right both about this and about the inevitability of inequality, then social inequalities are both a consequence and a virtue of the basic structure. Of course there are limits to how much inequality egalitarians are prepared to accept, which explains why they have distinguished permissible from impermissible ones. Many egalitarians have followed Rawls in holding that within a well ordered society only inequalities that work to the benefit of the least advantaged persons are permissible. Now that we have elaborated on the nature of the basic structure and its relationship to social inequality more generally and racial inequality in particular, and with the claim that racial inequality is a consequence of the basic structure in hand, we have all that we need to complete our argument for why citizens have forward-looking shared political responsibility for racial inequality.

FORWARD-LOOKING RESPONSIBILITY FOR INEQUALITY

One can adopt a backward-looking or forward-looking approach to grounding shared political responsibility for racial inequality: one that looks back to establish some normatively relevant causal connection between agents and particular outcomes, or one that looks forward to ground individual or collective obligations to bring about a state of affairs. The former is attractive because it takes personal responsibility seriously and squares with the intuition that persons should be responsible for what they *do*. The latter conception is sometimes disparaged for seemingly removing individual agency from consideration in grounding responsibility. Something to dislike about the backward-looking conception is that it too easily absolves us of responsibility where causation cannot be readily established. And something to like about the forward-looking conception is that it does not do this. A philosophically attractive account of shared political responsibility for racial inequality would be forward-looking but without entirely setting aside the significance of individual agency in assigning responsibility.

Young (2011) rejects Hannah Arendt's account of political responsibility but applauds her for distinguishing it from collective guilt. Young finds Arendt's account of responsibility deficient in two respects: it makes persons politically responsible for what they have not done, and it grounds political responsibility in merely being a member of some group such as a nation, family, race, or class and inheriting responsibility for the evils, wrongs, or injustice done by the group. Young proposes an alternative account of political responsibility rooted in an obligation to share responsibility for unjust social structures and processes and taking political responsibility for changing them. This obligation is rooted not merely in our *being citizens* but in our *participation as citizens* in a political system of social cooperation that facilitates the existence of structural injustices.

According to Young's conception of political responsibility, individual agency plays an essential role in accounting for our forward-looking shared moral responsibility for injustice. This is attractive because it preserves the moral intuition that persons should only be held responsible for what they *do*, whether construed narrowly as actions or more broadly as omissions. What is commendable about Young's conception is that political responsibility can play this role without being conflated with the backward-looking moral responsibility typically associated with finding individual persons guilty of—and blaming them for—causing social injustice. The social psychological data we have considered gives us compelling reasons for insisting upon a distinction between forward-and-backward looking conceptions of political responsibility and for preferring the former under nonideal circumstances.

Young develops her forward-looking account of shared political responsibility for injustice using the case of vulnerability to homelessness. She observes that persons can end up in this position due to *social-structural injustice*, which "occurs as a consequence of many individuals and institutions acting to pursue their particular goals and interests, for the most part within the limits of accepted rules and norms" (Young 2011, 52). And she argues that our active participation in social processes (of the sort that Wilson identifies), which facilitate these countless interactions, gives us political responsibility for this injustice. This argument can be adapted and developed to make a similar case for responsibility for inequality.

All citizens pursue their life plans and exercise and develop the capacities essential for citizenship within the basic structure of society. And this interrelated system of rules and processes, which regulate our political constitution and our markets and system of exchange, as well as the production, development, and education of future citizens within the institution of family, are essential for facilitating our social cooperation in pursuit of these aims over the course of a complete life. There is great variety in the life plans that people choose. These choices impact our individual share of primary social goods such as income and wealth, and they often figure in moral assessments of our individual conduct and character. Yet they are made within the opportunity set afforded to us within the basic structure of society, which allows some to amass advantage and others disadvantage based on their social position.

So, for example, our choices about raising a family, work, schooling, and housing are all constrained by rules and processes, such as taxation, inheritance, property, zoning and school finance, which impact the opportunities available to us given our class background, our talents, our luck, and our race—in societies such as the United States that are not well ordered. Young (2011, 55) observes that this feature of the basic structure need not be coercive. As she says: "Social structures do not constrain in the form of the direct coercion of some individuals over others; they constrain more indirectly and cumulatively as blocking possibilities." We should add, *pace* Rawls (2005, 269), that the basic structure also facilitates possibilities insofar as it is also an institutional scheme "for satisfying existing desires and aspirations" and "fashioning desires and aspirations in the future." It thus provides the structural context for determining who we are and who we want to be.

Given the profound, comprehensive, and inescapable impact of these institutions on our lives, and assuming that our life prospects within the cooperative practice of organized society are exceedingly better than fending for ourselves in the state of nature, we all have a fundamental interest in *sustaining* the institutions that make up the basic structure of society. The creation and continued existence of the major institutions and social structural processes that determine our life prospects and facilitate our actions in pursuit of various ends all require our social cooperation.

In the course of such cooperation, we must make, accept, and abide by, and moreover, enforce conventions, which we do in different ways depending on our system of government. We do these things through voting within a democratic society, which is why political liberties are counted among the primary goods by Rawls. But even if we do not vote, or find ways to evade active participation in democratic governance, we clearly still have an interest in sustaining these institutions and processes. Were it the case that many fewer people or no one voted or participated in democratic governance then the social practice of organized society would whither away and we would be stuck with our least preferable outcome of fending for ourselves in a state of nature. So, clearly, we all have an interest in the basic structure remaining intact and ensuring that our social cooperation takes place on fair terms. Therefore, on this forward-looking model of responsibility, our agency is absolutely essential for preserving the major institutions that set the terms of our social cooperation and we all share a political responsibility for bearing the costs of its unjust consequences.

Within the social contract tradition considerable attention has been placed on the *creation* of society and the establishment of institutions and rules that constitute its basic structure. This focus on origins may partly explain why philosophical accounts of political responsibility are backward-looking. For instance, if we focus exclusively on the extent to which parties helped to create the life-prospect shaping basic structure, we may be inclined to attribute whatever negative consequences flow from this to all who had a hand in creating the basic structure, and this encourages us to look back to make such determinations. The shift to a forward-looking account of political responsibility requires placing greater emphasis on the interests we all share in sustaining the major social institutions that so profoundly shape our life prospects—a point that Young does not fully appreciate in focusing on the complex way we contribute to injustices that flows from them. So even though we may not have created the basic structure—having inherited it from our ancestors—we nonetheless have a vital interest its endurance. Therefore, assuming with Rawls, Wilson, and Young that social inequality is an inevitable outcome of the basic structure, and further assuming that we share responsibility for its outcomes, we should also take political responsibility for inequality given our vital interest in sustaining the system of cooperation and institutions that give rise to both permissible and impermissible inequalities.

Unfair racial inequalities in the distribution of goods, resources, opportunities, or in the various benefits and burdens of our social cooperation are a paramount concern of social justice. Such inequalities can certainly stem from intentional efforts on the part of specific parties. Within the social sciences there is ongoing debate over the extent to which persisting racial inequalities in wealth, political power, education and other measures are due to such efforts. Where these efforts are motivated by social group animus or racial bias they are described as instances of discrimination. Although they can arise and be perpetuated without conscious intention (Adams et al. 2008), in post-racial America many believe that racial inequalities can only be judged unjust if they can be traceable to discrimination with racist intent.

Although formal and informal discrimination continues to account for racial inequalities, a point that is far from uncontroversial, they need not stem from such discrimination. In other words, we need not presume that bias is operative, or that some parties are not playing by the rules, or that government is out to get those most disadvantaged by racial inequalities to declare them unjust. The basic structure provides us with an alternative perspective from which to normatively

evaluate racial inequality. And provided that we remain focused on our individual
and shared interest in sustaining this structure, it affords us a forward-looking
justification of why we should take political responsibility for doing something
about it, which aims to circumvent blame-switching and other defenses by which
those who are not disadvantaged aim to absolve themselves of responsibility. This
is a virtue because, as Young (2011, 117) notes, when focused on structural injustice
(or racial inequality), "it is difficult to make blame 'stick' to anyone in particular,
because almost everyone is involved."

Thus, on this model, we have shared political responsibility for inequality
even if we have not acted unfairly in our dealings with others, have treated others
with equal respect and concern, have minded our business, and have not caused
their plight in the sense of being morally blameworthy for it. The basic structure
and processes can produce inequality even when individuals are acting justly.
Inequality can result, as Young (2011, 117) puts it, "from a complex combination of
actions and policies by individual, corporate, and government agents—actions and
policies that most people consider normal and acceptable, or even necessary and
good." As we noted earlier, Wilson (1999) offers a useful account of some of the
policies and processes that produce racial inequalities in the United States.

This forward-looking model of responsibility can be fruitfully elaborated
upon using Margaret Gilbert's (2006) notion of being jointly committed. We might
say that citizens have a "joint commitment" to sustaining the institutions and
processes that make it possible to pursue their aims cooperatively. How and why
they form, uphold, or breach this commitment is not germane to our present
purposes. All that matters is that this commitment be viewed as unifying citizens to
work toward a common project, namely sustaining the basic structure and processes that vitally shape the terms of their social cooperation, which all have an
interest in contributing to. Some accounts of collective responsibility are interested
in examining the relationship between the blameworthiness of the collective and
the blameworthiness of particular members; however, this would be unattractive
for our purposes. Indeed the reason to advance a forward-looking model of responsibility is precisely to avoid analyzing responsibility for inequality in personal
terms. But to eschew analyzing this in personal terms is not to reject the importance
of agency in establishing responsibility altogether. Hence the attractiveness of
rooting political responsibility in joint commitment is that it locates agency in
undertaking such a commitment. It is important to emphasize that this commitment only serves to locate a person within the relevant group, which shares responsibility, and not to hold them morally blameworthy for its action, or even for their
membership in this group.

We must be careful, however, about how we specify the content of this joint
commitment. For example, consider our premise that racial inequality is an inevitable consequence of the basic structure, which means that some will be disadvantaged in the distribution of income and wealth based upon their social position. To
say that citizens have a joint commitment to sustaining the basic structure will not,
then, be tantamount to saying that they have a joint commitment to a common
project of wronging certain members of society, say by subjugating them or treating
them unequal (Thompson 2006). This would negate the point that participants

within organized society might be acting in accordance with the prescribed norms and there still be unfair racial inequalities. Moreover, this way of understanding the content of citizen's being jointly committed amounts to an indirect way of interpreting shared political responsibility as a special case of *blameworthy* personal responsibility. Instead, the content of this joint commitment is, more generally, to sustaining the institutions and processes needed to pursue our individual aims. Because these have consequences such as creating inequalities when persons act in accordance with the rules, we must share the burden of these outcomes even in the absence of moral blame.

So the joint commitment, as we envision it, is not to be bound by the decisions of the authorities or the social contract (either past or present), but rather it is to sustaining the basic structure, which makes the common pursuit of ends in organized political society possible. The former envisions responsibility as backward looking to repair or to make amends for unjust acts and decisions. The latter conceives of it in a forward-looking manner to sustain the structures that make our collective life possible. Therefore, the notion of joint commitment for inequality allows us to treat citizens as being jointly committed to bearing the burden of sharing responsibility for doing something about racial inequality without also accepting personal responsibility for it. This is not ideal; but neither is the world we live in. And in our less than perfect world, this strategy is attractive given the evidence of the real problems associated with waiting for collective guilt to induce whites to take political responsibility for doing something about the pressing social problem of unjust racial inequality.

CONCLUSION

In this article we have argued for a forward-looking approach to grounding political responsibility for racial inequality. This enables us to avoid the pitfalls of a backward-looking approach, which empirical research in social psychology brings to light. Some critics will worry that our argument lets off the hook those who might be guilty of racial inequality–generating discrimination. They may also complain that it does not squarely confront the ideological assumptions that blame the victims of racial inequality for their disadvantage. These are serious concerns. However, if we attend to evidence concerning how people actually think and behave given their respective social identities, thereby taking persons as they are rather than as we wish or imagine them to be, it is clear that playing the blame game—regardless of where the blame is taken to rest—will not be a winning strategy in this day and age. Assuming that addressing unfair racial inequalities will require multi-racial collective action or shared burdens on the part of citizens who are differently motivated based on their social identities, the evidence we have considered justifies grounding political responsibility for racial inequality in a forward-looking manner. We have done this by rooting it in a joint civic commitment to do what we must to sustain the basic structure that makes organized society possible and productive. Forward-looking political responsibility for inequality may not give us all that we want but it gives us all that we can reasonably hope to get in our nonideal world.

136   *Derrick Darby and Nyla R. Branscombe*

REFERENCES

Adams, Glenn, Biernat, Monica, Branscombe, Nyla R., Crandall, Christian S., and Wrightsman, Lawrence S. 2008. "Beyond Prejudice: Toward a Sociocultural Psychology of Racism and Oppression." In *Commemorating Brown: The Social Psychology of Racism and Discrimination*, ed. Glenn Adams, Monica Biernat, Nyla R. Branscombe, Christian S. Crandall, and Lawrence S. Wrightsman, 215–46. Washington, DC: American Psychological Association.

Arendt, Hannah. 2003. *Responsibility and Judgement*, ed. Jerome Kohn. New York: Schocken Books.

Bandura, Albert. 1990. "Selective Activation and Disengagement of Moral Control." *Journal of Social Issues* 46: 27–46.

Banfield, Jillian C., Ross, Michael, and Blatz, Craig W. 2014. "Responding to Historical Injustices: Does Group Membership Trump Liberal-Conservative Ideology?" *European Journal of Social Psychology* 44: 30–42.

Bobo, Lawrence D. 2012. "Somewhere between Jim Crow & Post-Racialism: Reflections on the Racial Divide in America Today." *Daedalus* 140: 11–36.

Bobo, Lawrence D., Camille, Z., Charles, Camille Z., Krysan, Maria, and Simmons, Alicia D. 2012. "The *Real* Record on Racial Attitudes." In *Social Trends in American Life: Findings from the General Social Survey since 1972*, ed. Peter V. Marsden, 38–83. Princeton, NJ: Princeton University Press.

Branscombe, Nyla R. 2004. "A Social Psychological Process Perspective on Collective Guilt." In *Collective Guilt: International Perspectives*, ed. Nyla R. Branscombe and Bertjan Doosje, 320–65. New York: Cambridge University Press.

Branscombe, Nyla R., and Cronin, Tracey. 2010. "Confronting the Past to Create a Better Future: The Antecedents and Benefits of Intergroup Forgiveness." In *Identity and Participation in Culturally Diverse Societies*, ed. Assaad Azzi, Xenia Chryssochoou, Bert Klandermans, and Bernd Simon, 338–358. Malden, MA: Wiley-Blackwell.

Branscombe, Nyla R., and Miron, Anca M. 2004. "Interpreting the Ingroup's Negative Actions toward Another Group: Emotional Reactions to Appraised Harm." In *The Social Life of Emotions*, ed. Larissa Z. Tiedens and C. W. Leach, 314–35. New York: Cambridge University Press.

Branscombe, Nyla R., Slugoski, Ben, and Kappen, Diane M. 2004. "The Measurement of Collective Guilt: What It Is and What It Is Not." In *Collective Guilt: International Perspectives*, ed. Nyla R. Branscombe and Bertjan Doosje, 16–34. New York: Cambridge University Press.

Brooks, Roy L. 1999. *When Sorry Isn't Enough: The Controversy over Apologies and Reparations for Human Injustice*. New York: New York University Press.

Darby, Derrick. 2009. "Educational Inequality and the Science of Diversity in *Grutter*: A Lesson for the Reparations Debate in the Age of Obama." *The University of Kansas Law Review* 57: 755–93.

———. 2010. "Reparations and Racial Inequality." *Philosophy Compass* 5: 55–66.

Darby, Derrick, and Branscombe, Nyla R. 2012. "Egalitarianism and Perceptions of Inequality." *Philosophical Topics* 40: 7–25.

Darby, Derrick, and Saatcioglu, Argun. 2014. "Race, Justice, and Desegregation." *Du Bois Review* 40(1): 87–108.

Doosje, Bertjan, Branscombe, Nyla R., Spears, Russell, and Manstead, Antony S. R. 1998. "Guilty by Association: When One's Group Has a Negative History." *Journal of Personality and Social Psychology* 75: 872–86.

Epenshade, Thomas J., and Radford, Alexandria W. 2009. *No Longer Separate, Not Yet Equal: Race and Class in Elite College Admission and Campus Life*. Princeton, NJ: Princeton University Press.

Feagin, Joe R. 2000. *Racist America: Roots, Current Realities, and Future Reparations*. New York: Routledge.

Gilbert, Margaret. 2006. "Who's to Blame? Collective Moral Responsibility and Its Implications for Group Members." *Midwest Studies in Philosophy* 30: 94–114.

Horowitz, David. 2002. *Uncivil Wars: The Controversy over Reparations for Slavery*. San Francisco: Encounter Books.

Huo, Yuen J., and Molina, Ludwin E. 2006. "Is Pluralism a Viable Model of Diversity? The Benefits and Limits of Subgroup Respect." *Group Processes and Intergroup Relations* 9: 359–76.

Iyer, Aarti, Leach, Colin W., and Crosby, Faye J. 2003. "White Guilt and Racial Compensation: The Benefits and Limits of Self-Focus." *Personality and Social Psychology Bulletin* 29: 117–29.

Johnson, James D., Simmons, Carolyn, Trawalter, Sophie, Ferguson, Tara, and William Reed, William. 2003. "Variation in Black Anti-White Bias and Target Distancing Cues: Factors that Influence Perceptions of 'Ambiguously Racist' Behavior." *Personality and Social Psychology Bulletin* 29: 609–22.

Kaplan, Jonathan, and Valls, Andrew. 2007. "Housing Discrimination as a Basis for Black Reparations." *Public Affairs Quarterly* 21: 255–73.

McCarthy, Thomas A. 2004. "Coming to Terms with Our Past, Part II: On the Morality and Politics of Reparations for Slavery." *Political Theory* 32: 750–72.

McGarty, Craig, and Bliuc, Ana-Maria. 2004. "Refining the Meaning of the 'Collective' in Collective Guilt: Harm, Guilt, and Apology in Australia." In *Collective Guilt: International Perspectives*, ed. Nyla R. Branscombe and Bertjan Doosje, 112–29. New York: Cambridge University Press.

Miron, Anca M., Branscombe, Nyla R., and Schmitt, Michael T. 2006. "Collective Guilt as Distress over Illegitimate Intergroup Inequality." *Group Processes and Intergroup Relations* 9: 163–80.

Miron, Anca M., Warner, Ruth H., and Branscombe, Nyla R. 2011. "Accounting for Group Differences in Appraisals of Social Inequality: Differential Injustice Standards." *British Journal of Social Psychology* 50: 342–53.

Powell, Adam A., Branscombe, Nyla R., and Schmitt, Michael T. 2005. "Inequality as Ingroup Privilege or Outgroup Disadvantage: The Impact of Group Focus on Collective Guilt and Interracial Attitudes." *Personality and Social Psychology Bulletin* 31: 508–21.

Rawls, John. 1971. *A Theory of Justice*. Cambridge, MA: Belknap Press.

———. 2005. *Political Liberalism*. New York: Columbia University Press.

Schmitt, Michael T., Miller, David A., Branscombe, Nyla R., and Brehm, Jack W. 2008. "The Difficulty of Making Reparations Affects the Intensity of Collective Guilt." *Group Processes and Intergroup Relations* 11: 267–79.

Sigelman, Lee, and Welch, Susan. 1991. *Black Americans' Views of Racial Inequality: The Dream Deferred*. New York: Cambridge University Press.

Sidanius, Jim, and Pratto, Felicia. 1999. *Social Dominance: An Intergroup Theory of Social Hierarchy and Oppression*. Cambridge: Cambridge University Press, 1999.

Subašić, Emina, Reynolds, Katherine J., and Turner, John C. 2008. "The Political Solidarity Model of Social Change: Dynamics of Self-Categorization in Intergroup Power Relations." *Personality and Social Psychology Review* 12: 330–52.

Sullivan, Daniel, Landau, Mark J., Branscombe, Nyla R., and Rothschild, Zachary K. 2012. "Competitive Victimhood as a Response to Accusations of Ingroup Harm Doing." *Journal of Personality and Social Psychology* 102: 778–95.

Thompson, J. 2006. "Collective Responsibility for Historic Injustices." *Midwest Studies in Philosophy* 30: 154–67.

Triandis, Harry C. 1995. *Individualism and Collectivism*. Boulder, CO: Westview Press.

Tutu, Desmond. 1999. *No Future without Forgiveness*. New York: Image Books.

Wilkinson, Ricard, and Pickett, Kate. 2010. *The Spirit Level: Why Greater Equality Makes Societies Stronger*. New York: Bloomsbury Press.

Williams, David R., and Collins, Chiquita. 2004. "Reparations: A Viable Strategy to Address the Enigma of African American Health." *The American Behavioral Scientist* 47: 977–1000.

Wilson, William Julius. 1999. *The Bridge over the Racial Divide: Racial Inequality and Coalition Politics*. Berkeley: University of California Press.

———. 2009. *More than Just Race: Being Black and Poor in the Inner City*. New York: W. W. Norton.

Young, Iris Marion. 2011. *Responsibility for Justice*. New York: Oxford University Press.

Midwest Studies In Philosophy, XXXVIII (2014)

War "In Our Name" and the Responsibility to Protest: Ordinary Citizens, Civil Society, and Prospective Moral Responsibility

NETA C. CRAWFORD

War—the use of armed force to coerce others for political purposes—entails not only hardship but difficult moral choices and dilemmas. Who should determine the resort to war? What role should ordinary civilian citizens play in decisions about resort to war and its conduct?

Decisions about resort to war and conduct in it are usually limited to a small number of elected or appointed officials. In legitimate sovereign states governing executive authorities have a legal monopoly on judgments about the legitimate use of violence. Legislatures may set the parameters for uses of force, or decide their budgets, and judiciaries may determine when laws are broken, but presidents and prime ministers generally make the determination of resort to war and then attempt to persuade others in the government that their decision is right. As Michael Walzer notes, civilian citizens tend to defer their judgments on war to leaders and "go along." He writes:

> When a state . . . commits itself to a campaign of aggression, its citizens (or many of them) are likely to go along, as Americans did during the Vietnam war, arguing that the war may after all be just; that it is not possible for them to be sure whether it is just or not; that their leaders know best and tell them this or that, which sounds plausible enough; and that nothing they can do will make much difference anyway. These are not immoral arguments, though they reflect badly on the society within which they are made.[1]

1. Michael Walzer, *Just and Unjust Wars: A Moral Argument with Historical Illustrations*, 3rd ed. (New York: Basic Books, 2000), 301.

Bad citizenship is not, nor should it be, an international crime of war, although bad citizenship can enable war crimes, and so, when citizens "go along" the people's retrospective responsibility for wars of aggression may be asserted. In late 1945, the philosopher Karl Jaspers argued to fellow Germans that in addition to individual criminal guilt for specific crimes committed in World War II, "a people answers for its polity"; the people, he argued, are "collectively liable" for the "acts committed by their state."[2] Jaspers asserts that "we are politically responsible for our regime, for the acts of the regime, for the start of the war in this world-historical situation."[3] Walzer suggests that citizens could do better: "in democracies there are opportunities for positive response." However, the rest of his sentence—"and we need to ask to what extent these opportunities fix our obligations, when evil deeds are committed in our name"—is more of an invitation to consider the problems involved than an answer to the question of the extent of our political obligations.[4]

The idea of the citizens' shame or guilt for war assumes their prospective individual and collective moral agency—that citizens should have and could have acted beforehand to change the course of events and that citizens failed to constrain their governments. As Peter French argues, blame implies a prior failure. "By our lack of preventive action, by our willingness to be governed poorly, or by our failure to grasp the significance of what we were doing, we showed ourselves to be substandard, that is, either below the standard we set for ourselves, traditionally or below the standard expected of the people of all nations in regard international behavior. We should have known better."[5]

On the other hand, citizens are not always so agreeable. Just war scholar John Williams explored the meaning of the slogan, "not in my name," used by citizen opponents of the Iraq invasion led by the United States and the United Kingdom during their February 2003 protest march in London, suggesting that, " 'not in my name' challenges established notions of legitimate authority in just war thinking—that this is the authority of the sovereign."[6] Williams argues that citizen assent for war cannot be assumed but must be *retained*—citizens must be persuaded that a war is necessary and justified. Williams continues: " 'Not in my name' marks a clear desire to withdraw that consent in relation to war, arguably the most fundamental arena of policy for the idea of sovereignty."[7] The assertion "reminds the political leaders that they are beholden to a political process and that the authority that they

2. Karl Jaspers, *The Question of German Guilt* (New York: Fordham University Press, 2000), 55.

3. Jaspers, *The Question of German Guilt*, 72. Jaspers was clear that liability was not the same as criminal guilt or moral and metaphysical guilt.

4. Walzer, *Just and Unjust Wars*, 298.

5. Peter A. French, "The Responsibility of Monsters and Their Makers." In *Individual and Collective Responsibility*, ed. Peter A. French (Rochester, VT: Schenkman Books, 1972, 1998), 8.

6. John Williams, " 'Not in My Name'? Legitimate Authority and Liberal Just War Theory," in *Just War: Authority, Tradition and Practice*, ed. Anthony F. Lang Jr., Cian O'Driscoll, and John Williams (Washington, DC: Georgetown University Press, 2013), 65.

7. Williams, " 'Not in My Name'?" 65.

claim derives from the people whom they ostensibly represent and to whom they should be accountable."[8]

> The desire of so many people to dissociate themselves from their governments' action was not on the whole, a philosophical claim about the complex relationship between authority and obligation on the brink of war. It was a political protest about the proposed course of action, the way in which that course had been decided upon, and a perceived lack of accountability to those whose authority was being invoked.[9]

The London march and rally Williams describes was part of a much larger civilian protest over the weekend of 15 and 16 February 2003, involving millions of people in more than 600 cities in 60 countries. In New York, 400,000 people marched passed the United Nations in extreme cold against a court order. Although estimates of the number anti-war protestors in Rome ranged from 650,000 to 3 million, Italian "State television, RAI, did not broadcast the protest live, saying it would put 'undue pressure on politicians'."[10] As Williams argued, "Withholding consent, even if only rhetorically, was a powerful statement because of the way it highlighted the tendency to take such consent for granted, to see the decision over war as being something that takes place at the level of national governments negotiating in what are now the smoke-free rooms and corridors of power."[11]

Yet, although the citizens' obligation in wartime is arguably one of the most important questions of politics, consideration of citizen participation has rarely extended beyond the assertion that civilian citizens have some role in the process and may be blamed for not acting. As Walzer suggests, "insofar as we can recognize aggression, there should be little difficulty in blaming heads of state. The hard and interesting problems arise when we ask how responsibility for aggression is diffused through a political system."[12] If ordinary citizens either individually or collectively are *not* responsible, then they cannot be morally blamed, for as French argues, "an essential element of all blaming is the existence of standards of performance, either implicit or explicit."[13]

8. Williams, " 'Not in My Name'?" 68. " 'Not in my name' is also a powerful political rejection of the claim to legitimate authority by a government over its own people." Williams, " 'Not in My Name'?" 75.

9. Williams, " 'Not in My Name'?" 75.

10. Angelique Chrisafis, David Fickling, John Henley, John Hooper, Giles Tremlett, Sophie Arie, and Chris McGreal, "Millions Wordwide Rally for Peace: Huge Turnout at 600 Marches from Berlin to Baghdad," *The Guardian*, February 16, 2003, http://www.theguardian.com/world/2003/feb/17/politics.uk.

11. Williams, " 'Not in My Name'?" 75.

12. Walzer, *Just and Unjust Wars*, 292.

13. Peter A. French, *War and Moral Dissonance* (Cambridge: Cambridge University Press, 2011), 233. Institutions for post-conflict justice, such as the International Criminal Court, that call individuals to account for criminal behavior in war, assume moral agency—that someone could have made different choices before war and behaved differently in war. International law focuses on *individual* perpetrators. I argue that there may also be collective moral agency and collective responsibility for conduct in war, specifically for cases of collateral damage. The military is morally responsible for collateral damage to the extent that the harm was foreseeable, and often foreseen, and could be minimized or completely avoided through changes in rules and procedures. Neta C.

That is just the point: civilians are supposed to be doing something *before* states go to war, and they ought to act to halt immoral behavior during war, but just what is it that citizens are supposed to do to fulfill these roles and how can they do it? Further, "it seems unfair to ascribe collective responsibility to a group which is not clearly structured to receive responsibility."[14] How is it that citizens could be or should be organized as a collective to be responsible? If the problem is preventing states from launching wars of aggression, or using disproportionate or indiscriminate means in war, how could civilian citizens both foresee the harm and then act to prevent it?

Against the view that citizens should leave questions of war and peace to political and military leaders,[15] I argue that ordinary civilian citizens have a collective political and moral responsibility to participate in decisions about wars that are undertaken by their governments and they have a responsibility to protest unjust wars or immoral conduct during wars.[16] Specifically, citizen participation should be understood as more than passive consent to decisions about war taken by their political leaders. Further, just as the "war convention requires soldiers to accept personal risks rather than kill innocent people,"[17] citizens have a responsibility to accept some personal cost and risk rather than let their government harm innocent people.

War is a collective act, "an end that is not realized by one individual acting alone."[18] While the number of *decision makers* may be quite small, the number of actors required to make war is large: waging even nuclear war, but most certainly conventional war, requires that many government actors do their part to plan, mobilize, deploy, and prosecute war. What makes such a large-scale act, such as war, possible is individual consent and obedience within organizations. On the other hand, beyond the fact that the legitimacy of the state rests in large part on its ability to protect the citizen from violence, the mobilization of resources required to make war necessarily entails the formalization and institutionalization of various state apparatus—from systems of education and taxation to conscription. In other words, as Charles Tilly argued, wars make states and states make war.[19] States need legitimacy in the eyes of their publics. For E.H. Carr,

> manpower is not reckoned by mere counting of heads. "The Soldan of Egypt or the Emperor of Rome," as Hume remarked "might drive his harmless subjects like brute beasts against their sentiments and inclinations. But he

Crawford, *Accountability for Killing: Moral Responsibility for Collateral Damage in America's Post-9/11 Wars* (Oxford: Oxford University Press, 2013).

14. French, "The Responsibility of Monsters and their Makers," 9.

15. In the United States and most other countries in the world, this is not simply a view, it is the de facto reality of the control of military force.

16. I use the phrase civilian citizens to distinguish them from citizen soldiers acting in their civilian capacity.

17. Walzer, *Just and Unjust Wars*, 305.

18. Seumas Miller, "Collective Moral Responsibility: An Individualist Account," *Midwest Studies in Philosophy* 30 (2006): 177.

19. Charles Tilly, *Coercion, Capital, and European States: AD 990–1992* (Oxford: Blackwell, 1992).

must at least have led his *mamelukes* or praetorian bands like men by their opinions." Power over opinion is therefore not less essential for political purposes than military and economic power, and has always been closely associated with them. The art of persuasion has always been a necessary part of the equipment of a political leader.[20]

Because individual citizens cannot themselves halt a war, or by themselves make war happen, a responsibility to protest must be exercised by citizens acting in their capacities as not only individuals but also as collective moral agents in a civil society. Specifically, civilian citizens should become educated about war and peace and set the range of acceptable action by defining qualities of the self to be defended in peacetime. In the weeks or months of decision just before a potential war, citizens should act as the skeptical audience of the state's justifications for war and they should themselves deliberate about war. If the state, acting on our behalf and ostensibly at our behest, is about to embark on, or has begun a war that civilian citizens can reasonably foresee will be wrong, citizens are morally bound to object, protest, and perhaps even obstruct the implementation of that policy. And finally, at war's end, citizens ought to reflect on their, and their government's, decisions and the conduct of war. Thus, my argument is not only for a "responsibility to protest"—a phrase used here as shorthand; I argue that citizens have a responsibility to deliberate, monitor, and make judgments about war and its conduct. Not only *ought* citizens act on these questions, under well-structured conditions, collective civilian citizen participation has some advantages over elite decision-making about war.

Further, it is possible citizens to have some effect on the recourse to and conduct of war. In both the distant and recent past, civilian citizens have in fact acted to intervene to halt wars or prevent abuses in war, even in nondemocratic states. That is not to say that what I propose is easy. The exercise by citizens of forward looking responsibility at the collective level for war entails developing and enhancing the conditions for civilian moral agency—including both a sense of the stakes and roles for civilians and their enhanced capacity for deliberation, action and reflection—well before potential wars.

In what follows, I explore these questions: First, *should* civilians be collectively responsible for war? If so, what are the grounds and bounds of their responsibility? And second, is it *possible* for civilian citizens to exercise prospective moral responsibility for their government's war? What could we reasonably expect civilian citizens to be able to do? Because arguments that citizens ought *not* to be responsible for war are tied to the practical questions of whether they can act responsibly, these two questions are not so easily disentangled. Moreover, because I am arguing for citizens' *collective* moral responsibility, I must at least plausibly show that citizens are not simply individual moral agents but can be understood as imperfect collective moral agents.

Part I summarizes the competing views about civilian citizens' prospective moral responsibility for war. Part II considers the grounds for the authority and

---

20. E. H. Carr, *The Twenty Years' Crisis, 1919–1939*, 2nd ed. (London: Macmillan, 1946), 132.

responsibility of ordinary citizens with regard to resort to war and military conduct. Part III argues that citizens can act as collective imperfect moral agents. Part IV considers the obstacles to civilian collective moral agency in wartime. Part V describes how civilian citizens can, individually and collectively, overcome the barriers to their effective participation and suggests the form that collective civilian responsibility for war could take.[21]

I. SHOULD CIVILIAN CITIZENS PARTICIPATE?

Against Civilian Engagement

The main arguments for limiting citizen responsibility for decisions about war concern authority, prudence, and morality. The argument from authority in the just war tradition, since Grotius, is that citizens should defer to the state's leaders on questions of the resort to war and the conduct of war on the assumption that government officials are the best and only legitimate authority on the use of force in war.[22] In some polities there may be, as there is in the United States, a lively debate about "war powers"—whether, when, and for how long a political leader can use force without authorization by the legislature. But the role of the public in decisions about resort to war is usually absent from this conversation largely because, it is assumed, citizens have ceded their authority to representatives. The legitimately appointed or elected leaders of the state are "in authority"—not the citizen.[23]

Realist and liberal political traditions presume that in representative democracies political leaders are legitimately authorized to render decisions on the justice of war and its conduct. The paradigmatic social contract implies a division of labor and responsibilities: the state insures physical security from within and without and in exchange the people provide the resources in blood and treasure for war when war is necessary. The social contract implies a mental division of labor where the citizens trust the state to evaluate threats to the people and the state expects people to respect the executive's judgment. Citizens delegate their authority to decide about war. Further, the argument goes, since the state has the duty to protect its citizens, it must be authorized to do so by whatever means are necessary in cases of grave threat or "supreme emergency." Indeed, leaders may be trusted to know when it is acceptable to violate norms and international law in cases of supreme emergencies where the existence of the state as an on-going community is at risk.[24]

21. All of these issues are necessarily considered all too briefly, and with too few citations, and in some cases, almost in shorthand. Every one of these issues deserves much greater elaboration.

22. See James Turner Johnson, *Morality and Contemporary Warfare* (New Haven: Yale, 1999), 53.

23. On the distinction between being "an authority" by virtue of knowledge, versus being "in authority" because one is the holder of a position, see Richard E. Flathman, *The Practice of Political Authority: Authority and the Authoritative* (Chicago: University of Chicago Press, 1980).

24. Walzer argues that "moral communities make great immoralities morally possible. But they do this only in the face of a far greater immorality, as in the example of a Nazi-like attack on

The prudential arguments against citizen engagement in decisions about war suggest that involving civilians in "real time" before war is impractical and unwise.[25] The first version of the imprudence argument stresses time. Specifically, the formation of a citizen consensus and approval for war will be time consuming in just such a case where time is of the essence. Moreover, if government mobilization has to wait for civilian consent, the argument goes, all could be lost. As the sixteenth century Spanish theologian Francisco de Vitoria argued: "A prince is not able and ought not always to render reasons for the war to his subjects, and if the subjects cannot serve in the war except they are first satisfied of its justice, the state would fall into grave peril."[26]

The argument from prudence also stresses the epistemic limits of the public. Most citizens, it is argued, cannot grasp the moral and strategic complexities of war and strategy, especially if some information is (justifiably or not) held in secret. These issues are "too complicated" for nonspecialists to understand. Further, the argument from prudence stresses the passionate nature of the public. Political leaders worry that civilians citizens may be self-interested or sentimental, reluctant participants in war because they fear its costs or don't have the "stomach" to "do what it takes." In sum, these arguments conclude, it is prudent to leave war to the expert authorities who—by virtue of their training, access to specialized knowledge and restricted information, and dispassionate constitutions—are more capable than ordinary citizens of making the right decisions quickly, and it is presumed, correctly.

The third set of arguments against civilian moral responsibility for war concern moral innocence. Civilian citizens understandably want some distance between themselves and the moral responsibility for their government's war. Civilians want "clean hands" and expect their leaders to take on the moral burden of "dirty hands"—making the morally difficult decisions that will or may cause harm to innocent others or to one's own soldiers, but that are nevertheless necessary for the nation's security.[27]

Civilian leaders also benefit from the legal and moral prohibition on directly and intentionally attacking noncombatants, on the reasoning—and under the condition that—they are "innocent" and do not pose an armed threat to the adversary. Civilians have reason to worry that their moral and political responsibility for war could be used to justify armed attacks against them. Civilians *have* often been attacked on the view that they are responsible for their state's behavior in war and that attacking civilians is a justified punishment, or that attacking them could cause

the very existence of a particular community, and only at the moment when this attack is near success, and only insofar as the immoral response is the only way of holding off that success." Michael Walzer, "Emergency Ethics," in *Arguing About War*, ed. Michael Walzer (New Haven: Yale University Press, 2004), 50.

25. As a slogan, the argument might be phrased "democracy is a threat to the practice of war." For a general discussion see Robert Dahl, *Controlling Nuclear Weapons: Democracy Versus Guardianship* (Syracuse, NY: Syracuse University Press, 1984).

26. Quoted in Walzer, *Just and Unjust Wars*, 39.

27. See Michael Walzer, "Political Action: The Problem of Dirty Hands," *Philosophy and Public Affairs* 2 (1973).

citizens to withdraw their consent and support for the war, or even lead them to oppose a war.

Terrorists have specifically articulated this idea of civilian complicity as a justification for attack. In his 2002 "Letter to the American People" Osama bin Laden answered the question "Why are we fighting and opposing you?" with "Because you attacked us and continue to attack us." Bin Laden then makes an argument for American responsibility for al Qaeda's attacks. The "American people are the ones who chose their government . . . a choice which stems from their agreement to its policies . . . The American people have the ability and the choice to refuse the policies of the Government and even to change it if they want. The American people are the one ones who pay the taxes which fund the plans that bomb us in Afghanistan, the tanks that strike and destroy our homes in Palestine, the armies which occupy our lands in the Arabian Gulf, and the fleets which ensure the blockade of Iraq . . . That is why the American people cannot be innocent . . ."[28] Governments have also used civilian complicity as a justification for attack, as in the "terror bombing" of World War II.[29]

In sum, the arguments against civilian participation are that civilians have given their authority to the state; that it is imprudent for civilians to act on questions of war because time is short and civilians' cognitive and emotional capacities are limited; and that civilians should be kept away from the dirty business of war lest they be blamed for the decisions their leaders take. Civilian immunity rests on their innocence.

For Civilian Engagement

The first response to arguments against civilian engagement is to challenge the assumption that the state is the right or only legitimate authority on war (or anything else) and to vest ultimate authority in the citizen. These arguments about authority focus on two issues—determining who works for who in the principal-agent relationship, and questioning the authoritativeness of those in authority.

Specifically, liberals argue that states are themselves authorized by the consent of their citizens: in the principal-agent relationship, the citizens are the principal. Immanuel Kant frames authority for war in precisely this way in *Perpetual Peace* and *Metaphysics of Morals*. Kant suggests that while one might argue that "since most of his subjects are his own product, the supreme authority in a state, the sovereign, has the right to lead them into war as he would take them on a hunt, and into battles as on a pleasure trip,"[30] the leader cannot treat their citizens in this way. Kant writes that

---

28. Osama Bin Laden, "Letter to America," http://www.theguardian.com/world/2002/nov/24/ theobserver.

29. See articles in Igor Primoratz, ed., *Civilian Immunity in War* (Oxford: Oxford University Press, 2007).

30. Immanuel Kant, *The Metaphysics of Morals*, introd. and trans. Mary Gregor (Cambridge: Cambridge University Press, 1991), 152.

Although such an argument for this right . . . holds with regard to animals, which can be a man's *property*, it simply cannot be applied to men, especially as citizens of a state. For they must always be regarded as colegislating members of a state (not merely as means, but also as ends in themselves), and must therefore give their free assent, through their representatives, not only in waging war in general, but also to each particular declaration of war. Only under this limiting condition can a state direct them to serve in a way full of danger to them. We shall therefore have to derive this right from the *duty* of the sovereign to the people (not the reverse); and for this to be the case the people will have to be regarded as having given its vote to go to war. In this capacity, it is although passive (letting itself be disposed of), also active and represents the sovereign itself.[31]

John Ladd translates these last sentences differently: "we must be certain that the people have given their consent, and, in this respect, even though they may be passive (in the sense that they merely comply), they also still act for themselves and themselves represent the sovereign."[32] In sum, Kant argues that the state has no right to make decisions for the people, without their consent, on the question of war. While Kant suggests they must give their consent, he is not clear about how citizens can actually do this except through their legislators. Kant is not in favor of citizens *directly* deciding about war. Kant's "first definitive article of Perpetual Peace" states that the "constitution of every nation should be republican."

Related to the issue of who works for whom is a rejection or at least a questioning of the division of labor implied by the social contract understanding of citizenship on the argument that war is a special case because of the great material and moral costs and risks war entails. Whether or not citizens can give their authority to the state to make certain decisions in many other issue areas, they ought not to automatically or unreflectively do so when it comes to war because of the particular nature of war and its demands on the people. War entails the violent deliberate and unintended killing of other humans. It entails using humans on both sides of a war as means. And war usually demands much of *both* the state and its citizens—whether the steady accumulation of military power over decades, or the rapid mobilization of arms and soldiers, to paying for the long aftermath in human and economic costs. Civilian citizens not only make war possible by those contributions, they have an interest in the burden of war for themselves and their fellow citizens, including future generations, and they must pay the immediate and long-term costs of waging war. A decision to go to war, in other words, is not only the taking on of an immediate obligation to do grave harm to others, but the assumption of long-term economic, social and environmental costs—not least of which will be the burden of caring for wounded soldiers for many decades. So, John Finnis argues, war is "paradigmatically a social and public act" and that war is a "public

---

31. Kant, *The Metaphysics of Morals*, 152.
32. Immanuel Kant, *Metaphysical Elements of Justice: The Complete Text of the Metaphysics of Morals, Part I*, trans. and introd. John Ladd (Indianapolis: Hackett, 1999), 154.

policy which members of the society are invited or required to participate in carrying out."[33] For these reasons, Jeff McMahan argues, citizens bear some responsibility for unjust war in particular:

> Citizens have special responsibility for unjust wars fought by their own state for the simple reason that it is *their* institutions that are malfunctioning— institutions that operate on the basis of their labor, through their financial support, and ostensibly with their consent and for their benefit . . . [Citizens have] a special responsibility to ensure that the institutions are not a source of unjust harm to others.[34]

A second argument about authority is the claim that a state's leaders may not have the same interest in war as the civilian citizen, and citizens must therefore protect their material, political, and moral interests. Specifically, Kant argues, political leaders may be insufficiently attentive to the costs and risks of war when they do not have to consider the interests of the people. Kant is skeptical about the ability of the autocratic political leader to make prudent decisions about war. "[U]nder a non-republican constitution, where the subjects are not citizens, the easiest thing in the world to do is to declare war. Here the ruler is not a fellow citizen, but the nation's owner, and war does not affect his table, his hunt, his places of pleasure, his court festivals, and so on. Thus he can decide to go to war for the most meaningless of reasons, as if it were a kind of pleasure party, and he can blithely leave its justification (which decency requires) to the diplomatic corps, who are always prepared for such exercises."[35]

Arguments about the danger of limiting authority to the state have suggested that states' leaders can be captive to special interests, such as the "military-industrial complex" or other lobby groups. Because those interests may primarily be concerned about how they might benefit from something related to war, they may fail to adequately consider the wider public interest in their own actions. In other words, a defense contractor does not have to say that "our country should go to war against another country." The effects of an interest group on the decision to go to war may be indirect, for instance as when an arms manufacturer convinces legislators and military advisors that their weapon is highly accurate, with high reliability rates and that a certain number of these weapons systems will help ensure a quick victory with low cost in life to either side. If the costs and risks of war are perceived to be low and the hoped—for benefits are potentially great, then the interest group has indirectly contributed to framing the decision in a way that tilted toward war. Advocates of including a large number of voices with different perspectives in decision-making about war are suggesting that the outcome of a

---

33. John Finnis, "The Ethics of War and Peace in the Catholic Natural Law Tradition," in *The Ethics of War and Peace: Religious and Secular Perspectives*, ed. Terry Nardin (Princeton: Princeton University Press, 1996), 19.

34. Jeff McMahan, *Killing in War* (Oxford: Oxford University Press, 2009), 215.

35. Immanuel Kant, *Perpetual Peace: A Philosophical Sketch* (1795), sec. 351. In Immanuel Kant, *Perpetual Peace and Other Essays*, trans. and introd. Ted Humphrey (Indianapolis: Hackett, 1983), 113.

decision will be better because actors without a profit interest in a rose-colored view of the benefits of war will be included in the processes.

The arguments with perhaps the most radical implications about authority construes a prospective unjust war or immoral behavior in war as a failure of the political sovereign's responsibility, where sovereignty is defined not as control but "*sovereignty as responsibility* in both internal functions and external duties."[36] This is the view taken in the relatively new doctrine of a *Responsibility to Protect.*

> Thinking of sovereignty as responsibility, in a way that is being increasingly recognized in state practice, has a threefold significance. First, it implies that the state authorities are responsible for the functions of protecting the safety and lives of citizens and promotion of their welfare. Second, it suggests that the national political authorities are responsible to the citizens internally and to the international community through the UN. And third, it means that the agents of state are responsible for their actions; that is to say, they are accountable for their acts of commission and omission.[37]

When the state mobilizes to act aggressively outside its borders, it has also failed in its responsibility to respect international law and other members of the international community, and states have the right to defend themselves. Advocates of a "responsibility to protect" argue that when the state fails to protect its citizens or itself harms them, that state has also vitiated its sovereignty: "sovereign states have a responsibility to protect their own citizens from avoidable catastrophe—from mass murder and rape, from starvation—but that when they are unwilling or unable to do so, that responsibility must be borne by the broader community of states."[38] When states mobilize against their own citizens, and violate the rights of citizens they are legally and morally bound to protect, they have violated their duties and have vitiated their claim to legitimate authority.

The responsibility to protect argument is used to justify external intervention by international authorities. It can also be used vitiate claims of domestic sovereignty and to justify the assertion of political responsibility for citizens' intervention in unethical decisions about war—a responsibility to protest. If the "agents of states are responsible for their actions,"[39] then the principals—the citizens, are responsible agents.

Turning to the argument about prudence of civilian participation in decisions about war, John Finnis asserts that "individual citizens can, in principle, assess the public policy, the announced reasons for going to war, the announced war aims, and the adopted strategy (so far as they know it) and assess the justice of the war . . ."[40]

Yet time is sometimes short. In the case where the state is faced with imminent attack and the options are either to accept the blow or to wage a preemptive

36. International Commission on Intervention and State Sovereignty (ICSS), *The Responsibility to Protect* (Ottawa: International Development Research Centre, December 2001), 13.
37. ICSS, *The Responsibility to Protect*, 13.
38. ICSS, *The Responsibility to Protect*, viii.
39. ICSS, *The Responsibility to Protect*, 13.
40. Finnis, "The Ethics of War and Peace in the Catholic Natural Law Tradition," 19.

strike, time is indeed extremely short. If a state has already been attacked, a speedy mobilization and response will be imperative if a military response is indeed the best option. Some wars might receive pre-authorization by the people—such as when they approve of military doctrines that are capable of mounting an effective defense or preemption. Yet there are few cases of war that conform to this stylized scenario of what used to be called a "bolt out of the blue" attack. Many potential wars, and certainly the unjust wars of aggression we are concerned with, do not fall in to the category of the requirement of a speedy decision by the public. Rather, it is more often the case that tensions build for months, if not years, and there is time to deliberate and even avert a war. The citizenry can evaluate the causes of these wars and urge alternative solutions. Further, the argument from urgency fades once wars begin—deliberation is an ongoing project in war.

The other pragmatic objections to citizen participation are epistemic, namely the claim citizens will not and cannot make good decisions about war because they can't understand the issues, including the moral dilemmas, and the claim that citizens may be too emotional. How could civilian citizens be expected to do a better job than the state, or at least add something to the deliberative process that corrects for state biases? There are two responses.

First, we might be vastly over estimating the capacities of political authorities to make wise decisions about war and peace. Political and military leaders have deliberative weaknesses that are, in general, exacerbated by their position. Specifically, state's leaders are often *not* so well equipped to use the information in front of them because they may be influenced by the militaristic bias that assumes that the use of force is almost always effective. As Robert Pape found in his study of bombing in war, "Leaders are often drawn to military coercion because it is perceived as a quick and cheap solution to otherwise difficult and expensive international problems."[41] Further, "statesmen very often overestimate the prospects for successful coercion and underestimate the costs."[42] Political leaders often feel constrained by their political office to prioritize reasons of state, and may have been elected or promoted because they seemed to fit a soldier-statesman model.

Further, states' leaders may take the citizens' authorization for war and the justification of "reason of state" too far, as a license for extreme measures—including to violations of civilian immunity—on the grounds that they are charged with defending the state and promoting its interests by any means necessary. As Walzer argues, "We must resist the routinization of emergency, reminding ourselves again and again that the threats we force ourselves to live with, and live with ourselves, are immoral threats. Over the years we became habituated, callous, hardened against the crimes we were pledged to commit."[43] Further, C. A. J. Coady argues that "terms such as 'necessity' or 'supreme emergency' are very vague and open to diverse interpretations, not to mention exploitations." Coady cautions that the "exemptions from profound moral prohibitions" authorized by the invocation

41. Robert Pape, *Bombing to Win: Air Power and Coercion in War* (Ithaca, NY: Cornell University Press, 1996), 2.

42. Pape, *Bombing to Win*, 2.

43. Michael Walzer, "Emergency Ethics," in *Arguing About War*, ed. Michael Walzer, 49.

of necessity and supreme emergency "dangerously opens the door to the identification of the state's survival with that of its political leadership."[44]

Ample research suggests that the rational actor view of political authorities is at best a stylized representation of governmental decision-making processes. Leaders can and do make many cognitive and affective errors, especially under the stress that is characteristic in war.[45] Moreover, elite decision-making groups sometimes suffer "groupthink"—a tendency to value consensus over critical thinking and an unquestioning adherence to the beliefs and decisions of the group which often leads to a failure to consider a range of alternatives. When groupthink occurs, group members' "striving for unanimity override their motivation to realistically appraise alternative courses of action" leads to "deterioration in mental efficiency, reality testing, and moral judgment."[46]

Yet decisionmakers do not have to suffer from the pathology of "groupthink" consensus seeking because they already agree on major premises. Knowledge about war, weapons, and strategy is specialized and complex. The experts in the mobilization, deployment and use of force share a language and worldview, assumptions that, after a time, become unquestioned and whose logic may become closed to challenge, self-reinforcing or even circular. Although taken for granted by experts, some of those premises may be completely false, or if not false, quite risky. Nowhere is the danger of specialized language and unchallenged logic clearer than assumptions about nuclear strategy and nuclear war, where the big picture was often lost while attention was focused on the details of deterrent calculations.[47] On the other hand, while political authorities may have weaknesses and biases that make them less than ideal deliberators, they may be better equipped to deliberate than civilians because the authorities have access to information, specialized education, and the capacity to decide quickly.

Even as we acknowledge limits to the deliberative capacities of civilians, we may be overlooking and underestimating the advantages and strengths of collective civilian citizens' deliberation. Taken as a collective, civilians have three attributes that constitute comparative advantages over elite decisionmakers that could, in an institutional design that enhances those strengths, make them well suited to assume the responsibility to deliberate about war.

44. C. A. J. Coady, "Terrorism, Morality, and Supreme Emergency," *Ethics* 114, no. 4 (July 2004): 781.

45. In this sense, although political leaders may be extremely well educated, their information processing may be little different than the "average" person. See Daniel Kahneman, *Thinking Fast and Slow* (New York: Farrar, Strauss and Giroux, 2011).

46. Irving Janis, *Groupthink: Psychological Studies of Policy Decisions and Fiascoes* (Boston: Houghton Mifflin, 1982), 9. See also Paul 't Hart, Eric K. Stern, and Bengt Sundelius, ed., *Beyond Groupthink: Political Group Dynamics and Foreign Policy-Making* (Ann Arbor: University of Michigan Press, 1997).

47. See Lawrence Freeman, *The Evolution of Nuclear Strategy*, 3rd ed. (New York: Palgrave, 2003); Lynn Eden, *Whole World on Fire: Organizations, Knowledge and Nuclear Weapons Devastation* (Ithaca, NY: Cornell University Press, 2004); and Neta C. Crawford, "Policy Modeling," in *Oxford Handbook of Public Policy*, ed. Martin Rein, Michael Moran, and Robert Goodin (Oxford: Oxford University Press, 2006), 769–803.

First, as a *collective*, citizens are diverse and diversity tends to improve the deliberative processes.[48] Specifically, *more* information can be brought to bear. As Rawls notes, "The benefits from discussion lie in the fact that even representative legislatures are limited in knowledge and the ability to reason. No one of them knows everything the others know, or can make all the same inferences that they can draw in concert. Discussion is a way of combining information and enlarging the range of arguments. At least in the course of time, the effects of common deliberation seem bound to improve matters."[49] Further, in an intellectually diverse public setting, there is a greater likelihood that there will be a diversity of views about both the legitimacy of war and its effectiveness. Nonexpert civilians are not, for instance, captive of the organizational frames (or language games as Wittgenstein would say) that make nuclear weapons or conventional force deliberations both more complicated and subject to self-contained and sometimes dangerous assumptions. While homogenous groups experience "ideological amplification," in diverse groups, both experts and nonexperts will be forced to justify their views in the face of counterarguments and evidence: "mixing increases the likelihood that people will be aware of competing rationales and see that their own arguments might be met by counterarguments."[50]

Second, taken as a collective, the majority of civilians are attentive to costs and often less tolerant of extreme risks. Not only does war affect "their table" directly and indirectly—it affects many other aspects of citizens' current and future lives. As Kant suggests in *Perpetual Peace*, citizens are bound to be cautious about the costs and risks of war, not simply its possible benefits: "Among these are those doing the fighting themselves, paying the costs of war from their own resources, having to repair at great sacrifice the war's devastation, and finally, the ultimate evil that would make itself better, never being able—because of new and constant wars—to expunge the burden of debt."[51] While military and civilian leaders certainly weigh costs, there is ample evidence that leaders often underestimate the cost and duration of wars.[52] "The republican constitution also provide for this desirable result, namely, perpetual peace, and the reason is as follow: If (as must inevitably be the case, given this form of constitution) the consent of the citizenry is required in order to determine whether or not there will be war, it is natural that they consider all its calamities before committing themselves to so risky a game."[53]

48. See Aristotle, *The Politics* (1281b1–10) and Iris Marion Young, "Difference as a Resource for Democratic Communication," in *Deliberative Democracy: Essays on Reason and Politics*, ed. James Bohman and William Rehg (Cambridge, MA: MIT Press, 1999), 383–406.

49. John Rawls, *A Theory of Justice* (Cambridge, MA: Harvard University Press, 1971; rev. ed., 1999), 358.

50. David Schkade, Cass R. Sunstein, and Reid Hastie, "When Deliberation Produces Extremism," *Critical Review* 22, no. 2–3 (2010): 240.

51. Kant, *Perpetual Peace*, 113.

52. Experts may also tend to dismiss or discount risks and costs of foreseeable "normal" accidents. See Charles Perrow, *Normal Accidents: Living with High Risk Technologies* (Princeton: Princeton University Press, 1999); Scott Sagan, *The Limits of Safety: Organizations, Accidents, and Nuclear Weapons* (Princeton: Princeton University Press, 1993).

53. Kant, *Perpetual Peace*, 113. I regard Kant's argument against democracy as definitional rather than substantive: "*Republicanism* is that political principle whereby executive power (the

Third, civil society institutions, as discussed at greater length below, are removed from the pressure of direct causal responsibility, and more insulated from pressures to conformity and groupthink. Civilians are usually not thinking under the same duress as soldiers or even civilian leaders. Many venues in the public sphere can play a vital role as deliberative spaces when they are structured for reasoned deliberation. While, these potential advantages of civilian deliberation are often not realized, as I argue in part IV, the obstacles to civilian participation can be overcome, as I suggest in part V, through institutional design.

The last objection to increasing civilian participation in decisions about war, the concern that participation would blur the distinction between combatant and noncombatants which would make civilians liable to attack, is serious. If one agrees with the claim that "[p]olitical liability is graduated according to the degree of participation in the régime,"[54] then by arguing that civilian citizens should participate in decisions about war haven't we increased the both the political liability and potentially the vulnerability of the citizen to the charge of guilt?

While I cannot fully explicate the arguments here, there are several arguments against the claim that citizens' moral and political responsibility for war vitiates their right to immunity from attack—namely that such a policy is indiscriminate in practice, nearly always disproportionate, usually ineffective, and often counterproductive. While it may be that even if *some* civilian citizens were morally responsible for their state's behavior in the sense of authorizing an unjust war, not all are (e.g., children are not responsible), nor are all responsible to the same degree, and to attack civilians is, generally, to attack them indiscriminately. Indeed, although war is a collective act, many civilians may have objected to a particular war and are certainly not complicit. Second, even if the majority of civilian civilians do consent to war and may be considered morally and politically responsible for an unjust war, the prohibition on attacking civilians in war still applies because civilians do not pose a *direct military* threat to the other side and in that sense, have not lost their immunity.[55] Finally, hurting civilians does not tend to work—as the militaries that have intentionally and unintentionally attacked civilians have often

government) is separated from legislative power. In a despotism the ruler independently executes laws that it has itself made. . . . *Democracy*, in the proper sense of the term, is necessarily despotism. Every form of government that is not *representative* is properly speaking *without form*, because one and the same person can no more be at one and the same time the legislator and executor of his will. . . . everyone wants to rule." *Perpetual Peace*, 114.

54. Jaspers, *The Question of German Guilt*, 37.

55. Civilians are immune from attack unless they directly participate in armed action in ways that cause actual harm to enemy personnel and equipment. See Geneva Convention Additional Protocol II, Article 13, (1) and (3). For a discussion of "direct participation," see Nils Melzer, *Interpretive Guidance on the Notion of Direct Participation in Hostilities under International Humanitarian Law* (Geneva: International Committee of the Red Cross, 2009). Also see Kai Draper, "Self-Defense, Collective Obligation, and Noncombatant Liability," *Social Theory and Practice* 24, no. 1 (Spring 1998): 57–81; Igor Primoratz, "Civilian Immunity in War: Its Grounds, Scope and Weight," in *Civilian Immunity in War*, ed. Primoratz, 35; McMahan, *Killing in War*, 203–35; and Toni Erskine, "Kicking Bodies and Damning Souls: The Danger of Harming 'Innocent' Individuals while Punishing the 'Delinquent' States," in *Accountability for Collective Wrongdoing*, ed. Tracy Isaacs and Richard Vernon (Cambridge: Cambridge University Press, 2011), 261–86.

realized after the fact. Civilians do not usually capitulate; they tend to increase their determination to resist those who attack them.[56]

II. FOUNDATIONS OF CITIZENS' COLLECTIVE MORAL RESPONSIBILITY FOR WAR

Having argued that the objections to civilian participation are at least questionable, in this section I argue that there are good reasons for citizens, especially (but not only) in a democracy, to be responsible for authorizing war, protesting unjust wars, and monitoring and limiting the conduct of war. My argument for public moral responsibility rests on four interrelated pillars: war is public policy; citizens are implicated in the conduct of this public policy and have a form of collective moral responsibility for it; democracy is undermined if citizens do not play a role in this arena and strengthened when civilians participate; and war makes all civilian citizens vulnerable to harm. Indeed, for these reasons, collective civilian participation is an urgent moral responsibility.

First, while individual action is required to wage war, as an attempt to fulfill a public and collective purpose, war is a collective act. Thus, war is not simply violence, but by definition a social and political activity that publics undertake, which makes the killing in it different than murder or organized crime. The public collectively and individually bears the burdens and reaps the benefits of war because of and to the extent that war shapes the purposes, resources, and behavior of the state at home and abroad.

Second, citizens are implicated in war because collective action is an essential feature of war. Although war can be initiated without wide participation (in authoritarian states), whether or not the state is democratic, war cannot be waged without the collective participation of *both* military organizations and civilian citizens. The public and the private are thus thoroughly intertwined at a practical and moral level. In this sense, civilian citizens are both public and private actors.[57] As Iris Marion Young argues, "individuals bear responsibility for structural injustice because they contribute by their actions to the processes that produce unjust outcomes."[58]

But there are obviously different kinds of moral responsibility. While the state has the primary direct role in war, the civilian role is specific but indirect and secondary: democratic publics nominally authorize war, potentially benefit from a successful war, and contribute to war by providing resources (blood and treasure) that make war possible. The state has primary moral responsibility because it directs the action. Civilian citizens have secondary moral responsibility for war in

56. See Pape, *Bombing to Win*, and Crawford, *Accountability for Killing*, chap. 2.

57. As Barbara Herman argues, "we live in and through social institutions that shape our moral lives, sometimes in ways that empower us and sometimes in ways that challenge our will to act well." Barbara Herman, *Moral Literacy* (Cambridge, MA: Harvard University Press, 2007), vii.

58. Iris Marion Young, *Global Challenges: War, Self-Determination and Responsibility for Justice* (Malden, MA: Polity Press, 2007), 175.

their oversight and accountability role, the obligation to monitor those with primary responsibility and ensure that those institutions with primary responsibility take due care.[59]

Our individual contribution is usually not decisive, which is why this role of responsibility is collective: in waging war, states and their publics, the civilian citizens, *act as if* they are collective moral agents. Because individual citizens cannot by themselves halt a war, or for that matter, by themselves cause and conduct war, a responsibility to deliberate about and protest unjust wars must be exercised by citizens acting in their capacities as individuals and collective moral agents. By making the shape, functions and capacities of this collective moral agency explicit, its power and civilian collective agency can be both understood and exercised with better effect.

Third, when citizens are not engaged in decisions about war and its conduct, democratic institutions and the practice of democracy suffer. I am not the first to make this claim. Thirty years ago, Robert Dahl likened the effects of citizen alienation of their authority over nuclear weapons and other complex matters to experts, to the role of guardians in Plato's *Republic.* Dahl said, "We have in fact turned over to a small group of people decisions of incalculable importance to ourselves and mankind, and it is very far from clear how, if at all, we could recapture a control that in fact we have never had. Thus, in this crucial area, and maybe others, we have perhaps unwittingly adopted the principle of guardianship."[60] Similarly, Elaine Scarry argues that the concentration of the power to launch nuclear war in the presidency violates the U.S. Constitution's separation of powers and turned the United States into a "monarchy."[61] At a deeper level, there is a relationship between the too easy authorization and use of coercion abroad and at home. Randall Forsberg argued, "democratic institutions have prompted, or paralleled, a growing rejection of violence as a means of achieving political or economic ends within and between nations."[62] For Forsberg, democracy and a commitment to nonviolence are synonymous—"commitment to non-violence lies at the core of democratic institutions . . ." Forsberg argues, "Commitment to non-violence protects and preserves freedom of expression and other civil liberties by precluding intimidation or coercion by violence or the threat of violence. Within democracies, wherever nonviolence is not the rule . . . other democratic rights and freedoms are lost or severely compromised."[63]

Fourth, I return to the fact that civilians are often killed in war and the importance of the principle of civilian immunity. Harm to civilians in war is both likely and foreseeable. There is no way around that fact. We have good reason to be

---

59. On primary and secondary responsibility see Robert E. Goodin, *Protecting the Vulnerable: A Reanalysis of Our Social Responsibilities* (Chicago: University of Chicago Press, 1985), 151–52.

60. Dahl, *Controlling Nuclear Weapons*, 7.

61. Elaine Scarry, *Thermonuclear Monarchy: Choosing between Democracy and Doom* (New York: W.W. Norton, 2014).

62. Randall Caroline Watson Forsberg, *Toward a Theory of Peace: The Role of Moral Beliefs* (doctoral dissertation, MIT, 1997), 34.

63. Forsberg, *Toward a Theory of Peace*, 35.

both skeptical about the ability to prosecute "clean wars" and to be concerned for the other sides' civilians.

The claim that war is a contest between military forces seems obvious, indeed definitional. Strategists from Clausewitz to the present argue that what ought to and does determine the outcome in war is force on force battles on a battlefield between highly trained and massed military forces using increasingly sophisticated military technologies.

But recall the earlier argument against civilian participation in decision making about war: even though civilians ought *not* to be deliberately attacked in war, militaries threaten, attack and destroy the civilian population of the other side and their property quite frequently in war. Homes, fields, and food stores are burned, industries are destroyed, women are raped, and children are enslaved. The strategy of targeting civilians reached its peak in the twentieth century with terror bombing and nuclear deterrence threats but it has found expression in the twenty-first century as well in many wars.

Attacks on civilians are rooted in a view of influence—specifically that threats and harsh treatment make the fearful and brutalized civilian or political leader capitulate. Conquerors often say that the only thing their enemy under-stands is brute force. In other words, under the thumbscrew theory of military force, one need only ratchet up the pain to a level necessary to achieve submission. When coercion fails, it is because insufficient force was used. Further, it is better to be extremely brutal at the outset in order to bring war to conclusion sooner, rather than later. We can see this reasoning in the 1863 U.S. General Orders 100 of the American Civil War: "The more vigorously wars are pursued the better it is for humanity. Sharp wars are brief."[64] The argument is clear: "War is not carried on by arms alone. It is lawful to starve the hostile belligerent, armed or unarmed, so that it leads to the speedier subjection of the enemy."[65]

The belief that tightening the thumbscrews on civilians will lead to speedy capitulation is, as I suggested above, an optimistic assumption. Rather, as Pape found in his study of coercive airpower, the "citizenry of the target state is not likely to turn against its government because of civilian punishment." Instead, "the supposed causal chain—civilian hardship produces public anger which forms political opposition against the government—does not stand up."[66] In sum, people usually do not turn on their governments when under attack, but rather rally around the flag. Nevertheless, as Pape demonstrates, time and again leaders attempt to ratchet up civilian pain to achieve political gain.[67]

On the other hand, norms of civilian immunity sometimes constrain the behavior of military forces.[68] There is also the hope, indeed belief among those who

64. United States, *Laws of War: General Orders 100*, 1863, art. 29.

65. *Laws of War: General Orders 100*, art. 17.

66. Pape, *Bombing to Win*, 24.

67. Interestingly, and also time and again, military and political leaders rediscover that war is about winning hearts and minds too. They come to believe that ending wars is about persuasion.

68. Crawford, *Accountability for Killing*, discusses this in relation to U.S. behavior in its post-9/11 wars in Afghanistan and Iraq. Also see Benjamin Valentino, *Final Solutions: Mass Killing, and Genocide in the Twentieth Century* (Ithaca, NY: Cornell University Press, 2004).

advocate the use of particular weapons, that precision weapons and drone technologies for "targeted killing" will reduce civilian harm. Indeed, fewer people are
deliberately killed in many contemporary wars than in the past. Yet, these hopes
are not enough. Collateral damage can add up to many thousands of people. We
can foresee that many wars will, even if they begin with intentions to avoid civilian
harm, often fail to keep harm to civilians low. Indeed, although the numbers are
disputed, even "surgical" U.S. drone strikes have killed thousands of people in
Pakistan, including civilians, as President Obama recently acknowledged.[69]

In sum, the idea of a "clean war" that does not affect civilians on either side,
is wishful thinking, and in this way, authorizing war is a grave responsibility, in all
senses of the word grave. Although we are all members of a particular state, we are
also all human beings who would agree that noncombatants should be protected
from harm. We ought to be concerned about foreseeable harm to the other side's
noncombatants, even if we don't individually intend it or think we are authorizing
it when we consent to war. We ought to act as responsible citizens of our state
because we are not only citizens of our state.

III. CITIZENS AS COLLECTIVE AND IMPERFECT MORAL AGENTS

I have elsewhere argued that it was possible for complex organizations to have the
characteristics of what I called imperfect moral agency—organizational structures
and processes that enable organizations as collectives to deliberate and act in ways
that are analogous to individual moral agents—and that some organizations do act
as if they were moral agents. I suggested five qualities of imperfect moral agency
within governments and complex organizations: a shared purpose/organizational
intention; persistent roles; institutionalized decision-making procedures; the capacity to act; and the capacity to reflect upon and revise its purpose, roles, decision-
making procedures, and actions.[70] To the extent that civilian citizens act together
through the institutions of a civil society, and using the public sphere, they act as
imperfect moral agents with characteristics that are parallel to those found in
complex organizations and they become a legitimate and important participant in
the arguments about war. How is it that civilians could form a civil society with the
potential to act as an imperfect moral agent? What follows is a sketch for an
ideal-type understanding of civilian publics as imperfect collective moral agents.
The ideal type is further developed, with respect to the problem of citizen responsibility for war, in Part V.

First, just as complex organizations are organized around shared intentions
members of a public may have, formally or informally, articulated shared intentions
or a common purpose for which they agree to coordinate their actions.

Second, in complex organizations, action is organized around and through
persistent causal and normative beliefs, roles and rules. Individual members may

69. Barack Obama, "Remarks by the President at the National Defense University," May 23,
2013, http://www.whitehouse.gov/the-press-office/2013/05/23/remarks-president-national-defense-
university. For a longer discussion, see Crawford, *Accountability for Killing.*
70. See Crawford, *Accountability for Killing*, chap. 6.

come and go, but the institution remains functional over time because behavior, and, in particular, the understanding of roles are guided by beliefs (organizational knowledge and culture). Actions are prescribed by rules and roles, and the collective has the ability to enforce the role performance of members. So also the civil society to which civilians belong is a persistent entity and citizens have persistent beliefs and roles within that system—roles that will involve them in and implicate them in executing decisions about war.

Third, autonomous individuals and collective moral agents need a capacity to make decisions. While organizations may use *ad hoc* procedures in crises, decision-making procedures in complex organizations are generally institutionalized. In complex organizations, the organization has knowledge resources, the ability to generate new knowledge and process information, decision-making rules and roles, and deliberative capacity.[71] The decision-making capacity for individual civilian citizens may be highly constrained and, absent investment in moral education, we cannot expect many citizens to have the resources that will make it possible for them to make informed decisions. On the other hand, deliberation is possible if elements in a civil society can process and pool information, and make informed analysis.

Moreover, citizens probably become better deliberators and decision makers the more that they practice—by working through historical and contemporary cases. In an article that explores the arguments by Aristotle, Rousseau, de Toqueville, and Mill that participation in democratic decisions has benefits for citizens, Jane Mansbridge says that she believes "participating in democratic decisions makes many participants better citizens." She hastens to add that "I believe this claim because it fits my experience. But I cannot prove it. Neither, at this point, can anyone else."[72] Indeed, work by Diana Mutz, James Fishkin, Francesca Polletta, and others support the view that democratic deliberation can improve with practice as decision makers gain skills and pool their resources and talents.[73]

Fourth, moral agents must be able to act. Complex organizations demonstrate this feature of imperfect moral agency when they coordinate the efforts of members, deploy preexisting resources, or mobilize new resources. The actions in complex organizations are often based on routines, standard operating procedures, and scripted responses to expected scenarios. While it may seem as if

71. French calls this a "corporate internal decision structure." See Peter A. French, "The Corporation as a Moral Person," *American Philosophical Quarterly* 16, no. 3 (1979): 207–15.

72. Jane Mansbridge, "On the Idea that Participation Makes Better Citizens," in *Citizen Competence and Democratic Institutions*, ed. Stephen L. Elkin and Karol Edward Soltan (University Park, PA: Penn State University Press), 291.

73. See Diana C. Mutz, *Hearing the Other Side: Deliberative versus Participatory Democracy* (New York: Cambridge University Press, 2006); James S. Fishkin, "Consulting the Public Through Deliberative Polling," *Journal of Policy Analysis and Management* 22, no. 1 (Winter 2003): 128–33; James S. Fishkin and Robert C. Luskin, "Experimenting with a Democratic Ideal: Deliberative Polling and Public Opinion," *Acta Politica* 40 (2005): 284–98; Francesca Polleta, *Freedom Is an Endless Meeting: Democracy in American Social Movements* (Chicago: University of Chicago Press, 2002).

civilian citizens have little capacity to act there are many cases of direct action by civilian citizens that illustrate how "exit" and "voice" can be used to effect.[74]

Fifth, to be constituted as an imperfect moral agent, collectives should have the institutionalized capacity to reflect upon, and evaluate their purposes, rules and roles, knowledge-production and decision-making procedures, and the quality of their actions and their consequences. They must be able to critically reflect on their normative beliefs and the consequences of their beliefs, decisions and actions. In individuals and organizations, reflection and evaluation may lead to revision of intentions, or changes in structure or rules for action. The openness of the individual or organization to reflection and revision is often a function of its preexisting normative and causal belief system.[75]

IV. OBSTACLES TO CIVILIAN MORAL AGENCY IN WARTIME

The obstacles to citizens' collective participation in decision making in the period that precedes a possible war and during wartime are hurdles to citizens acting as effective albeit imperfect moral agents. These are barriers to the formation of shared intention and the development of deliberative roles, and the difficulties of developing the capacity to make decisions, act, and reflect upon intentions, roles, decisions and actions that tend to reinforce each other and may result in a spiral of apathy, nonparticipation, and discouragement about the prospects for effective collective action.

I argued above that an essential feature of collective imperfect moral agency is shared intention. Citizens should see themselves as intending to act responsibly and as having the substantive shared intentions of preserving their peaceful community and to insure that their state does not engage in an unjust war. Citizens have a shared intention to make self-defense possible in the face of threats.

Further, citizens should ideally have a dialogue and come to a shared view about the nature and the limits to the "self" to be defended. All too often an aggressor state has an enlarged understanding of the self—that the state deserves what the other has, or that their identity is threatened by the very existence of the other or their way of life—rather than definition of the self that is limited to their physical integrity. Patriotism or loyalty to the idea of the state and its particular manifestation is an important factor in determining whether and how people will exercise their voice or withdraw their participation from a regime.

The conception of the collective self affects how civilians understand the roles of civilians in time of war. Many people not only avoid questions about the virtue of a proposed war or their state's conduct in it, they want to obey what they understand to be legitimate authority; many citizens believe that they have a duty to follow laws and presume that the state is generally right. In other words, it is not only bureaucrats who believe in rule following and "just following orders." These

74. Albert O. Hirschman, *Exit, Voice and Loyalty: Responses to Decline in Firms, Organizations, and States* (Cambridge, MA: Harvard University Press, 1970).
75. See Kay Mathiesen, "We're All in This Together: Responsibility of Collective Agents and Their Members." *Midwest Studies in Philosophy* 30 (2006): 244–45. Paul Sheehy, "Holding Them Responsible," *Midwest Studies in Philosophy* 30, 85 and 92.

citizens may believe that patriotism requires that they not think too hard about the justice of a war or attend too closely to its conduct. Howard Zinn framed this as the "problem of civil obedience."

> As soon as you say the topic is civil disobedience, you are saying our *problem* is civil disobedience. That is *not* our problem. . . . Our problem is civil *obe-dience*. Our problem is the numbers of people all over the world who have obeyed the dictates of the leaders of their government and have gone to war, and millions have been killed because of this obedience. And our problem is that scene in *All Quiet on the Western Front* where the schoolboys march off dutifully in a line to war. Our problem is that people are obedient all over the world, in the face of poverty and starvation and stupidity, and war and cruelty. Our problem is that people are obedient while the jails are full of petty thieves, and all the while the grand thieves are running the country. That's our problem. We recognize this for Nazi Germany. We know that the problem there was obedience, that the people obeyed Hitler. People obeyed; that was wrong. They should have challenged, and they should have resisted; and if we were only there, we would have showed them.[76]

Further, the "rally-around the flag" effect is real. Leaders often see a boost in their approval ratings in times of war while patriotism can make those who oppose a potential war more timid. At the same time, potential activists may feel that the time is not ripe for them to speak out and hence their costly efforts might be wasted because patriotism has diminished the willingness of many citizens to hear the arguments of those who are brave enough to question a march to war.

Assuming that citizens agree on the shared intention—that one of their roles is to monitor the state and prevent unjust wars—there may still be dearth of citizen participants willing to take part in a public dialogue about war. This is the concern that that citizens won't use the democratic institutions and freedoms that they have even if they think they have a role responsibility to check an unjust war. For instance, Walzer suggests that too few Americans engaged in discussion about the Vietnam War—they saw the war as "merely an ugly or an exciting spectacle."[77] Thus, he says, "[t]he real burden of the American war fell on that subset of men and women whose knowledge and sense of possibility was made manifest by their oppositional activity."[78]

This is the familiar notion that individuals may be free riders either on the state or on activists because individual action, in this case, acquiring information about war and deliberating about it, is costly. Potential free riders hope they can avoid the actual and potential costs of their particular individual action.[79] Indeed,

76. Howard Zinn, "The Problem Is Civil Obedience," November 1970, in *Voices of a People's History of the United States*, 2nd ed., ed. Howard Zinn and Anthony Arnove (New York: Seven Stories Press, 2009), 483–84.

77. Walzer, *Just and Unjust Wars*, 303.

78. Walzer, *Just and Unjust Wars*, 303.

79. Mancur Olson, *The Logic of Collective Action: Public Goods and the Theory of Groups* (Cambridge, MA: Harvard University Press, 1965).

many people won't act if they hope or assume that others will act for them and that the others' action will be sufficient. Even those who want to encourage greater civic engagement will excuse inaction if action is seen to be too costly. For instance, John Rawls suggests that individual citizens should support and comply with just institutions and work to "further just arrangements not yet established, *at least when this can be done without too much cost to ourselves.*"[80]

In addition, if democratic deliberation requires democratic institutions, a free press, and a public sphere, political leaders and scholars have long observed that war and mobilization for it are a threat to democracy. The danger of permanent war mobilization is the long-term degradation and suspension of democratic practices. James Madison argued,

> Of all the enemies to public liberty war is, perhaps, the most to be dreaded, because it comprises and develops the germ of every other. War is the parent of armies; from these proceed debts and taxes; and armies, and debts, and taxes are the known instruments for bringing the many under the domination of the few. In war, too, the discretionary power of the Executive is extended; its influence in dealing out offices, honors, and emoluments is multiplied; and all the means of seducing the minds, are added to those of subduing the force, of the people. . . . [There is also an] inequality of fortunes, and the opportunities of fraud, growing out of a state of war, and . . . degeneracy of manners and of morals . . . No nation could preserve its freedom in the midst of continual warfare.[81]

In 1941, Harold Lasswell warned against the "possibility that we are moving toward a world of 'garrison states'—a world in which the specialists on violence are the most powerful group in society."[82] The dominance of specialists on violence, Lasswell argued, decreases civil liberties and sidelines democratic processes. "Decisions will be more dictatorial than democratic, and institutional practices long connected with modern democracy will disappear."[83] In a garrison state the symbols of democracy would remain, but legislatures and voting would "go out of use."[84] Lasswell warned against the gradual erosion of civil liberties.

> To militarize is to governmentalize. It is also to centralize. To centralize is to enhance the effective control of the executive over decisions, and thereby to reduce the control exercised by courts and legislatures. To centralize is to enhance the role of military in the allocation of national resources.

80. Rawls, *A Theory of Justice*, 293. Emphasis added.

81. James Madison, 1795, in *Letters and Other Writings of James Madison* (1865), vol. iv, 491–92. http://archive.org/stream/lettersandotherw04madiiala#page/490/mode/2up.

82. Harold Lasswell, "The Garrison State," *American Journal of Sociology* 46, no. 4 (January 1941): 455–468. Also see Lasswell, "The Garrison State Hypothesis Today," in *Changing Patterns of Military Politics*, ed. Samuel P. Huntington (New York: The Free Press, 1962), 51–70.

83. Lasswell, "The Garrison State," 461.

84. Lasswell, "The Garrison State," 462.

Continuing fear of external attack sustains an atmosphere of distrust that finds expression in spy hunts directed at fellow officials and fellow citizens.[85]

Iris Marion Young argues that "The security state ... constitutes itself in relation to an enemy outside, an unpredictable aggressor against which the state needs vigilant defense." The internal aspect of security states threatens democracy.

Internally, the security state must root out the enemy within. There is always the danger that among us are agents who have an interest in disturbing our peace, violating our persons and property, and allowing outsiders to invade our communities and institutions. To protect the state and its citizens, officials must therefore keep a careful watch on the people within its borders and observe and search them to make sure they do not intend evil actions and do not have the means to perform them. The security state overhears conversations in order to try to discover conspiracies of disaster and disruption, and it prevents people from forming crowds or walking the streets after dark. In a security state there cannot be separation of power or critical accountability of official action to a public. Nor can a security state allow expression of dissent.[86]

The sense that there are internal threats allied with external threats then feeds the passivity of the civilian citizen. As Lasswell argued, "Outspoken criticism of official measures launched for national defense is more and more resented as unpatriotic and subversive of the common good. The community at large, therefore, acquiesces in denials of freedom that to go beyond the technical requirements of military security."[87] Similarly, Young argues that in wartime security states can come to embody a "logic of masculinist protection," where the paternalistic state is defending a dependent and weak people: "Security states do not justify their wars by appealing to sentiments of greed or desire for conquest; they appeal to their role as protectors."[88] Young points to the important role of fear in sparking and cementing in what she calls the "protector-protected" relationship.

Citizens and residents who accept the security state because they fear attack allow themselves to be positioned as women and children in relation to paternal protector-leaders. At the same time, to the extent that we identify with a rhetoric of war for the sake of saving the victims of tyranny, we put ourselves in a position superior to those we construct as in need of our aid. Whether looking outward or inward, adopting a more democratic ethos entails rejecting the inequality inherent in the protector-protected logic.[89]

85. Harold Lasswell, "Does the Garrison State Threaten Civil Rights?" *Annals of the American Academy of Political and Social Science* 275 (May 1951): 111–16.
86. Iris Marion Young, "The Logic of Masculinist Protection: Reflections on the Current Security State," *Signs* 29, no. 1 (Autumn 2003): 8.
87. Lasswell, "Does the Garrison State Threaten Civil Rights?" 111.
88. Young, "The Logic of Masculinist Protection": 8.
89. Young, "The Logic of Masculinist Protection": 20–21.

A lack of consensus about the intentions and roles of citizens, or a wide-spread sense that the only legitimate role is passive acceptance of the state's authority, and compliance with the requests for obedience in wartime are already formidable obstacles. The protected-protector logic can also not only diminish the individual's sense of role responsibility, but weaken the sense of role responsibility among various institutions whose role it is, in time of peace, to provide a space for deliberation and the information and analysis necessary for information. Specifically, the press may self-censor as much as it is censored by the state. Universities may deny protestors access to their campuses or sanction the speech of student groups or faculty. And professional organizations may say that war is none of their business.

Collective civilian deliberation requires deliberators, the flow of accurate information and analysis, and the capacity to meet to discuss and weigh arguments. Without these pieces in place the two hardest parts of the exercise of civilian responsibility—evaluation and deliberation about war and mobilization to stop a war, if that is what is required—becomes all the more difficult.

Citizens' willingness to engage in deliberation may also be diminished if they also see a third obstacle to effective civilian citizen engagement: deliberation about future wars and the consequences of specific conduct not only requires willing interlocutors; citizens must have access to information on which to make their decisions. The institutions and practices that make the exercise of civilian's deliberation possible and more effective—the flow of accurate information and analysis, and the capacity to meet to discuss and weigh arguments—are diminished in war time by official secrets acts, and by censorship. Secrecy that long outlasts a war can also hinder the reflective aspect of collective imperfect moral agency.

How is it possible to know enough about the *potential* future consequences of a particular war in order to make informed decisions about the granting or with-drawal of consent? And even if citizens were able to come to consensus, how long would opinion and will formation take? It is arguable that such deliberation would be, as Vitoria feared, much too slow. In many instances, even experts may disagree about the nature of a threat and the best ways to deal with any potential threat.

Fourth, there is the problem of effective action. What could or should citizens who decide that a war is unjust or that the conduct of it will be immoral do? How far should citizens go to stop an unjust war? If many perceive the pressures to conformity and costs of speaking out to be high, is it reasonable to expect civilian citizens to act collectively to halt war?

Less dramatically, activists may become discouraged because political leaders often suggest that protests won't make a difference to them; leaders will do what is right no matter what the public says. U.S. National Security Advisor Condoleezza Rice exemplified this attitude on the day following the large anti-war mobilization of February 2003. Rice was asked by "Fox News Sunday" host Tony Snow: "There are some press accounts saying that the administration is rattled by street protests that occurred in the United States and around the world yesterday. You rattled?" Rice replied, "No. Nothing could be further from the truth. People have the right to protest. People can say what they think." Snow then asked, "Do you think the protesters are naive?" Rice answered: "I just think that it would be worthwhile to step back—it's fine to protest—but to step back and to remember the true nature of the Iraqi regime, to remember how they rape and torture, to remember how they kill women in front of their families to make a point, to remember that he's acquiring and has acquired weapons of mass destruction, that he's used chemical weapons on his own population and on his neighbors, and to ask yourself, 'Do you really want this regime to go unchallenged for the next 12 years, as we've done for the last 12 years?' "[90] The phrases, "people can say what they think," and "it's fine to protest" can reasonably be understood as a dismissal of citizen deliberation, speech and protest as relevant or effective.[91]

Finally, reflection is an important element of imperfect moral agency. While "rally around the flag" patriotism tends to diminish after wars are begun, it is usually difficult to look back upon decisions and actions that were wrong. As Jaspers observed, "people do not like to hear of guilt," they want to move on.[92] While the potential for prospective moral responsibility entails looking backward, it may be difficult to get citizens to engage in the kinds of formal inquiries—such as truth commissions—that might shed light on how things went wrong in their deliberations or in the deliberations and behavior of their government.

V. CONSTITUTING CIVIL SOCIETY AND THE PUBLIC SPHERE FOR DECISIONS ABOUT WAR

In Part III, I outlined an ideal type conception of civilian citizens as an imperfect moral agent. In Part IV, I articulated formidable obstacles to effective public participation in questions of war and peace: a potential dearth of civilian citizens who are willing to consider the questions at stake; disagreement about the individual's role and the role of particular institutions; the erosion of democratic norms and practices during wartime which exacerbates the epistemic difficulties of deliberating about war even with a functioning democratic public sphere; the question of action, what to do if doing something is required; and finally, the problem of reflection. An argument for citizens' responsibility to deliberate and if necessary protest unjust wars ought to suggest how citizen participation can overcome the obstacles to meaningful and effective participation. The elucidation of these problems suggests both a focus for action to improve collective citizen participation—indeed part of the answer lies in collective as opposed to individual action—and a reminder that in problems of war and peace expecting perfection may be setting the bar too high. Perfect may be the enemy of good enough.

---

90. Transcript, "Condoleezza Rice on Fox News Sunday," February 16, 2003, http://www.foxnews.com/story/2003/02/16/transcript-condoleezza-rice-on-fox-news-sunday/.

91. Protest appears to have had little or no effect on the United States' initial decision to invade Iraq in 2003 apart from perhaps delaying the timetable for invasion as the U.S. government attempted to rally support for the invasion. However, public opinion arguably affected the U.S. and its allies conduct in the Iraq war in several ways. Fear of negative public opinion may have diminished the number of allies the United States was able to find for the invasion and occupation of Iraq, and U.S. conduct in the war. Declining support may have also sped U.S. withdrawal.

92. Jaspers, *The Question of German Guilt*, 21.

Just as "you go to war with the army you have . . . not the army you might want or wish to have at a later time,"[93] states go into decisions about war with the legislators, presidents, and prime ministers the people have already selected, and with the civilian citizens already formed in their prejudices and decision-making capacities. I take the problem of time very seriously, as well as Robert Dahl's observation that "the democratic process is not well equipped to deal with questions of exceptional complexity."[94] If war and the months or weeks before they start constitute states of emergency, where the work of constituting a morally responsible civil society prepared for and capable of deliberation and action becomes more difficult even as the option to vote for new representatives may not be available in a reasonable time, then much of this work has to be done in peacetime *before* wars begin. While the minimization of these obstacles will take a concerted long-term effort, the obstacles to the exercise of civilian moral agency in war can be reduced and minimized well before wars begin. We are less likely to harm others and or be the accessories to intended and unintended harm if we take care to develop our moral agency.

First, civic education is essential for the formation and articulation of a shared intention. There are two types of shared intention, substantive and procedural, that are relevant. On the procedural side, for group agency to be manifest, citizens must share the intention to participate and a rejection of the view that it is illegitimate to act against government or that resistance is ineffective. On the substantive side, and at the most basic level, the shared intentions of citizens are security and justice. With regard to questions of war and peace, the civil society's (perhaps nascent) shared intention is rather minimal: to make wise decisions to preserve their peaceful community. The obverse of this intention is the desire not to be accessories or direct participants in causing insecurity and injustice to others.

But these are big words, open to interpretation—the concepts need exploration and elaboration so that what it entails to have these minimal shared intentions, and how they might themselves conflict, becomes clear and so that the public develops a commitment to these minimal concepts. They may also intend to perform a secondary moral responsibility role, as the moral second to government, judging the state, and acting for it when the state has failed in its primary responsibilities.

Second, while collective agency requires that participants play certain roles, it is too much to ask that every single person in the state have a specialized role in decisions about war. As Henry Shue argues with respect to the demands of dealing with global inequality, "we are all entitled to some off-duty time whether it improves performance on the job or not . . . I am only invoking the familiar point that the duties of ordinary people must be less demanding than the performance of saints and heroes because duty bearers are themselves right-bearers too and may

---

93. U.S. Secretary of Defense Donald Rumsfeld said, "As you know, you go to war with the Army you have. They're not the Army you might want or wish to have at a later time." Donald Rumsfeld, "Town Hall Meeting in Kuwait," December 8, 2004, Department of Defense transcript, http://www.defense.gov/transcripts/transcript.aspx?transcriptid=1980.

94. Dahl, *Controlling Nuclear Weapons*, 8. Dahl makes several proposals for how to improve deliberation.

justifiably choose not to be heroes."[95] Shue solves this problem by a division of labor, through institutionalizing roles so that no one individual is overwhelmed.

I follow Shue's lead and suggest a division of labor into three basic roles. First *citizen generalists* are ordinary citizens, who before the fact of war have become skilled in thinking about arguing about war and alternatives to war. Given the importance of war in the life of a state, we might put this responsibility on par with learning to read, write, and do math and science and say that we all should have these reasoning skills that are, of course, not realizable without the ability to reason more generally. In other words, public education should include moral education, what Herman calls "moral literacy" in different modes of reasoning about the justice of coercion and alternatives to coercion including pacifism and the just war tradition.[96] However, while they should know something about what war entails, citizens should *not* be required to become experts in military strategy or weapons; it is the very fact that citizens are able to "think outside the box" that should be prized.

The second role, *citizen expert*, is to be played by individuals, professions and institutions, that have developed particular knowledge relevant to questions of war and peace, namely religious leaders, academics, public intellectuals, nongovernmental organizations, activists, and scientists.[97] When members of those expert communities do relevant research on those questions, hold meetings, and develop a consensus on relevant knowledge, they should be understood as providing a vital public service. Walzer seems to have intellectuals in mind when he raises the issue in *Just and Unjust Wars* of the "way to get one's fellow citizens to think seriously about the war or to join the opposition." He says, "It is not easy to know what sort of action might serve these purposes. Politics is difficult at such a time. But there is intellectual work to do that is less difficult: one must describe as graphically as one can the moral reality of war, talk about what it means to force people to fight, analyze the nature of democratic responsibilities. These, at least, are encompassable tasks, and they are morally required of the men and women who are trained to perform them."[98]

The third citizen participant role might be called *protectors of the public sphere*, which entails the creation and maintenance of public sphere venues, including the preservation of public spaces, and the functions of mediation and facilitation of dialogue. The protector role is fulfilled by the individuals and institutions who we trust with providing the space and making it safe to have conversations about war. These nongovernmental institutions should open their media pages and broadcasts to a wide range of views, provide safe places for public deliberation, moderate debates and discussions, and protect whistle blowers and dissenters. The protectors of the public sphere should promote *civil* exchanges between citizens of different and multiple perspectives. The citizens who direct these venues, including

95. Henry Shue, "Mediating Duties," *Ethics* 98, no. 4 (July 1988): 687–704.

96. Herman, *Moral Literacy*. Education in moral reasoning about conflict and alternatives to war would start in preschool and continue through secondary school. See Nel Noddings, ed., *Educating Citizens for Global Awareness* (New York: Teachers College Press, 2005).

97. Dahl also proposes a division of labor, including the formation of advisory commissions analogous to the National Academy of Sciences. *Controlling Nuclear Weapons*, 82–85.

98. Walzer, *Just and Unjust Wars*, 303.

their boards of directors, ought to see it as a responsibility to open their venues to public speech and to mediate and facilitate conversations.

Anthony Lang proposes churches as an ideal venue for dialogue in part because they "stand outside the concerns of the nation and government [and] . . . are not bound by the official narratives of war that are so often presented in media accounts."[99] There are several other civil society venues where deliberation is possible, including nongovernmental organizations, public libraries, the press, religious institutions, and universities which may then be supplemented by informal conversations on street corners and in coffee houses. Private foundations are also protectors of the public sphere, but they have a particularly important role during times of both war and peace in supporting all three of these roles.

If the first two elements of collective moral agency—the agreement on shared intentions and the sense of the legitimacy and necessity of taking on certain roles with respect to deliberation about war occur, the third element of citizen deliberation, higher quality deliberation, will be more easily met.

Deliberation about war is certainly a demanding task, but not impossible in the appropriate conditions. With regard to assessing the justice of war, and the intended and unintended harm that is likely to result, each collective must have the potential to understand the likely consequences of using military force in any particular situation, and the ways the causal chains linking belief and actions are likely to produce specific outcomes—whether intended or unintended. The task of civilian deliberation before a war is to evaluate the evidence for a prospective war and to discuss the likely consequences of military action and inaction. Citizens must also continue to deliberate during war to evaluate its conduct. There are a number of moral frameworks available for these deliberations including pacifism, nonviolent direct action, consequentialism and the just war tradition. Indeed, citizens will likely argue about which framework is appropriate and this kind of argument is an important part of the deliberation because it challenges dominant frames and forces people to become clear about their reasoning.

But the issue is not just what we talk about when we talk about war, but how we talk about war, how we deliberate and make decisions. Many civilian discussions are likely to take the form of debate or arguments, where, in the best of cases, participants adhere to rules of evidence and standards of argumentation that more or less approach a discourse of ethical dialogue.[100] But discourse of ethical dialogue is certainly not the only way to engage in moral deliberation, nor should it be assumed that deliberation will be neatly "rational"/unemotional. Discourse always includes emotions, whether passions are acknowledged or not, and the understanding of how feelings of empathy, fear, revenge, and anger are in play, manipulated or

---

99. Anthony F. Lang Jr., "Narrative Authority," in *Just War*, ed. Lang, O'Driscoll, and Williams, 150.

100. See Jürgen Habermas, "Discourse Ethics: Notes on a Program of Philosophical Justification," in *Moral Consciousness and Communicative Action* (Cambridge, MA: MIT Press, 1990), 43–115.

discounted, can actually elevate the political argument.[101] While some civilian citizens may aim for consensus, others may take votes, and offer resolutions to policy makers.

Lang argues that the "just war tradition provides exactly the kind of framework that could guide the question-and-answer process of a pastoral interaction. Rather than a set of rules that the population demands the military or political elites to follow, the just war tradition could serve as a framework through which an entire society can narrate the moral dilemmas of war."[102] Lang proposes churches because the pastoral form of dialogue is well suited to moral deliberation. Lang describes the pastoral role this way.

> In pastoral contexts, clerics are trained above all to listen. Members of their community who find themselves in morally challenged positions will often approach a cleric looking for answers to their problems. Rather than mechanically apply a set of moral rules or even make a judgment of the person, clerics allow individuals to tell their stories, to narrate the problem through the concrete details of the situation. Throughout this process, the clerics role is to ask questions that arise from the religious tradition so that the person can place his or her dilemma into a context that will resonate with the tradition itself. It is this process of telling stories, guided by incisive and morally penetrating questions, that allows individuals to make judgments that are both morally informed but sensitive to their own situation.[103]

One might accept the pastoral approach to dialogue as well suited to moral deliberation, but suggest the just war tradition itself is too rooted in the Western Catholic tradition to have wide appeal in many contexts. Further, as Nicholas Rengger argues, it is possible to see the just war tradition as becoming, in the last several centuries, less critical of state authority—indeed closer to it—and less limiting of violence than in the past.[104] Indeed, as Rengger suggests, the just war tradition is embedded in the responsibility to protect doctrine, which Rengger argues authorizes interventions that are potentially both punitive and paternalistic. Thankfully, there is a range of religious and secular moral traditions available to citizens with which to consider the questions of war and peace.[105]

101. See Brent J. Steele, "Revenge, Affect, and Just War," in *Just War*, ed. Lang, O'Driscoll, and Williams, 197–211; Iris Marion Young, *Inclusion and Democracy* (Oxford: Oxford University Press, 2000); Neta C. Crawford, "*Homo Politicus* and Argument (Nearly) All the Way Down: Persuasion in Politics," *Perspectives on Politics* 7, no. 1 (March 2009): 103–24; and Neta. C. Crawford, "No Borders, No Bystanders: Developing Individual and Institutional Capacities for Global Moral Responsibility," in *Global Basic Rights*, ed. Charles R. Beitz and Robert E. Goodin (Oxford: Oxford University Press, 2009), 131–155.

102. Lang, "Narrative Authority," 149.

103. Lang, "Narrative Authority," 148.

104. Nicholas Rengger, *Just War and International Order: The Uncivil Condition in World Politics* (Cambridge: Cambridge University Press, 2013).

105. See, for instance, Terry Nardin, ed., *The Ethics of War and Peace: Religious and Secular Perspectives* (Princeton: Princeton University Press, 1996) and Sohail Hashmi and Stephen P. Lee, *Ethics and Weapons of Mass Destruction: Religious and Secular Perspectives* (Cambridge: Cambridge University Press, 2004).

Another, secular, mode of citizen engagement is to use elements of the "deliberative polling" process where a number of citizens, randomly and representatively selected so that the group is diverse, are given notice that they will participate in discussing an important issue. Participants are then given "balanced briefing documents, balanced panels, and random assignment to small groups with trained moderators."[106]

The fourth element of moral agency is the capacity for effective action. If citizens judge that a war is unjust or they can reasonably foresee that the consequences of a war are likely to be disproportionate or indiscriminate harm to civilians, they may decide that they should protest the proposed war. The question of effective action has two elements: whether citizens can be expected to act, and whether their actions can have any effect on policy before and during war.

If, as Michael Walzer argues, the war convention requires commanders to take due care not to harm the innocent and that soldiers are required to "accept personal risks rather than kill innocent people"[107] are citizens similarly bound to accept personal costs and risks? Whistle-blowers may be prosecuted, dissidents may be threatened, jailed or pilloried, and draft evaders may be imprisoned. What risks might we reasonably accept civilian citizens to take in order to prevent an unjust war? There are several options for both exit and voice. Exit is manifest in the withdrawal of civilian resources from a regime, including labor strikes, resistance to conscription, and emigration while voice includes petitions, vigils, and demonstrations. Further, nonviolent direct action can include physically blocking the operations of the state, such as encircling military installations or forming road blocks. Questions of action and activism are individual decisions, but they are greatly influenced by the social context and the conception of what is possible. Gene Sharp suggests that nonviolent direct action can work and that when it does work, it shifts power relations.

> When people refuse their cooperation, withhold help, and persist in their disobedience and defiance, they are denying their opponent the basic human assistance and cooperation that any government or hierarchical system requires . . . If people and institutions do this in sufficient numbers, for long enough, that government or hierarchical system will no longer have power. The persons who have been 'rulers' become simply ordinary people. Everything is changed because the human assistance that created and supported the regime's political power has been withdrawn. Therefore, its power has dissolved.[108]

How does citizen action work in specific cases? Can activism and protest ever be said to be effective? And is direct action of this sort only possible in robust democracies where citizens need not fear retaliation?

While it is common to stress how many people and governments went along with Nazi policies during World War II, there were many small pockets of

---

106. Fishkin, "Consulting the Public through Deliberative Polling," 130.
107. Walzer, *Just and Unjust Wars*, 305.
108. Gene Sharp, *The Role of Power in Nonviolent Struggle* (Boston: The Albert Einstein Institution, 1990), 9.

resistance in Germany and in German-occupied territories. There were heroic acts by individuals and small groups. But there was also large-scale civilian resistance that saved thousands of people from their deaths.

For example, from the first moments of their occupation by Germany in April 1940 Danish political leaders and citizens resisted by not cooperating whole heartedly with German orders. Indeed, it is when the martial law was declared in August 1943 and the Danish government dissolved that the citizens' collective action and organization escalated.[109] Work slowdowns, strikes, and sabotage eventually made occupied Denmark much more difficult to govern and reduced the Danish contribution to the German war machine. Danish officials had refused to cooperate with the administrative steps necessary to identify Jews for deportation and eventual killing in concentration camps. The Danish government's foot-dragging for several years slowed the process of extending the "Final Solution" to Denmark while civil resistance raised the costs of the occupation.

But it is the Danish *people* who acted spontaneously and collectively to get more than 90 percent of Danish Jews to safety when the order was finally given in October 1943 to round up the Jews for deportation to a concentration camp. Within a few weeks of the order, thousands of Jews were transported by ordinary Danes to fishing boats and then ferried to Sweden. Most of the few Jews who remained in Denmark were hidden by Danes and, to Adolf Eichmann's great distress, the Nazis were only able to transport about 400 Jews to the Theresienstadt concentration camp. Hannah Arendt argues that the Danes had an "authentically political sense, an inbred comprehension of the requirements and responsibilities of citizenship."[110]

Danish resistance between 1940 and 1945 illustrates Gene Sharp's observation that "habits of obedience and loyalty to authority may be threatened by widespread nonviolent action."[111] As Hannah Arendt says: "It is the only case we know of in which the Nazis met with *open* resistance, and the result seems to have been that those who were exposed to it changed their minds. They themselves apparently no longer looked upon the extermination of a whole people as a matter of course. They had met resistance based on principle, and their 'toughness' had melted like butter in the sun."[112] Arendt also reminds us that German officials were frustrated in implementing the "Final Solution" in Bulgaria when faced with open and stubborn resistance by Bulgarian officials and the "population of Sofia": not a single Bulgarian Jew was deported.[113]

Several scholars make the case that citizen activism was effective in curbing the superpowers during the Cold War and indeed may be credited with creating the conditions that led to the end of the Cold War. For example, Matthew Evangelista

---

109. See Nathaniel Hong, *Occupied: Denmark's Adaptation and Resistance to German Occupation 1940–1945* (Copenhagen: Danish Resistance Museum Publishing, 2012) and Bo Lidegard, *Countrymen: The Untold Story of How Denmark's Jews Escaped the Nazis and the Courage of Their Fellow Danes—and of the Extraordinary Role of the SS* (New York: Knopf, 2013).

110. Hannah Arendt, *Eichmann in Jerusalem: A Report on the Banality of Evil* (New York: Penguin, 1963), 179.

111. Sharp, *The Role of Power in Nonviolent Struggle*, 17.

112. Arendt, *Eichmann in Jerusalem*, 175.

113. Arendt, *Eichmann in Jerusalem*, 185–88.

shows how experts—nuclear scientists, engineers, and physicians spoke out about nuclear testing and nuclear war in the 1950s, 1960s, and 1980s—provided important information, perspective, and creative solutions that helped foster arms control and an end to the Cold War.[114] Jeffrey Knopf argues that citizen activism was an important impetus to several nuclear arms control agreements—the test ban treaty, and the SALT and START treaties.[115] Mary Kaldor argues that transnational citizen activism, which formed a new civil society in Europe, helped end the Cold War by simultaneously promoting a disarmament and human rights agenda.[116] And Karin Fierke suggests that activists were effective precisely because they challenged expert framings of the Cold War and citizen activists changed expectations about what was possible.[117]

Finally, imperfect moral agency is characterized by reflection and, when necessary, revision of structures and processes that went awry. The capacity for reflection is a crucial element of moral agency and essential for prospective or "forward-looking" moral responsibility. Reflection provides the material for moral and political education, highlighting the ways that moral decisions are rarely isolated.

Reflection should focus not only on the state's behavior, but on role performance and actions of civilian citizens, and this is the first step to preparing for the *next* time a collective may need to evaluate a war. Specifically, while professional historians and journalists reflect on the judgments and conduct of commanders, civilian leaders, and military organizations, civilian citizens operating within civil society organizations can reflect upon the way they participated in decisions about war. This reflection could occur in the press or other institutions that are typically sites for reflection—religious and educational venues. Reflection could include questions such as "did we adequately consider alternative options?"; "were we swept up in patriotic fervor, fear, anger or militaristic enthusiasm?"; "did we make an environment conducive to public discussion and listen attentively to skeptics?"; "what can we learn from the protest movements and resistance activities?" And here too, in asking these questions, ordinary citizens, operating in their roles as generalists, experts, and protectors of the public sphere, play an important role in constituting a cycle of collective moral agency.[118,119]

114. Matthew Evangelista, *Unarmed Forces: The Transnational Movement to End the Cold War* (Ithaca, NY: Cornell University Press, 1999).

115. Jeffrey W. Knopf, *Domestic Society and International Cooperation: The Impact of Protest on US Arms Control Policy* (Cambridge: Cambridge University Press, 1998).

116. Mary Kaldor, *Global Civil Society: An Answer to War* (Cambridge: Polity Press, 2003).

117. K. M. Fierke, *Changing Games, Changing Strategies: Critical Investigations in Security* (Manchester: Manchester University Press, 1998).

118. For a recent treatment of some of these issues see Bronwyn Leebaw, *Judging State-Sponsored Violence, Imagining Political Change* (Cambridge: Cambridge University Press, 2011).

119. I thank Anthony Lang Jr., Bronwyn Leebaw, Jane Mansbridge, Cian O'Driscoll, and John Williams for perceptive comments on an earlier draft.

Midwest Studies In Philosophy, XXXVIII (2014)

From Global Collective Obligations to Institutional Obligations

BILL WRINGE

I. INTRODUCTION

Although the notion of collective obligation rarely plays a significant role within analytic political philosophy as the subject is currently conceived, it seems easy to make a case that it should do so.[1] For political philosophy involves theoretical reflection on politics, and the political domain is, among other things, an arena in which groups of human beings come together to confront the problems that they face together. In other words it is a domain within which collective action plays a central role. If there are collective obligations, then these place constraints on the kinds of collective action in which we may permissibly engage. So, it seems, considerations about collective obligations should play a significant role in thinking about the kinds of political institutions we ought to have, and the kind of political action we should engage in.

In this article, I shall be concerned with a particular kind of collective obligation which has recently been discussed by Martha Nussbaum: collective obligations which fall on humanity as a whole, or what we might call the "global collective." Many people might be skeptical of the existence of such obligations. In what follows, I shall try to make a case for their existence, and address one kind of reason for being skeptical about them: namely, that the bearer of this obligation— the world's population as a whole—is not the kind of entity which has the capacity

---

1. For one significant exception, see Margaret Gilbert, *A Theory of Political Obligation: Membership, Commitment, and the Bonds of Society* (Oxford: Oxford University Press, 2006).

to act. However, my main concern will be with a second kind of reason that people might have for being dubious about such obligations. This is that it seems unclear what constraints, if any, such obligations might place on the actions of particular, concretely situated individuals such as you and me. I shall address this issue by arguing that some kinds of forward-looking global obligation give rise to obligations on individuals to bring into existence institutions that can enable those obligations to be met.

II. GLOBAL COLLECTIVE OBLIGATIONS: THE VERY IDEA

In recent years, a number of authors have explored the idea of a collective obligation.[2] They have not, primarily, been concerned with the idea that certain obligations might fall on individuals in virtue of the groups of which they are members, but rather with the idea that obligations might fall on some kind of collective body, existing over and above its individual members. Such obligations need not be reducible to the obligations of individuals; but they need not float entirely free of them. One might, for example, conceive of certain obligations falling on individuals in virtue of their being members of a collective on which certain kinds of collective obligation falls.[3] Thus, for example, we might see the obligations which parents have to care for their young children as falling, in the first instance on the parents collectively, and only subsequently and derivatively on one parent or other.

If the notion of a collective obligation is coherent, as the work of these authors suggests, then it is important to ask what kinds of entities such obligations might fall upon. One obvious set of candidates consists of entities that have a formal organizational structure, such as nation-states, business corporations, and smaller bodies such as committees within a larger organization.[4] We should expect that in cases like this, the relationship between the obligations which fall on the group and those which fall on individual members of that group will be complex and will depend on a number of different features both of the group concerned, and of the details of the relationship between individual group members and the group as a whole.

2. See for example, Peter A. French *Collective and Corporate Responsibility* (New York: Columbia University Press, 1984); David Copp, "On the Agency of Certain Collective Entities: An Argument from 'Normative Autonomy'," *Midwest Studies in Philosophy* 30 (2006): 194–221; Philip Pettit, "Responsibility Incorporated," *Ethics* 117 (2007): 171–201; Margaret Gilbert, *Membership, Commitment, and the Bounds of Obligation* (Oxford: Oxford University Press, 2008); Tracy Isaacs, *Moral Responsibility in Collective Contexts* (Oxford: Oxford University Press); Elizabeth Cripps, "Climate Change, Collective Harm and Legitimate Coercion," *Critical Review of International Social and Political Philosophy* 14 (2011): 171–93.

3. For the idea that the relationship between collective obligations and individual obligations might be one of justification or explanation, and an argument that this is incompatible with the idea that collective obligations can be reduced to individual obligations, see Bill Wringe, "Collective Obligations: Their Existence, Their Explanatory Power and Their Supervenience on the Obligations of Individuals," *European Journal of Philosophy* (advance online publication, doi:10.1111/ejop.12076).

4. See Gilbert, *Membership, Commitment, and the Bounds of Obligation*, French, *Collective and Corporate Responsibility*, and Copp, "On the Agency of Certain Collective Entities," respectively, for examples of each of these types.

Martha Nussbaum has argued that that there is another, more fundamental collective whose obligations ought to be of interest from the point of view of political philosophy. In *Frontiers of Justice*, she argues that we all have entitlements based on justice to a minimum of a number of goods which feature on a list of core human capabilities. She then suggests that "if this is so, we are all under a collective obligation to provide the people of the world with what they need. . . humanity is under a collective obligation to find ways of living and co-operating together so that all human beings have decent lives."[5] We might wonder exactly who is included in the collective which is subject to this obligation. One natural suggestion, which is consistent with, if not required by Nussbaum's text, is that it includes everyone currently alive. Call this collective the "global collective": I shall assume that it is this collective that Nussbaum takes to be the bearer of the collective obligation she has in mind.

Nussbaum does not give a detailed argument for the claim that "humanity" has a collective obligation in any detail. However, I have argued for this conclusion in detail elsewhere.[6] My argument starts from a well-known objection to the notion of subsistence rights, conceived of as rights on the parts of individuals to have certain basic needs attended to. One standard objection to the claim that such rights exist is that if they did, they would necessarily give rise to obligations on agents to see to it that such needs are fulfilled (or, more plausibly to see to it that individuals acquire the capacity to meet these needs). However, there seem to be cases in which it seems implausible to hold that such an obligation could fall either on any individual human being or on any salient collective body.

Consider, for example, the case of a starving individual in a drought-stricken region of a failed state such as Somalia. It may be quite implausible to think that any particular individual has an obligation to do something about her fate: Everyone nearby who is in a position to help may be in a similar plight. It may also be true that the most obvious collective bodies are in no position to help either (that is the point of focusing on an individual in a failed state). The state in question may

---

5. Nussbaum, *Frontiers*, 279–80. For a more detailed argument along the same lines, see Bill Wringe, "Needs, Rights, and Collective Obligations," *Royal Institute of Philosophy Supplement* 80 (2005): 187–206.

6. Wringe, "Needs, Rights and Collective Obligations." Not everyone would accept that the population of the world does constitute an unstructured collective of the sort Wringe suggests. One reason for this has been explored in detail by Thomas Pogge, in *World Poverty and Human Rights* (Cambridge: Polity Press, 2001), who suggests that global economic interconnectedness makes the world's population part of a structured political community. Whether or not Pogge is correct, I think the argument from the nature of rights suggests that it makes sense to think of there being collective obligations on the world's population considered in abstraction from any political structure that might fall on them (just as it might make sense to think of a group of individuals who were in fact the members of a particular club or social group having certain obligations when considered as a particular social organized group, and other obligations in virtue of some other form of social organization, or in virtue of their being placed in such a way as to enable them to act together collectively to address some pressing need. For further critical discussion of Pogge's suggestion, see Saladin Meckled-Garcia, "On the Very Idea of Cosmopolitan Justice: Constructivism and International Agency," *Journal of Political Philosophy* 16 (2008): 245–71; Bill Wringe, "War Crimes and Expressive Theories of Punishment: Communication or Denunciation?," *Res Publica* 15 (2010): 119–33.

lack the resources, the organizational capacity, or the territorial control which would be required to do anything about their situation.[7]

It would be unsatisfactory to say that individuals in such circumstances do not have the rights that more fortunately placed individuals—for example, those who are in a position to be helped by their compatriots—do have. To say so would be to say in effect that the protection that rights are supposed to afford individuals lapses in situations where they are most in need of it.[8] This unsatisfactory conclusion can be avoided if we think that obligations can fall on a global collective.[9] The global collective body acts as what one might call an "obligation-bearer of last resort." The existence of collective obligations which fall on this body is thus something which can be taken to be a presupposition of the claim that there is a right to have certain kinds of basic needs met. What we have is, in effect, a transcendental argument for the existence of obligations falling on a relatively unstructured body—namely, a global collective.[10]

III. THE AGENCY OBJECTION

One might respond to this argument for global obligations by denying that unstructured groups can be the subject of collective obligations. Call this the Agency Objection. The Agency Objection rests on a substantive claim about the kinds of entities on which collective obligations can fall: namely, that they must be collective agents. Call this the Agency Claim. The Agency Claim is a substantive claim, which we should not accept without argument.[11]

7. Onora O'Neill, "Hunger, Needs and Rights," in *Problems of International Ethics,* ed. Stephen Luper-Foy (London: Westview, 1986), 67–83, reprinted as "Rights Obligations and Needs," in *Necessary Goods: Our Responsibility to Meet Others' Needs,*" ed. Gillian. Brock (Lanham, MD: Rowman and Littlefield), 86–106. Gopal Sreenivasan, "A Human Right to Health: Some Inconclusive Skepticism," *Proceedings of the Aristotelian Society Supplementary Volume* 86 (2012): 239–65 has recently appealed to an argument along similar lines in defense of the claim that there is no human right to health. See James Griffin, *On Human Rights* (Oxford: Oxford University Press, 2008) for a useful discussion of the first of these.

8. Of course the protection that rights provide is only metaphorical. Rights can only protect individuals to the extent that individuals act in accordance with the obligations that those rights generate. But what would be entailed by the suggestion that people in desperate circumstances have fewer rights is not this uncontroversial claim, but that these individuals would be deprived of the protections which rights can, and should, provide.

9. See Wringe, "Needs, Rights and Collective Obligations" for arguments that this is the best way of avoiding the conclusion; and in particular that collective obligations falling on other bodies provide a less satisfactory solution.

10. For defenses of the view that unstructured collectives can have obligations, see Cripps, "Climate Change." For a more skeptical view, see Isaacs, *Moral Responsibility*, chaps 1, 2, and 5.

11. Isaacs, *Moral Responsibility*, chap 1; Holly Lawford-Smith, "The Feasibility of Collectives' Actions," *Australasian Journal of Philosophy* 90 (2012): 453–67; and Stephanie Collins, "Collectives' Duties and Collectivisation Duties," *Australasian Journal of Philosophy* 91 (2): 231–48 all endorse the claim that only collectives which are capable of agency can be the subjects of collective obligation. For an argument against this view, see Bill Wringe, "Global Obligations and the Agency Objection," *Ratio* 23, no. 2 (2010).

Here is an argument in favor of the Agency Claim. Call it the "Agency Argument."

(Agency Argument)

(P1) Only groups with a certain kind of internal structure are capable of collective action.

(P2). Only groups that are capable of collective action can have collective obligations.

C: Unstructured groups cannot be the subject of collective obligation.

The Agency Argument does not give us good reasons for accepting the Agency Claim. Both of its premises are questionable (and, in this context, contentious). The first premiss of the Agency Argument is problematic because the phenomenon of collective action has been analyzed in different ways by different authors. While it is true that on some accounts of collective action, collective action requires an agent with a certain amount of internal structure, there are other accounts, such as Christopher Kutz's "minimalist" account according to which this is not so.[12] In the absence of detailed argument about the nature of collective action, we cannot simply make an inference from lack of formal structure to the incapacity for agency.[13]

The second premise of the argument is also problematic. Several authors, including Isaacs, Collins, and Lawford-Smith, appear to take it to be self-evident.[14] However, it is not. In this context it is highly contentious. One might argue (and I have in fact argued) that the existence of collective obligations does not require that the collective on whom the obligation falls be an agent, but only that some agent or agents be answerable for the fulfillment or nonfulfillment of the obligation.[15] In the case of obligations which fall on unstructured groups, the agents in question are typically some or all of those who make up the group in question.[16]

---

12. Christian List and Philip Pettit, *Group Agency: The Possibility, Design, and Status of Corporate Agents* (Oxford: Oxford University Press); Peter A. French, *Collective and Corporate Responsibility*; Margaret Gilbert, *On Social Facts* (London: Routledge, 1989); Christopher Kutz, *Complicity: Law and Ethics for a Collective Age* (Cambridge: Cambridge University Press, 2000); Christopher Kutz, "Acting Together," *Philosophy and Phenomenological Research* 61 (2000): 1–31.

13. We might wonder whether apparently competing accounts of collective action are in fact competing accounts of the same phenomenon, or whether they are accounts of different, but closely related phenomena. In the latter case, then in the absence of an argument for the view that collective obligations require a capacity for collective action of one particular sort rather than another, it would be tendentious to insist that collective obligations can only fall on groups which are capable of performing collective action of a particular sort. But this, it seems, is what would be required in order to establish that collective obligations could only fall on groups with a particular structure. Cf. Gilbert "Collective Wrongdoing: Moral and Legal Responses," *Social Theory and Practice* 28 (2002): 167–87.

14. Isaacs, *Moral Responsibility*; Lawford-Smith, " Feasibility"; Collins, "Collective Duties."

15. Wringe, "Global Obligations."

16. Wringe, "Global Obligations."

Anne Schwenkenbecher has argued that this response is unsatisfactory.[17] She suggests that it involves conflating two distinct duties: a duty to act in a certain way (of which the subject is the collective) and a duty on individuals to see that the collective organizes itself in a way which would enable it to act in a certain way. However, we need not see things in this way. For it is plausible that there is a relationship between the duties of collectives and the duties of individuals which make them up which is weaker than that of identity, but nevertheless nonaccidental: the relationship of grounding. My suggestion is that a duty of a collective may ground (without being identical to) the duties of the individuals who make it up. The existence of this grounding relationship is shown up for us when we cite the existence of a duty falling on a collective in order to explain why some individual has a particular duty.[18]

One might wonder whether the second premise of the Agency Argument follows from the claim that "ought implies can." It would do so if we accepted that only agents have the capacity to carry out the actions which are necessary for collective obligations to be fulfilled. However, if we think that some collectives are potentially agents without being actual agents, then this claim seems false. For it seems plausible that if a collective is (merely) a potential agent, it is capable of doing any of the things which it would have the capacity to do if it were appropriately organized.[19]

Lawford-Smith has argued against this suggestion. She suggests that in general we should not attribute to an unorganized group the capacity to do things which it could do if organized. In cases where it is not practically possible for a group to organize itself, it lacks the capacity to do the things which it could do if appropriately organized.[20] Thus, she suggests that the German army under Hitler did not have the capacity to bring Hitler down even though it could have done so if appropriately organized. As a consequence, she suggests, we should not regard the army as being to blame for not bringing Hitler down.

Lawford-Smith draws the wrong conclusion from this example. It is plausible if the facts are as she describes them the army, considered as an institution, was blameworthy. We might resist this conclusion on the grounds that since no individual member of the army was in a position to be reasonably sure that others would have co-operated with them, no individual was to blame. However, we might want to allow for the possibility of cases where the blameworthiness of a collective

---

17. Anne Schwenkenbecher, "Joint Duties and Global Moral Obligations," *Ratio* 26 (2013): 310–328.

18. We might put the point by saying that the grounding relationship is thus the ontological counterpart of the explanation relationship, which is epistemological.

19. In general, if I am capable of acquiring the capacity to do X by a certain time, then, in the only sense of can which is of interest here, I can do it. It is in this sense, for example, that one might judge that the students who are being taught by a particular teacher can pass the final exam which she devised at the beginning of the semester, and that those who are in receipt of a scholarship stand under a moral obligation to do so: They may not be capable of doing it now, but they are capable of acquiring the necessary capacity.

20. Lawford-Smith, "Feasibility."

agent does not entail the blameworthiness of any particular members.[21] One reason for doing so would be if one regarded the structure or ethos of the institution or collective as playing a significant role in explaining the blameworthy behavior of the agent—something which seems highly plausible in the case Lawford-Smith describes.[22]

I have argued that both premises of the Agency Argument are problematic. Since there do not seem to be any reasons independent of this argument for accepting the Agency Claim, we should take this claim to be unproven. So we are justified in ignoring the Agency Objection.

IV. TWO PRINCIPLES ABOUT ORGANIZATIONS

It is not immediately clear what bearing the existence of a global obligation to satisfy subsistence needs might have on questions about what particular individuals should do in particular concrete situations. It is clear that such an obligation cannot give rise to an obligation on each individual to satisfy everyone's subsistence needs. For no individual can do this. Indeed, it is the fact that no individual can do this, taken together with the claim that ought implies can, that motivated the suggestion there is a global collective obligation to be considered here in the first place.

However, it does not follow from this that global obligations can give rise to no obligations on individuals. To draw this conclusion would be to overlook the possibility that collective obligations can give rise to obligations on individuals that are slightly more complex than those which we have considered so far.

Here are two plausible principles about the ways in which obligations which fall on a collective can generate obligations on the individuals who make up that collective.
(Organizational Principle 1)

> OP 1: A stringent obligation which falls on a collective, and which can only be fulfilled by collective action of a sort that is unlikely to come about in a spontaneous and uncoordinated manner generates an obligation on each of the members of that collective to promote modes of organization that would enable the obligation to be carried out, to the extent that it is in their power to promote such forms of obligation.

(Organizational Principle 2)

> OP 2: A stringent obligation which falls on a collective which is organized in such a way as to enable the co-ordination of collective actions that satisfy

21. For a view of this sort, see Margaret Gilbert, "Who's to Blame: Collective Responsibility and Its Implications for Group Members," *Midwest Studies in Philosophy* 30 (2006): 94–114.

22. A view of this sort helps to make sense of certain kinds of reactive attitude that one might have in this case: For example, one might think that the army deserved contempt in this situation, while reserving judgment on whether any particular individuals did.

global obligations generates a *pro tanto* obligation on individuals who form part of that collective to act in ways which are necessary for the fulfillment of those obligations.

OP 1 and OP 2 do not give rise to putative obligations on individuals that those individuals are unable to satisfy. Furthermore, they do appear to be capable of providing some kind of guidance concerning the ways in which particular individuals should act in particular concrete circumstances. However, these facts about OP 1 and OP 2 do not establish their correctness. I shall attempt to provide some arguments for them in Sections V and VI. However, before doing so, however, some clarificatory remarks are required.

Clearly, both these principles require considerable explication. For example, much more needs to be said about which obligations are "stringent obligations" and why both principles are restricted to the case of stringent obligations. The occurrence of the notion of a stringent obligation in these principles will also make a difference to the question of what counts as an adequate argument for them. Any such argument will at a minimum have to explain why it only applies to stringent obligations; ideally it should also say something about whether there are any related principles which apply to nonstringent obligations.

The intuitive case for the restricting the principles in some way is fairly obvious: There would be something wrong with a principle that generated, or threatened to generate, a need for a world state—or even a loose federation of states—out of a possible collective obligation to avoid littering sidewalks. The word *stringent* acts, to that extent as something of a placeholder. However, I shall take an obligation to be stringent provided that failing to meet it would result to a large number of significant violations of individuals' basic rights, where I use the term basic right in Henry Shue's sense to mean a right which individuals must have in order for any further assignment of rights to them to have any point.[23]

This characterization of stringency still leaves the content of OP 1 and OP 2 somewhat indeterminate. Further specification would involve discussion of which rights are basic rights; of what counts as a "significant" violation of them; and how many such violations are required to generate a stringent obligation. These are all important issues, which I shall not pursue for the time being. Even when these lacunae are acknowledged, it seems plausible that a good argument for OP 1 and OP 2 would go some way toward showing how claims about global obligation might give rise to relatively contentful requirements for action relating to particular individuals.[24]

23. Henry Shue, *Basic Rights: Subsistence, Affluence and US Foreign Policy* (Princeton, NJ: Princeton University Press, 1980/1986) argues—correctly in my view—that such rights must include both rights to a basic level of subsistence and to a certain level of personal security. For further discussion, see Charles Beitz and Robert Goodin, eds., *Global Basic Rights* (Oxford: Oxford University Press).

24. It is worth emphasizing that I shall be providing arguments in favor of OP 1 and OP 2; I shall not be claiming that they provide us with the full story about the ways in which global obligations might filter down to the individual level. One reason for this is that OP 2 fails to generate any obligations on individuals in situations where there is more than one way for a collective to carry out its collective obligations—as will often be the case. Nevertheless, a successful

OP 1 and OP 2 both assign individuals a duty to organize themselves in particular ways when they are members of collectives on which certain obligations fall. Stephanie Collins has also argued that individuals have a duty to organize in certain ways when faced with certain kinds of predicament which can only be solved by collective action.[25] She calls these duties "collectivization duties." However, my position differs from Collins in at least two respects. First, my principles leave open, in a way that Collins does not, the possibility that some predicaments are best dealt with by a multiplicity of collective agents.[26] Second, and more significantly, Collins appears to take the existence of collectivization duties to be a brute moral fact. This view seems implausible. By contrast, on my view the existence of the duties specified by OP 1 and OP 2 follows from more fundamental moral consideration, as I shall now argue.[27]

V: CONNECTING COLLECTIVE AND INDIVIDUAL OBLIGATIONS

In arguing for OP 1 and OP 2, I shall argue for a general principle connecting collective obligations to individual obligations. I shall then attempt to apply this principle to the particular case of global obligations. Section IV will be devoted to the first of these tasks; Section V to the second.

The principle connecting collective and individual obligations which I shall be appealing to is one on which all-out collective obligations entail, but are not equivalent to, certain *pro tanto* conditional obligations on the parts of the individuals who make up the collective. It is as follows:
(C to I)

> If in a particular situation a collective C has an all-out obligation to Phi, then, for any member M of C, and for any set S of possible actions of members of C that, if performed together, would constitute C's Phi-ing, if S includes M's doing A, then M has a *pro tanto* obligation to do A.[28]

It is natural to think that a principle which is like C to I but which applies to all-out obligations rather than *pro tanto* ones must be true, since if it were not, there would be situations in which all individual obligations were met, and in which some collective obligations remained unmet. Since the only way in which collectives can act is via the action of individuals, this seems absurd. However, David Copp has

---

argument for them would at least show how claims about global obligation might give rise to substantive claims about the obligations of individuals.

25. Collins, "Collective Duties."

26. Collins, "Collective Duties." Collins's use of an example involving a relatively small number of agents may explain why this possibility is not especially salient for her.

27. Collins's view seems to have something in common with the "primitive obligation to contribute" view which I discuss and argue against in Wringe, "Collective Obligations," Section VI.

28. This formulation of C to I owes a great deal to useful correspondence with David Copp (though he should not be blamed for the formulation I have settled on).

argued that cases of this sort can occur, giving as examples situations where a committee fails to carry out its obligations even though none of the individuals on it fail to carry out their obligations.[29]

It is much harder to devise cases which constitute a counter-example to C to I when it is formulated as a principle about *pro tanto* obligations. The cases that Copp discusses involve situations where the obligations of a collective body impose *pro tanto* obligations on its members, and these *pro tanto* obligations are themselves defeated by countervailing obligations. However, it is worth noticing that we do not say in general that when a *pro tanto* obligation is defeated by some countervailing consideration that that obligation no longer exists; merely that in this particular situation it does not yield an all-out obligation. Nevertheless, while this point is suggestive, it does not amount to much of an argument for the view that there is a connection between collective obligations and the *pro tanto* obligations of individuals.

Here is an argument for (C to I), based on a broadly Kantian account of morality. It starts from one of Kant's formulations of the categorical imperative—the formula of the kingdom of ends. Kant argues that any rational being should will as if they were the legislator for a kingdom of ends.[30] One plausible suggestion as to what Kant means by this is that a kingdom of ends is, among other things, a state of affairs where all rational beings are treated as ends-in-themselves. Since Kant also seems to hold that all of our duties can be derived from a duty to treat rational beings as ends in themselves, it seems as though a kingdom of ends would have to be a situation in which every obligation bearer fulfills all of their obligations.

If we are good Kantians, then the scope of the universal quantifier here is not simply the class of human beings, for Kant thinks that moral laws apply to all rational beings. One might think, as an alternative, that it ranges over all agents. But if the class of obligation holders is wider than the class of agents—as I have argued it is—it is hard to see why the quantifier in the suggestion should not range over all obligation bearers.

Kant also holds that "whoever wills the end wills also the means that are indispensably necessary to his action."[31] So, if there are collective obligations, and a legislator in a kingdom of ends necessarily wills that all obligations—including collective obligations—should be satisfied (as I have suggested), then such a legislator in a kingdom of ends wills the necessary means for satisfying collective obligations be satisfied. However, as I have already argued, the only means by which collective obligations can be carried out is through individual action. So a legislator in a kingdom of ends wills that individuals act in such a way as to enable the obligations of the collectives of which they are members to be carried out.

This establishes something very close to the conclusion that we want to reach. For, on a Kantian view, the moral law is given by the content of what a legislator in a kingdom of ends would will. So if we have established that a

29. David Copp, "On the Agency of Certain Collective Entities," 194–221.
30. Immanuel Kant, *Grounding for the Metaphysics of Morals*, trans. James W. Ellington (Indianapolis: Hackett, 1993), 40 (AK 434).
31. Kant, *Grounding*, 27 (AK 417).

universal legislator would will that individuals act in such a way as to allow collective obligations to be carried out by means of their concerted efforts, then we have established that there are moral obligations on individuals of the sort that I have been arguing for.

One might object that C to I runs into difficulties in situations where there is more than one way for a collective to fulfill a collective obligation. For C to I seems to imply that every individual has a *pro tanto* duty to do the action that would be doing their part, not just in a collectively selected way of fulfilling the collective's duty, but in every possible way of fulfilling the collective's duty. Since it seems plausible that some pairs of such individual actions will not conflict with one another, it seems to follow from C to I that individuals have undefeated *pro tanto* obligations to do both.

This objection is unpersuasive as it stands. If C to I meant that collective obligations could give rise to conflicting all-out obligations, this would clearly count against it. But there is no obvious reason for thinking that we cannot have conflicting *pro tanto* obligations. It would also count against C to I if the *pro tanto* obligations it gave rise to were all of the same strength: If so, this might give rise to a situation where collective obligations failed to generate any reasons in favor of a particular course of action which were not cancelled out by countervailing considerations againts it of exactly the same strength. However, there is no reason to think that all the *pro tanto* obligations generated by C to I should give rise to reasons of equal strength. There might be all sorts of reasons for preferring one way of meeting a collective obligation to others: One might be less costly, or more salient, or distribute the burdens involved more equally. Or one might be a means of fulfilling the obligation arrived at by a method of collective decision-making which we had independent reason to value.[32]

One might think that there are counterexamples to C to I. Suppose that it is extremely unlikely that a collective will fulfill the obligations under which it falls. Is it still true that members of the collective have a *pro tanto* duty to perform actions which would make it possible for the collective to perform the actions that it needs to in order to fulfill its duty? If the argument I have given suggests it is correct, then it is. One might think this courts absurdity. It certainly would, if the duties generated by C to I ended up outweighing other duties—and in particular, duties whose performance could reasonably be expected to benefit some particular individuals. However, it is not clear that there is any risk of this. *Pro tanto* duties can, after all, be outweighed by other duties. It seems reasonable to think that cases where it is unlikely that other members of a collective will act in the way that is required for a certain duty to be fulfilled will turn out to be relatively weak.

Pro tanto duties can be outweighed by other duties. Some people hold that they can also be outweighed by reasons which are not moral duties—for example, reasons generated by projects or values which are central to my identity. Someone who holds this view will have a response to the claim that C to I might require too much of me if it requires me to act in ways which would enable collectives to behave in certain ways even when the collective concerned is extremely unlikely to

32. The objection was raised by Henry Richardson.

act in that way and even if acting in those ways does not conflict with other duties. On the other hand, someone who does not hold this view should, I think, simply find the putative objection unpersuasive.

What about cases where my acting in a certain way makes it less likely that other members of a collective will do what is required to meet its obligation? It might initially seem absurd to think that I could have a duty to act in a certain way to enable a collective to fulfill a duty if the result of my doing so is to make it less likely that the collective will in fact fulfill that duty. However, C to I does not generate a conclusion which is absurd. Suppose it is true that although A is a member of a set of actions which, if performed together, would make it possible for a given collective to meet an obligation O, my doing A nonetheless makes it less likely that a collective of which I am a member will fulfill O. For this to be true, there must be a way in which the collective could fulfill O which involves my refraining from A. If so, then I have a *pro tanto* duty to refrain from A. Provided my duty to refrain from A is stronger than my duty to perform A, there is no obvious absurdity. And it seems that in fact my duty to refrain from A in this situation should be regarded as stronger than my duty to perform A: It is stronger precisely because my refraining from A makes it more likely that the collective of which I am a part meets its obligations.

VI. DERIVING OP 1 AND OP 2

Here is an argument intended to establish that OP 1 and OP 2 follow from C to I.

OP 1 talks about situations where a collective has an obligation which is extremely unlikely to be met by spontaneous action on the part of its members. Furthermore, if collective obligations are constrained by the principle that ought implies can, then such obligations can be met by some combination of actions. If the obligations cannot be met by spontaneous action, and can be met in some way, then the way they can be met is, presumably, by means of organized action. But organization of the required sort does not come out of nowhere: It needs to be put in place by the action of individuals. So if a collective can only solve a problem by acting in an organized manner, it can only solve that problem by doing what is required to organize itself in the requisite manner.

To say this is to say that if a collective has a duty which it cannot fulfill without organized action, then the ways in which it can meet that obligation involve organizing itself in a way that enable it to meet that obligation.[33] If there is a duty on the individuals that make up the collective to act in ways which would enable them to fulfill the obligation, and these ways involve organizing themselves in particular ways then, according to C to I they have a *pro tanto* duty to organize themselves in these ways. But this is what OP 1 says.

I have said that collectives that are unlikely to be able to meet their obligations in virtue of the spontaneous actions of individuals who make up the collective may be able to meet them by organizing themselves. One might wonder whether this is the only possibility. In principle it seems as though it might not be. A

---

33. Or perhaps acquiescing in having such a form of organization imposed upon it: see below.

collective might acquire the sort of organization required for meeting its obliga-tions not by organizing itself, but by having some form of organization imposed on it from outside. This possibility is clearly irrelevant to the main kind of case that I have in mind here—that of the global collective, for in that case there is *ex hypothesi* nothing outside the collective which could impose the requisite form of organization on it. It is certainly possible to imagine situations involving other unorganized collectives are concerned where the necessary form of organization might be imposed from the outside.

Suppose that the citizens of a nation comprehensively defeated in war have a collective obligation to institute some form of order which will perform the basic functions of a state (as one might hold of the people of Germany in 1945).[34] It may be that in some situations the required kind of order is likeliest to come through being externally imposed. Nevertheless, in general the chances of some external body imposing on a collective body just the forms of organization that it need to fulfill its collective obligations (as opposed to serving the interests of those who are imposing that form of order) seem small enough to be discounted. It may be optimistic, but it does not seem to be unduly optimistic to suppose that in general unstructured collective bodies are more likely to meet their obligations by finding their own form of organization than by having some form of organization imposed upon them from outside.

OP 2 is more complicated. However, in most cases where a collective is organized in such a way as to enable an obligation to be met, it seems likely that the way in which the obligation is most likely to be met will involve the individuals acting in accordance with the forms of organization that already exist and which would enable them to meet the obligations. (It need not be the only way; perhaps the institutions we have are sufficient to enable us to fulfill a certain duty, but are not the only ones which could enable us to do so.) Changing forms of organization is complicated, time-consuming, and unpredictable. In most cases, obligations which could be met by a changed form of organization are less likely to be met in that way. So in most cases a *pro tanto* duty to act in accordance with existing organizations to meet given collective obligations will not be outweighed by a competing and incompatible duty to come up with other forms of organization.

I noted in Section IV that OP 1 and OP 2 were stated in terms of "stringent" collective obligations. I also noticed a concomitant argumentative burden of explaining why this should be so. Nothing in the argument that I have given so far provides such an explanation. In fact, the argument seems to justify much more inclusive principles, applying to all collective obligations, and not merely to strin-gent ones. This might even be taken as an objection to the arguments: The objection would be that if the arguments given are correct, our collective obligations give rise to too many obligations on individuals to be plausible.

My response is that the argument does provide support for versions of OP 1 and OP 2 which are not limited to stringent obligations. However, I have also argued that the obligations on individuals which these collective obligations give rise to are only *pro tanto* duties, and that in some cases these *pro tanto* duties might

---

34. Wringe, "Global Obligations." Thanks to Lars Vinx for suggesting this example.

have a weight that is so low as to mean that they are almost always over ridden. The point of restricting OP 1 and OP 2 duties to situations where the obligations involved are quite stringent is that it is plausible that in these cases—and to a far lesser extent in other cases—the *pro tanto* duties generated by our collective obligations are likely to be strong enough not to be generally over ridden by countervailing considerations.

VII. OBJECTIONS AND REPLIES

The account I have given so far might give rise to a number of misgivings. For example, one might worry that OP 1 could generate an obligation on the world's population to organize itself in oppressive ways in response to pressing moral obligations. This objection seems unconvincing. In order to be moved by it, one would have to be simultaneously optimistic and pessimistic about human capacities in a way that seems difficult to reconcile. For one would have to believe both that an oppressive form of organization was the only way in which human beings could meet the moral obligations in question (hence the pessimism), and also that such a form of organization would not lead to large-scale violations of basic rights of a sort that would give rise to a global obligation to do what one could to disrupt its workings (hence the optimism). While there is nothing formally inconsistent about a combination of attitudes of this sort, it is difficult to see what could motivate it.

A second worry is that OP 2 might seem unduly conservative, since it requires individuals to support existing institutions, even when they are less than optimal, when these institutions provide individuals with ways of meeting collective obligations. Still, the conservatism of OP 2 should not be overstated. It is not clear that the institutions that we currently have do enable us to meet our existing global obligations. If so, then OP 2 does not have especially conservative implications as things currently stand: It simply does not apply (and OP 1 has potentially quite radical implications). Furthermore, whether or not OP 2 would be very conservative in practice will depend on what kinds of institutions would be required for us to meet collectively our collective obligations. It is at least arguable that such institutions would at least need to be fairly flexible, and open to reform in the long term. If so, then the charge of undue conservatism is unwarranted.

Finally, the structure of the account I have given might seem somewhat counter intuitive. I have argued that the existence of global collective obligations creates *pro tanto* obligations on individuals to create and support institutions which are capable of discharging those responsibilities. One might describe this as a "bottom to top to bottom to middle" account: We start off with particular individuals and their needs (at, as it were ground level), which generate obligations on a very large collective (metaphorically somewhere in the stratosphere), which generates obligations on individuals (back at ground level) which generate obligations to support institutions (at somewhere between ground and the stratosphere). It might seem as though a simpler account (where obligations only flowed in one direction) would be simpler, and to that extent preferable.

It is not clear how seriously we should take intuitions about the form which an account of our obligations "must" take, except insofar as those intuitions can be supported and articulated in arguments. But in any case, the account that I have given does not have the form which the objection takes to be problematic. The view that I have been developing is one on which we see the global collective as being a collective with no internal structure (other than the "structure" which it has insofar as different individuals belong to it), rather than as a collective body encompassing all of the world's population with some kind of political structure.

Global collective bodies of this latter form, such as a world state, or a federation of all the states of the world, could be brought into existence. Indeed, one might think that the arguments that I have put forward in the main body of this article show that we have an obligation to try to bring them into existence. If it existed, a body of this sort might be seen as having other institutions as subordinate parts which could have obligations which derived directly from the obligations of the organized collective body. However, it is not clear that we should see any existing global body as being an institution of this form. Furthermore, whether or not we do so, we should see such a body, with the political structure that it would have to have in order to confer obligations on subordinate bodies as being distinct from, and less fundamental form a theoretical point of view, than the unstructured global collective which gives rise to obligations on individuals summarized in OP 1 and OP2.

VIII. CONCLUSION

If the arguments of this article are correct, the existence of global collective obligations gives rise to obligations on individuals to institute and support forms of organization which would enable those obligations to be met. If so, then although the notion of a global collective obligation is a highly abstract one, recognizing that such obligations exist can nonetheless have practical implications for concretely placed human beings. This is a result with significant practical and philosophical implications.

Nevertheless, some readers might doubt whether arguments at the high level of generality which has been employed in this article can have much practical significance for particular individuals in concrete situations. However, it is worth distinguishing between different functions which a focus on concrete examples might fulfill. One is a more or less rhetorical function: that of showing to an audience that might be more or less skeptical of the power of abstract reflection that that reflection is not simply a piece of sophisticated word-play. A second is that of providing some sort of guidance about a particular practical situation. A third is that of providing some sort of check on the plausibility of a piece of abstract reasoning. These three functions are distinct from one another, and require different approaches to the use of concrete examples. In particular, what is required by the second and third functions is at odds with what is required by the first. Furthermore, the third function is most important from a purely philosophical point of view (although that may not be the only point of view worth considering in this context). Developing a concrete example in sufficient detail to achieve this would probably require a separate article.

A second reason for being skeptical about the practical implications of what I have said relates to the content of my conclusions. In trying to connect global obligations with concrete obligations falling on particular individuals, I have argued that global collective obligations give rise to *pro tanto* obligations. I have also conceded that some *pro tanto* obligations are relatively weak, and can easily be over-ridden, both by other obligations and perhaps even by considerations which are not obligations. One might wonder whether this nullifies any practical significance my conclusions might have.

One might respond to this concern by attempting to develop a plausible theory about the weights that different kinds of obligations have in different situations, and the circumstances in which one obligation can over ride another. Some philosophers—moral particularists—deny that any general account of this sort can be given; and, although there is no space to discuss this issue in great detail here, I am at least sympathetic to some of the arguments that they have given.[35] However, even if particularists are correct, I have shown both that some considerations which one might not otherwise take to have any moral weight do in fact have some, and explained why they do. This is not a trivial matter.

What is true is that I have said relatively little about the sorts of situations that give rise to global collective obligations and nothing at all about the form the requisite institutions might take for different kinds of collective obligations. If I am right then these are important questions, to be pursued in detail in future work.[36]

---

35. For more on moral particularism, see in particular Jonathan Dancy, "Ethical Particularism and Moral Properties," *Mind* 90 (1983): 367–85; Jonathan Dancy, *Moral Reasons* (Oxford: Blackwell, 1993); Jonathan Dancy, *Ethics Without Principles* (Oxford: Oxford University Press, 2004); and Brad Hooker and Margaret Little, *Moral Particularism* (Oxford: Oxford University Press, 2000).

36. I am grateful to audiences at a workshop on Forward-Looking Collective Moral Obligation organized under the umbrella of the MANCEPT workshops in Political Theory by Felix Pinkert, at a work-in-progress workshop at Bilkent University, and at a conference on Kantian Approaches to Moral Philosophy at Boğaziçi University; and especially to Sandrine Berges, Gunnar Björnsson, Kendy Hess, Tracy Isaacs, Selim Sazak, Joseph Savage, Ulrich Steinvorth, Lucas Thorpe, and Lars Vinx for helpful questions and suggestions.

Midwest Studies In Philosophy, XXXVIII (2014)

What We Together Can (Be Required to) Do

FELIX PINKERT

In moral and political philosophy, collective obligations are promising "gap-stoppers" when we find that we need to assert some obligation, but cannot plausibly ascribe this obligation to individual agents. Most notably, Bill Wringe and Jesse Tomalty discuss whether the obligations that correspond to socio economic human rights are held by states or even by humankind at large.[1]

The present article aims to provide a missing piece for these discussions, namely an account of the conditions under which obligations can apply to loose collections of agents that do not qualify as collective agents in their own right. I first explain the notion of joint obligations of loose collections of agents (henceforth "collections") as opposed to collective obligations of collections of agents that are collective agents in their own right (Section 1), and argue that the conditions under which agents can jointly have obligations are the conditions under which they are jointly able to do what is required (Section 2). I then build on Virginia Held's seminal work on the (backward-looking) moral responsibility of "random collections" to develop such conditions for joint ability (Sections 3–7). My discussion shows that collections of individuals can more easily be subject to moral obligations than previously assumed. It also shows that putative joint obligations need to

---

1. Jesse Tomalty, "The Force of the Claimability Objection to the Human Right to Subsistence," *Canadian Journal of Philosophy* (2014 advance online publication; doi:10.1080/00455091.2014.900211): 11ff. Bill Wringe, "Global Obligations and the Agency Objection," *Ratio* 23, no. 2 (2010): 217–31; Bill Wringe, "Needs, Rights, and Collective Obligations," in *The Philosophy of Need (Royal Institute of Philosophy Supplement)*, ed. Soran Reader (Cambridge: Cambridge University Press, 2006), 201–03.

be carefully time-indexed, and that it is largely an empirical question whether a given collection can be subject to a moral obligation to perform a given joint action at a particular time (Section 8).

1. COLLECTIVE OBLIGATION AND JOINT OBLIGATION

Ascribing obligations to collections of individuals faces the following "agency objection": Many collections to whom we may want to ascribe obligations, especially humankind at large, arguably lack collective agency. Moral obligation, so the argument goes, presupposes that the bearer of the obligation is an agent—after all, stones and trees do not have obligations. Consequently, it is a category mistake to ascribe obligations to collections of agents that do not form collective agents.[2]

Bill Wringe responds to this challenge by denying the agency requirement for obligations. On his view, claims like "humankind ought to provide the means of subsistence to all those in need" do not ascribe obligations to "humankind" as a supposed agent. Instead, such sentences make claims about how the world ought to be, for example, such that humankind helps all those in need, while leaving it unspecified who ought to see to it that the required state of affairs obtains. To use an example with an individual agent, the claim "Alex ought to get a severe punishment" does not assert any obligation on Alex's part.[3] Instead, it makes a claim that the world ought to be such that Alex gets a severe punishment, and leaves unspecified who ought to see to it that the world is such.

However, Wringe's response merely pushes the agency objection to another level: Admittedly, there may be true "unowned" oughts, like the claim that life ought not be so unfair, which only concern how the world ought to be, without saying anything about what agents ought to do.[4] But in most situations where we want to ascribe an obligation to a collection, the kind of obligation we need must be owned. In the case of socio economic human rights, the obligations corresponding to rights must be owned by someone, because otherwise the rights would not be claimable.[5] So with regard to obligations to assist all those in need, the question arises who ought to see to it that humankind assists all those in need.

Now Wringe ascribes obligations of assistance to humankind because ascribing the desired obligations to potential collective agents like states is riddled with problems.[6] For Wringe, it then makes no sense to say that states ought to see to it that humankind at large helps all those in need. Instead, Wringe ascribes ownership of this obligation to individuals, with one qualification: The resulting obligation of individuals are not individual obligations to see to it that humankind helps all those

---

2. Cf. Wringe, "Global Obligations," 220; Wringe, "Needs, Rights," 193ff.

3. John Broome, *Rationality through Reasoning* (Malden, MA: Wiley Blackwell, 2013), 12.

4. Cf. Ibid., 19.

5. Likewise, to make sense of ascriptions of blame, it is not enough that things ought to have been different, but that someone ought to have seen to it that things are different than they turned out to be.

6. Wringe, "Needs, Rights," 194–95, 199–201.

in need, as this would fall foul of ought implies can. Instead, for Wringe, the obligations are obligations to do something that contributes to making it the case that humankind helps all those in need.[7]

However, such individual moral obligations will not do: In a simple form "you ought to contribute," they imply that you ought to contribute even if not enough others contribute as well, but it is implausible that one ought to perform such pointless actions. In a more sophisticated conditionalized form "you ought to contribute if enough others do so as well," it turns out that everyone discharges their obligation if no one contributes. Neither of these individual moral obligations is a plausible candidate for obligations that are meant to correspond to socio-economic human rights. For this reason, we are back to ascribing ownership of the obligations to see to it that humanity at large helps all those in need to humanity at large, which again raises the agency objection.

A better response to the agency objection is to understand ascriptions of obligations to loose collections of agents as joint obligations that are jointly owned by these agents together. To clarify the logical structure of joint obligations, consider that owned obligations in general are relations between agents and propositions, of the form "a ought that p."[8] The fact that such a relation obtains can typically be rephrased as a property of the obliged agent, of the form "$F_p(a)$."[9] Now collective obligations are properties of a single collective agent, where "$F_p(c)$" means that collective agent c ought that p. By contrast, joint obligations are nondistributive plural properties of a plurality of agents, where "$F_p(aa)$" means that agents aa jointly ought that p.

For example, "to form a circle" and "to constitute a group" are such nondistributive plural properties of collections of agents. These properties are plural properties as opposed to properties that apply to singular objects, because for these properties to apply, it does not matter whether the agents together form a single collective agent. They are further nondistributive as opposed to distributive plural properties because they are not properties that all of the involved agents have individually, as no one individually constitutes a group or forms a circle. To say that an obligation is had by several agents jointly then neither means that each one of them individually has the obligation, nor does it mean that they are a collective agent who, as a single entity, has the obligation. Instead, the agents jointly have the obligation, which has the sui generis structure of plural properties.

Once we understand ascriptions of obligations to loose collections of agents as joint rather than collective obligations, worries about the lack agency of such collections become irrelevant, because joint obligations do not even purport to ascribe an obligation to a single integrated agent in the first place. This does not mean, however, that a given collection of agents can be required to do just anything. After all, in the individual case, there are no special worries about me being an agent who can bear moral obligations, but I cannot be required to jump to the moon. So with worries about the lack of agency of collections of agents put out of

7. Wringe, "Global Obligations," 226–29.
8. Broome, *Rationality through Reasoning*, 14.
9. Ibid., 15.

the way, we still need to ask under which conditions a given presumed joint obligation can apply to a given collection. These conditions, I contend, are simply the conditions under which the agents together are jointly able to do what they supposedly jointly ought to do. The reason why I cannot be required to jump to the moon is that I am not able to do so. Likewise, it may well be that all humans together cannot be jointly obliged to help all those in need, namely if we are not jointly able to do so. To evaluate this concern in any given case of a supposed joint obligation, we need an account of joint ability. The remainder of this article develops precisely such an account.

2. VIRGINIA HELD AND THE RESPONSIBILITY OF "RANDOM COLLECTIONS"

A distinguishing feature of joint ability is that a collection of agents is often jointly able to do much less than what it is possible for the sum of individual agents together to do. To see this point, consider the following example:

> **The Concert Audience:** A concert audience is awaiting a performance. Just before the performance starts, the conductor tells the surprised audience that the performance is interactive, which requires that in each row of seats, precisely half of the audience simultaneously stands up at the opening chord.

Now suppose that each person in the audience is able to stand up at that time, and that the number of people in every row is even. It is then possible that precisely half the audience in each row stands up at the opening chord, but it is not something that they are jointly able to do. The reason for this inability is that there are many ways for the audience to be such that half of them in each row stand up. It is then not clear to the individual members of the audience which of these ways should be implemented, and what they individually hence need to do. So a core task for developing an account of joint ability is to determine the conditions under which a collection of agents is jointly able to coordinate on one of several implementations of a joint action.

In a seminal paper, Virginia Held tackles this task by examining the conditions under which backward-looking responsibility for past actions can apply to collections of agents,[10] and in her recent paper on the claimability objection to socio economic human rights, Jesse Tomalty translates Held's view into preconditions for joint obligation.[11] Since the precondition of joint obligation is joint ability, we can then formulate the following Heldian position:[12]

---

10. Virginia Held, "Can a Random Collection of Individuals Be Morally Responsible?" *The Journal of Philosophy* 67, no. 14 (1970), 471–81, especially 476.

11. Tomalty, "The Force of the Claimability Objection," 11.

12. Held's discussion can be translated into the terms of joint ability and obligation, because the conditions under which we can hold a collection of agents morally responsible for failing to perform joint action Φ are precisely the conditions under which the agents could have been morally required to Φ. These conditions, in turn, are just the conditions under which the agents would have been jointly able to Φ.

Heldian conditions for joint ability: Agents *aa* are jointly able to perform joint action *Φ* if and only if there is at least one possible collective pattern of actions of *aa* that constitutes *aa* *Φ*-ing, and it is "obvious to the reasonable person" what part each of the agents needs to play for *aa* to *Φ*.

In terms of notation, I shall use *aa* to refer to collections of agents, for example, the listeners of the concert, and clauses of the form "one of the *aa*-s" to mean refer to the members of the collection *aa* individually, for example, to one of the listeners. By joint actions I mean things that a plurality of agents do together, for example, to form a circle, independent of whether or not they have any specific joint intentions. A collective pattern of actions of *aa* is a vector of agent-action pairs which assigns each of the *aa*-s an action. In a possible collective pattern of actions of *aa*, each of the individual *aa*-s is individually able to perform the action assigned to her independently of what others do, and it is possible that all of the *aa*-s play their part.[13]

The Heldian conditions for joint ability explain why in The Concert Audience, the listeners are not jointly able to satisfy the demands of the conductor. This is because it is not obvious to the reasonable person what each of the listeners needs to do at the opening chord. The individual listeners can only randomly decide whether to stand up or remain seated, but the chance that they will thereby manage to have precisely half of them in each row stand up is very small.[14]

The Heldian conditions, however, suffer from two crucial defects which make them extensionally inadequate for determining joint ability: First, the reference to "the reasonable person" makes the conditions pick out joint ability wrongly. Second, the conditions so far do not take into account how the availability of preparatory actions, for example, coordination mechanisms, affects agents' present joint ability to do something in the future. In the following, I improve upon the Heldian conditions in these two areas.

3. JOINT ABILITY AND THE "REASONABLE PERSON"

In the Heldian conditions, what individual actions need to be performed for the collection to perform a joint action must be "obvious to the reasonable person." I argue that the reference to "reasonable persons" is mistaken and should be removed. This is because it not only introduces problematically vague concept, but also makes the conditions for joint ability extensionally inadequate. To see this point, consider the following example:

13. To show why the second condition is necessary, consider the collective pattern of actions of all students of a university riding the very same bike at the same time. While each of the individual students can be able to ride the bike at that time, it is not possible for all of them to do so.

14. With an audience of 400 in ten rows, the chance is about 0.125 per row, and 0.0000000096 for all rows together. This means that inability in the morally relevant sense is weaker than sheer impossibility. To give another example, the very point of passwords is that only persons who know the password can access certain files or services. And while it is not impossible that I happen to enter the correct password to access your e-mail account, I am not able to access it without knowing the password.

The Treasure Hunters: A group of students study in a library, when one of them comes across an aged document and shows it to the others. The document indicates the location of a huge treasure. In order to retrieve the treasure, among other things, the students have to first discover the additional hidden script in the document, which contains crucial clues. They then have to travel to different locations on the globe to gather additional fragments with crucial information, and operate an ancient water-powered combination lock. The students do not yet know each other, and the group of students contains both chemists who are able to suspect and discover the hidden script, linguists who can read it, and mechanical engineers who can understand the lock. When finding the document, the students only know that it is a guide to finding a treasure, but do not know any other facts about the quest that may lie ahead of them.

First, the Heldian conditions are too strict, that is, they pick out some collections as jointly unable to do something which they are in fact jointly able to do. In The Treasure Hunters, it may not be obvious to some nondescript, average reasonable person who ought to play what part in order for the students to discover the hidden script. The Heldian conditions then judge that the students are not jointly able to discover the script. However, given the chemists' expertise, they may well be jointly able to discover it, because it is obvious to the chemists what they, possibly with the help of the other students, need to do to discover the hidden script.

Second, the Heldian conditions are too permissive, and judge that some collections are jointly able to do something which they are not in fact jointly able to do. For example, suppose that later in the quest the students fail to disarm a trap, and get hit by arrows that are poisoned with a hallucinogenic substance. For finally accessing the treasure, they need to lift the heavy lid of a sarcophagus. To the reasonable person, it is obvious that everyone should simply pick some spot on the lid, evenly spaced from the others, and then lift it when everyone else is in place. So the Heldian conditions judge that the students are jointly able to access the treasure. However, in their present state, they may not jointly able to access it. This is because due to their hallucinations, they may not be jointly able to assess the situation correctly, and may, for example, see hundreds of other students around the sarcophagus and think that they are not needed.[15]

The lesson from these two problems is that agents' roles need to be obvious not to some reasonable third party, but to the agents in question, and in the situation in which they find themselves. This claim, however, still needs to be specified further, because it can be understood in two ways: It can mean that

15. For a more real-world example, on the Heldian conditions, a group of agents with severe cognitive impairments can turn out jointly able to carry complex tasks that are beyond their grasp, because the part that any given agent needs to play is obvious to the reasonable person. But since reasonable persons are typically conceptualized as having average and not severely impaired cognitive abilities, this assignment of roles can be far from obvious for the agents in question. They are then in fact not jointly able to carry out the task, and the Heldian conditions then allow for mistaken and morally highly problematic ascriptions of joint obligations and backward-looking responsibility to groups of people with cognitive impairments.

everyone's role must be obvious to everyone, or that every agent must be such that her role is obvious to her.

To adjudicate between these two possibilities, consider again the first step in the students' quest, and ask whether the students are jointly able to discover the hidden script. Now suppose that for the students to discover the script, only the chemists are required. Call the chemists "relevant" and the remaining students "irrelevant" in this situation.[16] If the students are to discover the script, it must be clear to the chemists what they need to do, but it need not be clear to the remaining students what the chemists need to do. Furthermore, it need not even be obvious to the chemists what each other needs to do, as long as they know what they individually must do. So the Heldian conditions must be modified to only consider the roles of relevant agents, and to only demand that every relevant person's role be obvious to them individually.[17]

Taking into account these considerations, this gives us a first improvement of the Heldian conditions:

Heldian conditions for joint ability (2): Agents *aa* are jointly able to Φ if and only if there is at least one possible collective pattern of actions of the relevant *aa*-s that constitutes *aa* Φ-ing, and for every one of the relevant agents, it is obvious to her what she needs to do if *aa* is to Φ.

4. JOINT ABILITY AND OBVIOUSNESS

Having removed the problematic reference to the "reasonable person," the next task is to elucidate the notion of "obviousness." The main obstacle for individuals to know which role they need to play is the existence of multiple implementations of a given joint action. For example, in The Concert Audience, there are numerous collective patterns of actions which would all satisfy the demands of the conductor. In half of these patterns, a given individual's role is to stand up, and in the other half, to remain seated. Unless there is a way in which one of those collective patterns of actions gets picked out as the one to be implemented, there is no way for an individual to know which role she needs to play if the audience is to abide by the conductor's request.

More generally, if there are multiple collective patterns of actions that all implement the same joint action, then the agents face an equilibrium selection problem: Assuming that the agents want to see the joint action performed, they prefer situations where the action is performed to situations where it is not performed. All situations where a suitable collective pattern of actions is implemented are then at least weak equilibria in which no agent has an incentive to change her actions. The problem is that if agents have to decide what to do without knowledge of others' actions, they do not know which of the different equilibria to aim for, that

16. More precisely, irrelevant agents are agents who cannot make a difference to whether or not all considered agents together Φ, no matter what the other agents do. Note that I here exclude actively frustrating others' actions as a possible option.

17. Likewise, in the example of the concert audience, it is not required that every person knows what role everyone else needs to play, but solely whether or not she herself needs to stand up or remain seated.

is, they do not know in which of the different suitable collective patterns of actions they should play their part. What is required for joint ability in such a situation is that exactly one pattern somehow sticks out to all of the relevant agents. Now with regard to this salient pattern, every relevant agent does not need to have beliefs about what everyone else precisely needs to do. Instead, each relevant agent only needs to have a true belief about what her part is in that pattern, and to believe that if the collective is to perform the joint action in question, she must perform that part. That latter belief of a given relevant agent amounts to believing that if the other relevant agents want the collection to perform the action in question, they will try to do so via a pattern that includes the said relevant agent performing that particular action.[18] The salient pattern must be unique, because for coordination to be successful, every agent must have the same pattern in mind when forming this belief.[19]

Adding this condition, we get yet further improved conditions for joint ability. However, as I argue in the following, these conditions go wrong if applied to pick out joint ability simpliciter. This is because they focus only on subspecies of joint ability, namely immediate joint ability to do something without first having to perform any prior preparatory actions.[20] Restricting the scope of the present conditions accordingly, we get the following.

Conditions for immediate joint ability: Agents *aa* are immediately jointly able to Φ if and only if there is exactly one salient possible collective pattern of actions of the relevant *aa*-s that constitutes *aa* Φ-ing, and which is such that every relevant agent believes of the action which is her part in that pattern that she needs to perform this action if *aa* is to Φ.[21]

It is beyond the scope of this article to determine all the conditions under which a collective pattern of actions can become salient. However, two conditions are particularly relevant for the following discussion: First, a collective pattern of actions is salient if it is the unique most preferred collective pattern of actions for all agents, for example, if it is the least costly for all of them.[22] Trivially, it follows that any unique implementation of a joint action is salient. Second, a collective pattern of actions becomes salient if it is explicitly selected by a collective decision, where the content of the decision is common knowledge among all relevant agents.

18. I am indebted to Kai Spiekermann for pointing out the need for agents to have some sort of belief about other agents' perception of the salient collective pattern of actions.
19. For the concept of saliency, and understanding it as a "meeting of the minds" of the involved agents, see Thomas Schelling, *The Strategy of Conflict*, rev. ed. (Cambridge, MA: Harvard University Press, 1980), 54–59, 95–97.
20. Note that immediate joint ability allows for the available action to still take significant time, so it does not entail that the action can be immediately completed.
21. Note that the conditions state that each relevant agent believes of her part that she needs to perform it, rather than that she believes that she needs to perform her part in the pattern. I use this *de re* reference to agents' roles to make clear that the agents do not need to have beliefs about the salient collective pattern of actions as a whole, but only need to have beliefs about those actions that are their individual part of that pattern.
22. I remain unconvinced by approaches that hold that a unique worst equilibrium is also salient in a way that can aid coordination.

5. JOINT ABILITY AND MOTIVATION

Before turning to joint ability that is mediated via preparatory actions, note that the saliency conditions for immediate joint ability do not include any conditions on agents' beliefs about others' actions and willingness to play their part in making it the case that they together act in a certain way. This raises the worry that the conditions are too permissive, as they do not sufficiently take into consideration obstacles to agents' motivation.[23] To see this point, consider the following possible scenario during the students' quest:

> **The Treasurestan Meeting:** The students have figured out that the treasure is hidden in the country of Treasurestan, and have dispersed around the globe to find various further clues needed to determine the exact location of the treasure. They have agreed to meet up in the capital of Treasurestan at a given date. However, as they each go to their respective airports of departure, the news report that civil unrest has broken out in Treasurestan, and that traveling to the country has become very risky. The students each see the news, and believe that they all have seen it. They each still want to go through with the plan and want the team to meet in Treasurestan, but they are not able to get through to each other to communicate their views.

Each of the students is now faced with doubt about whether or not the other students will follow through on the agreement to meet in Treasurestan. This uncertainty arises first, because they may not be confident that all of the other students are still happy with the group going to Treasurestan under the changed circumstances. Second, even if they each had such confidence, they may not be confident that everyone else is likewise confident in each other. But if others lack such confidence, then they may fail to show up, not because they are not happy with the group going to Treasurestan, but because they may not be happy taking the risk of traveling there if it is possible that the other students do not show up. Third, similar considerations apply to a lack of confidence in others' confidence in one's confidence that others are happy with the group going to Treasurestan, ad infinitum.

The doubt that is sown by the news report may then make it less likely that the students all end up going to Treasurestan, even if they are all happy with the group going there under the new circumstances. This is because some students may then opt out because they do not consider it worth the risk of traveling to Treasurestan if they are not guaranteed that the quest will continue there. Their doubts can only be removed if the students can somehow form common beliefs about of each others' willingness to still go to Treasurestan with the group, which would typically be done by communicating with each other.[24] Such communication then not only assures the students of each others' willingness to go to Treasurestan

---

23. For getting me to think more about issues of motivation, I am again indebted to Kai Spiekermann.

24. The needed confidence could also be created by agreeing beforehand that they are all happy with continuing with the quest in case of a crisis in Treasurestan.

with the group, but also assures them of each others' confidence in each others' confidence, and so forth.

Because the lack of such common belief in each others' willingness to see a joint action performed may reduce the likelihood that agents end up performing the action, it is tempting to include such common belief as a condition of joint ability. More precisely, since it is perfectly possible for a collection of agents to be jointly able to do something even if none of the agents is willing to play her part, the condition would be that the agents are in an epistemic situation such that were everyone willing to play their part in the salient collective pattern of actions, they would have common beliefs about that. However, I contend that it is misguided to add such an additional condition, because a reduced likelihood to carry out a joint action does not necessarily indicate a reduced ability to carry it out. If the students in The Treasurestan Meeting do not meet up, this is because some of them did not put enough value on the meeting for it to be worth the risk of going to Treasurestan and ending up there alone. This problem, though, can easily be amended if only the students valued meeting up enough. In this respect, The Treasurestan Meeting is crucially different from The Concert Audience, where the probability that precisely everyone in each row stands up is extremely small, and will not rise no matter how much more the listeners value success.

The doubts sown by the news report then make it motivationally more demanding to meet up, in that a stronger motivation of each student is required if, as rationally deciding agents, they are in fact going to meet up.[25] But such motivational difficulty does not constitute any reduction of ability. To give an individual example, suppose someone gives you a large closed glass jar with some cash in it. You are able to unscrew the lid and reach in to get the money. Suppose further that as you are about to open the jar, the person tells you that it is also filled with a radioactive gas. Now you may think twice before opening the jar, and depending on how much you want the money, and how much you are concerned about your health, you may decide not to open it. However, you remain just as able as before to get the money.[26]

For these reasons, I conclude that the above saliency conditions for immediate joint ability do not need to be supplemented with further conditions about agents' motivations and beliefs about each other's motivations.

6. IMMEDIATE AND MEDIATED JOINT ABILITY

The saliency conditions for immediate joint ability together with the above discussion of saliency imply that if there is no salient implementation of a possible joint

25. Note that this motivational difficulty does not arise for irrational agents who fail to appropriately take risk into consideration. This further suggests that the problem faced by the students is not one of inability.

26. Matters are different if the jar is, for example, filled with spiders, and you simply cannot bring yourself to put your hand into the jar. In this case, the likelihood of you getting the money remains low no matter how motivated you are to get the money. In this situation, the problem is not one of motivational difficulty, but of psychological inability to perform the action in question. This kind of inability is taken into account in the understanding of possible collective pattern of action being patterns in which each agent is individually able to perform her part.

action of a collection of agents, then the agents are not immediately jointly able to perform the action. Now the most common way to create saliency is to coordinate by making a joint decision on which implementation to follow. Making such a joint decision is itself a joint action, and may be one which, according to the saliency conditions for immediate joint ability, the agents are immediately jointly able to perform. Such preparatory actions raise the question of what we should say about the agents' ability not only to coordinate, but also to carry out the joint action that requires such prior coordination.

For example, suppose that the conductor in The Concert Audience gives the audience one minute's time to determine who will stand up and who will remain seated, and tells them to start assigning the tasks of remaining seated and standing up to alternating people in each row, beginning on the left end. There is then exactly one salient collective pattern of actions of all listeners that constitutes them coordinating their actions at the opening chord, and they are immediately jointly able to carry out this coordination. The audience is then at the time of the conductor's demands immediately jointly able to coordinate, and once they have coordinated, they are immediately jointly able to have half of them in each row stand up at the opening chord. The remaining question is whether the audience is at the time of the conductor's request already jointly able to fulfil the request.

Held answers this question in the negative,[27] and Tomalty's discussion of whether socio economic human rights correspond to joint obligations to help the world's poor at least suggests that she would likewise answer in the negative.[28] Contrary to these positions, I contend that agents can already be jointly able to perform actions which first require them to coordinate. The Concert Audience shows why allowing for such mediated joint ability is necessary: Given that the listeners want to experience the best performance possible, they (rationally) ought to have half of them in each row stand up at the opening chord. If they do not fulfil the conductor's request, then we are in a position to afterward say that they spoilt the performance, and ought to have stood up as requested. However, if the listeners were at the time of the request not in some sense able to fulfil the request, and were only able to coordinate, then we could not make sense of this ought-ascription. We could only assert that they ought to have coordinated, but the most plausible explanation of this ought is that coordination was necessary for them to stand up as requested, which they ought to have done.

What we should thus say about The Concert Audience is first, that the audience is at the time of the request immediately jointly able to coordinate at the time of the request. Second, after coordinating, they are jointly able to stand up as

27. Held, "Can a Random Collection of Individuals Be Morally Responsible?" 476.
28. Tomalty, "The Force of the Claimability Objection," 11ff. Tomalty argues that short of a coordination mechanism, humankind cannot be jointly obliged to help all those in need. Likewise, since setting up a suitable coordination mechanism is a highly complex task, humankind can also not be jointly obliged to set up a coordination mechanism. Tomalty's brief discussion suggests that she does not think that present joint ability to coordinate on how to perform an action translates into present joint ability to perform the action later. She also does not seem to consider longer sequences of preparatory actions, which include coordinating on how to coordinate.

requested after coordinating. And third, they are at the time of the request also mediatedly jointly able to stand up as requested after coordinating.

The key to properly understanding joint ability in situations that require prior coordination, then, is to see that ability, as well as obligation, is (often implicitly) doubly time-indexed, namely to the time when the ability obtains, and to the time of the action one is able to do, and that the two times can come apart. Further, we need to acknowledge that joint ability comes in two species, namely immediate and mediated joint ability. The task for the remainder of the article is to determine under which conditions several agents are mediatedly jointly able to do something.

7. CONDITIONS FOR MEDIATED JOINT ABILITY

Before turning to the conditions for mediated joint ability, note that coordinating is only one kind of preparatory action that creates the needed saliency at the next step. Coordinating makes collective patterns of actions salient by creating new information, namely facts about what collective pattern of actions has been decided upon or otherwise designated. Another way to create saliency is to acquire new information, which typically makes entire joint actions, as opposed to their specific implementations, salient. For the purposes of the present discussion, it is then possible to subsume sequences of joint actions as one action, as long as relevant information that the agents have does not change during that sequence. Steps in a sequence of actions are then distinguished from each other by the information that agents have.

Returning to The Treasure Hunters, the students are at the time of finding the document not immediately jointly able to retrieve the treasure, because there is no salient collective pattern of actions of the team which constitutes retrieving the treasure, and which is such that each member of the team believes of her part that it is needed for the team to retrieve the treasure. For illustration, suppose that the quest consists of only three steps:

- deciphering the document (α),
- traveling to different locations to retrieve further fragments with crucial information and meeting in Treasurestan (β), and
- traveling to the right location in Treasurestan and operating a water-powered combination lock with the right code (γ).

Before the document is deciphered, the students do not know where to search for the treasure and where to look for the additional fragments. Further, before they do not gather the additional fragments, they do not know where to travel in Treasurestan, nor do they know about the lock and its combination. However, as the students progress on their quest, their information and immediate joint abilities change. Because of this change, their immediate joint ability to retrieve the treasure at the final step translates into mediated joint ability at earlier steps, in the following way:

First, once they meet in Treasurestan with the retrieved further information, they are then immediately jointly able to travel to the right location and operate the combination lock. This is because at this final step, there is exactly one salient collective pattern of actions that constitutes everyone traveling to the right location and then operating the lock in the way instructed in the retrieved fragments.[29] This pattern is further such that each of the students believes of her part in the pattern that she needs to perform it if the team is to retrieve the treasure.

Second, consider the moment after they decipher the document, and before they retrieve the additional information and meet in Treasurestan. At this point, they are immediately jointly able to retrieve the additional information and meet in Treasurestan. At the same time, they are not immediately jointly able to retrieve the treasure, because they do not yet know about the right location and the combination lock. However, this does not mean that their quest is futile and that they cannot retrieve the treasure simpliciter: After all, at this point, they are immediately jointly able to perform an action which will bring them into a situation in which they are then immediately jointly able to retrieve the treasure. Further, they know that they need to perform the first action if they are to obtain this future immediate ability. For these reasons, they are at this time jointly able to retrieve the treasure later on.

Further, consider the moment before they decipher the document. They are then immediately jointly able to perform a joint action which brings them into a situation in which they are mediatedly jointly able to retrieve the treasure later on. For this reason, they are already mediatedly jointly able to retrieve the treasure as they sit in the library and find the document.

Before generalizing the behavior of joint ability through time, note that in the above discussion I have assumed that at every step there is precisely one joint action (even though with multiple implementations) that facilitates joint ability at the next step. Now suppose that there are several totally distinct joint actions at one stage, that is, not just different implementations of the same action, for example, different ways to get to the location of the treasure, but different actions altogether, for example, first going to one location or first going to another location. In such cases, precisely one of the available joint actions must be salient to the agents that are relevant for that action. That is, all of those agents need to believe that if all agents together are to perform the final action, then they will jointly perform that salient preparatory action. So it must be salient both what, roughly, all agents together jointly should do, and how precisely they are going to do it. Typically, saliency of what roughly to do is easily given: First, there might be only one possible preparatory action, which is then trivially salient. Second, if there are apparently multiple options, then there is in fact a single and salient prior preparatory action, namely to together decide on which of those actions to take. Third, once such a decision is made, it makes precisely one of the multiple options salient.

Taking into account the double need for saliency, we can see that joint ability generally propagates backward in time in the following way: If in a situation s_2 at a time t_2, agents *aa* would be (immediately or mediatedly) jointly able to perform

---

29. More precisely, the students need to carry out further preparatory actions, for example, to agree on a way to travel to the right location, and to assign tasks in operating the lock. I simplify the example for ease of exposition.

joint action Φ_2 at time $t_2' \geq t_2$, and are at an earlier time t_1 immediately jointly able to perform an action Φ_1 at t_1 which would make it the case that *aa* find themselves in s_2 at t_2, and the relevant *aa*-s whose contributions can make a difference to whether or not *aa* perform Φ_1 believe that performing Φ_1 has this effect, and that if *aa* is to perform Φ_2, they will previously perform Φ_1, then (and only then) are *aa* at t_1 mediatedly jointly able to perform Φ_2 at t_2'. Allowing for longer sequences of preparatory actions, the conditions for mediated joint ability read as follows:

Conditions for mediated joint ability: Agents *aa* are at t_1 mediatedly jointly able to Φ_n at t_n if and only if

1. they are at t_1 immediately jointly able to perform action Φ_1 at t_1, where
2. performing Φ_1 at t_1 makes it the case that *aa* are at $t_2 > t_1$ immediately or mediatedly jointly able to Φ_n at t_n, and
3. the relevant members of *aa* believe at t_1 that *aa* performing Φ_1 at t_1 has this effect, and that if *aa* is to perform Φ_n at t_n, they will perform Φ_1 at t_1.

Note that these conditions are partly recursive, due to the reference to mediated joint ability in condition 3). Since joint ability simpliciter is the disjunction of immediate and intermediate joint ability, we get the following conditions for joint ability, where the recursion is more clear-cut and is indicated in boldface:

Recursive conditions for joint ability: Agents *aa* are at t_1 **jointly able** to Φ_n at t_n if and only if

A)   there is exactly one salient collective pattern of actions of the relevant members of *aa* that constitutes *aa* Φ_n-ing at t_n, and which is such that every relevant member of *aa* believes of the action which is her part in that pattern that she needs to perform this action if *aa* is to Φ_n at t_n,
or
B)   there is a joint action Φ_1 such that
1. there is exactly one salient collective pattern of actions of the relevant members of *aa* that constitutes *aa* Φ_1-ing at t_1, and which is such that every relevant agent believes of the action which is her part in that pattern that she needs to perform this action if *aa* is to Φ_1 at t_1, and
2. *aa* performing Φ_1 at t_1 makes it the case that *aa* are at $t_2 > t_1$ **jointly able** to Φ_n at t_n, and
3. the relevant members of *aa* believe at t_1 that *aa* performing Φ_1 at t_1 has this effect, and that if *aa* is to perform Φ_n at t_n, they will perform Φ_1 at t_1.

Applied to The Treasure Hunters with three steps, the conditions for joint ability then work as follows: At the time t_α when they find the document, the students are not immediately jointly able to retrieve the treasure at t_γ, so A) does not hold. Thus we need to check whether B) holds, that is, whether 1) the students are immediately jointly able to perform an action which 2) makes them jointly able at t_β to retrieve the treasure at t_γ, and 3) which the relevant students believe to have that effect, and which is the salient way for them to achieve that effect. The candidate for this action is deciphering the document. Now by the above considerations, the students are immediately jointly able to decipher the document, so 1) is given. As for the students' beliefs, if they believe that only deciphering the document has the said effect, for example, because they recognize that the document indicates the location of a treasure, then 3) applies, otherwise B) does not hold and the students are at t_α not jointly able to retrieve the treasure at t_γ. To check whether 2) applies and deciphering really does have this effect on the students' ability, we need to ask whether, after deciphering the document, the students are at t_β jointly able to retrieve the treasure at t_γ. We then need to recursively apply the same tests again at t_β.

Since the students are at t_β still not immediately jointly able to retrieve the treasure, A) again does not hold. B) holds if 1) the students are at t_β immediately jointly able to perform an action which 2) makes them jointly able at t_γ to retrieve the treasure at t_γ, and 3) which the relevant students believe to have this effect, and which is salient for them. The candidate for this action is retrieving the additional information and meeting in Treasurestan. Now they are immediately jointly able to perform that action, so 1) applies. Assuming that the students understand the retrieved information correctly, we can assume that they will form the right beliefs about the necessary next step in their quest, and 3) applies—otherwise, B) does not apply and the students are not jointly able both at t_α and t_β to retrieve the treasure at t_γ. To check whether 2) applies and retrieving the information and meeting in Treasurestan has the said effect, we again need to check whether, after performing these actions, the students are at t_γ jointly able to retrieve the treasure at t_γ.

At t_γ, A) applies and the recursion can stop, as we do not need to check for conditions B). So under the given belief assumptions, the students turn out to be at t_γ jointly able to retrieve the treasure at t_γ, and hence likewise also at t_β and t_α.

Lastly, note that I again do not add any conditions about agents' beliefs about each other's motivations, for the same reason as that given in Section 5: Suppose that for some reason the students come to doubt each other's willingness to carry out a given step in the quest, or each other's confidence in each other's willingness, and so forth. They may then be unwilling to invest by performing preparatory actions that create further joint ability which they suspect will not in fact be used to retrieve the treasure. However, the difficulty created by these doubts is again of a purely motivational nature, and can be overcome if the students place enough importance on retrieving the treasure. The students may end up not retrieving the treasure because someone pulls out when the insecurity about the quest's success arises, but they nonetheless are able to retrieve it.

8. CONCLUSION AND IMPLICATIONS

I have argued that collections of agents can be jointly able to perform not only joint actions which, via salient collective pattern of actions, are immediately available to them, but also joint actions which require preparatory coordinating actions. I have further proposed recursive conditions for when a collection of agents is jointly able to do something.

In Section 2, I have illustrated that collections of agents can be much less capable than the sum of their individual abilities. This claim now needs to be modified in light of the recursive conditions for joint ability: In the short run, when no coordination is possible, collections of agents can be less able than the sum of their individual abilities. But when agents have sufficient time to coordinate, then they can coordinate on and are able to implement any collective pattern of actions which is possible for them together to do. The question of whether a collection is able to do something is then not sufficiently specific, because in situations where the bottleneck is agents' coordination and acquisition and creation of information, the answer depends on the time frame set to perform the joint action. The question is then not whether the collection is able to perform the action, but by when it is able to perform it.

For practical application to supposed joint obligations of humankind to help all those in need, this means that given enough time, all coordination issues can be solved, and humankind together is able to do anything that is possible for us together to do. However, it remains an open question how long such coordination takes, and answering this question is largely an empirical matter.[30] Furthermore, from the need to coordinate, it follows that there are some things that we together are not able to do, namely to perform certain joint actions that require coordination and to do so without first coordinating. One important implication of this result is that there are some suffering people in the world that can no longer be saved, because coordinating on helping them will take longer than they can still wait. In the case of children for whom helping is already too late at the time of their birth, this raises the question if they were ever owed assistance. Philosophers who defend socio economic human rights on the basis of joint obligations of humanity at large are then forced to consider whether yet nonexistent future people can be owed obligations, and can hence have rights to assistance.

Lastly, considering how long it can take to coordinate ourselves on a global scale, the impression can easily arise that we are now able to perform many crucial joint actions, such as effectively mitigating anthropocentric climate change, only in the distant future. However, this impression is mistaken. How long it takes for a given collection of agents to coordinate to perform some joint action depends largely on the number of preparatory actions that must be taken, and the time it takes to carry out each of these actions. The reason why international negotiations, for example, in environmental matters often takes so long, however, is that such negotiations are not merely about coordinating on achieving a single set aim, but include negotiations that involve the individual aims and preferences of the negotiating parties. But the resulting delays are not due to a joint inability to coordinate more quickly, but instead a matter of not placing enough priority on getting coordination off the ground as soon as possible. So despite the formidable challenges of coordinating the world's population, we together are able to do a whole lot more than we currently do, and much sooner than we tend to think.

---

30. Cf. Schelling, *The Strategy of Conflict*, 162–65.

Midwest Studies In Philosophy, XXXVIII (2014)

Because They Can: The Basis for the Moral Obligations of (Certain) Collectives

KENDY M. HESS

There are undoubtedly situations in which understanding collective moral obligation will require new conceptual machinery—new ways of understanding agents and
agency, obligation, and responsibility. Many of the articles in this issue pursue just
such an approach, drawing on the influential theories presented by Margaret Gilbert
(1989, 2000, 2006), Michael Bratman (1987, 1999), Seumas Miller (2001, 2006), and
others. However, I think that much of the debate over collectives and collective
morality has missed the fact that a large class of collective actions can be simply and
easily addressed via the same theories that govern individual morality: namely, those
situations in which the collective qualifies as a moral agent in its own right.

A collective like those described below, which has its own "rational point of
view" and whose actions are driven by that RPV, qualifies as an agent in its own
right; to the extent that it is capable of taking morally relevant information into
account when it acts, it qualifies as a *moral* agent in its own right—one that can, and
therefore should, act morally. Such an entity has moral obligations in much the
same way and for much the same reason that human agents have moral obligations,
and its moral obligations can thus be understood in terms of the same theories. In
such cases the collective is what I call a "corporate agent,"[1] after the business
entities paradigmatic of the type. These corporate agents have forward-looking
obligations to act in ways that avoid harm, respect rights, pursue excellences unique

---

1. This is apparently becoming the favored terminology, and the phrase is appearing more
frequently. In addition to other usages, Christian List and Philip Pettit transition to this term over the
course of their influential *Group Agents* (Oxford 2011), and it seems to be gaining in popularity.

to their kind, or even bring the world closer to perfection for exactly the same reasons that human beings have them: because they can.

After addressing some preliminary matters (Section 1), I briefly outline my account of corporate agents before moving on to explain some of the mechanics by which they operate; I address this issue in some detail (Section 2). Certainly, there are a number of real philosophical issues at stake in this debate, some few of which are addressed below. Nonetheless, I've often found that what appears to be a philosophical disagreement arises out of confusion about how corporations and other corporate agents actually function. There's this rather charming idea that every corporate commitment is the result of some person or group of people sitting down at a table, considering options, and deciding to adopt it, and nothing could be further from the truth. It is crucial to develop a sense of at least some of the many mechanisms by which corporate agents commit to positions and goals, in order to understand the true weight of the claim that these are the commitments *of the corporate agent* rather than of its members. Building on this account, the remainder of the article will demonstrate that such corporate agents have the relevant capacities for belief (Section 3), desire (Section 4), and response to morally relevant information (Section 5) according to standard (non-collective) theories. I provide only a preliminary account of each capacity. A full demonstration or proof of even one capacity would be far too long, and my goal here is more modest. I aim simply to show that the holist claim of corporate moral agency is plausible—that in the case of large, highly organized and disciplined collectives (like corporations, governments, universities, nongovernmental organizations, etc.), we have no need for special pleading or the specialized accounts mentioned above.[2] In these cases, we can identify a single (albeit collective) moral agent, and this allows us to understand and justify claims of *collective* agency, morality, and obligation in exactly the same terms that we use to understand and justify claims of *individual* agency, morality, and obligation.

1. PRELIMINARY MATTERS

Let me begin by acknowledging two assumptions and introducing the general idea of a "corporate agent," as I use the term. First, for the purposes of this article, I simply assume a holist ontology without argument. I assume that there *is* "a corporate entity"—that in certain cases the collective exists as a single object, a whole. We humans have a strong bias toward experiencing the world at the level of concrete individual objects (despite knowing perfectly well that even those objects are assemblages of many pieces and parts). Building on this, many philosophers object to the idea that "extended" or "distributed" things like forests, families, and

2. In fact, the specialized accounts described above—from Gilbert, Bratman, Miller, and the rest—generally aren't applicable in situations involving corporate agents. In one way or another, all ultimately require that *all* participating members possess certain intentional attitudes. The requirements differ from theory to theory, and the relationship between the group attitude and the requisite intentional attitudes can be highly complex, but the ultimate requirement remains the same. And it is—to say the least—*highly* unlikely that the thousands (or tens of thousands) of members of a single corporate agent would possess the requisite mental states.

the solar system really exist.[3] These philosophers grant that the trees, people, and planets exist; the objection is to the idea that the larger things they constitute—the forest, the family, the solar system—exist in any proper sense of the word. Yet that is exactly my claim. When I refer to a corporate agent, therefore, I am referring to a single entity which meets standard criteria for existence: the (extended) material object constituted by its members.[4]

Second, I assume that a candidate entity must be capable of intentional action that takes morally relevant information into account, in order to qualify as a moral agent. I take it that this much is uncontroversial: one must be an agent (capable of intentional action) before one can be a *moral* agent, and an agent somehow incapable of taking morally relevant information[5] into account when it acted would be fatally incapacitated when it came to moral action. What is slightly more controversial is my further assumption (here) that these capacities are not only necessary but sufficient for moral agency—that additional capacities like emotion and empathy are not necessary.[6] For now, I simply assume that point and move on.

3. See Quinton (1976) for a skeptical discussion. David Copp (1979, 2006, 2007), Peter French (1984), Carol Rovane (1997), Deborah Tollefsen (2002), and Christian List and Philip Pettit (2011) also propose holist(ish) positions, but they seem to be "methodological holists." At the very least, all have shied away from making the kind of ontological claims I have made here, and I suspect they would be uncomfortable with the move.

4. The members quite literally "constitute" the entity in the sense established by Lynne Baker (2000, 2002) who notes that "when certain kinds of things are in certain kinds of circumstances, things of new kinds, with new kinds of causal powers, come into existence. . . . So, constitution makes an ontological difference" (Baker 2002, 593). Specifically, where Group is a group of agents and Acme is a given corporate entity, Group constitutes Acme iff:

(i) Group and Acme are spatially coincident at t; and
(ii) Group is in the circumstance of having members who are able to and disposed to effectively coordinate their actions in accordance with the imperatives of a particular rational point of view not (necessarily) associated with any single human agent at t; and
(iii) It is necessary that: if anything that has being a group of human agents as its primary-kind property is in the circumstance in which those agents are able to and disposed to effectively coordinate their actions in accordance with the imperatives of a particular rational point of view not (necessarily) associated with any single human agent at t, then there is something that has being a corporate entity as its primary-kind property that is spatially coincident with the group of human agents; and
(iv) It is possible that: Group exists at t and that no spatially coincident thing that has being a corporate entity as its primary-kind property exists at t.

Without getting too deeply into the many complexities involved in these commitments, let me acknowledge two implications. First, this has the result that corporate agents can be in more than one place at once; Wal-mart can be in both Boston and Beijing. Second, this suggests that the members are only a part of the corporate agent—only participate in constituting it—when their actions are guided by the corporate RPV discussed below. Both implications require more development than I can give them here.

5. "Morally relevant information" can be unproblematically cashed out in utilitarian (pain/pleasure), deontological (rights, respect), virtue (excellence), and other grounds.

6. See Hess (2014) for an argument that the corporate agents described here are capable of free will, and Björnsson and Hess ("Corporate Crocodile Tears," unpublished) for an argument that they are capable of reactive attitudes. For a very brief discussion of the irrelevance of phenomenal states, see Hess (2010), Björnsson and Hess ("Tears"), and Hess ("Does the Machine Need a Ghost?," unpublished).

Given that any entity capable of acting intentionally on the basis of morally relevant information *is* a moral agent and thus *ought* to do so, then, the question is whether corporate agents possess the necessary capacities. My claim is that they do.

Before we move on to the mechanics of how corporate agents operate such that they are capable of action on the basis of belief and desire, and of moral agency more generally, it may be helpful to provide a brief introduction to the basic idea of such an agent. Begin with the familiar fact that corporations (and other corporate agents) have complex, interlocking sets of goals and plans. Each corporation has its own distinctive set of goals and plans—they're pursuing different ends in different settings, subject to different constraints—but each behaves in its own distinctive manner because it has the goals and plans that it does. One corporation reacts to a drop in coal prices by raising the price of its own products, another responds by lowering its prices, and a third doesn't react at all. The reduced price of coal has different implications for each corporation because of how it affects their distinctive array of goals and plans.

Now of course, when we talk about the corporation acting—pursuing ends, reacting to scarcity—there is a more fine-grained description available that would talk about what the members are doing. Analogously, when we talk about *me* doing something there is a more fine-grained description that would talk about what my body (or its constitutive parts) is doing. Both descriptions, at the level of the whole and the level of the parts, will be true as far as they go, but the description at the level of the parts will be radically incomplete. As W. Teed Rockwell points out,

> If I told you I hit you in the face because a signal came down from my brain and triggered the neurons in my arm, you would not consider that to be an acceptable explanation no matter how detailed it was. What you want is an explanation that makes reference to my beliefs, desires, and emotions." (2005, 149)

A description that captures the mechanics of an action without identifying the reasons behind it is inadequate for moral purposes, and a description of corporate action that explained *how* the corporate agent performed its activity (listing the dozens—or hundreds—of members who contributed to the implementation) without identifying the reason behind it is no better. It would describe, in part, but it would neither explain nor predict. We cannot adequately account for corporate behavior *or* the collective behavior of corporate members without reference to the corporate goals and plans that drive it (or, for that matter, the corporate structures that coordinate it). When we speak of the *collective* behavior of corporate members *as members*—the collective behavior of agents acting from a position within the corporate structure, in accordance with the corporate goals and plans—then we are speaking of the behavior *of the corporate agent*.

These corporate goals and plans, unique to each corporate agent, form an integrated complex of commitments that drives the behavior of the corporate agent—commitments about how the world is and what matters, about fact and value, that guide the collective behavior of its members. In reference to human persons, Carol Rovane describes such a complex of commitments as a "rational point of view" or "RPV," and I take the phrase from her. An RPV is a logically coherent set of commitments about fact and value that drives rational action, a synthesized collection of reasons for action that, together, constitute "the point of view from which deliberation proceeds" (Rovane 1997, 23). When a human being has an RPV that guides her actions, she is an agent; when she acts on the basis of that RPV, she acts freely and the action is her own. When a group of people has an RPV (not necessarily held by any single person) that guides their collective actions, they constitute the single, supra-individual entity that I call a corporate agent. The purpose for which these people have united and the arena in which the corporate agent acts are irrelevant to the question of whether they form a corporate agent; governments, branches of the military, and large nongovernmental organizations are all likely to qualify. However, it is in the business arena that corporate agents are most obviously and consistently found and it is with the business entity that I am most especially concerned. For the purposes of this article I will speak solely of business corporations, though the points made apply to corporate agents wherever they are found.[7]

Corporate agents differ from less disciplined social entities (like groups and mobs) in the simple fact of possessing a complex RPV that guides their actions. What distinguishes corporate agents from smaller purposive groups is the independence of the corporate RPV. In Margaret Gilbert's plural subjects (1989) and the social groups defined by Seumas Miller's collective ends (2001), whatever RPV exists must be shared by the members: the plural subject or social group has no beliefs or desires that its members do not have in one sense or another. In corporate agents, by contrast, the members do not necessarily share the commitments that form the corporate RPV. As a corporate agent, Wal-Mart can have a commitment to greening its image without *any* of its members necessarily having such a commitment; in fact, as described below, Wal-Mart can have such a commitment without any of its members even being aware of the fact. The possibility of this lack of continuity between member commitments and corporate commitments is crucial. It reveals the independence of the corporate RPV, marking the corporate RPV as unique to the corporate entity and the corporate entity as an agent in its own right.

This is not to say that the members have no role to play. As described below, the corporate RPV comes into being as a result of member activity, its existence is sustained by the continuing activities of its members, and it is effective in the world only to the extent that the members act from it. (Look at that sentence again, and note that in all of these things, it is much like *my* RPV in its dependence on the capacities and activities of *my* body.) It is, however, neither identical to, nor reducible to, nor directly derived from the RPVs of any of the human agents that constitute it. We can say that the imaginary Acme "doesn't care about the environment" without making any claims about what Acme's members believe, desire, or care about; the truth of the assertion does not turn on facts about the members' intentional states. What makes it true, if it is, is a *pattern of behavior* enacted by Acme's members—a pattern that they can collectively and reliably enact without any intention of enacting it. In fact, as demonstrated below, they can repeatedly and

---

7. As the examples suggest, the existence of a corporate entity is a matter of metaphysics rather than law. It is irrelevant whether the group is legally incorporated or not.

reliably enact that same pattern without having any idea that they are doing so, while themselves being passionately committed to saving the environment.[8]

2. THE MECHANICS OF CORPORATE AGENCY

So how does the corporate RPV come to have commitments that do not match the commitments of its members? For now I will refer to these commitments as "beliefs" and "desires"—in scare quotes—saving the task of justifying those designations for the third and fourth section of this article. To recast that question, then: how does the corporate RPV come to have "beliefs" and "desires" that do not match the beliefs and desires of its members? For the most part, commitments are incorporated into the corporate RPV in at least three different ways: via explicit decision making, distributed decision making, and cultural shift.

In the first case, the decision making is quite intentional and explicit: the board votes, the majority wins, and the corporation adopts a new position.[9] What I'd like to point out with respect to these kinds of decisions is that the board members do not necessarily express their own preferences when they vote, nor are they supposed to. Instead they make their decisions from the point of view of the corporate agent, reasoning from the existing commitments of the corporate agent to determine what the new commitments should be.[10] Let's flesh out some of the details of the fictional Acme, for an example.

Say that Acme is a small, 100-year-old company with existing commitments to seeking profit, producing industrial chemicals, and being environmentally

8. To see this clearly, imagine what would be involved in *changing* Acme's "beliefs" about the environment. Simply convincing the members is neither necessary nor sufficient. It is not necessary because the corporate entity can change its beliefs without a change in the member's beliefs. Assume that at t_1, Acme and each of its members believes that *not x*: the environment is unimportant. At t_2 the board members learn that polling indicates that consumers will flee Acme's products in droves if Acme continues to pollute, violate, and destroy as it has in the past. Various new practices and policies are proposed and instituted, and by t_3 Acme's behavior is exemplary. On most accounts of belief (discussed in Section 3, below), Acme now believes that the environment is important, but it may well be the case that every member of Acme from top to bottom still thinks that it isn't. Their beliefs haven't changed, but Acme's clearly have: Acme now believes that x. Convincing the members that x is also not sufficient to make Acme believe that x. Take the same starting point where Acme and each of its members believe that the environment is unimportant, then imagine that one night every single member has a conversion experience: the scales fall from their eyes and they now realize that the environment is the most important thing in the world. This is great, but not enough to make it the case that *Acme* now believes the same. If everyone returns to work and keeps doing the same old things (while possibly spending all of their spare time restoring wetlands and doing grassroots campaigning), Acme will still pollute, violate, and destroy and thus, on most accounts, will still believe that the environment is unimportant.

9. The existing literatures on this topic, both in philosophy and in the business academy, focus almost exclusively on this kind of decision making, despite the fact that such decisions constitute only a tiny fraction of the decisions that actually structure corporate action. It gives a very misleading picture of the reality of corporate practice.

10. As Philip Pettit and Christian List have demonstrated at length, even if the board members (or whoever) *do* vote to express their personal preferences, it does not follow that the corporate commitments that result will reflect those personal preferences. See their work on the discursive dilemma, for example, Pettit (2002, 2003); and List and Pettit (2005, 2011).

responsible. Given Acme's prior commitments to profit and to producing industrial chemicals, the board members could easily conclude (and vote) that Acme ought to develop a new kind of steel additive. Acme's prior—and very public— commitments to environmental stewardship suggest that this be done in ways that are protective of the environment, but it is clear that Acme's commitments to profit and production are more central to Acme and take priority. And so Acme adopts a new commitment to developing a new kind of steel additive and the work goes forward. None of this requires any personal inputs from the board members—just familiarity with Acme's RPV and sufficient knowledge about the world to do the means-end reasoning to further the pursuit of Acme's goals. Should the commitment to environmental stewardship interfere unduly with the pursuit of Acme's core commitments, the board members may well vote to abandon it *despite* their personal commitments to environmental stewardship. Here the members reason from Acme's RPV, not from their own, and Acme's actions thus express its own commitments rather than those of its members.[11]

Or Acme may "vote with its feet" (as it were), abandoning the commitment to environmental stewardship through its actions rather than through any kind of formal decision making. In such cases the "decision-making" process is distributed over a number of people, sometimes over hundreds or even thousands. The process is thus much less explicit and often effectively opaque to the members involved, and the individual members are often unaware that they are establishing a commitment for the corporate agent—one that may nonetheless become a part of the corporate RPV and thus a part of "the point of view from which deliberation proceeds."[12] "Distributed decision making" is a bit like assembling a car, with each member contributing one fact or decision and then passing the project on to the next, without any of them necessarily seeing the collective actions that the corporate agent reliably enacts as a result of their individual choices.

To sketch an unrealistically simplistic example of this second method[13], assume that as a result of Acme's new "desire" to produce steel additives:

11. Obviously the members are always free to subvert this process, inserting their own preferences into the reasoning process and ignoring the obligations of their positions, and they may well do so out of principle, ignorance, laziness, or simple malice. If enough members do so, eventually Acme will be incapable of intentional action on the basis of its own RPV. At that point, the RPV is not longer embodied and the corporate agent ceases to exist.

12. None of the existing accounts from Copp (1979, 2007), French (1984), Gilbert (1989), Isaacs (2011), List and Pettit (2011), Miller (2001), or Rovane (1997) acknowledge or allow for this kind of distributed decision making, whether intentionally or unintentionally pursued by the members. It would not qualify as an act or decision of the corporate agent on their accounts, nor would the actions that flow from it. And yet it is indispensible to contemporary corporate practice. Corporate practice relies upon intense specialization to achieve its efficiencies, and it is rarely the case that everyone who needs to contribute to a decision has time to sit down and discuss the matter with everyone else who needs to contribute to the decision. Distributed decision making solves this problem, though it (obviously) carries its own costs.

13. To make this more realistic, assume that each "member" in the example is a department, and add further concerns—and additional steps—to address tax implications, public relations, supplier relationships, etc.

Member A requests proposals from Departments α, β, and γ.
Member B picks the one from α and modifies it slightly to reduce costs.
Member C modifies the proposal to improve materials handling.
D modifies the proposal to improve efficiency,
E modifies it to improve health and safety compliance (less worker exposure),
F modifies it to use different (nationally available) chemicals, and
G modifies it to reduce costs again.

In the end, as a result of these piecemeal modifications and others during implementation—each innocuous and rational enough within its own limited sphere—the new production line results in a continuing discharge that pollutes a local river. As a result of all these individual choices by its members, *Acme* is now engaged in the ongoing pollution of the river, and has taken a significant step toward abandoning its prior commitment to environmental stewardship.[14]

In the third method, corporate decision making is even more broadly distributed (and thus even more opaque to the members). Rather than a limited roster of members generating a new commitment seriatim, a diffuse shift occurs over time throughout the corporate body. Here, for example, it may be that scattered members cease to attend to the environmental aspects of their own jobs. Some may know that they are skipping environmentally relevant steps; some may know that they are skipping steps but not that they are environmentally relevant; and some may not even realize that they've modified their behavior. Nonetheless, as time passes and the habits spread, and the change is either not noticed or—if noticed—not corrected, it begins to become standard practice. And eventually, Acme becomes a corporation that has either lost its prior commitment to environmental stewardship or (more strongly) gained a positive commitment to *not* practicing environmental stewardship. This is effectively a cultural shift—a change that (interestingly enough) can start "at the bottom" and spread upward. Once the practices have hit a tipping point, both old members and (especially) new members coming in will incorporate this new commitment—consciously or not—into their work practices, and behavior that conforms to it will be rewarded or at least ignored. But who, in this latter case, decided that Acme shouldn't be environmentally responsible? Certainly not any of the individuals just described, none of whom knew or could have known—within the parameters of their job descriptions/expertise—that these tiny changes to their own practices would have such a result. And yet Acme's RPV now includes this commitment, future reasoning *from* that RPV (in the case of explicit decision making) will reflect it, and corporate action will conform to it.

In either case, again, the corporate agent has come to "*believe*" *that x* (that the environment doesn't matter) and to "*desire*" *that y* (that it produce steel additives) in a manner that has no necessary connection to the preferences, beliefs, or desires of its members regarding x and y. When its members act, they will tend to act in ways that (collectively) express these corporate "beliefs" and "desires" rather than their own, possibly contrary opinions. This can be done knowingly and

---

14. Note that this is only "a step" in the new direction; this by itself would not be sufficient to justify the charge that Acme no longer cares about the environment. But it *is* a step, and if Acme continues in this direction—as discussed in the next paragraph—then the situation may change.

deliberately, as in the case of the board vote, or it can be done unknowingly, by masses of people going through the motions of doing their jobs without ever being in a position to see the corporate commitments—the corporate "beliefs" and "desires"—that they create and then conform to by so doing.

3. CORPORATE INTENTIONALITY—BELIEF

Now it's time to get rid of the scare quotes. These corporate commitments—however they arise—are easily and casually spoken of as beliefs and desires: "Acme doesn't care about the environment," "Acme wanted to cut corners and believed it could get away with it," and so on. In this section and the one that follows, I suggest that these commitments literally qualify as beliefs and desires on the standard interpretationist, dispositionalist, and representationalist accounts developed to explain human belief and desire. Rather than choose a particular account of belief or desire, my method in the sections that follow is simply to outline several of the major options and demonstrate that corporate agents can believe and desire on *any* of these accounts.[15]

What is it for an entity to believe something? There is little consensus in the literature. In general, interpretationists[16] say that A believes that x when we can reliably predict and account for A's actions on the basis of a posited *belief that x*. A really does believe that x if A's actions are sufficiently consistent with the belief that x; there's no more to it than that. Dispositionalists[17] go a little further to say that A believes that x if A is *disposed* to act as if A believes that x—to act in ways that would typically be expected given a belief that x. This is a little more palatable, as it allows the entity to have beliefs that it hasn't acted on or that have not yet manifested themselves in its actions. Neither account is especially popular, but it should be relatively obvious that corporate agents—as described above—are capable of belief on these accounts. It's easy to predict and account for Acme's behavior in terms of a posited belief in the value of profits, or the secondary nature of environmental concerns, and Acme is certainly disposed to act as if it believes that profit is of primary importance and the environment . . . not so much.[18] (It is worth noting that predicting and accounting for Acme's behavior in terms of the

15. This seems a good place to acknowledge that there is no phenomenal aspect to these corporate beliefs and desires. While some may find this rather questionable, it would take us too far afield to address the matter in any detail here. Again, see Björnsson and Hess ("Corporate Crocodile Tears," unpublished) and Hess (2010) for limited discussion. All I will say here is that I have not modified any of the accounts I've presented here in order to achieve that result. The standard, widely accepted accounts of belief or desire simply do not include a phenomenal aspect (though some philosophers have argued that they should; see e.g., Horgan and Tienson 2002).

16. For example, Dennett (1987, 1991, 1996); Davidson (1963, 1984, 1993).

17. For example, Audi (1972, 1993); Marcus (1990); Pettit (1993); and Baker (1995).

18. Remembering, again, that to say that "Acme is disposed to act as if x" is to say that Acme's members are disposed to act in ways that yield *collective* actions consistent with the belief that x. There is no need for their individual actions to be consistent with the belief that x, nor indeed, with any belief at all. Dennett himself suggests that some groups will meet the interpretationist standard (1978, 269 n*); see Clark (1994) and Tollefsen (2002) for more extended interpretationist analyses. I am generally in sympathy with their approaches, though I have some reservations.

posited beliefs or dispositions of its members—*without* reference to the structures and commitments of the corporate agent—will be less than effective, especially in cases where the corporate commitments have diverged.)

While (again) there is no consensus, representationalist accounts are far more popular. Representationalists[19] argue that belief requires both an internal representation and (essentially) a disposition to act on the basis of that representation. Dretske (1988) describes such internal representations as "maps by which we steer" (79); a belief is thus an internal representation of the world (or some aspect of it) that guides our behavior. Given how easily corporate agents meet the "disposition to act" requirements, the main question left is whether they can have "representations" in the appropriate sense.

So what is it to have a representation? Taking Dretske's (1988) account as our exemplar, a representation is (1) an information-bearing state (2) internal to a system (3) that the system synthesizes from information gathered from the world. Dretske uses the example of a wolf tracking a crippled caribou: The wolf has the ability (via its senses) to take in information about the external world and "indicate" that information to a central system; in this case, information about visual, aural, and olfactory matters. The central system synthesizes this disparate information into a representation that both signifies "crippled caribou" and identifies its relevance to the wolf. Thus the complete representation is more likely "easy prey" or just "dinner." The important thing to remember is that representations are not direct reflections of the external world but *interpretations* of the external world based on reports—"indications"—which *are* direct reflections. Dretske emphasizes that representations are not (or need not be) mental images or pictures of any kind: "representations are not expected, even under optimal conditions, to *resemble* the objects they represent. . . . The wolf's internal representation of a sick caribou may or may not be a sick-and-fleeing-caribou representation, but it is certainly a representation *of* a sick, fleeing caribou. How the neural machinery represents *what* it represents is, to some degree, a matter of speculation . . ." (71) The representations necessary for belief are not—or need not be—pictorial. Thus, the wolf has a representation of the crippled-caribou-as-dinner once systems internal to the wolf gather up the disparate information and synthesize it into a coherent packet of information that has relevance or significance for the wolf; the representation consists of related bits of information synthesized into a single *significant* item, as something relevant to potential action. If the information is gathered, synthesized, and communicated in such a way that the wolf can *act* on the basis of it, then it is a belief.

From this account it seems unproblematic to say that corporate agents have representations. Moreover, it seems unproblematic to say that corporate agents have representations that are their own, that are not possessed by any member of the corporate agent. In fact, Dretske's emphasis on the distinction between indications and representations gives us exactly the concepts we need to

19. For example, Dretske (1988, 1993) and Millikan (1984, 1993).

account for the specific role that the members play in the *development* of the corporate belief that x, while distinguishing that behavior from any *member* believing that x.

Individual members take in information about the world and *indicate* to the corporate agent by their actions, transmitting information into the corporate structure. They may do so by making statements, filing reports, or performing certain actions within their own positions that effectively signal information to other parts/members of the corporate agent. This information is gathered from across the corporation and synthesized into a single representation which, again, is "an information-bearing state," *not* a mental picture. This representation may not (and need not) be present "in anyone's head." Various members of the corporate agent can know enough to know that some actions are available to them while others are not—and to act accordingly—without anyone seeing enough of the entirety to know the fullness of the representation. And yet this representation will still guide the activity of the corporate agent. (See Appendix A for a fully developed example of Acme's erroneous belief that it is low on coal.)[20]

4. CORPORATE INTENTIONALITY—DESIRE

With the work already done regarding corporate beliefs, we can move more quickly through the matter of corporate desires. On the interpretationist account, an agent *desires that y* to the extent (and only to the extent) that an observer would be entitled to impute the desire that y to the agent on the basis of the agent's actions. Like beliefs, desires are "indirect 'measurements' of a reality diffused in the behavioral dispositions of the brain (and body)" (Dennett 1991, 45). From the intentional stance, again, it is easy to account for corporate behavior in terms of desires, as is obvious from the ease, frequency, and predictive success with which we ascribe desires to corporate actors.[21] On the dispositionalist account, it would not be the overt actions of the purported agent but its *dispositions* to act that would be constitutive of desiring that y: Acme desires that y if and only if it is disposed to *act as if* it desires that y, presumably by pursuing y or striving to bring it about that y. Again, this is an entirely familiar phenomenon (though for all of the reasons previously discussed, "Acme desiring that y" is not equivalent to "the members of Acme desiring that y").

Representationalism is, again, more complicated and sets a more demanding standard, but corporate agents meet that standard in much the same way and for much the same reasons that they met the standard for having their own beliefs.

---

20. Like a human agent, a corporate agent may undoubtedly possess representations that it has not acted on; in such cases we would have no way of knowing that the agent or the entity in fact possessed the representation. For corporate agents, as for human agents, the only *evidence* of a representation lies in the dispositions of the agent or the entity to act in certain ways, affirming some statements, denying others, and so on.

21. Again, see Clark (1994) for a somewhat developed statement of interpretationism regarding desires in a corporate context.

Unlike the interpretationist and dispositionalist accounts discussed *supra*, Dretske's representationalist account does not treat beliefs and desires as analogous states. Beliefs and desires are importantly similar. Both are intentional states, referentially opaque,[22] and capable of accounting for action regardless of error on the part of the agent (we act on false beliefs and misguided or hopeless desires in exactly the same way that we act on true beliefs and proper/reasonable desires, though perhaps with less satisfaction). There is a crucial difference, however, in that desires are not representational states (Dretske 1988, 127).[23] Desires are nonetheless intentional states, and on the representationalist account that means that they have to have some kind of content. For the representationalist interested in avoiding the problems associated with requiring an *internal* representation for desires, there remains the problem of accounting for the content of desires *without* reference to an internal representation.

On Dretske's account, desires are above all *motivational states*. There are pure desires, which are simply "desires for x," and then ever more sophisticated layers of cognitive desires which are derived from beliefs about what will best achieve the goal identified by the pure desire. To have a desire, then, is to be in a certain kind of state ("D")—specifically, to be "receptive" to a specific "reinforcer" ("R," a condition or outcome) in such a way that this receptiveness becomes a structuring cause. Triggering causes, such as the availability of R, will (causally) lead to behaviors aimed at achieving R iff the entity is in state D. D's having R as its goal, its being *for R*, is not a triggering cause of behavior. It is a *structuring* cause.[24] It helps explain, not why D or movement ("M") is occurring now, but why, now, D is causing M (rather than something else) (114).

The *content*, the information, is contained in the state of the world that is sought by the entity possessed of the desire rather than in a representation. We determine the representational content of a desire (for others and sometimes for ourselves) by seeing what satisfies it. The content is thus *external* to the entity (in contrast to the content of a belief), but still motivating for the entity because the entity's internal states make it "receptive to" R.

Corporate agents are capable of desire on this account because they are capable of possessing motivational states as structuring causes: they can be

22. Dretske explains this quite succinctly: "The belief that *s* is *F* is not the same as a belief that *t* is *G*, although *s* = *t* and although the predicate expressions, '*F*' and '*G*', are co-extensional (are true of, or refer to, exactly the same things). The same is true of desire. Oedipus wants to marry Jocasta, but does not want to marry his mother (and perhaps even wants not to marry his mother), despite the fact that Jocasta is his mother" (1988, 127).

23. This is an important aspect of Dretske's account, but a full discussion would take us too far afield. The general concern is that if desires *were* representational states, we could only desire something we could clearly represent to ourselves. This leads to several problems. First, only highly sophisticated intellects would be capable of desire, with the result that children and animals can't desire things (which seems wildly at odds with our experience of the world). Second, it suggests that we can't desire things with which we are unfamiliar, and unconscious and subconscious desires become very problematic. Third, it suggests that we cannot desire (arguably) impossible-to-imagine but certainly attractive states of affairs like "world peace."

24. See Dretske (1993) for a full explanation of triggering and structuring causes.

receptive to R in a way that shapes their behavior, such that a triggering cause (such as the availability of R) will result in behavior aimed at achieving R. This is what it *is* to have a desire for R. Further, this state is once again unique to the corporate agent (as opposed to its members), in that the corporate agent can be receptive to—and thus motivated by—reinforcers that have absolutely no "pull" for the individual members; the corporate agent can be in state D[R] despite the fact that none of its members desire R. (See Appendix B for a fully developed example of Acme's desire for more coal.)

With this, it is easy to see how we can say both *that* corporate agents have desires and *how* they have desires—how the desires of the corporate agent are distinct from the desires of its members. Again, on the representationalist account desires are internal states of an entity which are incorporated as structuring causes that shape the entity's behavior, and they are defined at least in part by their content: by the state(s) of affairs to which they are receptive. It is entirely possible—even familiar—for Acme to be receptive to states of affairs that have no valence for its members, and for it to respond to events (which for it are triggering causes) that have no significance for its members (which do not solicit any response, or contribute to any causal chain involving the members; again, see Appendix B for a more detailed discussion). The members act on Acme's desires not because they share those desires but because they have *their own* desires, and Acme has established a system of rewards and penalties such that the members can best satisfy their own desires—for prestige, money, security, identity—by satisfying Acme's desires. The corporate agent doesn't replace the desires of the members with its own; it co-opts them for its own purposes. And when the members act on Acme's desires, Acme acts.

5. CORPORATE MORAL AGENCY—A BRIEF NOTE

The upshot of all this is that corporate action originates in, expresses, and is guided by a complex of beliefs and desires that are unique to the corporate agent. They are not the beliefs or desires of the members (of whatever rank), they are not reducible to the beliefs or desires of the members, and they cannot be properly attributed to the members as individuals separate from the corporate structure and context. The corporate agent has its own RPV, and the possession of an RPV coupled with the ability to act effectively on the basis of that RPV marks the existence of an agent. To the extent that this agent is capable of having and acting on beliefs and desires about morally relevant factors (however understood), it is a moral agent: one that is capable of—and thus should—take morally relevant information into account when it acts. With the sketch already provided, it should be relatively obvious how the corporate agent would do so.

Corporate agents (like human agents) act from an RPV—again, a coherent set of commitments about fact and value that forms "the point of view from which deliberation proceeds." This RPV is comprised of beliefs and desires; on a representationalist account, these beliefs and desires are anchored by representations synthesized from information gathered by the individual members and built into the corporate structure of incentives.[25] Once this much is securely established, it seems odd to suggest that these representations *couldn't* include morally relevant information. The members already contribute to the development of corporate beliefs and desires about profit, expansion, and survival by the information that they collect and report. If the members gather and report information relevant to pleasure and pain, rights and duties, excellence and inferiority, etc. such that the representations include that information, then the corporate agent will have beliefs and desires that take such morally relevant information into account. And when it acts on the basis of those beliefs and desires, it will—or at least, can—act morally. If a corporate agent is capable of doing X instead of Y *because* X causes less pain, respects rights, exemplifies an excellence, etc., then it is a moral agent. If it then fails to do X it acts not *a*morally but *im*morally.

I would like to briefly acknowledge that I have presented a radically simplified account of moral agency, in an effort to expose its most basic core and show how a corporate agent could perform those very basic functions. There are far more sophisticated accounts of moral agency, which require various kinds of knowledge, self-referentiality, specific attitudes (of care or respect), specific reactions (shame, guilt, indignation), and the like. Fortunately, corporate agents are likewise capable of far more sophisticated functioning than the very basic behaviors that I have outlined here, and I suggest that the capacities introduced above also enable them to manage these more sophisticated forms of moral agency as well.[26]

6. CONCLUSION

To close with the full technical statement: metaphysically speaking, all of this means that there *is* a corporate agent. There are discernible, effective commitments about fact and value that drive corporate behavior, and these commitments are not held by the members. They must be held by something—they cannot be free floating—and they are therefore held by the corporate agent; there is no other candidate. Further, this corporate agent has beliefs and desires (those same commitments about fact and value) and the ability to act on them. This entity is constituted by its members (see note 4); it is thus a material object in the sense of necessarily possessing material properties (though like any agent, it has nonmaterial properties as well). The beliefs and desires "coincide" (in Yablo's [1992] sense of the term) with specific member activity, just as my beliefs and desires "coincide"

---

25. All of this begins to get *really* interesting when we recognize that the corporate incentive structure itself—like everything about the corporation—can develop via *all three* of the mechanisms described in Section 2. The incentive structure itself can reflect corporate commitments that no individual explicitly chose or adopted, or even recognizes, but these unintended commitments can become just as firmly anchored and can guide member behavior just as effectively as the explicitly articulated ones—sometimes, even more effectively, because they are neither noticed nor questioned.

26. See the works listed at note 6 for some discussion.

with specific physical activity in my body.[27] And because this corporate agent *can* have beliefs and desires about moral matters, it *ought to* have (proper) beliefs and desires that take moral matters into account.

If we take the previous paragraph and replace references to "the corporate agent" with references to "the human agent," and replace references to "the members" with references to "the body (or its parts)," it describes a human agent as well as a corporate agent:

> Metaphysically speaking, this means that there *is* a [human agent]. There are discernible, effective commitments about fact and value that drive [human] behavior, and these commitments are not held by the [body (or its parts)]. They must be held by something—they cannot be free floating—and they are therefore held by the [human agent]; there is no other candidate. Further, this [human agent] has beliefs and desires (those same commitments about fact and value) and the ability to act on them. This entity is constituted by its [body (or its parts)]; it is thus a material object in the sense of necessarily possessing material properties (though like any agent, it has nonmaterial properties as well). The beliefs and desires "coincide" (in Yablo's [1992] sense of the term) with specific [bodily] activity. . . . And because this [human agent] *can* have beliefs and desires about moral matters, it *ought to* have (proper) beliefs and desires that take moral matters into account.

Such human agents are unproblematically considered to be moral agents with moral obligations, and I suggest we should extend the same courtesy—and expectation—to the corporate agents which share so many of their capacities.

REFERENCES

Audi, Robert. 1972. "The Concept of Believing." *Personalist* 53: 43–62.

———. 1993. "Mental Causation: Sustaining and Dynamic." In *Mental Causation*, ed. John Heil and Alfred Mele, 53–74. Oxford: Clarendon Press.

Baker, Lynne R. 1995. *Explaining Attitudes*. Cambridge: Cambridge University Press.

———. 2000. *Persons and Bodies: A Constitution View*. Cambridge: Cambridge University Press.

———. 2002. "Précis of *Persons and Bodies: A Constitution View*." *Philosophy and Phenomenological Research* 64(3): 592–98.

Bratman, Michael. 1987. *Intentions, Plans and Practical Reason*. Cambridge, MA: Harvard University Press.

———. 1999. *Faces of Intention*. Cambridge: Cambridge University Press.

Clark, Austen. 1994. "Beliefs and Desires Incorporated." *Journal of Philosophy* 91(8): 404–25.

Copp, David. 1979. "Collective Actions and Secondary Actions." *American Philosophical Quarterly* 16(3): 177–86.

———. 2006. "On the Agency of Certain Collective Entities: An Argument from 'Normative Autonomy'." *Midwest Studies in Philosophy* 30: 194–221.

———. 2007. "The Collective Moral Autonomy Thesis." *Journal of Social Philosophy* 38(3): 369–88.

Davidson, Donald. 1963. "Actions, Reasons, and Causes." *Journal of Philosophy* 60(23): 685–700.

---

27. Or possibly are emergent from. . . . The accounts works as well with emergence theory (from O'Connor and Wong 2005) as with Yablo's coincidence theory.

——. 1984. *Inquiries into Truth and Interpretation*. Oxford: Clarendon Press.

——. 1993. "Thinking Causes." In *Mental Causation*, ed. John Heil and Alfred Mele, 3–17. Oxford: Clarendon Press.

Dennett, Daniel C. 1978. "Conditions of Personhood." In *Brainstorms: Philosophical Essays on Mind and Psychology*, 267–85. Cambridge, MA: MIT Press.

——. 1987. *The Intentional Stance*. Cambridge, MA: MIT Press.

——. 1991. "Real Patterns." *Journal of Philosophy* 88(1): 27–51.

——. 1996. *Kinds of Minds*. New York: Basic Books.

Dretske, Fred. 1988. *Explaining Behavior: Reasons in a World of Causes*. Cambridge, MA: MIT Press.

——. 1993. "Mental Events as Structuring Causes of Behaviour." In *Mental Causation*, ed. John Heil and Alfred Mele, 121–36. Oxford Clarendon Press.

French, Peter. 1984. *Collective and Corporate Responsibility*. New York: Columbia University Press.

Gilbert, Margaret. 1989. *On Social Facts*. Princeton, NJ: Princeton University Press.

——. 2000. *Sociality and Responsibility: New Essays in Plural Subject Theory*. Lanham, MD: Rowman and Littlefield.

——. 2006. "Who's to Blame? Collective Moral Responsibility and Its Implications." *Midwest Studies in Philosophy* 30: 94–114.

Hess, Kendy. 2010. "The Modern Corporation as Moral Agent: The Capacity for 'Thought' and a 'First-Person Perspective'." *Southwest Philosophy Review* 26(1): 61–69.

——. 2014. "The Free Will of Corporations (and Other Collectives)." *Philosophical Studies* 168(1): 241–60.

Horgan, Terrence, and Tienson, John. 2002. "The Intentionality of Phenomenology and the Phenomenology of Intentionality." In *Philosophy of Mind: Classical and Contemporary Readings*, ed. David Chalmers, 520–33. Oxford: Oxford University Press.

Isaacs, Tracy. 2006. "Collective Moral Responsibility and Collective Intention." *Midwest Studies in Philosophy* 30(1): 59–73.

——. 2011. *Moral Responsibility in Collective Contexts*. Oxford: Oxford University Press.

List, Christian, and Pettit, Philip. 2005. "On the Many as One." *Philosophy and Public Affairs* 33(4): 377–90.

——. 2011. *Group Agency: The Possibility, Design, and Status of Corporate Agents*. Oxford: Oxford University Press.

Marcus, Ruth. 1990. "Some Revisionary Proposals about Belief and Believing." *Philosophy and Phenomenological Research* 50, Suppl. (Autumn): 133–53.

Miller, Seumas. 2001. *Social Action: A Teleological Account*. Cambridge: Cambridge University Press.

——. 2006. "Collective Moral Responsibility: An Individualist Account." *Midwest Studies in Philosophy* 30: 176–93.

Millikan, Ruth G. 1984. *Language, Thought, and Other Biological Categories*. Cambridge, MA: MIT Press.

——. 1993. *White Queen Psychology and Other Essays for Alice*. Cambridge, MA: MIT Press.

O'Connor, Timothy, and Wong, Hong Yu. 2005. "The Metaphysics of Emergence." *Noûs* 39(4): 658–78.

Pettit, Philip. 1993. *The Common Mind: An Essay on Psychology, Society, and Politics*. Oxford: Oxford University Press.

——. 2002. "Collective Persons and Powers." *Legal Theory* 8: 443–70.

——. 2003. "Groups with Minds of Their Own." In *Socializing Metaphysics: The Nature of Social Reality*, ed. Frederick Schmitt, 167–94. Lanham, MD: Rowman & Littlefield.

Quinton, Anthony. 1976. "Social Objects." *Proceedings of the Aristotelian Society* 76: 1–27.

Rockwell, W. Teed. 2005. *Neither Brain Nor Ghost: A Nondualist Alternative to the Mind–Brain Identity Theory*. Cambridge, MA: MIT Press.

Rovane, Carol. 1997. *The Bounds of Agency: An Essay in Revisionary Metaphysics*. Princeton, NJ: Princeton University Press.

Tollefsen, Deborah. 2002. "Organizations as True Believers." *Journal of Social Philosophy* 33(3): 395–410.

Yablo, Stephen. 1992. "Mental Causation." *Philosophical Review* 101(2): 245–280.

APPENDIX A. THE MISTAKEN BELIEF

The ability to have *mistaken* beliefs is often taken to be crucial for true intentionality, true agency, so what follows is an example of just that. It also presents Dretske's representationalist account in a little more detail, briefly addressing the matter of causation: how corporate beliefs cause the corporate agent to act in certain ways. On Dretske's account, I need to show that *the corporate agent itself* has representations, that (1) it has recruited indicators to gather information about the world; (2) that this information is synthesized into representations; and (3) that the representations can become structuring causes for the corporate agent, influencing its behavior in certain predictable ways. It is not enough to show that the individual members have beliefs that are reflected in the behavior of the corporate agent.

Back to the vile Acme Corp., maker of industrial chemicals and heedless polluter of the environment. One of the things that Acme needs to do, in order to ensure its continued successful existence, is to ensure that the right kinds of raw materials come in at the right times and in the right quantities. It needs some way to know which materials are needed, when, where, and in what quantity, and it needs some way to ensure that the materials end up at the right place. Let's say that it is opening a new factory, and now needs to make sure that all these new needs are taken into account. The corporation already has internal elements capable of indicating the lack of things needed, so it recruits them to do so: member A is now responsible for indicating a lack of coal (usually by writing a memo, or filling out a form, or making a phone call), member B is now responsible for indicating a lack of iron, and member C is now responsible for indicating a lack of additives. What A, B, and C believe, want, fear, and do on is irrelevant to the corporation because it is not available to the corporation. A may be desperate for a raise and so overly assiduous in renewing the coal supply; B may be close to retiring and so unduly lax in tracking the iron supply. As a result, A may indicate that Acme is low on coal before this is the case (and may even know she is doing so) and B may *not* indicate that Acme is low on iron when this *is* the case (and may know she is doing so). Further, A may be completely indifferent to whether Acme is a successful business, since A has a standing offer at a competing firm, and B may want very badly for Acme to be successful because it will affect her pension. None of this information is available to the corporate agent or a part of its representations or beliefs. The information regarding the electrical and chemical behaviors of the wolf's sensory systems is not available to the wolf or present in her representation of a crippled caribou, despite the fact that these processes were crucial to the *ability* of those systems to provide the information to the wolf. For that matter, information about the electrical and chemical behaviors of *our* internal systems is not available to *us* or present in *our* representations, despite being equally crucial to our ability to have and act on those representations. Similarly, none of the information regarding these internal factors about members A and B, which will undoubtedly affect A's and B's performances as indicators, will be present in the indications that A and B provide to the corporation. Thus, that information will not be a part of the representation or of the corporate agent's belief.

Once A and B (but not C) have successfully indicated a lack—the information has been made available in the proper ways and taken up in the proper ways so that it is then available to those members responsible for acting on it—the corporate agent will have developed a representation with the content "I need coal and iron, but not additives" and a belief to that effect.[28] Again, it is a belief because it is an internal representation of a state of affairs that is incorporated into the system in such a way as to shape the behavior of that system. Specifically, it is a "structuring cause": *because* the representation has the content that it has, the corporate agent will respond to "triggering causes" in one way rather than another. Further, it is a representation that is internal *to the corporate agent* rather than to any of its members. On the account given above, *A* knows that Acme doesn't really need coal but *Acme* doesn't know that, and it is Acme's belief that it needs coal that structures Acme's behavior. Bound by Acme's belief, member D will respond to the triggering cause of a drop in coal prices by making a phone call that results in Acme acquiring more coal. As long as the representation is *internal to* the corporate agent such that it *influences the behavior of* the corporate agent (as a structuring cause), it is a *belief of* the corporate agent.

APPENDIX B. THE DESIRE FOR COAL

Going back to the earlier example (Appendix A), members A and B had respectively indicated that Acme was low on coal and iron, and as a result Acme had developed the belief that it was low on coal and iron (despite the fact that it was not, in fact, low on coal). As a result, member D ordered more coal on Acme's behalf. Note, however, that Acme's belief by itself was inert, a structuring cause that had not yet been activated in any way. Simply believing itself to be low on coal and iron does not automatically lead to action by Acme any more than the knowledge that I am low on truffles automatically sends me running to the store. I must have a *desire* for truffles before the knowledge of a lack will lead to action, and Acme must have a *desire* for coal and steel before the knowledge of a lack will lead to action. Nor will the presence of a (potentially) triggering cause elicit action in the absence of a desire: again, a sale on truffles is irrelevant to me unless I want truffles, and a drop in the price of coal is irrelevant to Acme unless it wants coal. To the extent that the corporation responds to the triggering cause of a drop in coal prices by ordering more coal (via member D's activities), this is evidence that Acme has a desire for coal. In fact, this behavior is evidence of a *dual* structuring cause: there is a belief *and* a desire with closely related content. But what about

---

28. It is fair to say that Acme has a belief that it does *not* need steel additives because—again—on Dretske's account beliefs are structuring causes. Acme's belief that it does not need steel additives will structure its behavior in the event that some triggering cause (say, a drop in the price of steel additives) brings the belief into play (and it will fail to purchase).

member D? Member D likewise responded to the triggering cause of a drop in coal prices by acting to buy coal, so D must also have been in possession of a relevant belief/desire state as the structuring cause for *her* behavior. In what sense, then, does the relevant structuring state belong to Acme?

It is possible in any given instance that the individual member so deeply identifies with the corporate agent of which she is a member that her internal states *do* track those of the corporation. Member D may believe that Acme needs coal, want Acme to have more coal, and act for no other reason than to secure the coal for Acme. However, we need not suppose—as many individualists do—that this is always or necessarily the case.[29] D can act to procure more coal for Acme without having either the belief that *Acme needs coal* or the desire to satisfy that (reported) need. D may be fully aware that A makes a habit of over-indicating and thus lack the belief that Acme needs coal, and she may be utterly indifferent to the state of Acme's coal supplies but want very badly to keep her job. Her job is to order coal when A indicates a need for coal. More specifically, her job is to order coal when *Acme* believes that it needs coal; her job is to act on Acme's beliefs, not her own, and to satisfy Acme's desires.[30]

Desires are intentional states. They are essentially *about* something—they have content—and they are defined in terms of their content. Acme has a desire *for* coal because it is receptive to the acquisition of *coal*; nothing else will satisfy its desire, and the desire will not be satisfied until it has acquired more coal. Member D, on the other hand, has a desire to *keep her job*. This desire may or may not, at different times, involve ensuring that Acme acquires more coal, but it can and will be satisfied by any number of states of affairs; there is no reference to coal. At best we may be able to say that she has a derivative desire that *Acme acquire coal* (which is still importantly different from Acme's desire that *I acquire coal*), but to the extent she has such a desire or something like it at all, she gets this desire *from Acme*. It must be Acme's desire first, before it becomes hers. Not only is Acme's desire not identical to or derivative of the desires of its members—the desires of its members are in many cases derivative of the desires of Acme.

---

29. Seumas Miller (2001), for example, suggests that we imagine that "that workers in a car factory only work for their pay packets. They are not interested in whether or not any cars are produced. Certainly, they perform whatever tasks they are paid to perform, but they care nothing about the outcomes of the combined efforts of themselves and their workmates.... I suggest that such an organization would come to grief very quickly indeed.... Surely, in that case it would be unlikely, or at best fortuitous, if in general cars were produced in that car factory" (2001, 179). I am at a bit of a loss as to how to respond to this. My only suggestion is that Miller visit his local McDonald's, if he would like to experience the efficiency of an enterprise in which the workers have absolutely no personal investment in producing their product.

30. Corporations are typically structured this way because in the vast majority of cases the individual members do not have access to sufficient information to act effectively on the company's behalf in their own right. They're not *supposed* to act on their own beliefs and desires. They're *supposed* to act on the beliefs and desires of the company, as those beliefs and desires have been communicated to them through proper channels. This becomes less true at higher levels of management, but as we saw in Section 2, even the highest-ranking members of a corporation are subject to constraints and imperatives established by and instituted in the corporation itself.

Midwest Studies In Philosophy, XXXVIII (2014)

The Impact of Corporate Task Responsibilities: A Comparison of Two Models

AVIA PASTERNAK

In recent years there has been a growing consensus around the "corporate agency thesis": the view that groups can qualify as moral agents in and of themselves. This thesis rests on the observation that groups can possess relevant agential qualities: the ability to corporately form rational representational states (beliefs) and motivational states (desires), and to translate them into actions.[1] The corporate agency thesis opens the door for corporate responsibility, in the various meanings of that term. As moral agents, groups are morally responsible for their actions (in the sense of backward-looking attributions of blame and praise). And as moral agents groups can be task-responsible (in the sense of forward-looking duties and obligations).[2] For example, they may be charged with "remedial responsibilities" to invest resources into putting a bad situation right.[3]

But the claim that group agents can have forward-looking task responsibilities faces an important challenge, which relates to the distributive impact of corporate task responsibilities. As several authors have observed, when groups are set with forward-looking tasks such as paying compensation or making redress, it is individual members who are adversely affected. For example, when a business

---

1. See, for example, Peter French, *Collective and Corporate Responsibility* (New York: Columbia University Press, 1984); Christian List and Philip Pettit, *Group Agency* (Oxford: Oxford University Press, 2011).

2. The term "task responsibility" is borrowed from Robert Goodin, "Apportioning Responsibilities," *Law and Philosophy* 6, 2 (1987): 167–85.

3. On "remedial responsibilities," see David Miller, "Distributing Responsibilities," *Journal of Political Philosophy* 9, no. 4 (2001): 453–71.

corporation is encumbered with the forward-looking task of paying compensation out of its assets, its shareholders feel the sting.[4] This fact casts a shadow on the normative legitimacy of corporate task responsibility. There are those who are led to reject the practice of holding groups responsible, at least in some senses, in light of the adverse impact on group members.[5] Others suggest that corporate task responsibilities should be assigned only to certain types of groups, where their distributive impact can be normatively justified.[6]

This article contributes to that debate by reflecting on the nature of the impact of corporate task responsibility. Section 1 rejects some not too uncommon claims that corporate task responsibility is necessarily distributive. Instead, it argues that, like corporate moral responsibility, corporate task responsibility attaches to the group and not to its members. Sections 2 and 3 draw a conceptual distinction, hitherto unnoticed, between two very different readings of the impact of corporate task responsibility. The first reading, which I call "the membership-based duties approach," focuses on the duties imposed on individuals as group members by virtue of their agential involvement in the group (Section 2). The second reading, which I call "the side-effects approach," focuses on individuals as third parties who happen to be adversely burdened as a result of the group's corporate responsibility (Section 3). Juxtaposing these two readings sharpens our understanding of the distributive impact of corporate task responsibility, and helps to clarify the circumstances under which, and the reasons why, that impact can be justified.

1. REJECTING THE ASYMMETRY THESIS

This section points to what I think is a mistaken assumption of asymmetry between corporate moral and task responsibility. I mentioned the "corporate agency thesis" which suggests that groups can themselves be moral agents. Crucially, this thesis assumes the independence of the moral agency and responsibility of the group from the moral agency and responsibility of its members. This independence stands most starkly in structural groups, whose organizational structure and decision-making procedures create a clear ontological distinction between the desires, beliefs, and moral reasoning of the group and those of its individual members: What a group believes is not necessarily identical to what most, some, or even any

4. The impact of corporate task responsibility is discussed, for example, in John Parrish, "Collective Responsibility and the State," *International Theory* 1, no. 1 (2009): 119–54; Avia Pasternak, "The Distributive Effect of Collective Punishment," in *Collective Wrongdoing*, ed. Richard Vernon and Tracy Issacs (New York: Cambridge University Press, 2011), 210–30; Anna Stilz, "Collective Responsibility and the State," *Journal of Political Philosophy* 19, no. 2 (2011): 190–208.

5. For example, John Hasnas, "The Centenary of Mistake: One Hunderd Years of Corporate Criminal Liability," *Amercian Criminal Law Review* 46 (2009): 1329–58, which rejects corporate criminal liability.

6. For two such attempts, specifically in the context of state responsibility, see Avia Pasternak, "Limiting States' Corporate Responsiblity," *Journal of Political Philosophy* 21, no. 4 (2013): 261–81; Stilz, "Collective Responsibility."

of its members believe.[7] And what the group does is not necessarily identical to what most, some, or any of its members do. Group agents have a "collectivised reason" and "a mind of their own."[8] It follows then that moral responsibility for the group's actions attaches to the group itself and not to its members, since it is the group that forms the intention to do wrong and acts upon it. Of course, group members are likely to have contributed to the group's actions and omissions, and quite possibly these individual contributions are blameworthy in themselves. However, adherents of the separate agency thesis are united in their assertion that, given the separate moral agency of group agents, we must separate the moral blame of the group for the bad things it brings about, from the moral blame of group members for their complicity in those wrongdoings.[9]

But the picture becomes less clear when we turn to corporate task responsibility. For the purposes of the discussion here, I will focus on task responsibilities that are commonly assigned to groups that committed harmful wrongdoing.[10] Consider, for example, the case of environmental pollution. An oil company adopts defective procedures that results in an oil leak at one of its refineries. Quite likely, the company is morally responsible for its negligence. That responsibility attaches to the group and not to its members (who themselves may be at no fault at all). And the company is also remedially responsible for the environmental damage it caused: It ought to fix the leak, pay compensation to the victims, and clean up the mess. Do those responsibilities also attach to the group rather than to its members? Some suggest otherwise. Joel Feinberg, for example, argues that "group liability is inevitably distributive: what harms the group as a whole necessarily harms its members."[11] Anna Stilz writes in similar vein that "since (even when paid out of collective funds) the impact of compensation ultimately falls on individuals, [corporate] compensation treats collective responsibility like a pie that can be carved up."[12] John Coffee observes that "[a]xiomatically corporations do not bear the ultimate cost of the fine; put simply when the corporation catches a cold, someone else sneezes."[13]

---

7. For an elaborated discussion which revolves preference aggregation mechanisms, see List and Pettit, *Group Agency*, 65–72. The relationship between a group's beliefs and desires and its members' beliefs and desires is often described as a relationship of supervenience. See List and Pettit, *Group Agency*, and Alexander Wendt, "The State as Person in International Theory," *Review of International Studies* 30, no. 2 (2004): 289–316.

8. List and Pettit, *Group Agency*, 8.

9. For example, French, *Collective and Corporate Responsibility*, 44–47; Tracy Issacs, "Collective Moral Responsibility and Collective Intention," *Midwest Studies in Philosophy* 30 (2006): 59–73; List and Pettit, *Group Agency*, 65–72.

10. There are, of course, other reasons for assigning groups with remedial tasks. For example, group agents may have positive duties of assistance. But for brevity's sake, I focus on cases of wrongdoing.

11. Joel Feinberg, "Collective Responsibility (Another Defence)," in *Collective Responsibility: Five Decades of Debate in Theoretical and Applied Ethics*, ed. Larry May and Stacey Hoffman (Savage, MD: Rowman and Littlefield, 1991), 73. Feinberg refers here to task responsibilities.

12. Stilz, "Collective Responsibility," 194.

13. John C. Coffee, Jr., "No Soul to Damn, No Body to Kick: An Unscandalized Inquiry into the Problem of Corporate Punishment," *Michigan Law Review* 79 (1981): 401.

What these authors suggest is that it is difficult to draw a sharp conceptual distinction between a group's task responsibility and its members' task responsibilities. Notice that there are two different rationales for this claim (both of which I will reject). On the first rationale, a group's forward-looking responsibilities inevitably distribute to group members, because group agents can only act through the agency of natural agents. For example, if the oil company owes compensation, it will be its treasurer, lawyers, and managers who will have to act in order that compensation is paid. So in contrast with moral responsibility, task responsibility cannot stay at the level of the group.

But the claim that corporate task responsibility inevitably distributes to group members in that sense is too hasty. First, it's worth noting that even if groups must activate natural agents in order to act, it is not the case that they must activate their own members. Second, it is not clear that by definition they must activate any natural agent. One can imagine a computerized process that will enable groups to perform certain tasks (e.g., money transfers) without activating any natural agent in the world. Finally, even if such a process is a mere fantasy, I would argue that the fact that a group agent needs natural agents in order to act does not render its corporate responsibilities "distributive." After all, many (perhaps even most) *individual* task responsibilities share this feature as well: In order to pay my rent, I must activate a bank teller to transfer money from my bank account. But we do not commonly think that my obligation to my landlord is "distributed" to the bank teller because of that. It remains my obligation, even if in order to execute it I must authorize other individuals in the world to act on my behalf.

A second rationale for the claim that corporate task responsibilities are inevitably distributive focuses on the various costs that they entail for group members. Recall again the example of compensation paid out of a corporation's funds that decreases the market value of its shares. As Feinberg puts it, what "harms" the group, inevitably harms its members. But here, too, I would argue that, at least conceptually, it's possible that a group will be task-responsible without any of its members suffering as a result. Consider the following example: An incorporated church collects money from its members for an emergency fund. All the members who put money into the fund are long dead, and the money remained untouched. Now the church finds itself in a position where it owes compensation to a third party. The ministers decide to use the emergency fund to pay the debt. Should we conclude that the cost is *distributed* to the current church members? I don't think so. These members have not been asked to use their own resources to pay the corporate debt, and they have no claim on the church's emergency fund.[14] That money belongs to the church, an entity that is separate from them, and it can use it as it sees fit. The church could decide to use the money to benefit its current members, but it could also decide to use it for other purposes (humanitarian aid, spreading its message, or attending to debts). That the church used up this money does not necessarily harm its members, and may not even harm any individual in the world.

14. This is different from the business corporation where shareholders do have claims against the assets of the corporation.

To conclude the point, if we take the corporate agency thesis seriously, and accept that a group is an agent that is separate from its members, and can be morally responsible for its actions independently of them, there is no reason not to accept that it can also be found responsible in a forward-looking sense independently of its members. That said, it is nevertheless the case that when groups are held to certain tasks (e.g., pay compensation, assist in remedying a bad situation), it is quite likely that individuals who are related to the group will be affected as a result (in the same way that when a group will be morally blameworthy, it is likely that at least some of its member will share the blame). As we already saw, real-world cases provide ample examples: A corporation pays compensation out of its corporate assets. Shareholders suffer financial losses and some employees lose their jobs. A university department admits a cohort of PhD students, generating supervisory responsibilities for its academic staff.[15] Large compensatory fines are levied on a state, and its citizens are levied with additional taxes, or suffer from cutbacks in public services. The question I now turn to is how we should conceptualize these *likely* effects of corporate task responsibility. In the next sections I distinguish between two different and commonly offered readings of these effects.

2. THE "MEMBERSHIP-BASED DUTIES" APPROACH

A characteristic example of the first reading of the distributive impact of a group's task responsibility is offered by David Miller, who describes an employee-controlled factory that causes environmental pollution. The factory is encumbered with the forward-looking duties to clean up the damage and to compensate those who were harmed by its wrongful activities. These tasks, Miller observes, are distributed to the workers: They ought to pay up and/or take part in the cleaning operation.[16] The workers' tasks are derivative from the group's own corporate task responsibility: It is because the factory is held liable that its workers are encumbered with the clean-up tasks.

This and similar depictions of the distributive impact of corporate task responsibility have two important features.[17] First, they are restricted to group members. The key idea here is that group members, *qua* group members, inherit duties associated with their group's corporate liabilities. Membership in the group is a necessary condition for these specific duties to arise. However, membership is not a sufficient condition, since—as we saw earlier—corporate task responsibilities will not necessarily generate derivative duties for group members. And it may also be the case that a group's corporate tasks will generate derivative liabilities only to some of its members—for example, only in those who play a specific and relevant role in the group.

---

15. Feinberg, "Collective Responsibility," 74.

16. David Miller, *National Responsibility and Global Justice* (Oxford: Oxford University Press, 2007), 119.

17. Other expressions of the derivative duties approach appear in Christopher Kutz, *Complicity: Ethics and Law for a Collective Age* (New York: Cambridge University Press, 2000); List and Pettit, *Group Agency*, 163–64; Larry May, *Sharing Responsibility* (Chicago: University of Chicago Press, 1992); Stilz, "Collective Responsibility."

A second feature of the membership-based duties approach concerns the agents to whom these duties are owed. I would argue that the membership-based account defines the duty to do one's share in discharging the group's obligations as an associative duty, that is, a duty that exists between the group and its members, and between the group members themselves.[18] After all, on the "corporate agency" model it is the group itself that wrongs the victims, and is therefore under the direct forward-looking duty to address their plight. Group members, on the other hand, ought to do what is necessary so that the group is able to discharge its own duties, but these derivative duties are not generated from a direct relationship with the group's victims, but rather from the their membership status and their various roles and responsibilities within the group. Members who fail to comply with their derivative duties are failing the group and its members: They either undermine the overall ability of the group to discharge its responsibilities, or they engage in morally objectionable free-riding; by shirking their own duties, they create heavier burdens for other group members, who may have to take up the slack.

Finally, notice the justification that is offered for holding group members duty-bound in this way. Typically, such derivative duties are justified in light of the agential involvement of group members in the group and in its activities. One leading and oft-cited example for this move is found in Christopher Kutz's work. Kutz adopts the derivative duties approach, arguing that group members bear "a special duty to contribute to the aid of those who have suffered [from the group]."[19] These duties are justified in light of group members' "participatory intentions," to act as part of the group, or to contribute to a collective project or outcome. Kutz demonstrates at length that individuals participate in collective projects when they involve their agency in the group by structuring their actions around a shared project, thus becoming "inclusive authors" of that project.[20] The involvement of one's agency in the group agent generates duties to share in the group's remedial responsibilities, duties that "mirror the nature of [one's] participation beforehand."[21]

3. THE "SIDE-EFFECTS" APPROACH

I described one interpretation of the distributive impact of corporate task responsibility, read in terms of derivative duties for group members. But sometimes we find a different characterization of that impact. An expression of this alternative view can be found, for example, in Peter French's defense of the practice of holding corporations criminally liable. Addressing the objection that corporate punitive sanctions (e.g., punitive fines) ultimately fall on "innocent employees," French

18. Cf. Christopher Kutz, "The Collective Work of Citizenship," *Legal Theory* 8 (2002): 476–77.

19. Kutz, *Complicity*, 199.

20. Ibid., 105–06.

21. Ibid., 201. Larry May and Anna Stilz also ground their accounts of derivative duties in the agential involvement of group members, although their accounts differ from Kutz's. See Larry May, *Sharing Responsibility* (Chicago: University of Chicago Press, 1992) and Stilz, "Collective Responsibility," 198–205.

points out that "when a natural person commits a felony and is convicted and punished, his or her associates, often family members and dependants, are frequently cast into dire financial straits," but that "in many jurisdictions, little or no official interest is paid to these innocent sufferers." He concludes that "by analogy [. . .] indirect harm to corporate associates should not defeat [corporate] penalty."[22] This analogy between the costs imposed on employees as a result of corporate penalties and the costs imposed on the family of an incarcerated criminal, is evoked elsewhere in the literature.[23] It suggests that the distributive impact of a group's own task responsibility is a "spill-over" or a "side-effect."[24] The "side-effects approach" has several features that set it apart from the membership-based view.

First, in contrast with the membership-based duties account, the side-effects view is not focused exclusively on group members. Consider again the criminal analogy: When a criminal is jailed or forced to pay punitive damages, there are many agents in the world who may be affected: family, colleagues, friends, business associates. What these various individuals share in common is that they stand in some relationship to the criminal in light of which they are affected by his conviction. Similarly, when a group agent pays up for its wrongdoing, there can be various individuals in the world who will be adversely affected, but they need not necessarily be its members. Consider, for example, the wide-reaching ripple effects that sanctioning a corporation may have on consumers and on society at large (especially in cases of layoffs and closures). Membership in the group is neither a necessary nor a sufficient condition for being subject to the detrimental side-effects of a group's task responsibility.

Related to that, the analogy between the criminal and the group agent suggests that the side-effects view takes all affected individuals, whether group members or not, to be third parties. Like the criminal's family members, they are not involved in the crime for which the criminal is paying. This portrayal is essentially different from the one advocated by the membership-based account, which takes the affected individuals to be involved in a morally relevant way in the group and its activities.

For that reason, the side-effects view offers a different justification for the impact of corporate task responsibility. Since the side-effects approach portrays the affected individuals as uninvolved third parties, a main concern here is that of fairness: Why should *those* individuals be made worse-off?

There are various answers to this question, and what they share in common is the idea that there is something in the position of the affected third parties in light of which they can be expected to internalize the side effects of the group's

---

22. French, *Collective and Corporate Responsibility*, 189–90.

23. For example, Toni Erskine, "Kicking Bodies and Damning Souls: The Danger of Harming 'Innocent' Individuals while Punishing 'Deliquent' States," in *Accountability for Collective Wrongdoing*, ed. Tracy Issacs and Richard Vernon (New York: Cambridge University Press, 2011), 284; Francois Tanguay-Renaud, "Criminalizing the State," *Criminal Law and Philosophy* 7, no 2 (2013): 276.

24. The term "spill-over" is used by Erskine, "Kicking Bodies and Damning Souls," 283. Francois Tanguay-Renaud refers to it as "detrimental side effects" (Tanguay-Renaud, "Criminalizing the State," 276).

corporate task responsibilities. One such common fairness-mitigating argument concerns "voluntary risk takers": individuals (or other group agents) who have voluntarily exposed themselves to the risk of such burdens. A corporation's bond holders are a good example here. They do not classify as group members, since they are not orienting their activities around the group, nor do they authorize it to act on their behalf. And yet, they have a certain financial relationship to the group, from which they hope to profit, but from which they foreseeably may lose. Such individuals, if they suffer the side effects of corporate task responsibility, do not have a cause for complaint grounds of fairness (as long as the costs are proportional to the risk taken). They are paying for the risk they took upon themselves.

A second common fairness-mitigating argument refers to individuals who benefit from the group agent's activities (even if they have not voluntarily taken a financial risk).[25] There is growing support in the literature to the claim that the beneficiaries of wrongdoing can be expected to disgorge the benefits in compensation to the victims of the wrongdoing, even if they find themselves in that position involuntarily.[26] This view suggests that, to the extent that third parties (e.g., consumers or employees) benefited from a group's wrongful activities, they can be expected to incur some of the side effects when the group is made to pay for those activities (so long as that burden does not exceed the benefit).

These two characteristic justifications of the side effects of corporate task responsibility set limits to the amount of burden that an uninvolved individual may be expected to carry without that burden being deemed unfair. As we saw, the burden should be proportional to the risk one took, or to the benefit one derived from the group's activities. These limits are different from those set by the membership-based account, which apportions members' duties in light of their participation and role in the group agent. Indeed, the justifications offered by the side-effects view do not invoke the agential involvement of the cost-bearing individual in the group agent, and they do not propose that there exists an associative duty between that individual and the group members. The duty of third parties to internalize the side effects is an impersonal duty, to accept the reasonable requirements of fairness, rather than an interpersonal duty to fellow group members.

We can conclude at this point that the membership and the side-effects views offer a rather wide range of justifications for the impact of corporate task responsibility. But they also leave open the possibility that a group's corporate responsibility will have an adverse impact on individuals in the world, which could not be justified by any of the arguments discussed so far. Consider again the case of the family of the criminal, which is put into dire financial straits as a result of his conviction. Arguably, what this example highlights is that there is something deeply unfair about the fact that the children of a convicted criminal, who are neither complicit in their father's deeds nor benefited from them, stand to suffer as a result of them. Taking that concern onboard, one may be drawn to conclude that

25. French, *Collective and Corporate Responsibility*, 188; Miller, *National Responsibility and Global Justice*, 119; Tanguay-Renaud, "Criminalizing the State," 278.

26. For example, Daniel Butt, "On Benefiting from Injustice," *Canadian Journal of Philosophy* 37, no. 1 (2007): 129–52.

punishing criminals, or at least punishing them in certain ways, is a practice that should be abandoned. Alternatively, one may be drawn to conclude, like French, that the unfairness that punishment entails for the families of convicted criminals is not, overall, a sufficient reason to give up that practice. At the same time, one may recognize the moral cost that this practice involves, a moral cost that is unintentional, regrettable, and that should be avoided where possible. Perhaps the families of convicted criminals should be compensated for the disadvantages they suffer through no fault of their own.

Similar concerns could apply to the impact of corporate task responsibility. We may have good reasons to think that holding groups forwardly responsible is overall a desirable practice. But at the same time we may recognize that, at least under some circumstances, some of the side effects of corporate task responsibility are inherently unfair, and that we ought to do what we can to mitigate them.

4. CONCLUSIONS

I argued in this article that, while corporate task responsibility is not inevitably distributive, it is likely to have a distributive impact on individuals in the world. As we saw, that impact can be conceptualized in two different ways, distinguished by the set of people they apply to, their justification, and the moral expectations they generate. These differences should be taken into account when either reading is employed. For example, if one employs the side-effects view, one ought not restrict the analysis to group members only.[27]

To recapitulate, the analysis here does not suggest that either reading is superior to the other. Rather, it suggests that, given their differences, we ought to examine which of them is more appropriate in particular circumstances. For example, if one analyzes the impact that is experienced by group members, one ought to consider the applicability of the membership-based duties model. French's "innocent employees," to whom he applies the side-effects model, are quite possibly duty bound to share in the costs generated by their employer's liability, in light of their participatory membership in that group agent. Next, consider the much discussed case of citizens of authoritarian states who are disadvantaged when their state is fined for wrongdoing. To assess the legitimacy of this impact, one needs to examine which of the two models offers a more accurate reading of it. Does it make sense to argue that the citizens of authoritarian states are intentional participants of their state, and that their agency is involved in its activities? If the answer to this question is positive, we should understand the distributive impact on them in terms of derivative associative duties to share in the task of correcting that wrong. If the answer to the question is negative, then the impact should be conceptualized as a side effect. At this stage, we will be faced with a follow-up question: Is the imposition of that burden unfair? To answer it, we will need to examine, for example, whether or not they benefit from their membership in the state, and/or from the wrongdoing in question. If they did, then the side effect could be justified. If not, we may have to conclude that saddling them with those

---

27. As is done, for example, in Tanguay-Renaud, "Criminalizing the State."

costs is unfair. While this conclusion may not be a cause for a wholesale rejection of corporate responsibility in this case, it would suggest that holding the state corporately responsible involves a moral cost, which at least we ought to recognize. The conceptual distinction between the membership-based and the side-effects accounts does not offer a conclusive answer for whether and when the distributive impact of corporate task responsibility is justified, but it points to the correct procedure for determining the answer to that question.[28]

28. I am grateful for comments by Bob Goodin, Holly Lawford-Smith, and Zofia Stemplowska, and the participants of a workshop on collective obligations held in Manchester University in May 2013.

Midwest Studies In Philosophy, XXXVIII (2014)

Structural Injustice and the Distribution of Forward-Looking Responsibility

CHRISTIAN NEUHÄUSER

In recent years, Iris Young has systematically expanded the idea of a forward-looking and collective responsibility, which was previously developed by other authors on a rudimentary level only.[1] Young describes her approach as the social connection model of responsibility, and it is intended to be distinguishable from a traditional understanding of responsibility as liability.[2] Her central objection against the classical model is that responsibility as liability is directed only to the compensation of past damages and therefore remains a one-sided understanding of the concept of responsibility. Moreover, it is based solely on individual agents to which a causal connection to the action can be attested, which Young also finds problematic.[3] It seems worthwhile to look at the alternative model, which Young develops, since it is forward-looking and directed at collectives and therefore seems better equipped to deal with some of the very complex normative issues we are dealing with today.

---

1. Max Weber ([1919] 2004) and Hans Jonas ([1979] 1985) formulated early versions of a forward-looking responsibility. Hannah Arendt ([1968] 1987), a key author for Young (2011, 75–93), was the first to develop a collective account of a forward-looking responsibility in her reply to Joel Feinberg's (1968) attempt to formulate a backward-looking account of collective responsibility. Larry May (1996) developed an account of responsibility, which is in some respects quite similar to Young's and which she also discusses as still being too much backward-looking (Young 2011, 110–11). David Miller (2001, 2007, 2011) has used the rather loose concept of remedial responsibility, which is also forward-looking and collective in nature.
   2. Young (2006); Young (2011, 104–13).
   3. Young (2011, 97–104).

Young herself is clearly of the opinion that we are currently faced with practical issues of structural injustice that cannot be understood with the classic conception of responsibility as liability. Rather, it requires a new conception of responsibility in which the forward-looking and collective nature of responsibility is emphasized. She also speaks of a political responsibility to emphasize that her model is directed at changing the social structure through public action with others.[4] The basic idea of her concept of responsibility can probably be summarized as follows: the objective is to develop a normative approach that helps actors to collectively embrace their responsibility for future equitable conditions.

Given current issues of justice we are facing, this general approach seems attractive. Across the world, more than a billion people still suffer from absolute poverty; many of them are starving, at risk of dying from treatable diseases with little or no opportunity to adequately care for themselves. In the economically more developed countries, the financial markets are out of control, so that financial market players cash their profits privately while socializing their risks and costs. This leads to increasing social inequality and structural unemployment. Man-made climate change threatens to induce massive environmental changes and destruction, with considerably negative and often life-threatening consequences for many people.

In regard to such problems of justice, looking for responsibility does not just raise the question of who is liable for which damages, because (s)he has caused them, or at least benefited from them. It also raises the question of how future damages can be prevented, or how improvements for negatively affected people can be achieved, so that they are able to subsist adequately with a perspective of stronger justice claims for the future. I believe this is probably the reason why the ideas of Young have received considerable attention in the research literature.[5] I also believe that her efforts to develop the idea of a forward-looking responsibility can actually constitute a significant part of a normative theory for nonideal circumstances.

However, her approach on some key issues seems to be strongly underdetermined, or so I think. At first glance, her theory does possess great suggestive power, precisely because it promises a constructive approach to urgent issues of justice. At the same time, however, it requires conceptual sharpening. In particular, the strict separation of liability on one side, and forward-looking responsibility on the other, will prove to be problematic. Therefore, in this article, I aim to reveal a number of gaps and weaknesses in Young's concept of responsibility and in the end will make some suggestions as to the direction in which the concept could be further developed.

In a first step, I will provide a general analysis of responsibility as a four-place relation. This is not to say that this is the only logical-semantic correct use of the concept of responsibility. Understanding responsibility as a four-place relation is simply a sensible way of using the concept in many practical contexts. Therefore,

---

4. Young (2011, 90).
5. There are two recent collections of essays devoted on her work (Ferguson 2009; Niesen 2013).

this approach makes it possible, in a second step, to reveal a number of gaps in the social connection model of responsibility. First, Young has not sufficiently clarified whether or not her concept includes independent corporate agents. Second, the normative standard to which she refers remains underdetermined.

A third difficulty for Young concerns how to decide the fair distribution of responsibility to address structural injustice. I believe this third gap is the crucial weakness in the design of her theory. Therefore, in a third step, I will discuss this issue in greater detail than the others. In a fourth step, I will outline first thoughts on a constructive proposal to systematize the fair distribution of responsibility to address structural injustice. It will be shown that the categories of guilt and liability, contrary to Young's assumption, are of central importance. I want to show that a forward-looking collective responsibility cannot be systematically separated from questions of a backward-looking individual liability. Rather, an integrated approach is required to address structural injustices.

1. RESPONSIBILITY AS A FOUR-PLACE RELATION

Responsibility is often interpreted as a three-place relation.[6] This means that one speaks of responsibility in sentences where there is, first, an agent of responsibility; second, an event or a condition for which (s)he is responsible; and third, an addressee to whom (s)he is responsible. Examples of such sentences include: "The Prime Minister has to answer to the people for the miserable situation of the labour market"; "The doctor is responsible towards the patient for the smooth running of the operation"; "The CEO has publically taken responsibility for the human rights violations in the production chain of the company."

This concept of responsibility based on a three-place relation can also be reformulated in three questions: Who is responsible? For what is (s)he responsible? To whom is (s)he responsible? However, answering all three questions is not a necessary condition for an appropriate use of the concept of responsibility in everyday situations. And as I will show, there are also contexts in which this understanding of the concept is not sufficient. Responsibility is rather a relatively loose term that can be used effectively in different contexts and in quite different ways. Sentences operating with only two relations of responsibility are also mean-ingful, as these variations of the previous examples show: "All responsibility for the miserable job market situation lies with the Prime Minister"; "The doctors' primary responsibility is towards the patient"; "The CEO takes responsibility for the human rights violations."

Although all of these sentences name just two relations, they are meaningful because they say something interesting about practical responsibility issues. It apparently is not necessary to always designate all three relations when it comes to dealing with responsibility in practical matters. The other way around this might sometimes also not be sufficient, since there may still be other relations, which

---

6. This at least is true for the discussion in the German-speaking world, which probably is much more strongly influenced by Weber's concept of an ethic of responsibility than the discussion in the English-speaking world (Nida-Rümelin 2011, 179).

could also be important in other contexts. The German philosophers Hans Lenk and Mathias Maring see as additional relevant relations the following: the normative standard of responsibility; the operational framework of responsibility; and the institutional setting in which one is to be held responsible. This amounts to a total of six relations.[7]

I believe that a fourth relation is especially useful if we want to analyze a collective and forward-looking responsibility. This relation affects the normative standard of responsibility. This dimension can again be demonstrated with the sample sentences used previously: The head of government is responsible toward the people for the miserable job market situation, especially on a political level. However, he has no reason to fear legal consequences. The doctor, however, is legally responsible toward the patient, perhaps even morally. The CEO can probably not be held either politically or legally responsible, but perhaps he bears a moral responsibility and even accepts this. The fourth question for the determination of responsibility, which results from this relation, can be formulated as follows: On the ground of what normative standard is there a responsibility?

If responsibility is understood as a four-place relation, then in this sense complete statements about responsibility are able to answer this fourfold question: Who is accountable to whom, for what, and on the basis of which moral standard? Such a general and broad understanding of responsibility covers many practical uses of the concept of responsibility, I think. The key point here is that it allows an unbiased examination of the question, in what ways responsibility could be collective and forward-looking. This general framework can then be applied to any existing account of collective and forward-looking responsibility, just as I will apply it to Young's account of political responsibility in the following chapters.

Whenever the collectivity of responsibility is discussed, at first sight it seems to relate to the subjects involved. This means that there are groups that somehow bear a responsibility. However, collectivity could also refer to the addressees, the responsibility toward groups. To speak of collective normative standards, in contrast, seems to be a bit odd at first glance. However, we could speak of collectively established normative standards, for example, in political processes.[8] More important, on the other hand, is the issue concerning the responsibility for collective actions. As we will see, in the elaboration of Young's concept of collective responsibility, it makes a difference if we are speaking about the responsibility of collective agents for their specific actions or the shared responsibility of individual agents for shared actions. This is important for the approach of Young, because she is not sufficiently precise in this question.

The forward-looking dimension can also be applied to all four relations of responsibility. The orientation toward the future can refer to the futurity of the agents. If, for example, climate change occurs, because we will have failed to prevent it, then it will obviously fall to future agents to deal with the consequences

7. Lenk and Maring (1991).
8. Social constructivist accounts of normativity, like discourse ethics, for instance, do always assume that normative standards are developed in social processes (Apel 1990). Likewise some authors stress the dialogical character of responsibility whereby its normative standard is established through personal interaction (Levinas [1961] 1991).

in a more responsible way. It is more difficult again with the normative standards. What exactly could future normative standards mean? Although it might not be easy to give a general answer to this question, it at least is possible to think of future standards in certain contexts, for example, possible developments of positive international law. More interesting is that a forward-looking responsibility can relate to future actions and conditions, or to future addressees. Current agents could be responsible to present or future addresses. In addition, they might be responsible for present or future actions and conditions they cause. As we can see, understanding responsibility as a four-place relation opens up many possibilities for a collective and forward-looking understanding. What answer then does Young give to those many questions and possibilities in her model of responsibility?

2. ON POLITICAL RESPONSIBILITY FOR STRUCTURAL INJUSTICE

In a series of essays and a posthumously published monograph, Iris Young has developed a concept of responsibility, which she labels as political and calls it the social connection model of responsibility.[9] In my view, this model is to date the most advanced and best elaboration of the idea of a forward-looking collective responsibility. This is why I believe, that a critical examination of Young's model can enhance the theoretical analysis of this aspect of responsibility and help with future developments.

Young herself emphasizes that her social connection model of responsibility should not fully replace other concepts of responsibility, but rather complement them in a certain manner. Other models like the classical liability model of responsibility might for instance be better equipped to deal with certain crimes, like domestic homicide. Her model renders an important addition to those classical accounts, she argues, because it is especially powerful regarding issues of structural injustice. This particular attribute is due to three key features of her social connection model of responsibility. First, the model does not involve the concepts of guilt and blame, but rather emphasizes responsibility based on social relations that are not blameworthy. Second, responsibility is not assigned to individual acts, but rather collective ones, or as we will see later, to shared activities. Third, her model does not focus on backward-looking moral judgments, but on forward-looking political actions. Consequently, Young herself describes the central point of her concept as follows: "The social connection model does not isolate perpetrators. It brings background conditions under evaluation. Its main purpose for assigning responsibility is forward-looking. Responsibility under the social connection model is essentially shared. It can therefore be discharged only through collective action."[10]

How exactly this social connection model of political responsibility works, in what respects it is collective and forward-looking, but also what problems it brings with it, can be clarified through an analysis of her model with the help of the previously discussed four relations of the concept of responsibility. In this section,

9. Young (2003, 2006, 2007, 2011).
10. Young (2011, 105).

I will comment briefly on the normative standard, the addressee, and the agents of responsibility. The central question as to what exactly agents are responsible for in the social connection model will be discussed in the whole of the next section, because this is where the model shows the biggest gap and need for further elaboration, or so I will argue.

2.1 On the Normative Standard of Political Responsibility for Structural Injustice

For Young, the normative background of her model of responsibility arises from her conception of structural injustice, which she defines as follows: "structural injustice, then, exists when social processes put large groups of persons under systematic threat of domination or deprivation of the means to develop and exercise their capacities, at the same time that these processes enable others to dominate or to have a wide range of opportunities for developing and exercising capacities available to them."[11] Two aspects are of particular interest to this definition of social injustice as a normative standard of responsibility. First, there is a need to understand precisely what structural social processes mean, and second, it needs to be clarified how her understanding of injustice can function as a normative standard for her model of responsibility.

According to Young, social processes are structural when they involve large groups and systemic contexts. Such structural processes have four characteristics.[12] First, individuals perceive them materially and psychologically as objective social facts. These facts either hinder or enable them, and appear to them as given since they cannot be changed by them. Second, these processes structure various positions within the social space, which coexist in a normative relationship to each other, for example, employees and employers, mother and father, and so on. These positions go hand in hand with social expectations and limited or enhanced possibilities for action. Inequality—and this is important for Young—can be determined through a comparison of these different positions.[13]

Third, these are processes in which structures are created and maintained through the actions of many agents, but which at the same time cannot be reduced to these actions. To demonstrate the irreducibility of social structures, Young refers to the sociological structuration theory of Anthony Giddens.[14] Giddens argues that agents pursue specific goals through their actions, taking advantage of existing social structures that they thereby reproduce collectively at the same time as an unintended and unforeseeable consequence.[15] This is especially true for the validity of rules and the distribution of resources. When an employee, for example, enters into a contract of employment with an employer under certain conditions, say of employment at will, (s)he reproduces the legitimacy of these conditions.

11. Young (2011, 52).
12. Young (2011, 52–64. See also Owen (2013).
13. Young (2011, 37–38; 2003).
14. Young (2011, 60–61; 2007, 69).
15. Giddens provided a definite ouline of his theory in his major book *Constitution of Society* (1986). Young refers to the earlier *Central Problems in Social Theory* (1979).

Fourth, agents are often unaware of the fact that their actions contribute to or reproduce certain social structures. Many consumers, for example, know very little about the working conditions in the production process of the goods they consume and therefore do not know how they actually contribute through their consumption to the collective consolidation of these economic structures and for instance the unjust working conditions in sweatshops.[16]

This understanding of structural processes will later play an important role when it comes to the question of why Young asserts that it is not possible to find responsible agents for structural injustices in the sense that these actors have helped to create unjust structures in a blameworthy way. For now, we should continue to inquire into the normative standard in Young's model of responsibility, whereby it turns out that her understanding of structural injustice is strongly underdetermined. On the negative side, she distances herself firmly from certain theories of justice such as luck egalitarianism, normative nationalism, and cosmopolitan utilitarianism.[17] However, on the positive side, she does not develop which forms of dominance are problematic in her view and what renders a missing or uneven development as unfair. At least she does not do so in her work on responsibility. It seems that she leaves the question of the normative standard of responsibility relatively unanswered. She only gestures at domination and unfair development of capabilities, without further clarifying those concepts.[18]

Her reticence with regard to substantial normative statements about what constitutes particularly serious or urgent forms of structural injustice that demand resolution could stem from the fact that she considers particularly apparent forms of dominance, and the lack of the development of important capabilities, to be obviously unjust.[19] Her position in earlier work on the relationship between democracy and justice, however, suggests that she is also of the position that such questions would have to be settled in deliberative democratic processes. Then her model of responsibility would contain a collective element regarding the normative standard, because it could only be determined intersubjectively in political processes. However, Young does not discuss this question explicitly in the context of her social connection model of responsibility, so that all further considerations were to be purely speculative.

In this respect, it remains only to note that her model is compatible with both a substantial moral theory about structural injustice, as well as a more procedurally oriented democratic theory or a combination of both, whereas the latter option is

16. Young (2011, 140) refers approvingly to Thomas Pogge (2002, 91–117) in arguing that affluent people participate in the injustice of the global economic order. However, she seems to think, contrary to what Pogge assumes, that they do not do so in a culpable manner.

17. Young (2011, 27–35, 137–39).

18. It is not clear if Young refers to the capability approach as developed by Amartya Sen and Martha Nussbaum. She does not make an explicit reference to this approach and uses the term "capability" only loosely. Likewise, domination does not seem to refer to the concept as developed in neo-republican theories of liberty. However, both theories probably could function as a background for Young's account, especially since there is a considerable overlap (Pettit 2005).

19. In *Justice and the Politics of Difference* Young (1990, 48–63) identifies five forms of oppression, which could also function as a negative normative standard for identifying responsibility when it comes to structural injustices.

clearly supported by her earlier work on justice and democracy. [20] Anyhow, the fact, that she does not further address this question in her work on responsibility is not destructive to her social connection model, because in one way or another it surely can be determined what is to count as structural injustices, and where the priorities for the elimination of such injustices lie.

2.2 On the Addressees of Political Responsibility for Structural Injustice

As to the question to whom agents bear a responsibility in her model, Young gives a clear answer: "People who understand that they share responsibility in relation to injustice and justice call on one another to answer before a public. The political process consists in the constitution of a public in which members raise problems and issues and demand of one another action to address them."[21] The addressees of her model are thus the members of a political public. This reference to the addressee clearly has a collective dimension. Although the individual members of the public address each other mutually, the possibility of this addressability depends on the already successful collective constitution of a political public.

Young intentionally describes this political public not as a demos, because she thinks it should not to be seen as organized by government structures on a state level. Members of the relevant political public are simply those agents who are aware of the fact that they participate on the basis of a common responsibility regarding a certain structural injustice. They can form this public on many different levels from local to global depending on the form of injustice to be addressed and the coalition of responsible agents willing to address it.[22] It is the responsible agents willing to take up a forward-looking responsibility who are also the addressees of this responsibility. Within the social connection model, the responsible agents are only responsible to themselves as members of a political public. This fact might be somewhat surprising, because one could think that it is the victims of structural injustice who should be the primary addresses. This is not so, because any responsibility within the social connection model is voluntarily taken up, based on some social connection. Victims of structural injustice cannot point their fingers at guilty culprits and hold them responsible. This is also why the victims can and should be among those taking up responsibility to eradicate the structural injustice, as Young says.[23]

2.3 On the Agents of Political Responsibility for Structural Injustice

Regarding its standard and addressees, the collective dimension of the social connection model of responsibility should be clear by now. Yet and somewhat

20. This is especially clear in her *Inclusion and Democracy* (2000, 27–31) where she combines an inclusive procedural view of democracy with substantive assumptions about justice.

21. Young (2011, 122).

22. That is why, for Young, the otherwise tricky question of inclusion and exclusion when it comes to a political public is not central in her model of responsibility, since here public is formed by a sense of a shared responsibility and therefore can work on both the sub-state and supra-state regional or global levels.

23. Young (2011, 146).

surprisingly it appears as if the model is not collective in nature when it comes to the agents of responsibility, even though one might expect to find it most likely here. Young's answer to the question of who is responsible in the social connection model can be summarized as follows: Those actors in a social connection with a form of structural injustice can bear the responsibility together, but only as individual agents.

This short formula needs to be clarified regarding what type of agents Young is considering, and how these agents are jointly responsible. As we have seen, Young assumes that individual agents produce social structures. In line with her own assumption, she makes a general statement regarding the current theoretical landscape: "Few theorists of social structures deny that individual actors produce them."[24] Martha Nussbaum takes this statement to entail that Young was a methodological individualist.[25] However, this assessment is not quite right in two respects.

First, Young's reference to the structuration theory of Anthony Giddens should make clear that it is often not possible to analytically trace the emergence of social structures back to the actions of individual actors, even if they are causally related. Methodological individualism cannot explain the full social reality of those structures. One must accept the causal force of structural processes and regard them as simply given, or so Giddens argues.[26]

Second, and more importantly, Young speaks not only of individual human agents, but also of organizational agents. This becomes clear when she asks, for example: "how shall agents, both individual and organizational think about our responsibility in relation to structural injustice?"[27] Accordingly, as she makes clear in several places, she is of the opinion that companies in particular should bear the responsibility to improve the unjust working conditions in sweatshops.[28] It seems that Young knows of not only individual but also corporate or organizational agents, as she calls them.

The model, therefore, also possesses a collective dimension in relation to its agents. As the example with the companies and sweatshops shows, Young believes that not only individuals but also corporate agents can act. Unfortunately, Young does not clarify how she understands corporate or organizational agents and what kind of model of corporate action she utilizes. She can either understand "corporate agent" in a reductionist way as a term for the structured and thus collective action of individual agents as functionaries within organizations. Or alternatively, she can take a more constructivist approach and assume that organizations such as companies may act through their functionaries but still remain independent agents, because it is possible to ascribe to them plans and intentions of their own.[29]

---

24. Young (2011, 53).

25. Nussbaum justifies her claim in her foreword to Young's book (2011, xiv) with reference to this sentence, which certainly is not sufficient proof.

26. Giddens (1986, 213–20) explicitly rejects methodological individualism.

27. Young (2011, 95).

28. Young (2004; 2006; 2007,168–72; 2011, 125–34).

29. Peter French (1979) in one of his seminal papers first argued for this. I have tried to give an updated version of this argument without relying on the concept of a person (Neuhäuser 2011). See also for, in some respects, a similar position on this question, List and Pettit (2011).

This distinction is maybe not central, but also not unimportant for Young's theory of responsibility, since it determines whether organizations such as companies are only part of the unjust background structure that can (and perhaps should) be changed by the joint action of individual actors. Or corporate actors are actually responsible agents themselves who can take over a part of the forward-looking responsibility to overcome structural injustice. Then, for example, it could be part of the political responsibility of corporate actors to change their own structure so that it becomes easier for certain individual actors to comply with their political responsibility. Unfortunately, Young does not clarify this issue, and thus her social connection model of responsibility remains underdetermined in this aspect.

2.4 On the Subject of Political Responsibility for Structural Injustice

However, this is not the central problem of her approach and probably can easily be amended. In my view, the main problem in Young's approach lies in how she determines and thereby limits the last question of responsibility, which asks what agents can be held responsible for. At first, she seems to be moving within the framework of Mackie's straight rule of responsibility, since agents in her model are responsible only for their intentional actions.[30] However, in a way Young is more restrictive than Mackie, since agents in her model are not responsible for all of their intentional actions. Her primary concern is the elimination of structural injustice, and therefore agents are only responsible for possible actions that contribute to this elimination.[31]

Her model of responsibility is therefore strictly forward-looking, insofar as it always departs exclusively from the present perspective to the future elimination of structural injustice through future action. Agents ready to bear responsibility following her model always wonder what they can do based on a normative standard at least partly determined by them to make social structures fair or at least less unfair. It then turns out that this can often be achieved only through joint action because individual agents do not possess the ability to influence these social structures in a relevant way. This is the pragmatic reason why Young's forward-looking model of responsibility has a strong collective dimension regarding the question what actions are to be taken.

For Young, it is quite important to insist on individual agents including corporate agents when it comes to collective action.[32] She rejects the idea of any collectivization of these agents, such as Margaret Gilbert claims with her construc-

---

30. Mackie ([1977] 2011, 208–14).

31. In a way, she then puts responsibility before agency. Because we are responsible for certain things, we have to monitor some of our actions, but also omissions with extra care. For this see Stoecker (1997).

32. Here it is important to see the difference between shared, collective, and corporate responsibility. Corporate responsibility is the responsibility of corporate agents and can be individuated. Shared responsibility is the responsibility of individual and corporate agents for things they can only do together. Collective responsibility is the responsibility of groups whereby responsible agents cannot be individuated. Young seems to believe that there is shared and corporate, but no collective responsibility.

tion of states as plural subjects.[33] Young criticizes Gilbert on the grounds that in her model the collective entity achieves a moral standing of its own and members are responsible on the sole basis of their membership in this morally significant group. She rejects this idea that groups can have a moral standing in this sense, nations or states for instance do not have moral standing of their own, and therefore membership is not a sufficient reason for responsibility.[34] To her responsibility must always be traced back to some stronger kind of individual connection. In a post-nationalistic world this sounds plausible and certainly contributes to an important part of the attractiveness of Young's approach. However, her determination of what agents in her model are responsible for based on their social connections is also strongly underdetermined, as I will argue in the following section.

3. ON THE DISTRIBUTION OF FORWARD-LOOKING RESPONSIBILITY

Young argues that structural injustice is best eliminated by agents who collectively take on a responsibility to reform the underlying structures that cause injustice, so that future injustices can no longer occur, or at least occur less frequently. To her this responsibility is political, because it is collective, involves public discourse, and aims at changing the social structure.[35] The great advantage of this position is in her opinion that it puts the improvement of the situation of the victims of structural injustice at the centre of concern. This sounds somewhat appealing, but what remains rather underdetermined in her approach is how exactly she envisions the collective elimination of structural injustice. It remains unclear, in other words, who has to do what.

First, Young says little about how the shared responsibility is distributed between different agents, and what constitutes the criteria of eligibility. Although she argues that actors have to be in a social connection of some sort with structural injustice, this is a very weak condition that can be fulfilled, for example, in the case of unjust work by simply buying a T-shirt or maybe even passing by the factory. Since she does not further differentiate different forms of social connection, it remains quite unclear to what extends different forms of connection ground a responsibility.[36] Being the CEO of a company purchasing a large stock of T-Shirts certainly constitutes another type of connection than being a maybe unemployed

---

33. Young refers to a collection of essays by Gilbert (2000). See for states as plural subjects also Gilbert (2006).

34. Young (2011, 136). She also criticizes Hannah Arendt for deriving responsibility from membership alone (2011, 75–93).

35. Political responsibility can therefore rest on the same normative basis as moral responsibility, it just takes another form and involves some kind of political action as opposed to private action. This distinction is a bit curious and probably rests on Arendt's distinction between political and moral normativity or Weber's distinction of "Verantwortungsethik" und "Gesinnungsethik." It does not seem to be wrong, though, to think of what Young calls "political" as a form of political morality.

36. See Hahn (2009).

person buying a cheap T-shirt.[37] Although she does not differentiate different forms of social connection, Young lists four criteria with which the extent of the responsibility can be determined: power, privilege, interest, and collective capacity. However, she does not further extend these criteria into a theory of the allocation of collective forward-looking responsibility.

Second, Young says nothing about how to fulfill one's own responsibilities when others do so only to a limited extent. Do I have to comply only with a fair share, even if then the desired result does not occur? Or do I have to do as much as I possibly can to eliminate the structural injustice? Third, Young tells us little about what to do when others fail to meet their responsibilities and therefore make it less and less likely (or even impossible) to eliminate structural injustice. In the latter case, Young does not seem to want to hold on to a collective forward-looking responsibility, and instead finds it more appropriate to try to influence other agents so that they might be willing to fulfill their responsibilities.[38]

However, then the central question arises whether she thereby includes elements of the classical liability model of responsibility. After all, she suggests making public accusations of irresponsible agents, because they have not complied in the past with their forward-looking responsibility.[39] This is a first indication that Young's social connection model of responsibility relies to some extent on the classical liability model. This charge will be the main thrust of my criticism of her model in this section. I want to argue that Young is unable to answer the questions as to who should contribute what in a collective forward-looking responsibility, because she insists on categorically excluding guilt and thereby liability.

Young's approach can be seen as equally one-sided as the liability model she criticizes, inasmuch as she refers only to the forward-looking elimination of structural injustice and excludes all liability issues. In this way, her model loses its force of pragmatic applicability, which is exactly what her model promised in the beginning by overcoming the one-sidedness of the backward-looking liability model. The central problem of her approach has to do with the fact that structural inequities often can be eliminated only through collective action and that such a collective action has to be well organized, which includes issues of a just distribution of responsibilities.[40] Such a distribution includes an important point that Young omits entirely. The acceptance of responsibility for structural injustice often is costly for agents, and this leads to the question of who should bear the weight of responsibility and the costs coming with it. This relationship between the acceptance of responsibility and personal costs can be shown with a simple example.

Virginia Held has argued in one of her classic essays that even a random group of people can have a shared responsibility to help others in need.[41] If a tree

---

37. Kreide (2013) argues for the need of these kinds of differentiations in the context of consumer ethics.

38. Young (2011, 122).

39. Young (2011, 131). In some of her earlier work, Young took a more aggressive stance regarding this issue. In *Inclusion and Democracy*, for instance, she called for publicly shaming powerful actors (2000, 174–76).

40. David Miller (2001) made a convincing case for the importance of this question.

41. Held (1970).

has fallen on a hiker and a random group of hikers can raise the tree only together to save his life, then they are responsible to do just that. This is a case of forward-looking collective responsibility without guilt, even if it is not a case of structural injustice, but one of natural disaster. However, and this is the crucial point, what happens if this joint effort is dangerous for some of the helpers?

Suppose that two of the helpers must be positioned at a precipice and there is a certain probability that they could fall down. Suppose further that the abyss is not deep and a fall would not be life-threatening, but could end with a significant injury like a broken leg or arm. Who should be positioned at this dangerous place? Suppose further that two of the helpers are responsible for the accident because they caused the tree to fall through negligence. To me it seems obvious that these two responsible agents also bear a special responsibility to take the additional risk. Perhaps this is true even when they have caused the tree to fall without any culpable conduct. After all, their involvement in the disaster differs from that of the other hikers.[42]

If it is true that the responsibility involved in the removal depends on the type of entanglement, then in many cases it is not possible to clearly distinguish between a forward-looking and backward-looking responsibility. The distribution of forward-looking responsibility also depends on who bears how much blame for an injustice and therefore must contribute accordingly to the elimination and possible compensation of the wrongdoing. At this point, however, Young argues that in many cases this might indeed be true, but that this is not so with structural injustice. The structural nature of these forms of injustice consists precisely in the fact that it is not clear who is to blame to what extent for their existence.

Everything then depends on how well Young's arguments support the assertion that in cases of structural injustice there are no responsible agents, or that these cannot be determined, or that it would be counterproductive to even attempt to do so. She formulates three arguments, but, in my opinion, all three do not demonstrate what they ought to.

First, Young argues that the attempt to distribute responsibility in a backward-looking perspective merely leads to a destructive blame game. Agents are only self-referentially interested in their own innocence, or at least in their assertion of being innocent. They will push the responsibility onto others, which is a distraction from the actual goal of eliminating injustice.[43] This argument is sometimes dismissed as being too pragmatic and unphilosophical.[44] However, I think the problem with this argument is of a more substantial nature. I believe it fails, because Young cannot rid the world of the underlying problem with her model of responsibility. As we have seen also within a forward-looking model of responsibility, costs emerge that need to be distributed. Because of this, there is an incentive to push the forward-looking responsibility onto others, just as there is with blame, guilt, and liability. Some standard is needed in order to distribute costs fairly and resolve disputes, and the guilt, which caused the injustice, must obviously play a

---

42. Tracy Isaacs (2011, 76–79) might speak of metaphysical guilt here.
43. Young (2011, 100).
44. Barry and Ferracioli (2013).

role in this standard. For example, this can be seen in issues of environmental justice, whereby states are intensely busy accepting less responsibility themselves while assigning more responsibility to other countries.[45]

Second, Young complains that the assignment of guilt could lead to there being only a few visible agents who can be held accountable, while other agents (and the structural basis of injustice) remain neglected, which has the result that the injustice itself is not properly addressed.[46] However, this argument only applies if responsibility is understood one-sidedly as entirely backward-looking. Once the concept of forward-looking and collective responsibility comes into play to address structural injustice, and is even put into the foreground, the problem ceases to exist. I believe this argument only shows, if anything, that the elimination of structural injustice should be of considerable importance and maybe even have some normative priority and the allocation of blame should be subordinated to this goal, because then the counter-productive focus on some few perpetrators can be avoided. In and of itself, I think this is a strong point in Young's argument, but it does not show the need for eliminating liability for this model of responsibility altogether.

Third, Young argues that guilt always presupposes blameworthiness. However, blameworthiness cannot be determined in structural injustices because it is not clear who made what causal contribution, who profited in a blameworthy way from the structural injustice, and to what extent.[47] This is the central argument of Young. Her categorical separation of a backward-looking individual and forward-looking collective responsibility is based on the assertion that in structural injustice one cannot clearly determine any backward-looking individual responsibility.

Here Young is rightly criticized for presupposing a too narrow understanding of causality, in which one must be properly able to identify the definitive causes of injustice. By contrast, however, it is sufficient to prove participation in the causal chain, in order to examine to what extent this involvement was culpable.[48] It is also sufficient to prove that profit was made from the injustice to further inquire whether there is a culpable involvement associated with this profit.[49] However, this criticism should not be taken as a reason to fall back to the liability model of responsibility entirely. Young is probably right that in cases of highly complex structural injustice, first, not all of those involved are culpably entangled, and second, their contribution to compensation may not be sufficient to correct the injustice done.

---

45. Meyer and Roser (2010) discuss the complications for the assessment of a fair distribution of responsibility regarding climate change.

46. Young (2011, 106).

47. Young (2011, 97–104).

48. Young (2011, 103) argues against Kutz (2000) that in her cases people are not complicit in a blameworthy way, because they lack intent to produce the harmful outcome. However, negligence should be enough to ground blameworthy complicity—at least in some cases and especially in cases of serious injustice. Barry and Ferracioli (2013) make a strong argument in this respect.

49. Thomas Pogge (2002, 171) argues for this kind of blameworthy profiting.

Still, this is no basis to conclude that it is impossible to find any culpably entangled agents. If that were actually to be a defining criterion for structural injustice, then Young's approach would be burdened with the problem that many if not all cases of what we normally would accept as being some form of structural injustice would no longer fit into her narrow definition. In matters of global environmental justice, unjust disadvantage of social groups within states and unjust global economic conditions, for example, one can always find at least some agents who have causally contributed to their existence and/or benefited from them in a culpable manner.

A strict defender of Young's model of responsibility could concede this point and still insist that it would be pointless to make such accusations and that it would burden the idea of a forward-looking collective responsibility, if it were to be confronted with the classic issues of liability. That would have the unproductive effect of creating an excessive orientation toward the past at the expense of a concrete improvement of the situation of disadvantage, as could be insisted on her behalf. I think this defense fails and that even on a very pragmatic level it is important to integrate some form of liability based on guilt into Young's conception of a forward-looking and collective responsibility. This is so for two reasons.

First, it seems to me that the motivation of agents to embrace a forward-looking responsibility also depends on whether other actors contribute their fair share, or at least are held accountable if they do not. If this is so, then the appropriate consideration of backward-looking responsibility and liability becomes a condition of success for the effectiveness of a forward-looking responsibility to address structural injustice. According to my hypothesis, if liability is handled justly and the burden is distributed fairly, the likelihood increases that collective action problems will be overcome, and structural injustices reduced, because more agents will be willing to participate.[50]

Second, the strict separation between backward-looking guilt and responsibility on the one hand, and forward-looking responsibility on the other, can even be systematically misused. Selfish agents can consciously create or maintain unjust structures because they benefit from them and know that they do not have to bear the costs for their elimination alone, since these are covered by a larger group of stakeholders. Corporate agents in particular certainly have the ability to create and maintain structural injustice through collective action, particularly by influencing legislative and political regulatory processes. This is one way of looking at the behaviour of banks and other financial companies before and during the recent financial crisis. Many were, after all, bailed out by governments and apparently counted on it.[51] In addition, if some agents take advantage of the separation of guilt and responsibility, then this can probably cause other agents to be less willing to embrace a forward-looking responsibility without also

50. This hypothesis might be controversial, but it is supported by results of dictator and similar games in game theory, where players are even willing to accept losses in order to counter behavior they deem to be unjust.
51. Stiglitz (2010, 33–47).

negotiating debt and liability. Such an arrangement would probably be seen as rather unfair.

The strict separation of guilt, liability, and forward-looking responsibility is then, in my opinion, the major problem in Young's approach. The main reason for this is that this separation precludes exactly that pragmatic orientation to an effective improvement of structural injustices that is so strongly emphasized by Young herself. She does not discuss whether and how the willingness of stakeholders to contribute to a combined reduction of structural injustice is also dependent on a fair dealing with guilt and a fair distribution of burdens. This point should be at least clarified in a further development of her account. This would lead, in my estimation, to the insight that the separation of backward- and forward-looking responsibility cannot be maintained, not even in a pragmatic perspective.

4. ON THE ORGANIZATION OF FORWARD-LOOKING RESPONSIBILITY

The critical points on the social connection model of responsibility raised in the two previous sections should not be taken as a reason to disregard this approach altogether, or so I think. On the contrary, they may serve to further develop important aspects of the idea of a collective and forward-looking responsibility and combine them with a suitable concept of liability. Young's account still works as a good starting point for future developments of such an endeavor. She was successful in pointing out that the backward-looking model of responsibility as liability is too one-sided when it comes to structural injustice. This model alone is not suitable to address structural injustices in an adequate way, because it does not put the elimination or reduction of structural injustice at the centre of its attention.

In my opinion then the main strength of Young's position consists in her insistence on the normative priority of a forward-looking responsibility compared to backward-looking liability. The elimination of (structural) injustice should be more important than the identification of culprits, Young argues. Actions should be undertaken as soon as there is a possibility to eliminate injustices through collective action, rather than waiting to discover, through a lengthy and perhaps protracted processes, who bears what proportion of blame. Admittedly, Young does not support this position with a definitive argument. But her reference to the social connectedness with structural injustice, after all, provides a basis for why agents should bear a responsibility, even if the relative proportion of a causal involvement is not fully determined. Also, most of the individuals disadvantaged by structural injustice would probably agree that its elimination has a normative precedence before any final determination of the culpable causers and profiteers, and their voice should carry considerable weight. Anyhow, this point surely is one that should be further elaborated in an integrated approach of liability and forward-looking responsibility.

At the same time, the forward-looking model of collective responsibility would also benefit greatly if it were to integrate a process of determining culpable causers and profiteers. It is not necessary for the model to work, that all of them are determined. But where it is possible to make agents liable in due process, this can be done entirely without negatively affecting the strengths of the social connection model of responsibility, or so I think.

On the contrary, such integration possesses three advantages, which I quickly want to outline here as possible starting points for a future development of such an integrated account. First, the compensation claimed by culpably entangled agents could be used to compensate for other agents who have embraced a great deal of responsibility. Second, the motivation of these agents to embrace a forward-looking responsibility would be greater not only because they are hoping for compensation, but also because their sense of justice is fulfilled. Third, agents may be made liable if they act negligently. Thus, the forward-looking perspective actually gains though the integration of liability, because the prospect of future liability may deter agents from participating in further damages or benefiting from them. Perhaps structural improvements are thereby even made easier because they are opposed by fewer elements of resistance.

For such an integrative perspective of responsibility which connects liability and a forward-looking responsibility to eliminate structural injustice, it is necessary to further advance some underdeveloped aspects in Young's approach. In my discussion of her concept I have identified three points. First, an integrated concept requires a theory of the allocation of responsibility. Second, more needs to be said about how joint action takes place. Third, consideration should be given to a reasonable search process for truth with a view to culpable parties in the creation and maintenance of structural injustice.

Regarding the first point, Young refers to social connections as the basis for the allocation of responsibility, as we have seen. However, she gives no advice as to how responsibility can be distributed along the criteria of power, privilege, interest, and collective capacity. In an integrated model, we would still have to include culpable involvement as a further criterion for distribution. Then more will have to be said on what and how much identifiable agents should contribute to a forward-looking collective responsibility. This is not only a question of justice and motivation to contribute. It is also a question of guidance, since it probably is not easy for many willing agents to figure out what they should do in order to best battle structural injustice.

Maybe David Miller is right to argue that decisions over how responsibility is to be distributed must be made in each individual case.[52] This would apply to both his remedial responsibility and to Young's political responsibility for structural injustice. However, this solution also seems to be somewhat too quick. Even if in the end it turns out to not be possible to specify a definite set of abstract criteria for distribution beyond specific cases, it should at least be possible to say something more about the procedure of defining a just and reasonable distribution. This would likely show that what is required is not only a public discourse on the distribution of responsibility, but also the creation of institutions that structures this discourse and organizes the distribution.

---

52. Miller (2001, 471).

Something similar applies to the question of joint action. It certainly makes sense when Young argues that individual agents often cannot achieve the elimination of structural injustice on their own, since this requires joint efforts by several agents. But she does not engage further with the question of how this common action is to be organized, and how to deal with the usual problems of collective action such as free riding, windfall gains, and unintended consequences. A more structured and organized approach leading to an institutional setting seems to be necessary here too, in order to develop an effective forward-looking responsibility through collective action.

Also, any credible assurance that agents culpable for their involvement in structural injustice can be determined and will be held accountable obviously depends on a well-organized search for liability. Such an assurance appears credible only if it is sufficiently well backed by powerful and rule-based institutions. Such institutions probably must take the shape of at least quasi-legal forms of organization, as is the case, for example, with truth commissions.

It turns out that with all three further developments discussed—namely, distribution of responsibility, organization of collective action, and determination of culpably entangled agents—it is clear that proper institutions are needed to take on these tasks. Most likely not against the intention of Young, the model of political responsibility for structural injustice then proves to be one that presupposes the remodelling of the structure of political institutions themselves or so it seems. Organizing forward-looking collective responsibility would become almost the first virtue of at least some social institutions on a local, regional, and global level. At the moment the primary forward-looking responsibility of individual and corporate agents would then probably be to contribute to the development of such an institutional structure. This is actually something Young called for in her earlier work: "I propose a global system of regulatory regimes in which locales and regions relate in a federal system. These regimes lay down rules regarding the small but vital set of issues around which peace and justice call for global co-operation."[53]

REFERENCES

Apel, Karl-Otto. 1990. "Diskursethik als Verantwortungsethik—eine postmetaphysische Transformation der Ethik Kants." In *Ethik und Befreiung*, ed. Raúl Fornet-Betancourt, 10–40. Aachen, Germany: Augustinus Buchhandlung.

Arendt, Hannah. [1968] 1987. "Collective Responsibility." *Amor Mundi: Boston College Studies in Philosophy* 26: 43–50.

Barry, Christian, and Ferracioli, Luara. 2013. "Young on Responsibility and Structural Injustice." *Criminal Justice Ethics* 32(3): 247–57.

Feinberg, Joel. 1968. "Collective Responsibility." *Journal of Philosophy* 65: 674–88.

Ferguson, Ann. 2009. *Dancing with Iris: The Philosophy of Iris Marion Young*. Oxford: Oxford University Press.

French, Peter. 1979. "The Corporation as a Moral Person." *American Philosophical Quarterly* 16(3): 207–15.

Giddens, Anthony. 1979. *Central Problems in Social Theory: Action, Structure, and Contradiction in Social Analysis*. Berkeley: University of California Press.

53. Young (2000, 267).

————. 1986. *Constitution of Society: Outline of the Theory of Structuration*. Cambridge: Polity Press.

Gilbert, Margaret. 2000. *Sociality and Responsibility: New Essays in Plural Subject Theory*. Lanham, MD: Rowman and Littlefield.

————. 2006. *A Theory of Political Obligation: Membership, Commitment, and the Bonds of Society*. Oxford: Oxford University Press.

Hahn, Henning. 2009. "The Global Consequence of Participatory Responsibility." *Journal of Global Ethics* 5: 43–56.

Held, Virginia. 1970. "Can a Random Collection of Individuals Be Morally Responsible?" *Journal of Philosophy* 67(14): 471–81.

Isaacs, Tracy. 2011. *Moral Responsibility in Collective Contexts*. Oxford: Oxford University Press.

Jonas, Hans. [1979] 1985. *The Imperative of Responsibility: In Search of an Ethics for the Technological Age*. Chicago: University of Chicago Press.

Kreide, Regina. 2013. "Die Verantwortung für ein T-Shirt. Individuelle und kollektive Verpflichtungen bei Iris Marion Young." In *Zwischen Demokratie und globaler Verantwortung: Iris Marion Youngs Theorie politischer Normativität*, ed. Peter Niesen, 59–76. Baden-Baden, Germany: Nomos Verlag.

Kutz, Christopher. 2000. *Complicity: Ethics and Law for a Collective Age*. Cambridge: Cambridge University Press.

Lenk, Hans, and Maring, Mathias. 1991. "Verantwortung—normatives Interpretationskonstrukt und empirische Beschreibung." In *Ethische Norm und empirische Hypothese*, ed. Lutz H. Eckensberger and Ulrich Gähde, 222–43. Frankfurt: Suhrkamp Verlag.

Levinas, Emmanuel. [1961] 1991. *Totality and Infinity: An Essay on Exteriority*. Dordrecht: Kluwer Academic Publishers.

List, Christian, and Pettit, Philip. 2011. *Group Agency: The Possibility, Design, and Status of Corporate Agents*. Oxford: Oxford University Press.

Mackie, John Leslie. [1977] 2011. *Ethics: Inventing Right and Wrong*. London: Penguin Books.

May, Larry. 1996. *Sharing Responsibility*. Chicago: The University of Chicago Press.

Meyer, Lukas, and Roser, Dominic. 2010. "Climate Justice and Historical Emissions." *Critical Review of International Social and Political Philosophy* 13(1): 229–53.

Miller, David. 2001. "Distributing Responsibilities." *Journal of Political Philosophy* 9(4): 453–71.

————. 2007. *National Responsibility and Global Justice*. Oxford: Oxford University Press.

————. 2011. "Taking Up the Slack? Responsibility and Justice in Situations of Partial Compliance." In *Responsibility and Distributive Justice*, ed. Carl Knight and Zofia Stemplowska, 230–45. Oxford: Oxford University Press.

Neuhäuser, Christian. 2011. *Unternehmen als moralische Akteure*. Berlin: Suhrkamp Verlag.

Nida-Rümelin, Julian. 2011. *Verantwortung*. Stuttgart: Reclam Verlag.

Niesen, Peter, ed. 2013. *Zwischen Demokratie und globaler Verantwortung: Iris Marion Youngs Theorie politischer Normativität*. Baden-Baden, Germany: Nomos Verlag.

Owen, David. 2013. "Responsibilities for Justice: Reading Young on Political Responsibility and Structural Injustice." In *Zwischen Demokratie und globaler Verantwortung: Iris Marion Youngs Theorie politischer Normativität*, ed. Peter Niesen, 93–110. Baden-Baden, Germany: Nomos Verlag.

Pettit, Philip. 2005. "Construing Sen on Commitment." *Economics and Philosophy* 21: 15–32.

Pogge, Thomas. 2002. *World Poverty and Human Rights: Cosmopolitan Responsibilities and Reforms*. Cambridge: Polity Press.

Stiglitz, Joseph E. 2010. *Freefall: America, Free Markets, and the Sinking of the World Economy*. New York: W.W. Norton.

Stoecker, Ralf. 1997. "Handlung und Verantwortung—Mackie's Rule Put Straight." In *Analyomen 2*, ed. Georg Meggle and Julian Nida-Rühmelin, 357–64. Berlin: de Gruyter.

Weber, Max. [1919] 2004. *The Vocation Lectures*. Indianapolis: Hackett Publishing.

Young, Iris Marion. 1990. *Justice and the Politics of Difference*. Princeton, NJ: Princeton University Press.

————. 2000. *Inclusion and Democracy*. Oxford: Oxford University Press.

———. 2003. "Political Responsibility and Structural Injustice." Lindley Lecture on Philosophy. Department of Philosophy, University of Kansas.

———. 2004. "Responsibility and Global Labour Justice." *Journal of Political Philosophy* 12(4): 365–88.

———. 2006. "Responsibility and Global Justice: A Social Connection Model." *Social Philosophy and Policy* 23: 102–30.

———. 2007. *Global Challenges: War, Self-Determination and Responsibility for Justice*. Cambridge: Polity Press.

———. 2011. *Responsibility for Justice*. New York: Oxford University Press.

MIDWEST STUDIES IN PHILOSOPHY 1976–2014

Volumes XXIII onwards are available through Wiley Periodicals, Inc. Previous volumes may be available through University of Notre Dame Press or University of Minnesota Press.

Contributors

Gunnar Björnsson, Philosophy, Universities of Umeå & Gothenburg
Neta C. Crawford, Political Science, Boston University
Derrick Darby, Department of Philosophy, University of Michigan
Nyla Branscombe, Department of Psychology, University of Kansas
Kendy M. Hess, Philosophy, College of the Holy Cross
Tracy Isaacs, Department of Philosophy, The University of Western Ontario
Ludger Jansen, Department of Philosophy, Rostock University
Christian Neuhäuser, Department of Philosophy and Political Science, University of Dortmund
Avia Pasternak, Department of Political Science, University College London
Felix Pinkert, Philosophy, St. Andrews
Linda Radzik, Philosophy, Texas A&M University
Carol Rovane, Department of Philosophy, Columbia University
Anne Schwenkenbecher, Philosophy, Murdoch University
Marion Smiley, Department of Philosophy, Brandeis University
Kai Spiekermann, Political Philosophy, London School of Economics
Bill Wringe, Department of Philosophy, Bilkent University, Ankara, Turkey

Peter A. French, Ph.D., L.H.D. is the Lincoln Professor of Ethics and Professor of Philosophy at Arizona State University. He is the Founding Director of the Lincoln Center for Applied Ethics and its Director from 2000 to 2013. Before that he was the Cole Chair in Ethics, Director of the Ethics Center, and Chair of the Department of Philosophy of the University of South Florida. He was the Lennox Distinguished Professor and Chair of Philosophy at Trinity University, and served as Exxon Distinguished Research Professor in the Center for the Study of Values at the University of Delaware. During his distinguished 50-year career in academia he has also been a professor of philosophy at the University of Minnesota, Dalhousie University (Nova Scotia), and Northern Arizona University. Dr. French earned a BA from Gettysburg College, an MA from the University of Southern California, and a Ph.D. from the University of Miami, and did post-doctoral work at Oxford University. He was awarded a Doctor of Humane Letters (L.H.D.) degree for his work in philosophy from Gettysburg College in 2006.
Dr. French has an international reputation in ethical and legal theory and in collective and corporate responsibility and criminal liability. He is the author of twenty books including *War and Moral Dissonance; The Virtues of Vengeance;*

Cowboy Metaphysics; Ethics and College Sports; Corporate Ethics; Responsibility Matters; Collective and Corporate Responsibility; Ethics in Government; The Scope of Morality; Corporations in the Moral Community; The Spectrum of Responsibility; Corrigible Corporations and Unruly Laws; and *War and Border Crossings: Ethics When Cultures Clash.* He is a founding editor with Howard Wettstein of *Midwest Studies in Philosophy.* As a single author, co-author, and editor he has contributed 61 books to the philosophical literature.

Dr. French has lectured at locations around the world. Some of his works have been translated into Chinese, Japanese, German, Italian, French, Serbian, and Spanish. Dr. French also was the editor of the *Journal of Social Philosophy* for 16 years and general editor of the *Issues in Contemporary Ethics* series. He has published scores of articles in the major philosophical and legal journals and reviews, many of which have been anthologized. In 2002 Dr. French was appointed to the Board of Officers of the American Philosophical Association. In 2008 the APA's *Newsletter on Philosophy and Law* dedicated an issue to him, and at its 2014 Central Division meetings in Chicago the APA honored him with a session on his work.

Howard K. Wettstein is Professor of Philosophy at the University of California, Riverside. He holds a M.A. and Ph.D. from the City University of New York and a B.A. from Yeshiva College. In 2013 his book, *The Significance of Religious Experience,* was published by Oxford University Press. Earlier books include *Has Semantics Rested On a Mistake? and Other Essays* (Stanford University Press, 1991) and *The Magic Prism: An Essay in the Philosophy of Language* (Oxford University Press, 2004). He has edited or co-edited several volumes including *Themes From Kaplan* and *Diasporas and Exiles: Varieties of Jewish Identity*. He is currently writing a new book on the philosophy of religion.

In normative political and social discourse it is often said that some collective or group of people morally ought to or is morally responsible to perform a certain action or bring about a certain outcome. One way such expressions are asserted is say that such collectives have a moral responsibility to do something going forward or from now on. This volume explores various aspects of the concept of forward-looking collective responsibility and its application. The 2006 *Midwest Studies in Philosophy* volume (*Shared Intention and Collective Responsibility*) concentrated primarily on collective responsibility for past actions and events. This volume serves as a companion piece to that volume by extending the philosophical discussion of collective responsibility and collective morality towards future collective action. It contains fifteen articles written by leading philosophers from around the world.